Analecta Gregoriana

Cura Pontificiae Universitatis Gregorianae edita

Vol. 131. Series Facultatis Theologicae: sectio B, n. 43

ROBERT L. RICHARD, S. J.

The Problem of an Apologetical Perspective in the Trinitarian Theology of St. Thomas Aquinas

GREGORIAN UNIVERSITY PRESS

4, PIAZZA DELLA PILOTTA

ROME

1963

IMPRIMI POTEST

Romae, die 26 Iulii 1963.

R. P. Paulus Muñoz Vega, S. I.
Rector Universitatis

IMPRIMATUR

E Vicariatu Urbis, die 10 Augusti 1963.

✠ Aloysius *Card. Provicarius*

TYPIS PONTIFICIAE UNIVERSITATIS GREGORIANAE - ROMAE

FOREWORD

So much has been written on both the doctrinal detail
and broad themes of Aquinas' trinitarian theology, a contemporary investigator setting himself the task of examining a
point of basic perspective in this theology assumes the burden
of proof that the examination is really called for. One would
think, for instance, that the Thomist concept of theological
science, its methodological ideal, the scope and limitations of
rational process within this ideal, were all questions that had
been more or less settled by previous criticism. The fact is,
however, that only recently no less a scholar than Dom Cyprian Vagaggini, in a contribution to the Anselmian commemorative volume *Spicilegium Beccense* (Paris, 1959), confronted
the traditional interpretation of St. Thomas' trinitarian expositions with a most interesting and academically stimulating
challenge.

As Dom Vagaggini reads the text, St. Thomas reached
a point in his more mature works where he had, for every
practical purpose, made quite his own St. Anselm's "rationes
necessariae" and the ideal of rational demonstration based
on the notion of ' pure perfections '. For in the matter of
the Trinity, St. Thomas eventually comes to argue the existence of the procession of the Divine Word from the universal
necessity for such procession in intellectual being. If this is
not meant to be a strict demonstration, Vagaggini concludes,
and one must also consider Aquinas' constant protest that
demonstration in this area was not possible, then it is at
least its close imitation.

A question has been raised, therefore, and in the writer's
judgment it is deserving of an answer — all the more so,
inasmuch as Vagaggini's purpose seems to have been, not so
much to propose a solution, much less a definitive solution,
than to call attention to a yet unsettled problem. Moreover,
as the further account of the academic dialogue in the first
part of this study will reveal, what has been said on the same

point by other modern interpreters of Thomist theology has been said rather summarily and indirectly in the course of discussing some quite different topic.

In the final analysis, the question will prove to be methodological. So far as the writer could determine, it had not yet been given any truly adequate treatment in this precisely methodological context.

TABLE OF CONTENTS

PART ONE

MODERN THEOLOGICAL OPINION AND THE
STATE OF THE PROBLEM

CHAPTER ONE

THE CHALLENGE OF DOM CYPRIAN VAGAGGINI

It was the recent and lively contribution of Dom Cyprian Vagaggini to the commemorative volume *Spicilegium Beccense*, that became the immediate occasion for the present study.[1] In view of the clarity and force with which Vagaggini expresses himself, an objective presentation of his position will serve quite neatly as the introductory chapter to the larger questions of Thomist interpretation to which his challenge gives rise, and which the purpose of the present work is to discuss.

Disagreeing with such as H. Paissac, who would attach Aquinas' doctrine on the two trinitarian processions directly to Augustine, Vagaggini finds that the significant antecedents of Aquinas' own theory derive rather from Anselm.[2] It is historically incorrect to see in Anselm merely a repetition of Augustine's doctrine on the procession of *Verbum* and *Amor*. Moreover, it is precisely what is new and distinctive in the development achieved by Anselm himself that had so profound an influence on St. Thomas. For, though Aquinas may come to cite Augustine almost exclusively, he remains, both in his

---

[1] CYPRIAN VAGAGGINI, " La hantise des *rationes necessariae* de saint Anselme dans la théologie des processions trinitaires de saint Thomas, " trans. J. Evrard, *Spicilegium Beccense. Congrès International du ixe centenaire de l'arrivée d'Anselme au Bec* (Paris : Librairie Philosophique J. Vrin, 1959), pp. 103-139. Inasmuch as the whole first chapter of the present study is confined to an objective presentation of this contribution by Dom Vagaggini to the *Spicilegium Beccense* volume, it will suffice to indicate simply the page number for all succeeding references and citations.

[2] p. 103.

1

formation of the state of the question, and in his prevailing methodological ideal, a true follower of St. Anselm.[3]

To recall, then, what had been the salient points in Anselm's treatment of the processions, Vagaggini notes first of all that Anselm approached this particular problem from within his general theological ideal : that is to say, the intention of proving through apodictic arguments addressed to unaided reason — such as would be accessible even to the unbeliever, and would make methodological abstraction from faith — the rational truth of at least the existence of the Christian mysteries.[4] From theodicy, Anselm borrowed the distinction between simple and mixed perfections, and the great novelty in his personal contribution to trinitarian theology, and to the theology of the processions in particular, was to have realized in this narrower field, through use of this distinction, the same ideal of rational demonstration that was ever his preoccupation.[5]

As the first and most important step in achieving his objective, Anselm turned to the concept of the Word, which he treated as a simple perfection, for all practical purposes substantially the same as the divine wisdom, or some other attribute. By means of the Word so considered, he passed in demonstration from the unity of the one God to the Trinity of Persons.

Thus in the *Monologion*, just as earlier in this work he had demonstrated in a purely rational way the existence of God, so did Anselm go on to apply the same apodictic method to the existence of the Divine Word. God, not only as Creator, but also in His act of self-knowing, must necessarily utter a distinct Word. For Anselm supposes that an inner word proceeds in every act of intelligence, as an instance of simple

---

[3] p. 104.

[4] " C'est la volonté de prouver, par le moyen de raisonnements apodictiques, face à la raison nue, s'agisse-t-il même de l'incrédule — et par conséquent en faisant méthodologiquement abstraction de la foi — la vérité rationnelle au moins de l'existence des dogmes de la foi elle-même. " Qualifications, as Vagaggini adds, have to be made in view of the judgment of recent scholarship upon the traditional, or patristic, context sometimes framing these demonstrations. Nevertheless, " ... c'est à partir de deux prémisses de raison qu'Anselme veut retrouver au moins l'existence des vérités imposées par la foi. Et ceci même s'il s'agit de ce que nous appelons aujourd'hui mystères proprement dits. " p. 105.

[5] p. 106.

or pure perfection. He supposes as well that this word must be really distinct from the one who utters it in understanding.[6]

Subsequently, after having applied what Vagaggini considers the same deductive process to the chief properties of the Divine Word, Anselm then took up the procession of the Holy Spirit. One who knows himself and remembers himself must necessarily love himself. This simple fact, which Anselm did not further analyse, was sufficient for him to demonstrate, and in a purely philosophical manner, the existence in God of a Third Person.[7]

In the same basic fashion, Anselm will carry through his demonstrations to include further elements of doctrine. The Third Person must proceed necessarily from both the Father and the Son as from a single principle. This second procession, moreover, is not properly called generation, nor can the Holy Spirit Himself be called Son.[8]

In concluding his recollection of the Anselmian position, Vagaggini concedes that there has been throughout a large dependence upon Augustine. But there is also a great difference. When Augustine sought in man images of the Trinity, his state of the question, judged in the light of a later theology, lacked precision, for want of a clear distinction between the analogy of metaphor and the analogy of proper proportionality. Anselm, on the other hand, transposes the *verbum* and *amor* of Augustine from their indeterminate condition within a contemplative aim to entities involving at once both no admixture of imperfection and real distinction, and which, as a consequence, compel the human reason to affirm the existence of a Trinity, without, at the same time, permitting its exhaustive comprehension.[9]

---

[6] p. 107.

[7] " Qui se connaît soi-même et se souvient de soi-même s'aime aussi nécessairement soi-même ; donc l'Esprit Suprême s'aime nécessairement soi-même. Ce simple fait, qui n'est pas analysé ultérieurement, prouve déjà pour Anselme, et par pure voie philosophique, l'existence d'une troisième Personne en Dieu. Il suppose par conséquent, sans l'expliquer ni le prouver il est vrai, que l'amour de soi-même est une perfection simple et qu'il implique en même temps une distinction réelle entre l'aimé et l'aimant, laquelle, en Dieu, ne pourra être que personnelle et relative. " p. 108.

[8] pp. 108-109.

[9] " Elle [la différence] consiste foncièrement en ceci : lorsque S. Augustin cherche des ' images ' de la Trinité dans l'homme, tout

The position of St. Anselm, therefore, represents a clear-cut break from the Platonic dialectic of Augustine in favor of the apodictic proof of the dialectic of Aristotle. All that was lacking in Anselm's achievement, and would have to wait for the day of Aquinas, was the special psychological analysis necessary to substantiate the supposed character of the simple perfections that had been claimed, and to handle satisfactorily the objections that could be adduced, as, for example, the difficulties arising from Anselm's failure to distinguish between *intelligere* and *dicere verbum*.[10]

There remains, finally, the problem of mystery as such. Anselm was quite aware that the Trinity was a mystery of faith transcending human understanding. Nevertheless, having distinguished between the *quia sit* of the mystery, which was accessible to human reason through the *rationes necessariae*, and the *quomodo sit*, which continued to be inaccessible, Anselm believed that he had sufficiently safeguarded the mystery itself. When it is further asked, however, just how Anselm understood this distinction, it appears, according to Dom Vagaggini, that Anselm wished to exclude from the competence of human understanding only the same exhaustive and direct knowledge that had to be denied to reason with respect to the divine wisdom or the divine being. It cannot

---

son état de la question — jugé à la lumière de la théologie postérieure — reste indéterminé parce que, en cette matière, en parlant d'" images ' il n'a jamais conçu une distinction nette entre ce qui fut appelé, dans la suite, analogie métaphorique et analogie de proportionalité propre.... Ainsi le verbe et l'amour d'Augustin, comme bases pour ' l'intelligence ' de la Trinité, étaient placés dans un perspective précise dont le Docteur africain n'eut jamais conscience. Non plus degrés suprêmes dans l'échelle des images terrestres pour s'élever à la contemplation pu Dieu Trine, mais entités qui, parce qu'elles n'incluent de soi aucune imperfection et impliquent en même temps une distinction réelle relative, obligent inéluctablement la raison à affirmer en Dieu le fait de la Trinité et des autres points que la foi catholique impose concernant celle-ci, même si elles n'en permettent pas la compréhension exhaustive. " pp. 109-111.

[10] " En ne distinguant pas entre ' intelligere ' et ' dire le verbe ', il ne se rend pas compte, parmi d'autres choses, de la difficulté qu'il y a à prendre comme base de cette analogie formelle des processions divines qu'il cherche, le fait d'un acte qui procède de sa propre puissance en l'homme, bien que cette procession implique formellement un passage de la puissance à l'acte qui ne peut se trouver proprement en Dieu. " p. 111.

be proved, therefore, that Anselm considered the Trinity of Persons an essentially greater mystery than these others.[11]

With this, Vagaggini addresses himself to the text of St. Thomas. Aquinas, he maintains, was not unaware of the *Monologion* when composing his own commentary on the *Sentences*, but his initial reaction to the Anselmian ideal is extremely negative. First and foremost, Aquinas flatly rejects the possibility of proving by apodictic arguments the existence of a plurality of Persons in the divine essence. For the human reason has no natural knowledge of God except through creatures, and whatever is said of God in this respect pertains to the divine essence, not to the distinct Persons. Reason, therefore, cannot penetrate beyond the attributes of the divine essence, and arguments seeming to do so are merely *adaptationes* of sorts, not demonstrations leading to necessary conclusions.[12]

Vagaggini concludes his discussion of the *Sentences*, however, by noting that, despite this categorical denial of rational demonstration within the Trinity of Persons — a stand, more-

---

[11] " Il savait parfaitement que la Trinité est un mystère qui transcende l'intelligence humaine. Mais il a fait une distinction entre le *quia* ou l'*an sit* et le *quomodo sit*, et il a estimé qu'au *quia sit* de la Trinité l'intelligence humaine pouvait parvenir par ' *raisons nécessaires* ', mais que le *quomodo sit* restait toujours inaccessible. Mais quand on cherche ce qu'Anselme entend par *quomodo sit*, on voit que pour lui cela consiste simplement dans le fait que l'intelligence humaine n'arrive jamais à une connaissance exhaustive et directe de la Trinité, de la même manière qu'elle n'arrive jamais à une connaissance directe et exhaustive de la sagesse divine ou de l'être divin. Ainsi on ne peut prouver que pour S. Anselme le mystère de la Trinité soit essentiellement plus grand que le mystère de la sagesse ou de l'être divin. " pp. 111-112.

[12] " Avant tout, il [S. Thomas] repousse nettement la possibilité de pouvoir prouver avec des arguments apodictiques l'existence d'une pluralité de Personnes dans l'essence divine. Le motif essentiel est le suivant : ' Naturalis ratio non cognoscit Deum nisi ex creaturis. Omnia autem quae dicuntur de Deo per respectum ad creaturas, pertinent ad essentiam et non ad personas. Et ideo ex naturali ratione non venitur nisi ad attributa divinae essentiae.... Omnes rationes inductae sunt magis adaptationes quaedam quam necessario concludentes '. (*In I Sent.*, d. 3, q. 1, a. 4c. et ad 3m.) Saint Thomas répètera cette affirmation dans tous ses ouvrages. Il dira toujours ne vouloir autre chose qu'expliquer de quelque manière la nature des processions divines à partir de l'admission de leur existence supposée par la foi. " p. 112.

over, Aquinas would reiterate again and again to the very
end of his works — the basic approach to the question, and
the scientific ideal here seen to be operative, is already quite
clearly Anselmian.[13]

In Dom Vagaggini's view, the commentary on Boethius'
De Trinitate offers a much more complete and profound handling of the same problem : can pure philosophy attain knowledge of the Trinity of Persons ? [14]

An objection contains what is, in fact, the position of
St. Anselm in the *Monologion* : " Ex hoc quod (Deus) est
intelligens sequitur quod verbum concipiat quia hoc est commune omni intelligenti. " St. Thomas dismisses this objection by pointing out the great difference in this regard between
God and creatures : since in God " idem est intellectus et intellectum, " one cannot argue from the mere fact that He
is understanding to the existence in God of a really distinct
concept, as one can of human beings. At the time of writing
the treatise *In Boethii de Trinitate*, therefore, St. Thomas was
persuaded, contrary to the theory of St. Anselm, that the inner
word conceived as implying a real distinction could not be
considered a simple perfection, but was rather a mixed perfection. It is precisely this principle, that leads him to reject the Anselmian argument for the first procession.[15]

Yet, according to Vagaggini's analysis, this is the same
principle Aquinas is on the point of abandoning once and
for all.

---

[13] Vagaggini notes, for instance, that even in the *Sentences*, it is
no longer a case of the Augustinian images, " mais bien des raisons
formelles des processions avec argumentation scientifique dans le sens
aristotélicien. Après S. Anselme, et déjà avant S. Thomas, ce pré-
supposé fut communément accepté par les scholastiques. " p. 113.

[14] Referring to St. Thomas' treatment of this question, Vagaggini
adds : " Et il le fait d'une façon beaucoup plus complète et plus
profonde que dans le Commentaire sur le Lombard. " p. 114.

[15] The objection itself is taken from *In Boet. de Trin.*, q. 1, a. 4,
ob. 6, and is quoted in note no. 47 : " Ex hoc quod est intelligens
sequitur quod verbum concipiat quia hoc est commune omni intelligenti. " Vagaggini maintains that this is exactly the position of *Monologion*, 32, 38, 49. He comments : " De la façon dont cette position
est résumée par S. Thomas, il ressort aussi clairement qu'en celle-ci
les processions du verbe et de l'amour sont considérées comme des
perfections simples. " In the immediate passage, Vagaggini supplies
the text of the important reply : " In Deo idem est intellectus et
intellectum ; et ideo non oportet quod ex hoc quod intelligit ponatur

The break comes with the fourth question of *De Veritate*. Discussing whether in God the *verbum* is meant properly, and whether its predication is essential or personal, St. Thomas is led by the testimonies of scripture and St. Augustine to affirm that at least the *verbum cordis* in the strict sense is a proper, as opposed to merely metaphorical, designation. Vagaggini sees here both recognition, on Aquinas' part, of the true character of the inner word as pure perfection, and a complete about-face from the negative position he had defended in the commentary on Boethius.[16]

The problem for Aquinas was to remove from the notion of inner word all potentiality and imperfection — the potentiality and imperfection that had made it necessary for him to reject Anselm's demonstration the first time he had confronted it. Here in the *De Veritate*, however, this is exactly what Aquinas has accomplished. By distinguishing the act of operation, which perfects the operator, from the *operatum*, which proceeds from the act of operation itself, St. Thomas discovered the solution to his original problem. The reality that proceeds from the act of operation is not only really distinct from the act of operation, as its principle, but entails in itself no potency or imperfection.

At this particular juncture, Vagaggini observes, St. Thomas does not immediately extend his solution to the doctrine

---

in eo aliquid conceptum realiter distinctum ab ipso, sicut est in nobis. Trinitas autem personarum requirit distinctionem realem." (*Ibid.*, ad 6m.) From this, he concludes : " Contrairement à l'opinion de S. Anselme, avec laquelle subsiste ou s'écroule toute sa construction théologique concernant les processions divines, S. Thomas était donc persuadé, lorsqu'il écrivait le Commentaire sur Boèce, que le verbe conçu comme impliquant une distinction réelle ne peut être considéré comme une perfection simple, mais qu'il est une perfection mixte. C'est pourquoi il repousse l'axiome affirmé dans l'objection à laquelle il répond, à savoir qu'en tout acte d'intelligence il y a nécessairement production d'un verbe. " p. 115.

[16] " Ici, pour justifier cette assertion qu'il pense être de foi que *Verbum* en Dieu est dit proprement et non pas métaphoriquement, S. Thomas affirme, et il faut bien le noter, le caractère de perfection simple du Verbe, même à la lumière de sa seule analyse philosophique. On notera aussi comment, en agissant ainsi, S. Thomas était amené à accepter ce qui est la position-clé de la doctrine des processions de S. Anselme en antithèse avec ce que le même Docteur Angélique avait écrit dans son Commentaire sur le *De Trinitate* de Boèce. " p. 116.

on processions.   Nevertheless, so far as the fundamental point
of the comparison is concerned, the new teaching of *De Veritate* amounts to acceptance of Anselm's notion of the inner
word as a reality involving at once both real distinction from
its source and simple perfection.   Moreover, through application of the distinction, hitherto unknown, between *per modum operationis* and *per modum operati*, Aquinas has supplied the psychological analysis lacking in Anselm's treatment,
whereby the concept of an *operatum* both immanent to intellection and really distinct from it could be philosophically
defended.[17]

Vagaggini concludes his discussion of the *De Veritate*
period by pointing out instances to show that St. Thomas
had not yet arrived at the moment when he would bring the
full force of this distinction to bear upon a theory of procession, and that even the perfect expression of the inner word
as distinct from the act of intellect, and term of this act,
would first be found in the fifty-third chapter of *Contra Gentiles I*.[18]

---

[17] After noting St. Thomas' doctrine that " l'opération est la perfection de l'opérant, " Vagaggini continues : " Mais une chose qui procède de l'acte de l'opération n'implique pas seulement une distinction
réelle de cette chose d'avec son principe, mais en outre, par soi, ne
dit pas imperfection. "   He refers also to Père Paissac's contention
that in *De Veritate* Aquinas had not yet arrived at the notion of
verbum as " chose-terme de l'acte de l'intellection. "   Be this as it may,
in Vagaggini's view comparison of *De Veritate* with the *Monologion*
brings out that " ... sur le point fondamental du verbe comme réalité
impliquant une distinction réelle et comme perfection simple, il faut
dire que selon toutes les apparences, non seulement il l'a acceptée
pleinement, mais en autre qu'il y a ajouté ce qui manquait encore
dans S. Anselme, à savoir une analyse de nature psychologique et philosophique justificative, basée sur la distinction *per modum operationis* et *per modum operati* ; grace à elle — chose inconnue jusqu'alors
— on eut le concept d'un *operatum* immanent à l'intellection et réellement distinct d'elle. " p. 117.

[18] St. Thomas, in the author's judgment, " ... n'a pas encore du
tout l'intention d'appliquer à la procession de l'amour en général ce
concept de procession *per modum operati* — et par conséquent de perfection simple — qu'il avait découvert dans le *verbum cordis*. "   The
only cause Aquinas can assign why the Spirit " ... procède-t-il par
voie d'amour, est qu'il procède de deux personnes, ce qui suppose le
consentement de deux volontés. "   Further on, Vagaggini continues :
" La doctrine philosophique du verbe comme chose réellement distincte de l'acte d'intellection et comme terme de celui-ci trouve pour la

It would not be long, however, before Aquinas would once again take up the question of the trinitarian processions, and this time, he would employ the refined *verbum* doctrine just seen in *De Veritate* to effect a seemingly rational demonstration of the plurality of Persons. Turning to the text of *De Potentia*, q. 8, a. 1, Vagaggini calls attention to the fact that St. Thomas continues to protest against the Anselmian pretension of attaining the Trinity of Persons through apodictic demonstration.[19]

Nonetheless, the process of argumentation Aquinas himself develops in this passage seems to be in conflict with his protest. If there are real relative distinctions in God, such distinctions must be founded upon some divine action. Since transient actions could not found a relation that would be real in God Himself, one is left necessarily with the immanent actions of intellect and will — the sole immanent actions of which a purely spiritual nature is capable.

Analysis of the human intellect, then, shows that the human intellect can be related to the following entities: to its external object, to its impressed species, to its act of understanding, and to its inner word. Of these four, however, only the last mentioned, the inner word, is pertinent. For only the inner word could be a proper image of that reality in God which is at once really distinct from its principle (the *dicens*) but no less consubstantial with its principle.[20]

Vagaggini is willing to concede that it is not altogether clear whether or not the demonstration just referred to is based

---

première fois sa parfaite expression dans le *Contra Gentiles I* 53 ... " p. 118. See also note no. 55, where Vagaggini observes that St. Thomas does not exploit here to the full his new theory on the *verbum* to reply to the question why only the Son proceeds *per viam intellectus*.

[19] " Encore dans le *De Potentia VIII* a. 1, il proteste comme toujours contre la prétention de S. Anselme à vouloir prouver d'une façon apodictique la pluralité des Personnes en Dieu en parlant du fait qu'en Dieu il y a intellection. " p. 119.

[20] Such, in substance, is the account of St. Thomas from *De Pot.*, q. 8, a. 1c, as reported here by Dom Vagaggini. The same passage will be studied later on in the present study, though from quite a different point of view, when in the final section of the study the opportunity will have been taken to compare the trinitarian ' order of analysis ' in *Contra Gentiles* and *De Potentia* with the corresponding ' order of synthesis ' in the *Summa* and *Compendium*. It may be useful to contrast this alternative interpretation of the text with Dom Vagaggini's, pp. 119-120.

upon the Anselmian principle of the simple perfection. He
maintains, however, that the passage in *De Potentia*, q. 9,
a. 5 ("Utrum numerus personarum sit in divinis.") removes
all doubt.[21]

According to Dom Vagaggini's analysis, St. Thomas, in
this second passage of *De Potentia*, begins by laying down
the general principle upon which he is going to base his argument: the principle, namely, that whatever is perfect in
creatures can be assigned formally and absolutely to God.
Next, he makes the application to intelligence. Intelligence
must belong to God in everything that comprises its essential
perfection. But it is of the essential perfection of intelligence
as such, that there be both *intelligens* and *intellectum* — or,
as Vagaggini suggests it might be rendered, that there be
distinction between the knowing subject and the internally
known object, the concept, that is to say, or inner word. In
the case of God's self-knowledge, then, reason is forced to admit in God the existence of that inner word which is necessary
to the essential perfection of intellect as such.

In Vagaggini's judgment, moreover, it is very difficult to
see how this demonstration of St. Thomas differs in any substantial way from the process of argument whereby St. Anselm
had sought, in the *Monologion*, to prove apodictically, by
pure reason, the procession of the Second Person, taking his
start in the concept of the inner word considered as a simple
perfection.[22] Vagaggini feels that this comparison is brought

---

[21] p. 120, ad fin.

[22] The *corpus articuli* in the passage referred to, *De Pot.*, q. 9, a. 5,
is quite lengthy. After asserting once again that the plurality of
Persons is a matter of faith, Aquinas continues: " Ad manifestationem
ergo aliqualem huius quaestionis, et praecipue secundum quod Augustinus eam manifestat, considerandum est quod omne quod est perfectum in creaturis oportet Deo attribui, secundum id quod est de
ratione illius perfectionis absolute. " It is here, in Vagaggini's judgment, that St. Thomas " ... pose avant tout le principe général sur
lequel le raisonnement se basera." Aquinas himself goes on: " Oportet ergo quod intelligere Deo conveniat et omnia quae sunt de ratione
eius, licet alio modo conveniat sibi quam creaturis. De ratione autem
eius quod est intelligere, est quod sit intelligens et intellectum. " Vagaggini considers this the application (" Par conséquent on passe à
l'application. "), and suggests a proper translation for the principle
that has just been enunciated: " On pourrait traduire: qu'il y ait
distinction entre le sujet qui comprend et l'objet qu'il comprend. "

out more clearly still when, in the same article, Aquinas extends his purely deductive procedure to establish the chief differences between the Divine Word and the word of human understanding.[23]

A further advance — Vagaggini considers it the high point in the evolution of St. Thomas' thought on the processions — is reached in the fourth book *Contra Gentiles*. From this moment on, there will no longer appear the formula *per modum naturae* to describe the procession of the Son. Moreover, the system of explanation already devised for the Word is now extended to the Holy Spirit, with the effect that the two processions are treated in perfect parallel.[24]

---

note no. 63. After continuing with St. Thomas' proof that the *intellectum* in this context, that which is " primo et per se intellectum, " is the intellectual conception, Vagaggini states his position clearly : " On voit vraiment difficilement en quoi ce raisonnement diffère essentiellement de celui avec lequel S. Anselme, dans les chapitres 32 et 38 du *Monologion*, croyait pouvoir prouver de façon apodictique, avec la seule raison, l'existence d'une seconde Personne en Dieu en partant du concept de verbe compris comme perfection simple. " p. 121.
    [23] p. 122.
    [24] " Au sommet de l'évolution de S. Thomas on peut situer les chapitres 11 et 19 du livre IV du *Contra Gentiles* qui furent certainement écrits après les articles du *De Potentia* cités plus haut. Ces chapitres perfectionnent le *De Potentia* d'une façon essentielle : d'abord en tant que, concernant la procession du Fils, ils laissent tomber complètement la formule *per modum naturae* dont on trouvait encore quelques traces dans le *De Potentia* ; ensuite en tant qu'ils étendent aussi à la procession de l'amour le système d'explication de la procession du Verbe, de sorte que les deux processions sont traitées d'une façon en tout parallèle. " p. 124. In what concerns specifically the divine generation, Vagaggini finds St. Thomas making here for the first time the perfect identification of generation with conception, but otherwise only confirming the position he had already reached in the ninth question *De Potentia*. " Encore une fois, cette façon de raisonner à partir du : *Deus seipsum intelligit*, coincide essentiellement avec celle du *De Potentia* IX a. 5. La conclusion est déduite de deux prémisses de raison pure : Dieu se comprend lui-même ; quiconque se comprend soi-même, produit un verbe mental immanent, réellement distinct de soi-même. On ne voit pas en quoi tout ceci diffère, en substance, du raisonnement de S. Anselme dans le *Monologion*. Dans le *Contra Gentiles IV*, il n'y a même plus trace de la formule : *per modum naturae*. C'est pourquoi S. Thomas dit clairement : ... *quum autem in divinis nihil aliud sit Filii generatio quam Verbi conceptio ...*, et ainsi il rejoint parfaitement le principe de S. Augustin qui constitue également la base des raisonnements de S. Anselme et qui identifie formel-

Scripture bears witness to the existence in God of a Holy Spirit, Who is not a creature, but truly God, subsistent, a Person really distinct from both the Father and the Son. But observe, Vagaggini continues, the reasoning process whereby St. Thomas will demonstrate, in the nineteenth chapter, how this testimony of scripture should be understood.

First, there is the general philosophical foundation : in every intellectual nature, there is will ; in every instance of will, there is that love which is the source of all its other acts. Then Aquinas attempts to discover in the interior of the act of love itself something really distinct from it, whereby the beloved exists in the one loving as the intrinsic term towards which love is tending — all, therefore, in a manner similar to the existence in intellect of the inner word as term of, and really distinct from, the act of understanding. Since Aquinas does not explain this presence of the *amatum in amante* as really distinct term any further, Vagaggini surmises this is because he is supposing such a condition as the necessary consequence of the act of love itself, or simply that he is treating the act of love as a simple perfection.

In any case, St. Thomas next makes the application to God. God is intelligent — Vagaggini underscores the simplicity of this point of departure — and hence there is in God both will and love. But since the beloved must somehow exist in the will of the lover, and since God certainly loves Himself, it is necessary that God exist in His own will as beloved in the one loving. Because of the identification in God between will and being, this existence must be strictly substantial. Finally, since every love of a being presupposes the intelligence whereby it is known and consequently conceived, there is nothing in the will as *amatum in amante*, unless as derived from the conceiving intelligence and the intellectual conception, or inner word.[25]

---

lement en Dieu génération et le fait de dire le Verbe : *Eo quippe Filius quo Verbum et eo Verbum quo Filius.* (S. Augustin, *De Trinitate*, VII 20, 27.) '' p. 126.

[25] '' Voici avec quel raisonnement S. Thomas atteint son but dans le chapitre 19. D'abord les fondements philosophiques généraux : dans toute nature intellectuelle il y a volonté et dans toute volonté il y a l'amour qui est source de tous ses autres actes. Ici S. Thomas essaie de découvrir à l'intérieur de l'acte d'amour lui-même quelque chose qui soit réellement distinct de lui et par quoi l'aimé soit dans

In Dom Vagaggini's opinion, therefore, the doctrine on the Spirit in *Contra Gentiles IV* reestablishes the position Anselm had originally worked out beginning in the forty-ninth chapter of his *Monologion* — but with this significant difference, that St. Thomas has introduced a psychological analysis of the act of love (patterned after his analysis of the inner word), which was totally lacking in Anselm.[26]

Since it is Vagaggini's declared judgment that later works of Aquinas add nothing in particular to the position assumed in *Contra Gentiles IV*, it should be permissible to pass on immediately to the author's conclusions.[27] Vagaggini finds that there are two fundamental points to be recognised even in works previous to *De Potentia*.

First, the general viewpoint of St. Thomas in his approach to trinitarian theology is dependent upon the state of the question as it had already been determined by St. Anselm. St. Thomas, that is to say, is not preoccupied with the loose images of Augustine, but rather sets himself the objective of reaching, and in some way justifying rationally, the metaphysical reality of the intratrinitarian processions. For his precise intent is to determine their *principium formale quo proximum*, as this principle is understood in Aristotelian science.

Secondly, Aquinas has accepted the Anselmian distinction between simple and mixed perfections, with the persuasion

l'aimant comme le terme intrinsèque à quoi tend l'amour, d'une façon semblable au verbe de l'intellect comme terme réellement distinct de l'acte de l'intelligence. Il dit : ' Quod amatur non est solum in intellectu amantis sed etiam in voluntate ipsius ... ' A propos de cette présence dans l'acte d'amour lui-même de la chose aimée comme terme réellement distinct et auquel il tend, S. Thomas ne donne pas d'autres explications ni d'autres preuves. Par conséquent, toutes les apparences laissent au lecteur l'impression qu'il suppose que cela se passe en tout acte d'amour en tant qu'amour, et que de soi, il s'agit d'une perfection simple. Après les bases philosophiques générales, l'application à Dieu. Dieu est intelligent (qu'on note bien cette simple constatation comme point de départ), donc en lui il y a volonté et amour. " pp. 126-127.

[26] " On assiste donc dans le *Contra Gentiles IV* 19 à une revalorisation des chapitres 49 et suivants du *Monologion*, principalement moyennant une analyse plus poussée de la psychologie philosophique de l'acte d'amour, en parfait parallèle avec le concept de verbe, ce qui manquait totalement chez S. Anselme. " p. 128.

[27] Of subsequent works, Vagaggini remarks that " ... elles n'en font au contraire qu'une simple reprise dont la pleine intelligence requiert la lecture des chapitres qu'on vient d'examiner. " p. 128.

that only the simple perfections bring one into formal contact
with the divine being.   It is significant, in fact, that precisely
what motivates St. Thomas' denial of the possibility that pure
reason could penetrate into the Trinity of Persons is the absence of any simple perfection including, at the same time, or
in its absolute formality, a real distinction.[28]

Beginning, however, with the development of the concept
of inner word in *De Veritate* and *Contra Gentiles I*, Aquinas
makes the sharp about-face described above.   From now on,
he will consider the *verbum cordis* as a simple perfection, and
straight away, in the *De Potentia*, he will incorporate this understanding of the inner word as simple perfection into a process of reasoning that has at least every appearance of being
a strictly rational demonstration of the first trinitarian procession.   It is not, of course, the general principle that has
changed.   The general principle — the 'major' — stands
firm : only simple perfections can lead to formal knowledge
of the divine reality.   But the particular instance — the 'minor' — is now, in Vagaggini's judgment, provided with precisely that quality of simple perfection which had always been
required, though Aquinas had heretofore been unable to locate it, as is evidenced by his earlier rejection of Anselm's
argument.

The result of this change in attitude, Vagaggini goes on,
is that, beginning with *De Potentia*, St. Thomas' treatment
of the divine processions is characterised by three simultaneous
affirmations.   (1) Unaided reason cannot advance in any apodictic fashion from the divine unity to the plurality of Persons.
For the Trinity is a mystery, and the theologian's task is solely

---

[28] Referring to St. Thomas' appropriation of the Anselmian perspective in preference to that of Augustine, Vagaggini writes : " ...mais
il veut atteindre et en quelque sorte justifier rationnellement la réalité
métaphysique des processions intratrinitaires dans le sens de la science
aristotélicienne, en en déterminant si possible le principe formel *quo*
prochain.   Fondamentale aussi dans la matière présente, et d'origine
anselmienne, est la distinction réfléchie entre perfections simples et
perfections mixtes, avec la persuasion que seules les perfections simples nous introduisent formellement dans la réalité divine.... Au contraire, l'affirmation que la raison nue ne peut arriver à la Trinité est
ici basée d'une façon cohérente sur l'unique fondement qui puisse la
justifier, à savoir qu'il n'existe pas une perfection simple qui inclue
en même temps, par propre essence formelle, une distinction réelle. "
p. 133.

to 'manifest' this mystery in some way, and to defend it against the attacks of unbelievers. (2) Nevertheless, first apropos of the inner word, and subsequently to 1263 of proceeding love as well, Aquinas makes assertions, which, if taken literally, indicate that he is considering both the inner word and proceeding love as simple perfections, but such as include, at the same time, the element of real distinction. (3) To 'manifest' trinitarian belief, St. Thomas has recourse to certain demonstrations, which, still supposing the literal intention, involve apodictic rational passage from the divine unity to the Trinity of Persons, through a process based precisely upon the understanding of the inner word and the term of love as simple perfection together with real distinction.[29]

What is ultimately at stake here, Vagaggini observes, is the mystery as such. For if the inner word, as term really distinct from the operation of intellect to which it is immanent, is a simple perfection, then quite necessarily the mystery of the Trinity ceases to be a mystery. Aquinas himself insists, in *De Potentia*, q. 9, a. 5, that every simple perfection found in creatures be attributed formally to God according to the strictly absolute character of the perfection in question.[30]

---

[29] " A partir du *De Potentia* (vers 1263), dans les ouvrages de S. Thomas qui traitent des processions divines, on peut lire simultanément ces trois affirmations : 1º) S. Thomas dit que la raison nue ne peut passer, d'une façon apodictique, de l'unité à la pluralité des Personnes en Dieu ; la Trinité est un mystère ; la tâche du théologien est seulement de la ' manifester ' de quelque façon et d'en défendre la foi contre les non-croyants. 2º) Toutefois concernant le verbe (et à partir du *Contra Gentiles* IV — après 1263 — également concernant le produit de l'amour), il fait des affirmations décidées qui, prises à la lettre en elles-mêmes, signifient qu'il le considérait comme une perfection simple incluant toutefois une distinction réelle. 3º) Pour ' manifester ' la foi trinitaire, il a recours à des raisonnements qui — toujours pris en eux-mêmes à la lettre — incluent le passage rationnel apodictique de l'unité à la Trinité sur la base précisément du concept de verbe (et du terme de l'amour) comme perfection simple incluant toutefois une distinction réelle. '' pp. 133-134.

[30] " En effet, si le verbe, comme terme réellement distinct de l'acte même d'intelligence auquel il est immanent, est perfection simple, alors nécessairement s'évanouit le mystère de la Trinité. Car c'est une nécessité métaphysique de fer — rappelée par S. Thomas lui-même dans le corps de l'article 5 du *De Potentia* IX — que l'on doive attribuer formellement à Dieu toute perfection simple que nous trouvons dans les créatures, selon le caractère formel précis de cette perfection, bien que non pas selon le mode accidentel qu'elle revêt dans les créatures.'' p. 135.

Yet, that St. Thomas was actually free from such an outright and serious contradiction, Vagaggini finds clearly proved from the nature of his reply to an objection in the important passage *S. T.*, *I*, q. 32, a. 1, ad 2m.[31]

The problem focused in this famous article is : " Utrum Trinitas divinarum personarum possit per naturalem rationem cognosci. " In the second objection, Aquinas poses Richard of St. Victor's claim for *necessaria argumenta*. He goes on to note that to demonstrate the Trinity of Persons, some have argued from the infinity of divine goodness, which communicates itself infinitely in the processions. Others have appealed to the principle that there can be no joyous satisfaction in the good possessed without companionship. And finally, Augustine went on to manifest the Trinity from the procession of the word and love in the human spirit — the ' way ', St. Thomas adds, he himself has followed in the foregoing sections of the *Pars Prima*.

In replying to this objection, Aquinas draws a distinction between two possible uses of rational argument. On the one hand, there is the process of reasoning which is sufficient to demonstrate a certain supposition in reality. He adduces the proof which natural science offers for the constant uniform velocity of celestial motion. On the other hand, there is the process of reasoning which is not sufficient to demonstrate such a basic supposition, but which, once the supposition is granted, can go ahead to show that consequent effects are congruent with it. He adduces the eccentricities and epicycles of astrology, on the basis of which certain phenomena of celestial motion can be accounted for.

In theology, it is the strictly demonstrative process of the first type, St. Thomas explains, that proves the divine unity. But it is only the process of the second type — not sufficient for adequate demonstration of the supposition — that can be used to manifest the Trinity of Persons, once the revelation of the Trinity, so Vagaggini interprets Aquinas' meaning, is presupposed.

---

[31] The reader may wish to refer to the examination that will be made of this same text in the last part of the present study, when the ' *de Trinitate* ' of the *Pars Prima* will be analysed in detail. The article in question is situated in St. Thomas' discussion of the Persons as the first point treated under the problem of cognoscibility.

Then, after commenting on the two arguments from infinite goodness and companionship in the possession of the
good, St. Thomas turns to the third and most important argument, Augustine's analogy.   But this likeness of the human
intellect is not adequate, to prove anything about God (the
context, of course, being trinitarian), inasmuch as intellect is
not found to exist univocally in God and in men.

Vagaggini reads this passage as follows.   For St. Thomas,
the entire process of reasoning which he has brought to bear
upon the trinitarian processions is not to be taken for an
apodictic proof.   All that he has written, and which, at first
sight, has every appearance of being such a proof, cannot be
accepted literally.   Nor can the expressions *oportet, necesse
est*, and the like, be cited to the contrary.[32]

What has not been given sufficient attention up to the
present, Vagaggini continues, is that if one accepts St. Thomas' protestations against intending to put forth apodictic
arguments and not merely those of a more or less probable
and illustrative type, then one must also admit that Aquinas
no longer wishes his remarks on the inner word as a simple
perfection to be taken at face value.   For the reply just cited
from the *Pars Prima* resumes the position previously espoused
in the *In Boethii de Trinitate*, to the effect that rational argument from the divine unity to the Trinity of Persons is impossible precisely because the inner word as such involves poten-

---

[32] " Voir la seconde objection : ' Augustinus vero procedit ad
manifestandum Trinitatem personarum ex processione verbi et amoris
in mente nostra ; quam viam supra (I q. 27 et dans les autres œuvres
à partir du *De Veritate*) secuti sumus'.   Quand S. Thomas dit qu'un
tel procédé ne peut être retenu comme preuve apodictique, il faut
donc comprendre que tout ce qu'il a écrit et qui, à première vue, donnerait l'impression d'une preuve de telle nature, ne doit pas être
pris à la lettre.   Que des expressions comme : oportet ... necesse est ...
et autres semblables, n'impliquent pas toujours dans l'esprit de S. Thomas une conséquence apodictique, on en a, entre tant d'autres, un bel
exemple déjà dans le commentaire sur le Lombard 1 d. 10, q. 1, a. 1c.
Là il dit clairement que la pluralité des personnes en Dieu est admise
seulement par la foi.   Toutefois, immédiatement après il dit : ' *oportet* quod inquantum processio creaturarum est ex liberalitate divinae
voluntatis, reducatur in unum principium, quod sit quasi ratio totius
liberalis collationis.   Haec autem est amor, sub cuius ratione omnia
a voluntate conferuntur ; et ideo *oportet* aliquam personam esse in divinis procedentem per modum amoris, et haec est Spiritus Sanctus '. "
p. 136, note no. 96.

tiality, and hence must be classified as mixed, not simple, perfection.[33]

In accepting this solution, however, one has still to explain the disconcerting procedure whereby St. Thomas has time and again treated the inner word as a simple perfection, and then incorporated this principle to manifest the mystery of the trinitarian processions in a way that appears to confirm the very Anselmian argument he has repudiated. Vagaggini concludes his discussion, therefore, with the suggestion that on this last point, only one answer is possible : the ideal of Anselm's *rationes necessariae* had come to obsess the medieval School, St. Thomas included.

Thus, even where Aquinas clearly sees that he cannot apply this rigorously deductive ideal in its purity, he will nonetheless imitate this ideal as closely as possible, and present a sort of substitute process giving at least its aesthetic illusion.[34]

---

[33] " Ce qui, à mon avis, n'a pas été assez remarqué jusqu'ici, c'est que si on croit sincèrement ces affirmations de S. Thomas où il dit qu'il n'entend pas du tout proposer les arguments qui semblent faire le passage rationnel de l'unité à la Trinité comme des arguments apodictiques mais seulement comme plus ou moins probables et ' illustratifs ', il faut admettre nécessairement qu'il n'entendait pas non plus prendre à la lettre ses affirmations sur le verbe perfection simple. La *Somme* I q. 32, a. 1, ad 2 rejoint parfaitement le *In Boetii de Trinitate*, Proem. q. 1, a. 4, ad 6 où S. Thomas dit que le motif pour lequel il ne peut y avoir passage apodictique de l'unité à la Trinité moyennant le concept de verbe, est que le verbe inclut nécessairement une potentialité et donc qu'il est perfection mixte. " p. 137.

[34] " Mais alors, comment expliquer la façon de procéder de S. Thomas, pour nous si déconcertante pour ne rien dire de plus, avec laquelle tant de fois il a présenté le verbe comme une perfection simple, et qui pour ' manifester ' la Trinité a eu recours à des raisonnements rigoureusement enchaînés sur la base du verbe perfection simple, paraissant ainsi confirmer pleinement S. Anselme au moment même où il le repoussait ? A cela il ne peut y avoir qu'une réponse : ' Les *necessariae rationes*, à la suite de S. Anselme, hantèrent toujours l'école '. Cette hantise de l'idéal anselmien de la preuve déductive par ' raisons nécessaires, ' comme l'idéal le plus parfait de toute science, fut telle chez S. Thomas lui-même que plus d'une fois, même lorsque d'un autre côté il se rendait parfaitement compte que cet idéal ne pouvait être proprement atteint dans sa pureté, il fut poussé à en présenter au moins une imitation, la plus parfaite possible, qui le remplacerait en quelque sorte et en donnerait comme l'illusion esthétique. " pp. 137-138.

Vagaggini's contribution to the academic dialogue :

Dom Vagaggini addresses himself directly to the problem of some degree of *de facto* rational demonstration in St. Thomas' treatment of the trinitarian processions. His answer to the basic question amounts to a qualified no.

In the opinion of the present writer, however, it is less than clear exactly how far this qualification is meant to go. For it seems that Vagaggini's final judgment on the matter could be summed up in two points. First, despite the many appearances to the contrary, Aquinas did not, in the last analysis, intend to include in his trinitarian exposition any apodictic, strictly and purely rational demonstration for the processions. Nevertheless — and this is the second point — the appearances themselves require a better explanation than has thus far been given.

Vagaggini, therefore, makes a suggestion of his own. One is forced to recognize the profound influence of Anselm's deductivist ideal and the *rationes necessariae*, which so obsessed the mind of Aquinas himself, that he would strive at least to imitate the apodictic demonstration when he could not apply it simply.

But what exactly is the nature and extent of this imitation? If Anselm began with the processions as a mystery of faith whose existence was learned from revelation, and then went on to demonstrate in an apodictic fashion the a priori necessity of these same processions, did Aquinas himself imitate Anselm to the extent of accepting the revealed mystery, and then going on to demonstrate — but this time not apodictically — the a priori "convenience" of the mystery? In other words, was Aquinas' focus the same as Anselm's, at least insofar as it was somehow directed to the existence or basic fact of the mystery, instead of, or as well as, its theological elaboration?

In the writer's view, Vagaggini's eventual conclusions do not pretend to answer these questions. The reader remains uncertain as to whether or not, in Vagaggini's mind, St. Thomas had employed rational demonstration, however qualified or softened, to penetrate to the very existence of the revealed mystery in some sort of apologetical a priori. Furthermore, the reader does not have a perfectly clear picture of whether or not, again in Vagaggini's mind, Aquinas actually considered the inner word a simple perfection.

It seems, however, especially in the light of these uncertainties, that Dom Vagaggini's own purpose all along was rather to pose a problem, than to offer a solution.

Chapter Two

LIMITED DISCUSSION OF THE PROBLEM
BY OTHER THEOLOGIANS

As seen in the preceding chapter, it is Dom Vagaggini's contention that the problem of some species of rational demonstration in the Thomist ' *de Trinitate* ' has not yet really been settled. It is time, then, to ask whether among the various theologians who have treated Aquinas' trinitarian doctrine in recent years, other authors have at least touched upon the same problem, even though less directly and explicitly than Vagaggini himself.

I. Père Paissac's "Théologie du Verbe"

A look should be taken first of all at H. Paissac's well known treatise *Théologie du Verbe. Saint Augustin et saint Thomas*.[1]

After discussing the passage in *C. G., I*, c. 53, where St. Thomas demonstrates the necessity for an inner word in every act of intellect, so that the act of intellect might have its proper and immanent term, Père Paissac appends a lengthy note on the universality of this principle. It is his judgment that Aquinas does, in fact, wish to show that the presence of an inner word is verified even in divine intellection. If this is so, Paissac observes immediately, one has answered affirmatively, it will be claimed, the delicate question whether there is an inner word in every instance of intellection.

---

[1] H. Paissac, o.p., *Théologie du Verbe. Saint Augustin et saint Thomas* (Paris : Les Editions du Cerf, 1951). In the following section of the present study devoted exclusively to an analysis of what is immediately pertinent in this work, only the page numbers will be given for references and citations.

Paissac feels that it would be beyond the purpose of his treatise to discuss the various points this question suggests. Nevertheless, he takes a moment to argue, following Sylvester of Ferrara, that the crucial question is simply to determine the exact reason why the inner word is required in intellectual operation. If the reason assigned is the absence of an object, or its disproportion, then the word will be verified only in imperfect instances of understanding. Paissac, however, believes that the necessity here is more profound : namely, that intellectual operation must have an object, a term, distinct as such from even the principle of the operation, and this, in the most perfect instance of intellectual activity as well as in any other.

In Paissac's analysis, St. Thomas' appeal to the absent object and material object to prove the necessity of an inner word in human understanding does not mean that absence and materiality constitute the ultimate necessity for inner word, but serve rather to disclose with certitude that there must be an inner word immanent to the human intellectual operation as such. But through this process of argument, would not one demonstrate the existence of a personal Word in God ? Paissac replies that one would not. All that is demonstrated — and he finds support in *C. G., I*, c. 53, where the Trinity is not as yet presupposed — is that in God, since there is intellection, there must necessarily be both principle and term of this intellection, but with no suggestion at this point that principle and term be really distinct, much less that the term be personal.[2]

---

[2] " En ce ch. LIII, en effet, saint Thomas pensons-nous, entend bien montrer que dans l'intellection divine elle-même, comme en toute intellection, se vérifie la présence d'un verbe. C'est, dira-t-on, répondre affirmativement à la délicate question de savoir s'il y a un verbe en toute intellection. Sans vouloir ici nous engager dans les discussions auxquelles a pu donner lieu cette question, ce qui dépasserait le but précis de notre travail, disons seulement que nous ne voyons pas de raison péremptoire de rejeter l'affirmation de Sylvestre de Ferrare dans le commentaire qu'il fait de ce chapitre. Toute la question revient en somme à savoir quelle est au juste la nécessité de poser un verbe dans une opération intellectuelle. Si l'on admet qu'il faut un verbe en raison de l'absence de l'objet ou de sa disproportion, le verbe ne se vérifiera que dans l'intellection imparfaite, c'est bien clair. Mais il nous semble que la raison de cette nécessité est plus profonde : c'est simplement qu'il faut un *objet* à l'action intellectuelle,

A few pages later, Paissac distinguishes very sharply between what is proper to the human word as human, on the one hand, and what analysis of the human word reveals as essential to the nature of inner word as such, on the other hand. In men, the inner word is distinct from the act of intelligence as an accidental reality, as the term issuing from a principle whose action is accidental. But it is no more essential to the basic nature of the inner word to be accidental, than it is to the basic nature of intelligence or intellectual operation. Rather, essential to the nature of inner word, is simply that it be that which issues from the intelligence in act, the term of an intellectual operation standing in relation, therefore, with the principle of this operation.

If, then, these notions are transposed to the divinity, the inner word retains what is essential to itself as inner word without being an accidental reality, and without being distinct from the divine essence as an accident from its substance. There remains, consequently, only the distinction of relation between the word and its principle : the word being that which issues *from* its principle, but this, only on the supposition it should somehow become necessary to affirm such a distinction in God in the first place.[3]

_____

un *terme*, distinct, comme tel, du principe même de cette action, et ceci dans l'intellection la plus parfaite ... L'absence de la chose, ou sa matérialité, n'est pas ce qui rend nécessaire un verbe, mais ce qui nous fait déceler avec certitude la nécessité qu'il y ait un verbe immanent à notre action ... Mais en Dieu, dira-t-on, si l'on conclut ainsi à la présence d'un verbe, ne démontre-t-on pas l'existence du Verbe personnel ? On démontre simplement (et ce nous semble être le sens de ce ch. LIII, où la Trinité n'est évidemment pas encore supposée connue) qu'en Dieu, il y a nécessairement, puisqu'il y a intellection, principe et terme de cette intellection ; mais principe et terme (ou verbe) ne sont pas distincts réellement, du moins on ne le sait pas encore, et nulle allusion ne peut encore être faite à un Verbe *personnel*. De même on démontrera qu'en Dieu il y a nécessairement, puisque Dieu est esprit, une intelligence et une volonté ; mais intelligence et volonté ne seront pas, en lui, distinctes réellement. " pp. 167-168, note no. 1.

[3] " Si le verbe en effet, se distingue, en nous, de l'intelligence, c'est que le verbe, en nous, est accidentel, comme le terme provenant d'un principe dont l'action est accidentelle. Mais il n'est pas essentiel au verbe d'être de nature accidentelle, non plus qu'à l'intelligence ni à l'opération intellectuelle. Ce qui appartient essentiellement à la nature du verbe, c'est d'être *ce qui provient de* l'intelligence en acte, le *terme* d'une action intellectuelle, en *relation* par conséquent avec

Moreover, Paissac observes in a note, this is the precise limit beyond which unaided reason cannot probe. Reason is unable to show that such a distinction of relation is actually verified in God, or that it would be real. On the other hand, reason cannot prove that to conceive such a real distinction would be impossible.[4]

So far, the observations and comments of Père Paissac, in the two sections of his treatise just referred to, have been incidental to his main purpose. In a third and last section, however, which stands as the conclusion to the lengthy historical analysis of the Thomist *Verbum* texts, the initial impression is of a much more direct and thorough treatment of the problem of a priori demonstration in the area of mystery. For here, the author proposes the question: what precisely was the value, in terms of certitude, that St. Thomas himself assigned to his own *Verbum* doctrine? In his discussion, Paissac allows the further question — the quite subordinate question really — of rational demonstration to figure somewhat prominently.

St. Thomas' process of verification has been so careful, his argumentation so solidly worked out, one might be tempted to accord to the *Verbum* theory as finally developed an absolute value. Has not Aquinas, Paissac continues, actually elaborated the true demonstration certain modern authors persist in finding in his text? Does not the *Verbum* theology of the *Summa* extend to the point of proving, by itself alone, the reality in God of a Divine Word, a Person distinct from its principle?

Once again, this time following St. Thomas' own handling of the objection in *S. T.*, *I*, q. 32, a. 1, ad 2m, Paissac shows

---

le principe même de cette action. Si donc on transpose ces notions en Dieu, le verbe garde en lui son essence de verbe sans être un accident, et sans se distinguer de l'essence divine comme un accident de sa substance. ' Reste pourtant la seule distinction de relation ' entre le verbe et son principe : le verbe est ce qui provient *de* son principe,... [sic] à supposer qu'il faille en Dieu affirmer d'une certaine manière quelque distinction. '' p. 175.

[4] '' C'est à ce point précis, nous semble-t-il, que peut conduire la raison seule. Au delà, rien ne peut, du point de vue de la raison, prouver que la distinction de relation se vérifie en Dieu et soit réelle, ou au contraire prouver que la réalité de cette distinction soit impossible à concevoir. La discrimination entre l'une ou l'autre hypothèse ne relève plus de notre pouvoir. '' p. 175, note no. 3.

the radical incompetence of pure reason to penetrate the plurality of Persons.[5]

It will not be necessary to review the entire discussion at this point. The element in Aquinas' reply that Père Paissac wishes to stress in particular, however, is the scientific hypothesis — in the sense of supposition. Every science has its hypotheses, the basic principles upon which the ensemble of scientific knowledge is erected. These hypotheses express the reality hidden under sensible appearances, with rational intelligence allowing facts accessible to observation to be understood. Their rôle is to sustain the facts which by themselves would be without reason for being, to plead their cause and to defend them. Paissac then cites St. Thomas' familiar example from astronomy.[6]

Faith itself proposes the existence of Three Persons in God, and this hypothesis constitutes the foundation of the whole treatment of the Trinity in scientific theology. Now one of the objectives of theology, as science, is to manifest the harmony possible between this basic affirmation and cer-

---

[5] " Est-il possible de préciser la façon dont saint Thomas apprécie la certitude de sa propre doctrine ? Le contrôle entrepris par le théologien a été si consciencieux, ses raisonnements si fermes qu'on pourrait être tenté d'accorder une valeur absolue à la théorie proposée au sujet du Verbe divin. Saint Thomas n'a-t-il pas, en fait, élaboré une véritable démonstration, comme certains auteurs persistent à le penser aujourd'hui ? La théologie du Verbe exposée par l'auteur de la *Somme* ne va-t-elle pas jusqu'à prouver, à elle seule, la réalité d'un Verbe en Dieu, Personne distincte de son Principe ? L'objection est formulée par saint Thomas lui-même : n'a-t-on pas démontré l'existence des Personnes au terme de cette ' voie ' utilisant le verbe mental, tout comme on a prouvé l'existence de Dieu en suivant les ' cinq voies ' à partir des créatures ? " p. 219. (In note no. 1 on the same page, the reference is given as *S. théol.*, Ia, qu. 23, art. 1, 2e obj., instead of Ia, q. 32, through an error in printing.)

[6] " Toute science suppose ses ' hypothèses '. De tels principes constituent le fondement sur lequel s'édifie l'ensemble du savoir scientifique. Ils expriment la réalité cachée sous les apparences visibles, la raison intelligible permettant de comprendre les faits donnés à l'observation. Leur rôle est, dans l'immense procès intenté par l'intelligence au monde sensible, de soutenir les faits qui par eux-mêmes n'ont pas raison d'être de plaider leur cause, et finalement de les sauver. Ainsi pour sauver les apparences on posera comme principe ou ' hypothèse ' en astronomie que les planètes se déplacent suivant des cercles homocentriques à la Terre. " p. 221. See also p. 220, note no. 2, for Paissac's rendition of *radices* by " hypothèses. "

tain observable data, and in this fashion to "give account" of what faith has taught.   But it is likewise true that human sciences must in some cases furnish proof of even their basic principles.   Is it not to be expected, then, that the scientific theologian, despite himself, will fall victim to the temptation of doing the same thing, and in the Trinity more than anywhere else?   What of St. Thomas in this regard?   Did the development of the *verbum* theory lead Aquinas to the same excesses as a similar theory had once led Augustine? [7]

For Père Paissac, however, St. Thomas makes his own position on the matter most precise.   It is true that reason will seek to prove even the foundations of a given science.   On the other hand, this is not always possible.   A decisive demonstration of fundamental principles would require the introduction of that reason sufficient to impose certitude, and thus verify the hypothesis in this strictly scientific manner.   Thus, for example, while faith proposes the existence of God, or the immortality of the human soul, the theologian is also able to verify these hypotheses with reasons that are sufficient to induce certitude.

In other instances, however, as in the affirmation of the astronomical eccentricities, no reason is sufficient to prove the basic hypothesis.   This time, the effort to give account of the principle leads, not to the demonstration of the principle, but only to the manifestation that certain facts are in accord with the principle.   Thus too, extending the analogy from natural science to theology, there is no sufficient and purely natural reason that can verify, as hypothesis, the Trinity of Persons.   For, as already seen, the hypothesis or radical supposition in this case lies quite outside the entire compass of demonstration. [8]

---

[7] " La foi pose en principe qu'il existe Trois Personnes en Dieu, et cette ' hypothèse ' ou ' supposition ' constitue le fondement de tout le traité de la Trinité.   L'un des buts de la théologie, comme science, est de manifester l'accord possible entre cette affirmation fondamentale et certains faits d'observation courante : ainsi l'on pourra ' rendre compte ' de la foi....   Mais les sciences humaines ne doivent-elles pas fournir en certains cas la preuve de leurs principes, et le théologien ne serait-il pas tenté, comme malgré lui, de suivre cet exemple, dans le traité de la Trinité plus encore que partout ailleurs ?   La théorie du verbe n'aurait-elle pas été pour saint Thomas comme pour saint Augustin l'occasion de tomber dans cet excès ? " pp. 221-222.

[8] " Saint Thomas précise sa pensée.   Il est assez au courant des sciences de la nature pour savoir qu'en effet les ' hypothèses ' sur les-

In the judgment of Père Paissac, therefore, the analysis of the *verbum cordis* developed by Aquinas following Augustine does not furnish a sufficient reason for affirming in God the reality of a Word personally distinct from its principle. One is left, then, with nothing more than a *ratio convenientiae*? Paissac suggests this would be going too far.

Aquinas himself, he says, reserves the notion of *convenientia* to such cases as are ultimately contingent — where the principle supposed represents a contingent reality, dependent upon the free will of God, as the creation of the world, or the Incarnation. In these instances, there can be a certain 'convenience' satisfying the reason. To affirm as principle, however, a reality that is not contingent, that cannot not be, as the mystery of the Three Persons in God, is to go beyond this : to a 'concordance', which is more than a simple 'convenience', but itself still quite short of being a proof. [9]

---

quelles elles se construisent ont été parfois, depuis Aristote, l'objet de discussions passionnées. Il connaît le problème des excentriques et des épicycles en astronomie. La raison cherche donc à prouver les fondements mêmes de telle science donnée. Mais cette preuve n'est pas toujours possible. Pour démontrer de façon décisive, il faut nécessairement ' apporter la raison suffisante ' imposant la certitude. Le principe est dès lors prouvé, l'hypothèse est vraie. Ainsi le théologien démontre avec toute la rigueur désirable certains fondements de sa science. Il pose en principe : Dieu existe, ou : l'âme de l'homme est immortelle, c'est de foi. Puis il fournit la preuve de ces ' hypothèse ', les raisons apportées sont suffisantes. Mais la même rigueur ne peut être observée dans tous les cas. L'affirmation de l'excentrique, en astronomie, n'est pas susceptible de preuve. Aucune raison ne peut être apportée pour prouver l'hypothèse. On peut dire seulement : de tels principes peuvent rendre compte, comme c'est le rôle de tous les principes, de faits apparemment inexplicables. Une telle raison n'est pas une preuve. L'effort fait pour rendre compte du principe aboutit cette fois non plus à le démontrer, mais à montrer simplement que certains faits concordent avec lui.... La science théologique peut donner lieu à des remarques analogues. S'il est question d'un principe tel que la supposition de Trois Personnes en Dieu, aucune raison décisive, indépendamment de la foi, ne peut être fournie prouvant sa vérité, on a vu pourquoi. Ce qu'on pose en ' hypothèse ' est en ce cas hors de portée de toute démonstration. " pp. 222-223.

[9] " L'analyse du verbe mental, conduite par saint Thomas à la suite de saint Augustin, ne fournit donc pas une raison suffisante pour affirmer en Dieu la réalité d'un Verbe personnellement distinct de son principe. Dira-t-on : il s'agit simplement d'une ' raison de convenance" ? Ce serait aller trop loin, semble-il. Saint Thomas réserve la notion de ' convenance ' pour le cas où tel principe supposé

These observations on aprioristic demonstration concluded, Père Paissac proceeds to develop the more strictly theological theme of *de facto* value. The question at this point is no longer whether, or to what extent, the Thomist trinitarian theory supplies proof for the root existence of the processions, but whether, and to what extent, as an achievement of speculative theology, the same theory, based frankly upon its source in the revealed word of God, offers a true, however imperfect and obscure, explanatory account of the revealed mystery. [10]

Extrinsically, of course, and Paissac clearly recognizes the fact, the dogmatic value of the Thomist trinitarian analogy hinges upon the place accorded this development in and by the Church. [11] Intrinsically, however, or arguing from the internal merits of the theory without explicit reference to authority, the ultimate theological value of the Thomist analogy derives from the fact that the analogy is just that: analogy, and not merely metaphor. [12]

Nevertheless, and of particular interest to the present inquiry, Paissac makes an important qualification. This qual-

---

représente une réalité contingente. Par rapport à ce qui aurait pu être ou ne pas être et dont l'existence dépend de la libre volonté de Dieu, comme le commencement du monde, l'Incarnation, l'institution d'un sacrement, on montrera, par l'observation de certains fauts, une certaine convenance capable de satisfaire la raison. Il y a plus si l'on affirme à titre de principe l'existence de ce qui ne peut pas ne pas être, comme le mystère des Trois Personnes. On ne dira pas seulement que certaines observations conviennent à l'affirmation révélée, mais qu'elles concordent vraiment avec elle, sans pour autant suffire à la prouver. La concordance dont on parle, et qui paraît différente de la simple convenance, n'est donc pas une preuve. Elle signifie que la supposition faite est, aux yeux de la raison, vraisemblable, mais non pas nécessairement vraie. " pp. 224-225.

[10] The change of focus is clear throughout these final pages. At the point marking the transition from a discussion of the possibilities of a priori demonstration to the discussion of *de facto* value, Paissac begins : " La valeur de la spéculation théologique à partir du texte de saint Jean peut être par là même évaluée. " p. 225, ad fin. Toward the end of the same section, he will ask the question : " Le travail de spéculation accompli dans la lumière de foi pour purifier la notion de conception mentale, pour manifester la solidarité de cette notion avec le donné révélé, ne pourrait-il être consideré come l'occasion providentielle de quelque précision déclarée par l'Eglise ? " p. 230.

[11] pp. 229-231.

[12] pp. 225-229.

ification, moreover, brings out the fact that, at least in Père Paissac's judgment, no contradiction is involved should a theologian wish to consider the Thomist exposition of higher value, in terms of certitude, as a theological account of what has been revealed, than as a demonstration to verify the primary hypothesis.

The name *Verbum*, when used of God, is spoken not metaphorically, but properly. And the reason for this, as St. Thomas' analysis has uncovered it, is that the finite *verbum mentis*, being simply the terminal act of the intelligence, does not involve, *de se*, any imperfection. One can speak, therefore, of the Word in God, just as much as one can speak of His intelligence or His goodness. [13]

Yet, there is also this difference. In the case of God's goodness, the human mind is led from a consideration of creatures to the affirmation of the divine nature through recognition of an efficient causality operative here and imposing itself with certitude. In the case of the inner word, on the other hand, there is no such causal principle making it possible for the human mind to transcend its own psychology and enter the mystery of divine life.

The human soul is simply the image of the Trinity, and an image reveals nothing to the observer for so long a time as the observer remains in total ignorance of the one the image represents. By itself, in other words, an image does not lead necessarily to knowledge of the one whom it represents. Once again, therefore, notwithstanding even the fact that the inner word is spoken of God and men in proper analogy as opposed to metaphorical comparison, there is still no possibility of advancing from human psychology to recognition of the existence or personality of a Divine Person apart from revelation. [14]

---

[13] " Or, le nom de Verbe se dit en parlant de Dieu non pas à titre de métaphore, mais au sens propre. Et la raison donnée, cherchée et obtenue par analyse, est la suivante : le verbe mental est dans le monde des créatures une réalité ne supposant, de soi, aucune imperfection, étant seulement l'acte terminal de l'intelligence. On peut parler de Verbe en Dieu, comme d'Intelligence ou de Bonté, en laissent à ces mots l'essentiel pe leur signification authentique. " p. 226.

[14] " Mais dans le cas de la bonté, l'esprit se trouve nécessairement conduit de la considération des choses créées à l'affirmation de la nature divine, en vertu même du rapport de *causalité efficiente* intervenant ici et et s'imposant avec certitude. Lorsqu'on parle du Fils de Dieu au contraire, et par analogie avec notre verbe mental, aucun

* * *

Père Paissac had published his treatise on the *Verbum*
(1951) eight years before the appearance of Dom Vagaggini's
challenge in the *Spicilegium Beccense* (1959). His treatment
of the matter can hardly be expected to have assumed the
precise focus and approach of the later contribution — all the
less so when one recalls that Vagaggini's own starting point
would be that here was a problem whose most significant critical aspect, the dependence of Aquinas on Anselm's *rationes
necessariae*, authors, among them and very explicitly Paissac,
had rather seriously neglected all along. [15] Nevertheless,
inasmuch as the present study has been occasioned by Vagaggini's appeal for further investigation into the matter of the
Thomist demonstrations, it should be noted that, in some
respects, the earlier writing — Paissac's, that is — had already
thrown some light on what could well be the precise point
that would have to be investigated should the challenge ever
arise.

In Paissac's analysis, St. Thomas distinguished two moments, or two functions, within the larger compass of scientific
theology. One of these functions — does Paissac at least
imply that he considers it the chief function ? — is to work
out from radical suppositions in the direction of giving these

---

rapport causal efficient ne permet de passer de notre psychologie au
mystère de la vie divine. Notre âme est simplement l'image de la
Trinité. Or, une image ne dit rien à celui qui la regarde tant qu'il
ignore tout de celui qu'elle représente. Une réalité prend valeur
d'image à l'instant seulement où se révèle ce dont elle est l'image ; elle
ne conduit pas nécessairement par soi à la connaissance de ce qu'elle
représente. La raison en est, sans doute, que le rapport entre
l'image et son modèle est un pur rapport de *forme* et comme tel un
rapport d'identité. Il n'y a pas à développer ici ce point de vue.
Ainsi l'observation la plus attentive de l'âme humaine, et la plus parfaite analyse du verbe mental ne peuvent conduire à reconnaître l'existence ou la personalité d'une Personne divine, indépendamment d'une
révélation toute gratuite. " p. 228.

[15] Vagaggini criticises Paissac's bypassing of Anselm in showing
St. Thomas' development of the Augustinian analogy. " La hantise, "
p. 103. Vagaggini also finds contradiction in Paissac's discussion of
the *verbum*, on the grounds that he makes of it a simple perfection
— involving even real distinction from its principle — to be predicated apodictically of every intelligence, but still claims that unaided
reason cannot demonstrate from such a *verbum* principle a distinct
and personal Divine Word. *Ibid.*, pp. 134-135.

latter an explanatory and intelligible account. The other function of scientific theology is to double back, wherever this is possible, on the radical suppositions themselves in the direction of verifying their simple existence.

This distinction is of no little importance. For Paissac's use of it in the critical context already seen clearly suggests that, in his own view, the question whether Aquinas' arguments could give, or were intended to give, a purely natural demonstration of the revealed hypothesis is a question that could be determined only through analysis of the basic methodological perspective elected by Aquinas in a given passage, and exercising full control over the process of scientific development. Explicitly, Paissac does say that at least the two objectives — explanation of hypothesis, verification of hypothesis — are distinct. Implicitly, he appears to consider the two processes, or methodologies, distinct as well. For he is quite willing to assign a higher degree of certainty, even aside from the element of external authority and ecclesiastical absorption, to the *verbum* principle as deployed in the interests of explanatory analogy, than to the same principle as an instrument for verifying the primary supposition, or hypothesis.

Père Paissac does not elaborate on the place of the verification function in St. Thomas' trinitarian theology : whether it is operative within the explanatory function, or apart from it in comparative isolation ; whether it is of frequent or only rare occurrence ; whether, when all is said and done, it even exists. For he points out how and to what extremely limited extent the Thomist analogy *could be* applied to verification of the processional hypothesis. But he does not say, certainly not explicitly, that to do at least this much was ever the intention, or part of the intention, of Aquinas.

What Paissac does establish, however, and what is of significance for the investigation at hand, is that the authentic Thomist notion of science in general, and of theological science in particular, distinguished in some way between explanation and verification as just explained. If, therefore, St. Thomas recognized the verification objective as theoretically possible, a further and quite legitimate question would be to ask whether the distinction in theory is reflected in his own practice. But did not Aquinas himself, in the very reply cited by Père Paissac, positively exclude the possibility of verification in the trinitarian processions? Actually, no. What Aquinas excluded was a process of verification that would engender certitude.

It is here, moreover, that Vagaggini's question is seen to be yet unanswered. St. Thomas did not pretend to give an apodictic demonstration for the procession of the Son and Holy Spirit. Nevertheless, he did propose — this is Dom Vagaggini's claim — to imitate the Anselmian process of apodictic demonstration to the fullest extent possible in any particular area of Christian belief. Vagaggini asks, what is one to make of these appearances of strictly rational proof? Or in terms of Paissac's analysis, what place within the total field of Thomist trinitarian theology must one assign to rational proof as verification, however qualified or restricted, of the primary hypothesis?

On the point of the *verbum cordis*, and whether Aquinas, as Vagaggini argues, considered the *verbum cordis* a simple perfection, Paissac's position is less detailed. There must be an inner word in every act of intellect, because there must be principle and term in every intellectual operation. Unaided reason, however, would not have cause even to suspect that in God this principle and term would be distinct, to say nothing of being personally distinct. It is not altogether clear, therefore, what Paissac makes of the element of real distinction in the *verbum* axiom formulated with true universal extension.

II. DOM H. DIEPEN ON ANALOGICAL KNOWLEDGE
     .OF THE TRINITY

If the question of real distinction in the *verbum* axiom occupied less the attention of Père Paissac, this was, on the other hand, the precise question that Dom H. Diepen had discussed quite specifically a few years earlier in an article appearing in two successive volumes of *Angelicum*. [16]

---

[16] H. DIEPEN, O.S.B., " De Analogica Nostra Sanctissimae Trinitatis Conceptione, " *Angelicum*, XXIII (1946), pp. 89-125 ; XXIV (1947), pp. 33-46. As this section of the present study is given over entirely to an account of Dom Diepen's article, it will suffice in future references and citations to indicate simply the periodical (*Ang.*) and the proper year of the volume in which the two halves of the article are contained, plus page numbers. (As will be seen in due course,

In point of fact, Dom Diepen's main preoccupation is not with the inner word as really distinct from its principle, but with the inner word as providing an analogical ground for trinitarian consubstantiality. [17] It is not surprising, therefore, that in the course of his rather highly technical analysis, he will seek to emphasize the immanence of the *verbum* procession, and this, no less in the human context than in the divine. [18] At the same time, however, Diepen presents a sufficiently elaborated and detailed demonstration to prove that the distinction between the inner word and its principle is unequivocally real, and that real distinction, moreover, is *de ipsa ratione formali verbi.*

The point of the author's first thesis is unmistakably clear : The inner word, not in virtue of any attendant potency, but from its proper formality taken in the strictest sense, is so necessarily really distinct from the act of knowledge giving it utterance, that one who posits a Word in God, by this alone posits a Person distinct from the Father. [19]

The first step in Diepen's demonstration is to show that the activity of intellect is not, in its proper perfection, the passive reception of an intelligible form, but rather the vital apprehension of an object. It is in this vital apprehension of an object, that the *ratio formalis* of intellectual operation consists. Of course, at least in most cases, vital apprehension presupposes the passive reception of an intelligible form (the impressed species), and the act of intellect itself follows upon

---

there is much in the precision and sharpness of Diepen's analysis to recommend it to the reader's attention. Hence, it is felt that the various forms of emphasis with which his text is so liberally embellished might more conveniently be omitted in transcription.)

[17] A long section is devoted to a thesis on consubstantiality, along with corollaries. *Ang.*, 1946, pp. 108-125. The thesis itself reads : " Cum verbum in intellectu nostro conceptum de sua formali ratione habeat, quod coessentiale maneat actuali notitiae a qua procedit : fundamentum praebet ad consubstantialitatem divini verbi analogice concipiendam. " *ibid.*, p. 108.

[18] The root of the author's argument lies in his interpretation of the Thomist formula " Quum intentionis intellectae esse sit ipsum suum intelligi. " The discussion of the formula apropos of the passage *C.G., IV*, c. 11, is worth noting. *Ang.*, 1946, p. 112.

[19] " Thesis. Verbum cordis a notitia actuali ipsum dicente non ratione potentialitatis adiunctae sed ex ipsa sua formalissima ratione tam necessario realiter distinguitur, ut qui in Deo poneret Verbum, eo ipso poneret Personam distinctam a Patre. " *ibid.*, p. 95.

the accidental information of the operator. If, however, intellect is already in possession of the intelligible form, as in angelic
self-knowledge, such intellectual operation is completed without
the need of any passive information. From this it is clear that
passive information pertains to the *ratio formalis* of intellectual
activity only presuppositively and accidentally. [20]

Next, Dom Diepen goes on to show that two modes of
intellectual apprehension are to be distinguished. There is
the act of simple intelligence or immediate vision, whereby the
outside object is grasped in its proper reality, at once both
physical and intelligible. There is the act of intellectual conception, whereby the faculty forms within itself the quiddity
of the object understood and brings forth the expressed species,
or concept. [21] In point of fact, however, every last instance
of finite intellection — the beatific vision alone excepted —
is conception, or diction, involving the utterance of an inner
word. [22]

Diepen then comes to the proposition of his first thesis.
To show that the inner word is, to start with, really distinct
from the act of intelligence that utters it, he turns to the

---

[20] " Intellectus et ipse vitaliter apprehendit obiectum intellectum,
et in hoc consistit formalis ratio intelligendi. At illud supponit, saltem
ut in pluribus, passivam receptionem formae intelligibilis seu speciei
impressae, et ipsum intelligere sequitur ad hanc formam intelligibilem,
sicut actio transiens sequitur ad quamdam formam accidentalem operantis (ut calefacere ad calorem), et sicut esse naturale sequitur ad formam substantialem. Si vero intellectus iam tali forma intelligibili
formatus est (sicut intellectus angelicus est ad sui cognitionem naturaliter determinatus, connaturaliter vero, i.e. per species infusas ad
totum ordinem universi cognoscendum), tunc sine ulla passione completur huiusmodi perfecta intellectio. Ex quo patet, passionem non
tantum praesuppositive sed et accidentaliter se habere ad formalem
intelligendi rationem. " *ibid.*, pp. 98-99.

[21] " Similiter ergo in intellectu duo actuum genera distinguere
oportebit (quare non duas potentias, mox dicemus), actum meri intelligere seu ' visionis ' immediatae, qua res extra nos in sua entitate
physica et simul in sua ratione intelligibili apprehenditur, et actum
' conceptionis ' intellectualis, qua potentia format in seipsa quidditatem rei intellectae atque speciem expressam foecunda parit. " *ibid.*,
p. 102.

[22] " Omnis igitur intellectio creata, praeter visionem beatam (quae
revera aptissime visio, non conceptio appellatur) omnis, inquam, alia
intellectio creata fit per modum conceptionis seu dictionis. " *ibid.*,
p. 103.

demonstration contained in *De Potentia*, q. 9, a. 5, and q. 8, a. 1, respectively. [23]   It is not necessary to review this part of the argument here. What is, on the other hand, of considerable importance for the study being undertaken, however, is the part of the argument immediately following, where Diepen attempts to prove that not only is the distinction between inner word and the act of understanding real, but that to be such is of the very essence of inner word.

The proof Dom Diepen offers here is relatively simple. It is of the essence, or strictly formal aspect, of the inner word to proceed from the act of understanding just as human speech proceeds from the mouth.   But if this is true, it automatically follows that the real distinction between inner word and understanding cannot rest ultimately on any imperfection, potentiality, or limitation, proper to the creature's special condition.   The real distinction can only be essential to the concept of inner word as such.   The reason for this necessity is simply that it is quite impossible to think of something that would be its own principle, would be simultaneously cause and caused, producer and produced.   Such a reality would have to enjoy at least a priority of nature with respect to itself, and this is absurd. [24]

Since, then, procession from another is essential to the human inner word, not as human, but precisely as inner word, it is not even possible to think of an inner word that would not necessarily include real distinction from its principle. Consequently, if a Word must be affirmed of God — a thing that cannot be done apart from revelation of the fact — by the same token, one must affirm a Word that really proceeds. Still more : since everything that exists in God is God and wholly God, one must also affirm that this Divine Word is a reality subsisting in the divine nature, a Divine Person, there-

---

[23] *Ibid.*, pp. 104-105.

[24] " Simul inde colligitur, non imperfectionis seu limitationis vel potentialitatis esse talem distinctionem ; non eam convenire verbo quia est quid creatum, sed quia est verbum.   Est enim de ipsa formali ratione verbi, quod sit quid prolatum ab intelligere, sicut sermo est ab ore prolatus.   Non tamen invenitur neque est possibile neque intelligibile, quod aliquid sit principium sui, quod sit simul causa et causatum, producens et procedens, oporteret enim quod esset (saltem natura) prius seipso, quod est absurdum. " *ibid.*, pp. 105-106.

fore, and really distinct from the Person who utters the Word,
the Son of God born of the Father. This, moreover, is the
clear teaching of St. Thomas himself. [25]

It is important to note at this point that, in claiming as
authentically Thomist doctrine the concept of an inner word
which would involve real distinction from its principle *ex ratione
formali*, and then going on to show how, on such a ground,
one would need merely the revelation of the Divine Word to
be able to conclude to a Son personally distinct from a Father,
Diepen is not asserting, either for himself or for St. Thomas,
the possibility of demonstrating the first trinitarian procession
from pure reason. The supposition all along is that the Divine
Word has been revealed, or at least would have to be revealed,
so to speak, for such a process even to begin to have any
meaning.

Nevertheless, there is a problem here, and Dom Diepen
is explicitly aware of the fact. For if a theologian argues that
real distinction from its principle is an absolutely necessary
note of the inner word as such, and if he maintains at the same
time that analysis of human psychology suffices to prove this
point, has he not automatically, and regardless of any contrary
protests, laid the foundation for a purely rational demonstration
of the Eternal Word proceeding in the Trinity? Diepen recognizes this objection, and devotes a separate thesis to its
detailed discussion. [26]

He recalls, first of all, his earlier proof that real distinction
is of the very essence of the inner word. He notes also that
when, in the same previous section, he had compared the
Divine Word to the conception of the human intellect, the
analogy of proper proportionality had been the constant pre-

---

[25] " Cum ergo verbum cordis in nobis de sua formali ratione habeat, quod ab altero procedat, sine distinctione reali a dicente ne intelligi quidem poterit. Unde si Verbum in Deo ponis, quod absque
Revelatione non potes, eo ipso Verbum realiter progrediens posuisti,
et cum omne quod est in Deo sit Deus et totus Deus, ponendo Verbum, posuisti quid subsistens in divina Natura, posuisti Personam divinam ab alia Persona, quae Verbum dicit, realiter distinctam : posuisti
Filium nascentem a Patre. Quae omnia in diserta doctrina Angelici
Doctoris habetur. " *ibid.*, p. 107.

[26] " Thesis. Existentia Verbi et Amoris procedentis in divinis ex
analogia praedicta ideo demonstrari nequit, quia nulla necessitas apparet has processiones immanentes ponendi in eo, qui est suum intelligere et sua veritas, suum amare et sua bonitas. " *Ang.*, 1947, p. 38.

supposition. But it is the well-known principle of theodicy that wherever a simple perfection is discovered in creatures, this same must be said to pre-exist in God, in an eminent, but nonetheless proper and formal, manner. Therefore, inasmuch as the inner word is one of these simple or pure perfections, it must be affirmed to exist in God. Moreover, since in the *ratio formalis* of this particular perfection there is included real distinction from its principle, it follows immediately that in God also there must be real distinction between the Divine Word and the Person who utters the Divine Word. [27]

Dom Diepen grants, of course, that the conclusion cannot stand. It is impossible to demonstrate by unaided reason the generation of the Second Person. Yet, it is also impossible, and certainly false to the text of Aquinas himself, to deny either that real distinction pertains to the essence of inner word, or that inner word is predicated of both men and God through an analogy of proper proportionality. Diepen proposes, therefore, what he considers to be St. Thomas' own solution to this dilemma.

When all is said and done, does St. Thomas take the inner word to be a simple perfection or not ? More accurately, Diepen asserts, Aquinas considers the inner word as a particular mode of that simple perfection which is intelligence.

Dicere, for St. Thomas, signifies not merely *intelligere*, but *intelligere* with this special addition or qualification : to express a conception. Human reason, then, can go so far as to show that God is intellect, but human reason cannot sufficiently discover the particular mode of the divine intelligence. As reason can know that God is, without knowing what God is, so can reason know that God comprehends, without knowing

---

[27] " Diximus distinctionem realem esse de formali ratione verbi. Ex alia vero parte semper analogiam proportionalitatis propriae supposuimus, comparantes Verbum Dei isti conceptioni intellectus nostri. Haec vero duo simul enuntiata, vera analogia, et distinctio realis in ipsa analoga ratione contenta, fidei supernaturali derogare videntur. Notissimum est enim principium illud theodiceae, omnem perfectionem quae in creaturis invenitur, praeexsistere oportere in Deo, idque iuxta modum eminentiorem quidem, sed tamen vere ac proprie seu formaliter, si agatur de perfectione simpliciter perfecta, ut sunt esse et unum, verum et bonum. Verbum igitur, cum dicat perfectionem simplicem, Deo formaliter tribuimus ; et cum distinctionem realem contineat, statim colligimus, esse in Deo distinctionem realem Verbi et dicentis Verbum. " *ibid.*, pp. 38-39.

how God comprehends.   In other words, that the divine intelligence involves the formation of a concept, is, or would be, understanding of the particular mode, and therefore inner essence, of the perfection that is God's intelligence, and not merely the affirmation of the existence of this perfection. [28]

Diepen does not consider this the end of the matter, however.   Someone could easily press the dilemma : but what of the particular mode itself ? Is not the mode of intelligence which is *dicere*, and which involves the expression of a distinct concept, itself either a matter of potentiality, or, once again, a simple perfection ? If the former, it can have no place in God at all ; if the latter, unaided reason continues to demonstrate the first procession.   But St. Thomas, in Diepen's analysis, will simply not accept this further statement of the dilemma.

Expression of a concept (*dicere*) is not a matter of potency, but of richness and actuality.   For communication pertains to form, to act, and hence to the excellence of things.   Expression of a concept remains, therefore, a simple perfection, but with a significant qualification : wherever this mode of intelligence is discovered in creatures and grasped by the human understanding, it is linked to a certain potentiality, from which, in the eyes of the human reason, it does not seem possible that this mode of intelligence could ever be separated. [29]

------

[28] " Maneat ergo analogia, maneat et distinctio realis in ipsa analoga ratione importata.   Qui vero putat ita divinam Generationem demonstrari, audiat S. Thomam disputantem secum [this dialogue, of course, is the author's literary device] : ' Tu verbum dicis perfectionem simplicem.   Ego illud modum quemdam perfectionis simplicis appello, scilicet ipsius intelligere.   Nam " dicere non solum importat intelligere, sed intelligere cum hoc quod est de se exprimere aliquam conceptionem, " (*De V*, q. 4, a. 2 ad 5).   Et exinde sic arguo : " Licet ratio naturalis possit pervenire ad ostendendum, quod Deus sit intellectus, modum tamen intelligendi non potest invenire sufficienter.   Sicut enim de Deo scire possumus quod est, sed non quid est : ista de Deo scire possumus quod intelligit, sed non quomodo intelligit.   Habere autem conceptionem in intelligendo pertinet ad modum intelligendi.   Unde ratio haec sufficienter probare non potest, sed ex eo quod est in nobis aliqualiter per simile coniecturare. " (*De Pot.*, q. 8, a. 1, ad 12) '. " *ibid.*, p. 40.

[29] " Sed merito instabit [the speaker is still the objector of the fictitious dialogue] : Iste modus intelligendi, quo intelligens ex se exprimit aliquam conceptionem, aut est modus potentialis, aut est et ipse perfectio simplex.   Si prius, Deo convenire nequit, et fides affir-

As a final consequence, then, Dom Diepen flatly rejects the charge that to make of the distinct inner word a simple perfection, is automatically to lay the sufficient rational ground for a demonstration of the Word proceeding in the Trinity.

* * *

A full decade later, when the time would come for Vagaggini to suggest that this entire problem of the Thomis demonstrations surrounding the inner word as a simple perfection should be reexamined from the start, the solution proposed by Diepen would come in for rather pointed criticism.

First, Vagaggini wonders how Diepen can claim that the expressed species belongs, *ex ratione sui*, to every instance of intellection, despite the fact that one might consider it as not produced in the beatific vision. [30] Secondly, apropos of Diepen's qualification — inner word is a simple perfection, but the unaided human reason is incapable of separating it from the potentiality with which it is connected in creatures — Vagaggini remarks that this is actually to verify of the inner word, so construed, the philosophical definition of a mixed perfection. [31]

---

maret quod ratio negat ; si alterum, in Deo esse efficaciter probatur, et ita semper mysterium per rationem naturalem investigari poterit. S. Thomas vero dilemma istud simpliciter non accipiet. Modus enim dictionis non est modus potentialis, sed dicit foecunditatem et per consequens actualitatem : ' Communicatio enim sequitur rationem actus : unde omnis forma, quantum est de se, communicabilis est, et ideo communicatio pertinet ad nobilitatem ', (*I Sent.*, d. 4, q. 1, a. 1). Dictio ergo est perfectio simplex : ita tamen, ut ubicumque in creaturis inveniatur et a nobis comperiatur, potentialitati cuidam alligetur, a qua separari omnino non posse nobis videatur. " *ibid.*, pp. 40-41.

[30] Vagaggini comments : " Diepen (l.c. 1945-46, p. 102 suiv.) estime que, malgré le principe que la *species expressa* appartient *ex ratione sui* à toute intellection, on peut toutefois penser que dans la vision béatifique il n'y a pas production de *species expressa*. Il reste alors à expliquer comment sauver encore la nature d'une chose si on lui enlève ce qui lui appartient *ex ratione sui*. " " La hantise, " pp. 134-135, note no. 93.

[31] " Non moins claire est la contradiction que l'on trouve chez Diepen ... Une perfection que l'analyse philosophique de l'homme ne peut arriver à séparer mentalement de la potentialité avec laquelle elle se vérifie dans les créatures est par définition, pour le philosophe, une perfection mixte et non une perfection simple. " *ibid.*, p. 135, note no. 94.

There is no intention here to engage in controversy, or to discuss whether Vagaggini has correctly interpreted Diepen's position. What is of more importance for the present study, is that Diepen, as also Paissac, had already succeeded in putting a finger on one of the points that would have to be tested and developed at some future date, when an occasion such as Vagaggini's article would arise calling for a more satisfactory explanation of St. Thomas' thought.

Paissac took up the problem of rational demonstration in scientific theology, and observed that Aquinas distinguishes, at least on the level of theory, between theological argumentation as explanatory, and theological argumentation as verifying a primary hypothesis. Diepen addressed himself to the problem of the inner word being a simple perfection, and concluded that, for St. Thomas, the human reason must indeed consider the inner word a simple perfection, but with a serious qualification. For the same unaided human reason cannot remove the element of potency and imperfection which is involved in the real distinction between inner word and its principle on the finite level.

In the mind of the present writer, there seems to be in Dom Diepen's analysis at least the suggestion that the inner word as distinct from its principle is *de facto* a simple perfection, but only then fully recognized to be such when the procession of the Second Person has been revealed. But this suggestion leads immediately to a still further question. Does Aquinas himself admit the instance where A can be *de ratione formali* of B, without this *de facto* truth being evident to merely rational or philosophical analysis? It might well be that the ultimate solution to the *verbum* dilemma would depend on the answer to that question. For if the answer were yes — if Aquinas does admit that something can pertain to the *ratio formalis* of a certain perfection or reality, without unaided reason being able to arrive at the fact relying exclusively on its own resources — it could then be asked whether the whole problem of the ' simple perfection ', raised and discussed both pro and con by so many authors, actually has a valid place in the interpretation of the true Thomist doctrine on inner word.

In any case, both Diepen and Vagaggini begin with the understanding that if the really distinct inner word is a simple perfection, fully accessible to purely rational analysis, it is difficult to explain how the first procession is not thereby demonstrable. But at this point, the two theologians part ways. For Vagaggini, to say that A belongs to the *ratio formalis* of B, to say that the reality so described is a simple perfection, and to say, finally, that the truth in question lies fully within the reach of unaided reason or philosophical analysis, appears to be all very much the same thing. [32]

For Diepen, however, there seems to be an attempt to break down these identifications — at least to the extent that what was still of the *ratio formalis*, and in the order of simple or pure perfection, would not necessarily involve philosophical conclusions based entirely on what was evident to reason. The difference in viewpoint here seems to show that the ultimate problems surrounding the appearance of rational demonstration in Aquinas' trinitarian theology are quite methodological, and that it is precisely in this area the reexamination called for by Vagaggini would have to be conducted.

More concretely, the problem can be expressed in terms of a network of dependencies. The precise focus and scientific value of an author's demonstrations should be determined by the principles upon which the demonstrations actually depend. These principles in turn depend, for selection and meaning, upon the basic intention, the prevailing scientific ideal, objective, or end, in the interests of which they were to be employed. Thus, in the order of the original composition, it is first the ideal or end, then principles (*principia demonstrationis*, that is), and finally demonstration. In the order of historical criticism, the process is understandably reversed : first, examination of the demonstration to discover, one might say isolate, its internal principles, and then the attempt to expose from a study of these principles the scientific ideal.

---

[32] Vagaggini's identifications in this regard are basic to the entire argument of " La hantise. " But one might note in particular a passage such as that in which he wishes to show that the demonstration in *De Pot.*, q. 9, a. 5, involving the formula " est absolute de ratione eius quod est intelligere, " is to all appearances an apodictic proof derived from the concept of inner word as simple perfection. He remarks here : " On voit difficilement en quoi ce raisonnement diffère essentiellement de celui avec lequel S. Anselme.... croyait pouvoir prouver de façon apodictique, avec la seule raison, l'existence d'une seconde Personne en Dieu en partant du concept de verbe compris comme perfection simple. " " La hantise, " p. 121.

The historian must be wary, however. When analysis of the Thomist demonstrations begins to reveal their internal principles, a certain similarity in idiom and structure may tempt him to presume right away that the principles thus emerging slowly from his analysis have identical equivalents in other methodologies — but methodologies quite possibly based on a different, perhaps radically different, scientific ideal. But this is presumptive criticism.

The historian's labor is a labor of patience. The principles must first be examined in their own right, so to speak, painstakingly and objectively, according to the cast of thought and fundamental methodology strictly textual evidence shows to have been the author's own. They cannot be examined in some system of equivalents brought in to simplify things, but before what was truly the scientific ideal of the author in question can possibly be established.

Part of the purpose of the present study, then, will be to determine, if possible, whether analysis of the Thomist notion of inner word in terms of 'simple perfection' involves introducing precisely such a system of equivalents.

III. ABBÉ PENIDO'S JUDGMENT ON THE VALUE
      OF THE THOMIST ANALOGY

It is the basically methodological aspect of the problem that had been set in relief a full generation before Dom Vagaggini's challenge in certain observations made by the Abbé Penido.[33]

Taking issue with what he feels is the unwarranted skepticism of de Regnon on the point, Penido contests the assertion that no theory could ever pretend to give an account of the mystery deserving to be called a true account, inasmuch as the mystery itself is beyond the possibility of such access. [34]

---

[33] M. T.-L. PENIDO, " La valeur de la théorie ' psychologique ' de la Trinité, " *Ephemerides Theologicae Lovanienses*, VIII (1931), pp. 5-16. For a parallel and substantially identical treatment of the same point, but with much of the matter most pertinent to the present inquiry discussed rather in the notes, see also Penido's well-known book : *Le rôle de l'analogie en théologie dogmatique*, Vol. XV of *Bibliothèque Thomiste* (Paris : Librairie Philosophique J. Vrin, 1931), pp. 295-311.

[34] " La valeur, " p. 6.

For, as he goes on to observe, divine revelation would be quite meaningless and futile, were it not for the fact that the revealed mystery, or the reality that is so revealed, still belonged to the universe of being, and maintained, therefore, some real degree of intelligible continuity with human reflection. [35]

Turning, then, to the Augustinian-Thomist psychological analogy, Penido poses first the question of possibility. Can this analogy express formally, however imperfectly, the divine reality?

In its preliminary stages, where metaphysical development has yet to be introduced, the analogy has the character of similitude. Once, however, the metaphysics of being has refined the human notions of personality, intelligence, or will, one may safely affirm these realities of God. Nor is there any species of anthropomorphism here. For the affirmation is made on a basis of analogy, not univocity. Thus, even in the Trinity, where the same predication is no less valid, theology attributes to God Himself, not, of course, the inner word of human understanding, but the analogous notion of inner word as such, proportioned, in this instance, to the divine nature. [36]

The theologian, therefore, accepts from revelation that there are in God two immanent processions, one of which terminates in a Word. His task is then to proportion these processions and this Divine Word to that Being which is the supreme among all intelligences. The process, consequently, is not psychological — except in its origins — but strictly ontological. At this point, however, Penido draws an important distinction between the analogical process of theodicy and the similar, but yet quite different, analogical process of theology.

---

[35] Penido expresses the idea of God and supernatural mysteries being nonetheless *de ratione entis* : " ... la réalité révélée, *étant encore de l'être*, n'est pas radicalement hétérogène à notre pensée. " *ibid.*, p. 7.

[36] " Considérée avant son élaboration métaphysique notre analogie n'est qu'une vulgaire *comparaison* ... En revanche, après l'intervention de l'analyse métaphysique, nous avons affaire à une *analogie de proportionalité propre*, d'ordre dynamique, avec distance simplement infinie entre les rapports semblables.... Une fois établie la connexion entre l'être et nos notions de personalité, d'intelligence ou de volonté, nous pouvons en toute sécurité les réaliser en Dieu : nous évitons l'anthropomorphisme du fait qu'en passant par l'être nous quittons l'univocité pour l'analogie. Il en va tout de même en théologie trinitaire. Nous n'attribuons pas à Dieu le ' verbe ' *humain* mais nous proportionnons à sa Nature la *notion analogique de ' verbe-comme tel '*. " *ibid.*, pp. 8-9.

Theodicy's analogy — *intelligentia participata* stands to *ens in fieri* as *Intelligentia Prima* stands to *Ens sine fieri* — is itself proportional to theology's analogy — *conceptus creatus* stands to *intelligentia participata* as *Verbum Divinum* stands to *Intelligentia Prima*.

Penido completes this graphic representation with a detailed account of the primary terms of difference between the two methodologies. In theodicy, the analogy moves out through apodictic demonstration from the unique notion of *Ens Necessarium*. The process here, inasmuch as it employs only highly intelligible concepts and restricts itself to the universal modes of being, is much more evident. In theology, on the other hand, the analogy rests rather upon divine revelation. In place of the highly intelligible concepts of philosophical theodicy, the focus is now upon the intimate life of God that is hidden from human view. The process, consequently, is more reserved, and the forward movement must be regulated by constant appeal to revealed data. [37]

At the same time, Penido is quick to point out, these differences must not be exaggerated. It is true that there can be no strict univocity within the analogical structure. But the proportional likeness just described suffices to guarantee

---

[37] " Tout ceci ne doit pas faire l'ombre de difficulté pour quiconque admet les analogies de la théodicée : *notre méthode est proportionnellement la même*. Proportionnellement disons-nous, car ces deux séries de rapports :

1º *intelligence participée*	=	*Intelligence première*
être en devenir		Etre sans devenir
2º *concept créé*	=	*Verbe divin*
intelligence participée		Intelligence première

ne sont qu'*analogues* entre soi. L'une s'appuie sur une démonstration apodictique, l'autre sur la révélation ; la première sera donc beaucoup plus évidente que la seconde ; en effet la théodicée traite de Dieu sous l'angle des notions éminemment intelligibiles, la théologie sous l'angle de la vie intime qui nous est cachée. La première s'en tient aux modes universels de l'être, la seconde descend à une détermination particulière qui nous échappe : ' Potentiam intellectivam esse primam potentiam satis naturali ratione considerari potest, non autem *hanc* potentiam intellectivam esse potentiam generativam. ' (10 de Ver., a. 13, ad 2). Tandis qu'en théodicée l'analogie épand majestueusement ses modes, immense sorite tout entier suspendu à l'unique notion d'Etre-nécessaire, en théologie au contraire, l'analogie est timide, sans cesse elle fait appel aux données révélées pour progresser comme pour contrôler ses conquêtes. " *ibid.*, p. 10.

methodological unity. If, then, it be presupposed that there are two processions in God, one intellectual, the other volitive, the Augustinian-Thomist theory worked out along the lines of this method would be quite capable of leading to proper and analogical knowledge of even the mystery itself.[38]

Penido's next task will be to examine the supposition that there is, *de facto*, in God the procession *per modum intellectus*, and *per modum voluntatis*.

Insofar as St. Thomas' own position is concerned, Penido claims that there is not even a possibility of doubt. One need consult only those passages where Aquinas discusses the possibility of there being in God more than two processions. The answer is always negative — and negative, not only in the sense of a mere probability or verisimilitude, but in the absolute sense that the opposite alternative is excluded as simply impossible. For St. Thomas, the sole immanent processions that could ever be affirmed of a spiritual nature are these two, and these two alone : by way of intelligence, and by way of will.[39]

No sooner has Penido stated this conclusion, however, than he faces the objection of *rationes convenientiae* that will surely be adduced from the famous passage, *S. T.*, *I*, q. 32, a. 1, ad 2m, where Aquinas himself replies to the question : can unaided human reason demonstrate the Trinity of Per-

_____

[38] " Ces différences ne doivent point nous étonner : l'univocité ne pouvant régner au sein de l'analogie, une similitude proportionnelle suffit pour assurer l'unité de la méthode : d'autre part il ne faudrait pas conclure à l'inefficacité de la théorie ' psychologique '. Celle-ci sera plus obscure que la théodicée, c'est entendu, mais plus obscur ne veut pas dire nul.... Tout nous pousse donc à conclure que le thomisme *peut* pretendre exprimer analogiquement la réalité même du mystère ... Conclusion hypothétique, car elle repose sur cette supposition que la fécundité divine s'épanche selon les deux voies que lui assignent Augustin et Thomas d'Aquin. " *ibid.*, pp. 10-11.

[39] " Quiconque lira S. Thomas avec un esprit non prévenu, aboutira en ce qui le concerne, à des conclusions semblables. Qu'il nous suffise de renvoyer aux endroits où est agitée la question de savoir s'il y a place, en Dieu, pour plus de deux processions. La réponse est toujours négative. Et pourquoi ? Est-ce en vertu de probabilités, de vraisemblances ? — Pas le moins du monde. S. Thomas soutient que cela est *absolument impossible* ; dans une nature spirituelle il ne peut y avoir que deux processions immanentes et deux seules : par voie d'intelligence et par voie de volonté. " *ibid.*, p. 11.

sons? [40] It is Penido's exegesis of this text, in broad structure similar to, yet in certain significant particulars much
more incisive than, Père Paissac's, that makes the earlier contribution — though written thirty years ago — of considerable value in settling upon the precise point, or points, that
must still be investigated to do justice to Dom Vagaggini's
challenge. This exegesis bears close scrutiny.[41]

It is an utterly false interpretation, Penido begins, to take
St. Thomas' remarks in this passage as equivalently assigning
his own trinitarian doctrine to its lawful place — the place,
that is, of the purely philosophical *ratio convenientiae*. For
what Aquinas discusses in this passage is not an analogical
explanation of the mystery, but the attempt to demonstrate the
very existence of the mystery. It is to Anselm and especially to
Richard of St. Victor, that his attention is directed here, and
to their claim that God's being Three Persons was a necessity
not only *quoad se*, but even *quoad nos*, and that therefore one
could demonstrate the Trinity through *rationes necessariae*.

Penido next observes that such an attempt to demonstrate
the existence of the mystery could take place at one of two
distinct moments, so to speak. In the first moment, before
the revelation of the Trinity is presupposed, none of the arguments that could be constructed would have any proper value
at all. In the second moment, the revelation of the Trinity
now being presupposed, arguments could in fact be constructed, which would have a certain limited degree of value, but
only as *rationes convenientiae* — or to use St. Thomas' actual
description: "Posita Trinitate congruunt huiusmodi rationes." Nor is the so-called psychological theory in trinitarian
theology any exception to this rule. For the attempt to force
a strict demonstration out of this theory is simply to argue
from the twofold procession in human psychology to the existence of the same in God. But this is to turn analogy back
into univocity.[42]

---

[40] As noted before, this key passage, *S.T.*, *I*, q. 32, a. 1, ad 2m,
will be discussed in the final section of the present study, according
to its proper place in the *Summa* structure.

[41] See also Penido's parallel discussion in *Le rôle de l'analogie*, p.
302, note no. 2. The treatment here in the book is more brief than in
the article "La valeur," but refers back to the earlier part of the
treatise to substantiate the historical material.

[42] "Là notre Docteur aurait enfin remis son explication à sa

In short, then, the theological elaboration that is struc-tured upon the analogy of proper proportionality can never as such demonstrate an existence, a *quod sit*, but enjoys rather, in Penido's judgment, the sole function of being able to explore a nature, a *quomodo sit*. And this, moreover, is the real sense of the Augustinian-Thomist trinitarian theory.

There is no intention, there is no possibility in fact, of demonstrating the processions. Rather, with the revealed processions standing as the ' major ', the psychological analogy acts as the ' minor ' and thus serves to explain or elucidate the revealed datum. Furthermore, the movement here is not toward the mere probability or *convenientia* that would be the outside limit of demonstration in the area of proving in apologetical retrospect the existence of the mystery, but toward the certitude proper to a theological explanation guided completely by the revealed mystery.[43]

---

vraie place : pure ' raison de convenance philosophique '. (Regnon) Erreur totale d'interprétation. En réalité il s'agit dans ce passage célèbre d'une *démonstration* de *l'existence* du mystère et non d'une explication analogique. Anselme et surtout R. de St-Victor sont visés qui semblaient croire que Dieu était nécessairement trine non seulement ' quoad se ' mais encore ' quoad nos ' et que, par suite, on pouvait prouver la Trinité ' rationibus necessariis '. Une telle démonstration peut être tentée ' ante revelationem ' — et alors toutes les raisons ne valent proprement rien ; ou bien ' post revelationem ', une fois connu le fait qu'il y a en Dieu trois personnes — ' posita Trinitate ', comme dit S. Thomas — ainsi quelqu'un qui commence par croire à l'existence de Dieu, puis la démontre : dans ce cas les preuves ont quelque valeur, mais seulement comme raisons de convenance : ' posita Trinitate congruunt huiusmodi rationes. ' (I. q. 32, a. 1, ad 2). Et la théorie ' psychologique ' elle-même ne fait pas exception, pour cet excellent motif qu'alors elle cesse d'être analogie pour se changer en univocité puisqu'elle argue de la double procession spirituelle en nous, pour conclure à leur existence en Dieu, ce qui constitue le péché caractérisé d'univocité. " " La valeur, " p. 12.

[43] " Il est constant en effet, qu'une analogie de proportionalité propre ne peut jamais comme telle prouver une existence (quod sit) : non seul rôle est d'explorer une nature (quo modo sit). Et tel est bien le sens de la doctrine augustino-thomiste. Elle ne montre pas, et ne peut pas montrer, qu'il existe en Dieu deux processions, que ces processions aboutissent en Dieu à deux termes substantiels etc. ; tout cela elle le *présuppose* : c'est la majeure de foi ; notre analogie fournit la mineure de raison qui *explique* la prémisse révélée ; la conclusion ne sera pas probabilité ou simple convenance mais *certitude théologique*.... En réalité ce passage c'est la révélation qui l'accomplit, l'explication analogique ne vient qu'*après.* " *ibid.*, pp. 12-13.

Finally, having restored, as he believes, the authentic aim and deployment of the Thomist analogical theory to its true sense and intention, Penido considers the problem of assigning a more or less precise evaluation to this theory in terms, now, of strictly theological certitude. Inasmuch, however, as this last question touches only indirectly on the point at issue in the present inquiry, it will suffice to note that Penido approaches this evaluation from two distinct aspects. From an exclusively metaphysical perspective, the Augustinian-Thomist theory might not be able to lay claim to more than a serious probability. Even so, Penido continues, once the perspective is enlarged to encompass the teaching of Christian faith and the implications of the long history of Scholastic Theology, it might well be asked if this probability is not transformed into certainty.[44]

* * *

It was Père Paissac's suggestion, as seen earlier, that St. Thomas recognized in theological science two distinct movements, one toward verification of the hypothesis, the other toward its explanation. But this was to transpose the question that would eventually be posed by Dom Vagaggini to a more basic level of methodological perspective. Whether Aquinas did, in fact, demonstrate the existence of a mystery, or at least develop his theological doctrine in close imitation of such a process, would depend on whether or not to demonstrate, or imitate demonstration, in this way had really been part of this scientific ideal and basic methodology.

It is here that the observations of the Abbé Penido are especially significant.

Writing on the same point twenty years before Paissac, Penido's position had been more emphatic. Paissac is content to observe St. Thomas' theoretical distinction between verification of the hypothesis and its simple elaboration. He discusses the text in *S. T.*, *I*, q. 32, a. 1, ad 2m, to bring out Aquinas' awareness of the fact that science cannot always verify its primary suppositions, and that this restriction extends to trinitarian theology in particular. For no reason can be adduced sufficient to prove with any certainty the

---

[44] *Ibid.*, pp. 13-16.

trinitarian hypothesis. In the line of verification, therefore, reason can go no further than to indicate *convenientia*. As already noted, however, Paissac does not say whether, in his own judgment, such a restricted process of verification was the objective, or at least part of the objective, of Aquinas.

Penido, on the other hand, argues much more explicitly that the distinction drawn by St. Thomas in *S. T.*, *I*, q. 32, a. 1, ad 2m, was meant to describe the great difference between his own system and that of Anselm and Richard of St. Victor.

If revelation is not presupposed, the demonstration would have no value at all. If revelation is presupposed, the demonstration has the strictly limited, non-probative, value of being able to show how these reasons accord with the trinitarian supposition. But in either case — and this is where Penido had gone further than Paissac — the remarks of St. Thomas in this passage of the *Pars Prima* are directed solely to the demonstrative or apologetical attempts of his Anselmian and Victorine adversaries, and are simply not intended to be a description of his own theological elaboration. For Penido, then, verification of the trinitarian supposition, even in the legitimate and carefully restricted sense of the ' congruence ' Aquinas explains here, has no place at all in the ' *de Trinitate* ' of the *Summa*. Unfortunately — that is, in line with the purpose and scope of the present study — Penido limits his comments to the general structure of the Augustinian-Thomist analogy, often calling it simply that. Consequently, it is not possible to cull from these general observations what Penido thought of the really distinct inner word as a pure perfection, or what he most likely would have replied to Vagaggini's claim that the way St. Thomas himself attributes the character of pure perfection to this inner word means, when all is said and done, that there is more of the apodictically demonstrative in the Thomist achievement than the author's declarations to the contrary can quite explain away.

Nevertheless, it remains that Penido understood the apologetical problem, to the brief extent he actually considered it, to be a problem of scientific method, one that should be discussed, therefore, in the strict context of the theological ideal and perspective that was Aquinas' own. As Penido sees it, Thomist trinitarian theology had left behind the apologetical objective of demonstrating the revealed hypothesis — even in the qualified sense of applying merely suasive reason-

ings, and that, only after the initial revelation of the mystery
is presupposed.   Moreover, he draws his conclusion from within
the fundamental dynamics of Aquinas' theological method.
The process constructed upon the analogy of proper proportionality, he asserts, can never have the function of demonstrating a primary supposition or hypothesis, but only the function
of explaining — to whatever degree — its nature.

IV. Father Lonergan's Formulation of the Problem in its Exclusively Theological Perspective

The same fundamentally methodological approach to the
problem taken by the Abbé Penido is also seen to have been
assumed, but with considerably greater precision, in Father
Lonergan's studies on the Thomist trinitarian analogy.[45]

Actually, Lonergan's specific discussion of the question at
hand — the possibility, that is, of demonstration being applied to the revealed datum in its radical existence — is absorbed inside of a very few pages within a much more extensive account of Thomist trinitarian doctrine.   Nevertheless, the observations made in these few pages reflect so clearly
the integration and consistency of the author's synthesis, their
importance for the present study is much greater than might
otherwise appear.

In his fifth and concluding article of the series devoted
entirely to the Thomist notion of inner word, Lonergan takes
up explicitly the question of the necessity for word, first in

---

[45] The following works are directly pertinent. See BERNARD J.
F. LONERGAN, S. J., " The Concept of *Verbum* in the Writings of St.
Thomas Aquinas, " *Theological Studies*, VII (1946), pp. 349-392 ; VIII
(1947), pp. 35-79, 404-444 ; X (1949), pp. 3-40, 359-393. Also, the
same author's two university texts, *Divinarum Personarum Conceptio
Analogica* (Romae : Apud Aedes Universitatis Gregorianae, 1957), and
the companion volume, *De Deo Trino, Pars Analytica* (Romae : Apud
Aedes Universitatis Gregorianae, 1961). It should likewise be noted
here that, while the comprehensive statement of Lonergan's personal
synthesis is not formally a commentary on Aquinas' theological achievement, and precisely as synthesis of understanding, this latter element
is certainly implicit in the background of the work, and noted *passim*
by the author himself. See also, therefore, *Insight. A Study of Human Understanding* (New York : Philosophical Library, 1957).

human understanding, and secondly in God.[46]   He explains at
the beginning that the necessity for word is not shown merely
on the demonstration of the necessity for an object in a cog-
nitional act.   In human understanding, what Lonergan terms
the strictly " essential " necessity of the inner word rests on
a highly refined analysis of man's need to effect " the transition from the preconceptual *quidditas rei materialis*, first, to
the *res*, secondly, to the *res particularis*, thirdly to the *res
particularis existens*," in achieving knowledge of external
things.[47]

Then, coming directly to the question whether unaided
reason can demonstrate the existence of a Divine Word, Lonergan treats separately the two possible bases upon which
such a demonstration might be attempted.   The first possibility concerns God's intimate self-knowledge.   But God is
simply intelligible — there being in God no distinction between essence, existence, intellect, operation of intellect, or
even between *esse naturale* and *esse intelligibile*.   One could
not argue, therefore, on the basis of any distinction between
the divine essence and the proper object of the divine understanding.   Nor, since it cannot be proved that objective confrontation is essential to knowledge, could one argue on the
basis of a necessary confrontation of knowing subject with
known object.[48]

What, then, of divine knowledge of the other ?   Here,
it might seem, there is a significant difference.   Inasmuch as
whatever God knows outside of Himself is not objectively
identified with Himself, nor always in act, nor simply intelligible, is not the identity principle less clearly applicable ?

Lonergan grants that some of the best *verbum* passages
of St. Thomas are to be found in discussions of divine knowledge of the other.   This connection, however, rooted in Christian Platonism, represents, for St. Thomas, a merely traditional association.   Aquinas had parted ways with the Platonist
view of knowledge as essentially confrontation, in favor of the
Aristotelian position that knowledge was essentially by iden-

---

[46] See " The Concept of *Verbum* in the Writings of St. Thomas
Aquinas, V. *Imago Dei*," *Theological Studies*, X (1949), pp. 366ff.

[47] *Ibid.*, pp. 366-368.

[48] *Ibid.*, p. 369.

tity, and his treatment of the secondary objects of divine knowledge was strictly in accord with this latter principle.

To indicate in some detail precisely how God's knowledge of the other is contained in His knowledge of His own essence and in one, utterly indivisible, act of understanding, Lonergan finds it useful to cite the parallel of human understanding of the one, unique substantial form that is the human soul. As this soul in its proper reality is primarily and formally intellectual, and only secondarily and virtually sensitive and vegetative, so understanding of the same human soul is primarily of its strictly formal perfection, and of the inferior virtualities only as comprehended within the simple act of understanding that is of the intellectual soul as such.

The comparison is then drawn to the divine essence. Formally, this divine essence is, of course, simply itself. At the same time, however, the divine essence contains eminently all other perfection. What God understands primarily, is His own divine existence or essence. But involved in this one act of understanding, as the secondary objects of God's knowledge, are all other perfections which are eminently precontained in the divine essence.

In the human model, the single act of understanding — primarily of the intellectual soul, secondarily, but without multiplicity of act, of its lesser virtualities — comes to be expressed, however, in several inner words, whereby the virtualities are defined and thus acquire intelligible existence. In the divine self-comprehension, on the other hand, the Word that is *de facto* uttered remains simple and unique, expressing at once both the divine essence and also everything else that God knows as virtually precontained in this essence.

Again, in the human model, as inner words expressing understanding of the lesser virtualities come to be uttered, intelligible existence is, so to speak, acquired. In the divine instance, on the other hand, since there is in God no distinction between *esse naturale* and *esse intelligibile*, the divine ideas uttered in the unique Divine Word do not acquire this *esse intelligibile*.

There is, therefore, no real distinction between either the divine essence and all that it eminently contains, or the primary and secondary objects of the divine knowledge. It stands as a final consequence, then, that divine knowledge of the other provides no more ground for a rational demonstration of the first trinitarian procession than the divine knowledge of self.[49] The concluding paragraph in Lonergan's treatment of the possibility of demonstrating the procession of the Word can be quoted in full :

> Hence, though our *intelligere* is always a *dicere*, this cannot be demonstrated of God's. Though we can demonstrate that God understands, for understanding is pure perfection, still we can no more than conjecture the mode of divine understanding and so cannot prove that there is a divine Word. Psychological trinitarian theory is not a conclusion that can be demonstrated but an hypothesis that squares with divine revelation without excluding the possibility of alternative hypotheses. Finally, Aquinas regularly writes as a theologian and not as a philosopher; hence regularly he simply states what simply is true, that in all intellects there is a procession of inner word.[50]

In keeping with the scope and purpose of his larger topic, Lonergan does not further explain how something might be " simply true " of all intellects without being, for that reason alone, a simple perfection. He does, however, suggest the key to this dilemma when he observes, immediately before taking up the problem of demonstrating the Divine Word, that the question of the necessity of this Word has, so to put it, two moments.

There is the question of what is necessary in God *quoad se*, and the quite different question of what is necessary in God *quoad nos*. The first of these offers no special problem in the present context : whatever exists in God is necessary, and that is the end of the matter. But the second question — whether in a particular instance this necessity can be established by rational or philosophical analysis — is quite a different affair. [51] As has been seen above, Lonergan devotes a compressed, but still rather detailed and closely reasoned examination to its solution in the case of the Divine Word.

---

[49] *Ibid.*, pp. 369-371.
[50] *Ibid.*, p. 371.
[51] *Ibid.*, p. 367.

Eight years later, in the first of his twin volumes on the
Thomist ' *de Trinitate* ' appearing in the Gregorian University
texts series, Lonergan will again take up the question of apologetical demonstration, and once more present the same basic
solution. [52]   Finally, in the companion volume published only
in 1961, and therefore after Dom Vagaggini's challenge, he
will do so still a third time, inserting the delicate observation
that, for St. Thomas, the *propositio per se nota quoad nos* adds
to the fact that the *praedicatum* is *de ratione subiecti*, that one
knows both *quid sit praedicatum* and *quid sit subiectum*.   But
knowing *quid sit Deus* would mean knowing God *per essentiam*,
which is simply impossible short of the beatific vision. [53]

* * *

Writing, therefore, in 1949, Father Lonergan had anticipated what would become, ten years later, the central point
in Dom Vagaggini's argument : that St. Thomas treats the
distinct inner word as a simple perfection, and goes on to
build upon this premise a seemingly rational, or purely philosophical, demonstration of the first procession.

Lonergan's position, on the other hand, and much more
clearly and unequivocally than Diepen's rather hesitant step
in the same direction, is simply that, while intelligence is a
pure perfection, and as such accessible to the philosopher,
the particular mode of intelligence, *dicere*, that would involve
the procession of an inner word cannot be treated in quite
the same way.   *De facto*, it is true that in every act of intellect there proceeds an inner word.   But this is not to make
of the inner word a simple perfection in the philosophical
sense of the notion.   Consequently, where Diepen, in speaking

---

[52] See *Divinarum Personarum, Conceptio Analogica*, pp. 82-84.

[53] " Quare, S. Thomas inculcat nos hac in vita non cognoscere quid
sit Deus.   Nam apud eum idem dicit cognoscere quid sit ac cognoscere per essentiam ...   Prcinde, propositio est *per se nota*, ubi praedicatum est de ratione subiecti ; et propositio est *per se nota quoad
nos*, ubi nos cognoscimus quid sit praedicatum et quid sit subiectum.
Quia ergo hac in vita non cognoscimus quid sit Deus, nullae sunt nobis propositiones per se notae quoad nos, quarum subiectum est Deus."
De Deo Trino, Pars Analytica, p. 278.   Referring, in the same place,
to Vagaggini's position in " La hantise, " Lonergan appends the observation : " Quod parum perspexisse videtur Dom. C. Vagaggini. " p.
278, note no. 12.

of the inner word, retains the vocabulary and analytical frame
of the simple perfection, though with a labored attempt to
qualify its application in this particular instance, Lonergan
drops it altogether.

In subsequent statements, including *De Deo Trino* published (1961) two years after Vagaggini's " La hantise, " Lonergan does not return to the specific question of simple perfection,
or, even this aside, discuss explicitly the genesis and classi-
fication of the Thomist generalization : it is of the very essence
of intellect (" de ratione eius quod est intelligere ") that there
proceed within intellect, upon the act of understanding a
really distinct inner word. Nevertheless, in the particular
case where the same generalization is applied directly to the
divine intelligence, Lonergan's solution to Vagaggini's problem
is at least clear, if not developed. For Lonergan does take a
moment to reemphasize, in certain respects more clearly than
in the fifth article of his " *Verbum* " series, that with regard
to the divine, the *propositio per se nota* is not, and cannot possibly be, a *propositio per se nota quoad nos*. It is true, therefore, that the predicate inner word belongs to (" est de ratione ") the subject God. But for this proposition to be *per se
nota quoad nos*, man would have to know the *quid sit* of both
the predicate and the subject. Outside of the beatific vision,
however, man does not know *quid sit Deus*.

Vagaggini, of course, would counter — or more correctly,
this is the position taken in " La hantise " — that one still
has more to reckon with in the text of Aquinas than the simple
statement of fact that there is procession of inner word in
every instance of intellect. It is the generalization as such
— that procession of inner word is essential to the very nature
of intellect — and the function of this generalization in
St. Thomas' theological exposition, that disturbs Vagaggini.
For it is precisely from this universal and apparently rational
principle, as he sees it, that St. Thomas appears to conclude,
as from the major premise of his argument, the procession of
a Word in God.

The ultimate question would seem to be, then, and it is
the purpose of the present study to attempt to answer this
question, how can one explain, from the text of Aquinas himself, the introduction at the beginning of a process at least
superficially resembling demonstration from necessary reasons

of the universal principle that procession of inner word is proper and essential to intellect as such?

If the principle is conceived rationally, what is left except apodictic demonstration, or, since this is impossible and contrary to Aquinas' explicit protests, its aesthetic imitation? If the principle is not conceived rationally, what could possibly have been the intention and perspective of St. Thomas in assigning it, in his later works, the first position, or the rôle of the 'major', in a process of argumentation that has the rationally consecutive structure of 'major', 'minor', and 'conclusion'?

V. The Question of 'Apologetical Perspective' as Determined from the Foregoing Account of the Theological Dialogue

In the second and third parts of the present study, the Thomist ' de Trinitate ' will be examined as carefully as possible to see whether or to what extent an ' apologetical perspective ' had been present in the original intention of Aquinas. A problem arises immediately, however.

The scientific historian, relying, one might say, upon many centuries of experience, is today well aware of the fact that analysis of author A to discover whether he thought along lines B may tend to yield a conclusion which a less pointed investigation would perhaps not have discovered at all. Fidelity to sources, unflinching preoccupation with text in context, may not always provide a sufficient guarantee that the initial framing of the question will not have effected a selection and organization of the raw material which can so easily prove prejudicial to scientific objectivity.

It was to anticipate, and if possible remove, such an objection, that led to the decision to commence the present study with a somewhat lengthy and detailed account of the state of the question in contemporary historical and theological criticism. For, in the mind of the writer, that account has issued in the following preliminary conclusions.

First, the direct and utterly candid challenge of Vagaggini, but also the more indirect *obiter dicta* of Paissac, Diepen, Penido, and Lonergan, serve to prove, it would seem, that, at least on first reading, the idiom and structure of the Thomist trinitarian elaboration might give rise to the problem of whether some element of rational demonstration touching on the existence of the mystery itself is present here. Secondly, from these same contributions to the academic dialogue, one would likewise seem to be justified in concluding that any more specific and detailed examination of this problem would have to concentrate on determining, if possible, the precise methodological perspective that St. Thomas had made his own in the composition of his ' de Trinitate'. To put it more particularly, was this perspective apologetical ?

The designation ' apologetical perspective', moreover, intends merely to describe in a single brief and convenient formula the scientific perspective that would aim, whether intentionally and explicitly, or at least de facto and implicitly, to demonstrate in some real, though perhaps only suasive, manner the a priori necessity of the mystery — in this instance, the mystery of trinitarian procession. From the foregoing account of contemporary theological criticism, however, it should be evident that to approach the text of Aquinas with this question in mind, is not at all to superimpose upon the text an arbitrary or foreign point of view. For apropos of the comments of the authors cited above, especially those of Vagaggini, key passages from works of St. Thomas have already been put in focus which give sufficient warrant from the text itself at least for posing the question, and for posing it precisely in these terms.

It is also clear, but should perhaps be stated explicitly, that ' apologetical' is not being used in the present study to describe such purely theological demonstrations as seek to refute objections brought against Christian faith by proving, with the assistance of even strictly rational and philosophical principles and arguments, the fallacy inherent in these objections. That this latter species of apologetics is clearly present in the works of Aquinas, is here taken for granted. It will also be brought out per transennam in the course of the investigation to follow, as when, for example, the process will be seen to have a significant rôle in the ' de Trinitate' of Contra Gentiles IV.

Again, ' apologetical' is not being used in the present study for the demonstrations customarily associated today with discussion of the praeambula fidei. That this further species of apologetics is present in the works of St. Thomas himself, at least in some fashion, is also being taken for granted.

'Apologetical' as used in the present study, then, is quite precise, and it has already been noted that this precision has been supplied from the contemporary theological dialogue. The formula 'apologetical perspective' corresponds simply to the mentality Vagaggini asks if one must not recognize in Aquinas, who, as he would have it, was so obsessed with the deductivist ideal of Anselm's *rationes necessariae* as to have followed Anselm in attempting to demonstrate the a priori necessity of the revealed processions, or at least in wishing to approximate and imitate demonstration to whatever degree possible.

And, of course, it is with this last mentioned nuance, that the present study will occupy itself. The real question is not at all whether St. Thomas actually planned to demonstrate the Trinity of Persons! In the concluding pages of his critique, Vagaggini himself is most insistent in rejecting such an idea. The question is rather, was *de facto* demonstration of a qualified sort somehow unavoidably involved in whatever else it was that St. Thomas did plan to achieve — involved, to pinpoint the decisive moment in Vagaggini's argument, in his assertion and use of the universal principle that procession of inner word, as a simple perfection, was essential to intellectua nature?

That the general plan and objective of Aquinas was, in fact, something else, Vagaggini concedes, therefore, but always with the suggestion that Aquinas still longed for the apodictic demonstration, still concentrated on proving the basic datum, if not with reasonings that would be certain, at least with those that were suasive, and might thus substitute for certitude in a process seeking to imitate demonstration where it could not simply reproduce it. For Vagaggini finishes by describing the Thomist achievement as demonstration's "illusion esthétique."

Vagaggini, then, not only calls for a reexamination of the text to determine what had actually been the scientific intention and perspective of St. Thomas, but suggests in addition the most likely — perhaps only? — area in which he believes that the final solution will be found. Demonstration, or its aesthetic illusion, seem to be the only alternatives he is prepared to consider.

For other theologians who have touched upon the same point, however, there would be a wider field of choice. Paissac appeals to Aquinas' distinction between the theological argument that aims to verify the hypothesis and can do so with probative certitude, on the one hand, and the explanatory argument that, in the line of verification, can be no more than suasive, on the other. The Thomist ' *de Trinitate* ' as constructed upon the analogy from inner word is an instance of the second type. Its objective, at least its primary objective, is not to verify, but to explain. Whether, along with explanation, there is also, as part of St. Thomas' own design, the verification that would be no more than suasive, Paissac, in the writer's judgment, does not make perfectly clear.

Penido, however, goes further. Arguing from his personal interpretation of the famous reply in *S. T.*, *I*, q. 32, a. 1, ad 2m, he sees St. Thomas making a definitive break from his Anselmian and Victorine adversaries, and positively excluding as a valid description of his own theological intention and perspective even the much restricted, though otherwise legitimate, verification in terms of congruence.

On the same point of Aquinas' basic theological ideal, Lonergan's position is still more refined, and encompasses as well a more decisive stand on the question of simple perfection than that already assumed by Diepen. For Lonergan, the distinction between verification and explanation is absorbed into the more precise distinction between the quest of certitude and the quest of understanding as the ideal of theological science. This distinction is not only fundamental in Lonergan's personal synthesis, but also, and antecedently, in his analytical criticism of St. Thomas' own achievement. [54]

Turning, then, to the question whether procession of the really distinct inner word is proper to intellectual nature as a simple perfection, Lonergan does not accept Diepen's answer — yes, provided that the notion of simple perfection is itself restricted and qualified — but simply dismisses both the question and the notion as not immediately pertinent. In

---

[54] The theme is basic to Lonergan's personal synthesis, *Insight. A Study of Human Understanding*. For the same author's discussion of the distinction according to its place in Aquinas' own thought, see also " The Concept of *Verbum* in the Writings of St. Thomas Aquinas, V. *Imago Dei*, " *Theological Studies*, X (1949), pp. 384-385.

Lonergan's reading of the text, the generalization made by
Aquinas was made by a theologian speaking precisely as a
theologian, and must be interpreted exclusively in this light.

* * *

In view of the contributions others have made to the
same problem, therefore, it cannot be assumed at the beginning
of the present investigation that the two alternatives suggested
by Vagaggini — demonstration or its aesthetic illusion — are
the only choices possible. For both of these alternatives seem
to imply that, in Vagaggini's mind, the ideal of theological
science, at least as conceived by Aquinas, must in any case be
an ideal of certitude. Others, however, see the further alternatives, the ideal of explanation, and the ideal of understanding.
Nevertheless, in the opinion of the writer, Dom Vagaggini's question deserves to be answered — all the more so,
since the object of his challenge seems to have been, not to
offer a solution, but rather to draw attention to a yet unsettled
problem, and to invite a reexamination of the Thomist text.
Whatever the basic intention and perspective of Aquinas had
been — demonstration's " illusion   esthétique ? ",   explanation ?, understanding ? — one must endeavor to give account,
if possible, from the text itself, and from its inherent methodology and design, for the peculiar, and judged by contemporary
standards, perhaps unusual, procedure, whereby St. Thomas
introduces at the beginning of his more mature trinitarian
exposition, in the idiom and structure of the syllogistic ' major ', the universal principle that procession of inner word
pertains to the *ratio formalis* of intellect as such.

PART TWO

EVOLUTION IN THE STRUCTURE
OF THE THOMIST 'DE TRINITATE'

Chapter One

EMERGENT METHODOLOGY IN THE
SCRIPTUM IN I SENTENTIARUM

On four separate occasions during the course of his teaching career, St. Thomas set out to present an explicit, at least to some degree unified and systematically coherent, account of the mystery of the Divine Trinity. It is to these four writings, then — *In I Sententiarum, Contra Gentiles IV, Pars Prima*, and *Compendium* — along with the methodological treatise *In Boethii de Trinitate*, and discussion of several particular topics in certain of the *Quaestiones Disputatae*, that attention will be given throughout the second and third parts of the present study.

As the examination of the text progresses, however, there are two conditions to be kept in mind. First, there is no intention in this study to give a complete or detailed analysis of the Thomist '*de Trinitate*' as a *corpus doctrinae*. At the same time, there is the intention of examining the indicated texts as a whole, rather than merely singling out questions and articles that on first sight might appear to be the only passages directly pertinent to the problem of the Thomist demonstrations and the possibility of an apologetical perspective. The distinction is of some importance.

The subject of this investigation is not Thomist trinitarian theology in all its doctrinal complexity, but the much more particularized question of whether, or to what extent, the process of exposition and development characteristic of this theological achievement had involved the intention, or at least the implicit consequence, of applying some measure of purely rational demonstration to the revealed mystery itself. The immediate question, therefore, is quite specific. But it is specific rather as an aspect, than as a part, of the whole.

If it were possible, for instance, to absolve Aquinas' doctrine on *processio ab utroque* by concentrating more or less exclusively, though still in context, upon those passages where this theme was the matter directly treated, it would not be possible to approach the problem of apologetical intention and perspective in the same simple fashion.

It is necessary here to recall the preliminary conclusions of the previous section. For, as already seen, pinpointing the passages of the original text in which the divine processions might appear to be demonstrated is not, by itself, sufficient to determine whether or not there is demonstration of this sort in fact. The reason is simply because the question keeps going back to what had been the basic scientific intention, or ideal, in virtue of which St. Thomas himself would have selected and defined his principles of demonstration.

But what, it could be suggested, if the passages directly concerned with the two trinitarian processions were coupled with introductory passages concerned with the problems of theological method? Unfortunately, such a procedure would tend rather to dismiss, than to answer, the more subtle question imposed upon the writer by what has hitherto been said in the contemporary theological dialogue.

Whatever might be claimed for the presumption of perfect consistency on the part of St. Thomas, such a presumption is quite out of order in a critical investigation of the text which must cope with the double question, not only whether Aquinas actually intended to demonstrate apologetically, but also whether the doctrinal elaboration he presented, and the scientific principles upon which this was based, involved *ipso facto*, one might say automatically, the species of demonstration that would still have been *praeter intentionem*, or even *contra intentionem*.

The process of elaboration, therefore, must be examined in itself. Moreover, it must be examined precisely as a process — that is, with primary attention being focused throughout on what exactly is the *terminus a quo*, the *terminus ad quem*, and the *media* through which, or in virtue of which, the movement between successive points will have been accomplished.

The method chosen in the present study, then, is as follows. In the four presentations of the Thomist ' *de Trinitate* ', beginning with the tract in the *Sentences*, analysis of the text will start wherever Aquinas himself actually poses and commences to discuss the trinitarian theme, and will continue — or after an interruption, resume — its course until that point in the text has been reached beyond which there remains only such detail as could no longer substantially affect the process of development at the point or points where this latter might have involved some sort of apologetical demonstration for the two revealed processions.

In a certain respect, of course, it is less satisfactory to have to begin this analysis of the Thomist text with a work bearing the external structure, if indeed not more, of a commentary. In a work of this nature, it might well be asked, will not the order and outline of the original so regulate the commentator's personal treatment as to render the basic movement of his own account an uncertain affair at best?

On the other hand, the time is passed when the historian could look upon St. Thomas' *Sentences* as simply a commentary on Peter Lombard. For among the more immediate predecessors of Aquinas himself, emphasis had already begun to shift from exegetical exposition to the discussion of sundry theological topics in a scheme of *quaestiones* only loosely related to the underlying text. [1] Furthermore, even where St. Thomas is thus indebted to certain of his forerunners for the suggestion of such appended topics, nevertheless a good measure of originality attaches to the scientific attitude and techniques with which he will treat them. In this light, as Père Chenu has remarked, the *quaestiones* of Aquinas transform his commentary into the first organic construct of his personal thought. [2]

It remains, then, to see whether this general observation of Père Chenu would have any peculiar relevance for the extremely long section of St. Thomas' *Sentences* which might conveniently be called its ' *de Trinitate* '.

---

[1] See M.-D. CHENU, O.P., *Introduction à l'étude de saint Thomas d'Aquin* (2e éd. ; Montréal : Institut d'Etudes Médiévales - Paris : Librairie Philosophique J. Vrin, 1954), pp. 231-232.

[2] *Ibid.*, pp. 233-237.

I. FROM THE DIVINE ESSENCE AND ATTRIBUTES TO PLURALITY OF PERSONS

It is in the second distinction, immediately after having presented a rather detailed outline of the Lombard's Trinity, that St. Thomas presents the single *quaestio* which brings him to begin his own treatment of the same theme. [3] His approach to the statement of the mystery consists in three simple steps, moving out from the oneness of the divine essence, to the plurality of the rationally distinct attributes, and finally to the plurality of the really distinct Persons.

The first article asks whether God is only one. The reply in the *solutio* could hardly be more brief. Since every multiplicity proceeds from some unity — or in the obvious sense of the principle attributed here to Dionysius, from some ' oneness ' — the multiplicity of the whole universe must necessarily be reduced to the one unique principle of all things. For, St. Thomas adds, this is presupposed by faith, and demonstrated as well by reason. [4]

The second article asks whether, notwithstanding the oneness of the divine essence, there is yet in God a plurality of attributes. To answer, St. Thomas first notes that whatever is of strictly positive reality in creatures comes entirely from the Creator. It follows, therefore, that, inasmuch as the cause of a thing always possesses this thing in a more excellent degree, God Himself must possess in the most excellent degree possible all the endowments of creatures. But since every imperfection proper to the creature's ontological status is to be excluded, God must possess these same endowments — wisdom, goodness, and the like — in the indivisible simplicity and perfect unity of the divine essence, with no possibility here of any real distinction.

At the same time, however, each of these perfections exists in God according to its proper formality (*ratio*) in the truest sense. Hence, inasmuch as the formality of wisdom as such is not the formality of goodness, these divine perfections must be rationally distinct — with a distinction, moreover, derived not from mere reason considered subjec-

---

[3] *In I Sent.*, d. 2, div.
[4] *In I Sent.*, d. 2, q. 1, a. 1 sol.

tively, but from what is seen to be objectively proper to the thing itself. Whence it is, that God stands in relation to His creation, not as an utterly equivocal cause, but as one producing analogically similar effects according to His own form. In the same manner, God is likewise the exemplary cause of all things, not only, that is, with respect to the *rationes ideales* existing in the divine wisdom, but also with respect to the perfections existing in the divine nature, that is to say the attributes. [5]

In the text of the *Sentences* as it now stands, there follows a third and quite lengthy article, in which St. Thomas goes on to give a further explanation of just what is meant by saying that the formal perfections (*rationes*) of wisdom, goodness and the like exist in God, and that the plurality of such formal perfections is radicated objectively in the divine essence. The text itself, however, presents a problem. For according to the evidence collected and rather convincingly presented by Père Antoine Dondaine, it is highly probable, if not certain, that this third article had been inserted into the text of the *Sentences* from a *quaestio* St. Thomas would have disputed at Rome all of ten years later. [6]

---

[5] " Respondeo dicendum, quod quidquid est entitatis et bonitatis in creaturis, totum est a Creatore : imperfectio autem non est ab ipso, sed accidit ex parte creaturarum, inquantum sunt ex nihilo. Quod autem est causa alicujus, habet illud excellentius et nobilius. Unde oportet quod omnes nobilitates omnium creaturarum inveniantur in Deo nobilissimo modo et sine aliqua imperfectione : et ideo quae in creaturis sunt diversa, in Deo propter summam simplicitatem sunt unum. Sic ergo dicendum est, quod in Deo est sapientia, bonitas et hujusmodi, quorum quodlibet est ipsa divina essentia, et ita omnia sunt unum re. Et quia unumquodque eorum est in Deo secundum sui verissimam rationem, et ratio sapientiae non est ratio bonitatis, inquantum hujusmodi, relinquitur quod sunt diversa ratione, non tantum ex parte ipsius ratiocinantis, sed ex proprietate ipsius rei : et inde est quod ipse non est causa rerum omnium aequivoca, cum secundum formam suam producat effectus similes, non univoce, sed analogice ; sicut a sua sapientia derivatur omnis sapientia ... Unde ipse est exemplaris forma rerum, non tantum quantum ad ea quae sunt in sapientia sua, scilicet secundum rationes ideales, sed etiam quantum ad ea quae sunt in natura sua, scilicet attributa. " *In I Sent.*, d. 2, q. 1, a. 2 sol.

[6] See ANTOINE DONDAINE, O.P., " Saint Thomas a-t-il disputé à Rome la question des ' Attributs Divins ' ?, " *Bulletin Thomiste*, X (1933), Notes et communications, pp. 171⁰-182⁰. Some years later, Père Dondaine further developed his position and discussed in detail

Nevertheless, this (now) third article must still be examined in some detail. As the writer intends to show, what is especially significant in St. Thomas' handling of his material in the second distinction now being considered — unity and simplicity of the divine essence, plurality of the rationally distinct attributes, plurality of the really distinct Persons — is the marked difference of approach at the moment he passes from the essence and attributes to the Persons. That this difference is not substantially affected by the interpolation of article three, and the point of the contrast therefore rendered less valid, would have to be indicated with sufficient clarity.

Aquinas begins, then, by nothing that the *ratio* as here used is simply the definition of a thing, where definition is possible, or at least what intellect grasps from the designation of a term, where it is not. [7] To say, therefore, that a certain *ratio* exists in a certain reality, means that what is signified by the word or term exists in the reality itself — properly, in the case where the intellectual conception is the similitude of the thing. [8] Moreover, and according to the tradition for

the questions of origin and authenticity : " Saint Thomas et la dispute des attributs divins (I Sent., d. 2, a. 3), authenticité et origine, " *Archivum Fratrum Praedicatorum*, VIII (1938), pp. 253-262.

[7] " ... ratio, prout hic sumitur, nihil aliud est quam id quod apprehendit intellectus de significatione alicujus nominis : et hoc in his quae habent definitionem, est ipsa rei definitio ... Sed quaedam dicuntur habere rationem sic dictam, quae non definiuntur, sicut quantitas et qualitas, et hujusmodi, quae non definiuntur, quia sunt genera generalissima. Et tamen ratio qualitatis est id quod significatur nomine qualitatis ; et hoc est illud ex quo qualitas habet quod sit qualitas. Unde non refert, utrum illa quae dicuntur habere rationem, habeant vel non habeant definitionem. Et sic patet quod ratio sapientiae quae de Deo dicitur, est id quod concipitur de significatione hujus nominis, quamvis ipsa sapientia divina definiri non possit. " *In I Sent.*, d. 2, q. 1, a. 3, sol, par. 3. (Where the convenience of citation makes subdividing a *solutio* advisable, paragraph distribution is included, as here, in the reference. The distribution is according to the 1929 Lethielleux edition.)

[8] Having explained the three degrees of objective correspondence — proximate foundation, when the conception is of an existing reality ; remote foundation, when the conception is due to the mode of understanding an existing reality ; no foundation, in the case of a chimera — Aquinas summarizes as follows : " Unde patet ... scilicet quod ratio dicitur esse in re, inquantum significatum nominis, cui accidit esse rationem, est in re : et hoc contingit proprie quando conceptio intellectus est similitudo rei. " *In I Sent.*, d. 2, q. 1, a. 3, sol, par. 5.

which Aquinas cites Dionysius and Anselm, this is verified no less of human knowledge of the divine essence. For the conceptions which the mind forms from the terms or names of the divine attributes are truly, however imperfectly, similitudes of that reality which is God Himself. Such *rationes*, therefore, exist not merely in the human intellect, but in the extramental, objective order of things as well, because their proximate foundation is found to be in the divine reality. [9]

Finally, even the plurality of these *rationes* rests upon the same strictly objective foundation. For to say that this plurality derived solely from the human mind considering the effects of God's creation, would be true to the extent that the cause of multiple predication was the intellect's inability to conceive God's infinite perfection in a single conceptual act, but false to the extent that the *rationes* thus attributed to God are proper to His own being, and quite independently of whether or not He had ever created.

God is not good, St. Thomas observes, because He makes what is good, but rather He makes what is good because He is good in Himself. Consequently, while there is no question of real distinction among the divine attributes, there is nevertheless in the divine reality something — His infinite perfection — which corresponds objectively to these multiple conceptions of the human mind. Thus it is, that every name or term designating such conceptions is predicated of God both truly and properly. [10]

---

[9] " Secundum ergo hanc opinionem [Dionysius and Anselm are cited several lines before], conceptiones quas intellectus noster ex nominibus attributorum concipit, sunt vere similitudines rei, quae Deus est, quamvis deficientes et non plenae, sicut est de aliis rebus quae Deo similantur. Unde hujusmodi rationes non sunt tantum in intellectu, quia habent proximum fundamentum in re quae Deus est. " *In I Sent.*, d. 2, q. 1, a. 3 sol, par. 7.

[10] St. Thomas concludes : " Quid ergo dixerunt, quod pluralitas ista est tantum ex parte intellectus nostri, vel ex parte effectuum, quodammodo verum dixerunt, et quodammodo non. Si enin hoc referatur ad causam multiplicationis, sic verum dicunt, quod est ex parte intellectus nostri, et effectuum quodammodo, ex eo quod intellectus noster non potest concipere divinam perfectionem una conceptione, sed pluribus ; cujus una ratio est ex hoc quod est assuefactus ad res creatas. Si autem referatur ad modum quo istae rationes attribuuntur Deo, falsum dicunt. Non enim ex hoc quod bona facit, vel quia ad modum bonorum se habet, bonus est ; sed quia bonus est, ideo bona facit, et alia participando ejus bonitatem ad modum ejus se habent.

In the very next article (the present a. 4, but which, as noted above, most probably followed immediately a. 2 in the original composition of the *Sentences*), St. Thomas passes on from discussion of the divine essence and the plurality of the rationally distinct attributes within the one, simple divine essence to discussion of the plurality of Persons. When he does so, the process of scientific development will take a well defined methodological turn. To evaluate the profound significance of this turn, one should first reflect a moment on what has been the basic movement up to the point where the question of personal and real plurality is about to be introduced.

As was remarked previously, St. Thomas approaches his trinitarian theme in three simple steps, advancing from the oneness of the divine essence, through the reality and plurality of the attributes, to the reality and plurality of the Persons. The scheme of analysis is neat and manageable, and recalls to mind that Aquinas was ever the teacher. At the same time, however, this simplicity in external structure must not be allowed to obscure the fact that, from another and scientifically more pertinent viewpoint, the passage effected from the divine essence to the rationally, but not merely subjectively, distinct attributes — a passage, moreover, fully completed independently of the interpolation in article three — constitutes, in fact, a doctrinal exploration of the divine essence itself.

Starting with the uniquely simple divine essence as the ' given ', so to speak, Aquinas proceeds to develop this initial supposition. Not only can the human intelligence affirm the oneness of God, presupposed by faith and demonstrated also by reason, but the same human intelligence can somehow penetrate the divine essence to affirm, as well, the existence in

---

Unde si nullam creaturam fecisset nec facturus esset, ipse in se talis esset ut posset vere considerari secundum omnes istas conceptiones, quas habet nunc intellectus noster ipsum considerando. Et sic patet quartum, quod pluralitas istorum nominum non tantum est ex parte intellectus nostri formantis diversas conceptiones de Deo, quae dicuntur diversae ratione, ut ex dictis patet, sed ex parte ipsius Dei, inquantum scilicet est aliquid in Deo correspondens omnibus istis conceptionibus, scilicet plena et omnimoda ipsius perfectio, secundum quam contingit quod quodlibet nominum significantium istas conceptiones, de Deo vere et proprie dicitur ; non autem ita quod aliqua diversitas vel multiplicitas ponatur in re, quae Deus est, ratione istorum attributorum. " *In I Sent.*, d. 2, q. 1, a. 3 sol, par. 9.

God of perfections such as wisdom and goodness, of attributes that are rationally distinct, but with a distinction rooted ultimately and objectively in the divine nature itself. This is the conclusion already reached in article two, though the precise quality of this objective foundation as ' proximate ' is brought out only in the more detailed and more refined explanation of the interpolated *quaestio disputata* which now stands in the text as article three.

There is, then, and even confining the analysis to articles one and two, a clear process of doctrinal development. It is important to observe the manner in which it is achieved.

At this stage in his treatise, St. Thomas does not include at any point in his *solutio* of the second (or third) article even so much as a reference to the divine goodness or wisdom as data of revelation. At this stage, what he seems intent on emphasizing is rather that God, as the first cause of all creation, stands in strict analogical continuity with His creatures — the principle explicitly enunciated at the end of the *solutio* of the second article.

Because the cause must precontain in a more eminent degree the perfection discovered in its effect, God must precontain all the perfections of all His creatures in the most eminent degree possible Because the cause, in this instance, is separated from its effects in the utter exclusion of all potentiality and imperfection, these perfections must exist in God in unqualified ontological identity with the divine essence. Nevertheless, and with serene confidence, St. Thomas does not hesitate to affirm, with sole appeal to the foregoing strictly rational or philosophical principles, that the same ineffable identity of God's essence is that which gives objective correspondence and value to the *rationes*, and to the very distinction and plurality of *rationes*, which human intelligence assigns to the divine being, and in this fashion explores some of the secrets of the divine essence.

But then St. Thomas asks, is there also in God a plurality of Persons ? First, he poses three introductory objections, each of them philosophical.[11] Next, the *contra* presents Dionysius' argument based on the self-communication of the *Summum Bonum*, which is followed by the argument according to which the highest degree of joy would demand companionship,

---

[11] *In I Sent.*, d. 2, q. 1, a. 4, obj. 1, 2, 3.

and by the still further argument according to which the most
perfect charity would consist in a gratuitous love of the other,
where, however, the love could not be of the highest order if
the beloved were merely a creature.[12]

The *solutio*, however, despite its brevity, could not be more
emphatic: that there is in God a plurality of Persons or supposits in the unity of the divine essence, must be admitted
without the least equivocation, and this, not on the strength
of the reasons offered in the *contra*, for these do not conclude
with necessity, but simply because such is the truth of faith.[13]

But is this plurality of Persons real or merely rational?
In the *contra* of the fifth and final article, St. Thomas first
cites the authority of St. Augustine, and then adds on his own
that personal distinction cannot possibly be merely rational.
To say so, is simply to revive the heretical position denying
a true plurality.[14]   In the solution immediately following, he
keeps this same primary focus on the authority of Christian
faith: to say that the Divine Persons are only rationally
distinct, recalls Sabellianism, and hence it must be asserted
without qualification that the plurality of Persons is real.
But one should also consider how this can be.[15]

The personal property, Aquinas explains, or the relation
distinguishing one Person from another, is really identical
with the divine essence, and only rationally distinct from it
— he recalls what he had said earlier on the attributes.   Yet,
inasmuch as the *ratio* of a relation is that it be referred to the
other, there is a twofold possibility in what concerns the divine being.   The relation may be compared to the divine
essence; in this case, it is merely *ratio*.   Or it may be compared to its immediate opposite; and in this case, in virtue
of the proper *ratio* of a relation, the particular relation in
question is really distinct from its opposite.   Moreover, it is

---

   [12] *In I Sent.*, d. 2, q. 1, a. 4, contra.
   [13] " Respondeo : concedendum est, absque ulla ambiguitate, esse
in Deo pluralitatem suppositorum vel personarum in unitate essentiae,
non propter rationes inductas, quae non necessario concludunt, sed
propter fidei veritatem. "   *In I Sent.*, d. 2, q. 1, a. 4 sol.
   [14] *In I Sent.*, d. 2, q. 1, a. 5, contra.
   [15] " Respondeo dicendum, quod dicere personas distingui tantum
ratione, sonat haeresim sabellianam : et ideo simpliciter dicendum
est, quod pluralitas personarum est realis.   Quomodo autem hoc possit
esse videndum est. "   *In I Sent.*, d. 2, q. 1, a. 5 sol, par. 1.

in terms of this latter comparison — not to essence, but to corresponding Person — that the divine Persons are distinguished from each other, and consequently the plurality of Persons is not merely rational, but real.[16]

To have given so detailed an account of the five articles comprising this apparently simple *quaestio unica*, might possibly have left some impression of labouring the obvious. To comment still further on the same passage, might seem even more superfluous. Surely, no one needs to be shown that St. Thomas Aquinas accepted the Trinity as revealed, or that he had at least no explicit intention of demonstrating the existence of the mystery by the light of unaided reason, or that, on the other side, he did include in certain of his works an account of the divine essence and attributes that made impressive use of philosophical principles and argument. The point, however, has not been to repeat, much less stress, such facts, but rather to make as certain as possible that the indications for prevailing scientific perspective and methodology would be set in proper relief. Otherwise, what will be presumed in later stages of the investigation might all too easily appear to lack solid substantiation from the text.

What precisely, then, are these indications? First, there is the contrast that has already been observed. Where the essential oneness of God as the unique and utterly simple cause of all creation is concerned, St. Thomas maintains that this supposition is accessible to rational demonstrations — not only in its primary affirmation, but also in its subsequent development as objective foundation for the rationally distinct attributed perfections. Where, on the other hand, the plurality of Persons is in question, not rational proof, but only the authority of faith, can establish the basic supposition.

---

[16] " Sciendum est igitur, quod proprietas personalis, scilicet relatio distinguens, est idem re quod divina essentia, sed differens ratione, sicut et de attributis dictum est. Ratio autem relationis est ut referatur ad alterum. Potest ergo dupliciter considerari relatio in divinis : vel per comparationem ad essentiam, et sic est ratio tantum ; vel per comparationem ad illud ad quod refertur, et sic per propriam rationem relationis relatio realiter distinguitur ab illo. Sed per comparationem relationis ad suum correlativum oppositum distinguuntur personae, et non per comparationem relationis ad essentiam : et ideo est pluralitas personarum realis et non tantum rationis. " *In I Sent.*, d. 2, q. 1, a. 5 sol, par. 2.

Secondly, but still within the terms of the same contrast, a further and extremely significant difference is to be noted in the nature of the process through which the initial supposition in each instance will be developed. This difference is not simply that in scientific elaboration of the divine essence rational principles will be employed, while in scientific elaboration of the plurality of Persons they will not. Such a statement of the case would be a gross oversimplification. The difference lies rather in the use of rational principles as found in each instance. For even at this very early point in the *Sentences*, there is already some positive indication of what this difference is, and the direction one might legitimately expect it to take later on.

When speaking of the divine essence and the attributes of wisdom, goodness and the like, the philosophical principles in virtue of which alone St. Thomas argued to the existence and distinction of such attributes in the divine nature — the laws of analogical continuity, and cause as eminent source — served not only to explain, in some fashion, the basic supposition, but also to discover specifically new ' data '.

The starting point here had been the one, indivisible essence of God. The process of development led to the ' addition ', so to speak, of the divine goodness, the divine wisdom, and other attributes. Ontologically, of course, the divine goodness and the divine wisdom are simply the divine essence. There is no real distinction. But there is the rational distinction Aquinas was careful to elucidate — even, though briefly, in article two — and this rational distinction, as he explicitly asserted in the same passage, has its strictly objective foundation in the divine essence itself. It is precisely in terms of that explanation, moreover, that the ' addition ' is to be understood.

But when, on the other hand, St. Thomas set out to show how there could be in God a plurality of Persons without the least compromise to essential simplicity through the philosophical principles he introduced to achieve this step in theological development — the laws governing relations — the step itself was marked, not by any ' addition ', in the sense of discovery of data, but solely by that species of ' addition ' that transposes the already given datum to a different level of understanding — the strictly scientific — by exposing, to whatever degree possible, its formal cause. The Person can be really identical with the essence, yet at the same time really distinct from another and corresponding Person, because the Person — at this point, he says rather the personal quality — is relation. But quite clearly, relation does not ' add to ' person in the same fashion wisdom and goodness ' added to ' essence. The process of development, therefore, at least in this instance, is rather different. In the case of the divine essence, there was both explanation and new discovery. In the case of the Divine Persons, there was only explanation, understanding.

Thirdly and finally, it should be noted that in treating both the divine essence and the plurality of Persons, St. Thomas scarcely more than affirms the basic supposition itself. Faith presupposes and reason demonstrates the oneness of the divine essence. Faith alone assures the plurality of Persons.

In the first case, the process of reason — causality and analogy — is briefly outlined ; in the second, the fact is merely affirmed in the *solutio*, with a passing reference to Augustine in the *contra*. At the moment, therefore, when one might normally expect it, that is to say at the very beginning of his treatment with the first statement of the trinitarian mystery, St. Thomas is not in the least preoccupied with its apologetical confirmation, or even with an account of its positive sources.

The point of departure is simply the revealed mystery that there is in God a plurality of Persons. The first and only progressive movement of theological development is in the strictly forward direction of analytical understanding — as opposed to any doubling back upon the basic supposition to verify or support its claim in the manner associated with an apologetical perspective.

II.   DIVINE COGNOSCIBILITY AND THE PROBLEM OF 'SIMILITUDO EXPRESSA '

The next distinction affords St. Thomas the opportunity of approaching the same questions — the existence of God and the Trinity of Persons — once again, this time from the precise aspect of the divine cognoscibility. In the first article of the first question, he establishes the general fact that God

can be known, at least in some way, by the created intellect.
Actually, the solution merely affirms the fact, together with
a double qualification : first, that immediate vision is not
here being considered at all ; secondly, that even in such
knowledge as the creature can achieve, there is still no comprehension of the divine essence, for knowledge is always
restricted to the mode of the knower.[17]   By implication, then,
one is left to consult the *contra* and the *responsa* for the positive argumentation.

In the *contra*, St. Thomas cites Aristotle's doctrine that
the end of human life is the contemplation of God. Man
would have been created in vain, therefore, if this end were
not attainable.[18]   In the first *responsum*, he recalls the law
of analogical continuity throughout the whole universe of
being. Contrary to what was supposed in the objection, the
nature of being (" natura entitatis ") belongs, granted in an
eminent manner, to God Himself. God, that is to say, does
not exist in any total isolation from the universe of being ;
nor, by the same token, from the universe of the known or
knowable.[19]

This first article, then, is hardly more than a clear re-
statement of God's infinite intelligibility with its necessary ontological implications for the spiritual creature. In the second
article, St. Thomas begins to explore these basic implications
in greater detail. Is the existence of God, he goes on to ask,
per se notum ?

Aquinas' solution is quite clear. If the question is meant
to ask whether God's existence is *per se notum* with reference
to God Himself, then yes, God is known in and through Himself, as already understood and already perfectly intelligible.
If, however, the question is meant to ask rather whether God's
existence is *per se notum* with reference to human beings, a
further distinction must be made. In what concerns the similitude and participation of divine reality, His existence is *per*

---

[17] *In I Sent.*, d. 3, q. 1, a. 1 sol.
[18] *In I Sent.*, d. 3, q. 1, a. 1, contra.
[19] " Ad primum ergo dicendum, quod sicut Deus non est hoc
modo existens sicut ista existentia, sed in eo est natura entitatis emi-
nenter ; unde non est omnino expers entitatis ; ita etiam non omnino
est expers cognitionis, quin cognoscatur ; sed non cognoscitur per
modum aliorum existentium, quae intellectu creato comprehendi possunt. "   *In I Sent.*, d. 3, q. 1, a. 1, ad 1m.

se notum for human beings — in the sense that all creatures
are known through the truth of which God is the exemplar,
and the existence of truth itself is *per se notum*.   But in what
concerns the divine supposit directly, considering God, that
is, in His own incorporeal nature, His existence is not *per
se notum* for human beings.   In fact, many have been found
to deny it simply.   For things are *per se notum quoad nos* only
when they are rendered such directly through the activity
of sense.   A man needs merely to see the whole and its part
to be able to know instantly, without any inquisition, that
every whole is greater than its part.   Knowledge of God, on
the other hand, is obtained from sensible objects, not through
this simple intuition, but only through a process of argument.[20]

The *responsum* to the fourth objection is also to be noted,
inasmuch as it throws light on what was the attitude of St.
Thomas at this early point in his career on the value of purely
conceptualist reason in arriving at conclusions pertinent to
the extramental, real order.   The objection had proposed the
famous argument of the *Proslogion* for the existence of God
as that greater than which nothing can be thought.[21]   Aquinas
observes, however, that such an argument is valid only if it
presupposes right from the start the actual existence of such
a being than which nothing greater can be thought.[22]   The

---

[20] " Respondeo, quod de cognitione alicujus rei potest aliquis
dupliciter loqui : aut secundum ipsam rem, aut quoad nos.   Loquendo
igitur de Deo secundum seipsum, esse est per se notum, et ipse est
per se intellectus, non per hoc quod faciamus ipsum intelligibile, sicut
materialia facimus intelligibilia in actu.   Loquendo autem de Deo per
comparationem ad nos, sic iterum dupliciter potest considerari.   Aut
secundum suam similitudinem et participationem ; et hoc modo ipsum
esse, est per se notum ; nihil enim cognoscitur nisi per veritatem suam,
quae est a Deo exemplata ; veritatem autem esse, est per se notum.
Aut secundum suppositum, id est, considerando ipsum Deum, secundum quod est in natura sua quid incorporeum ; et hoc modo non
est per se notum ; immo multi inveniuntur negasse Deum esse ... Et
hujus ratio est, quia ea quae per se nobis nota sunt, efficiuntur nota
statim per sensum ; sicut visis toto et parte, statim cognoscimus
quod omne totum est majus sua parte sine aliqua inquisitione. ... Sed
visis sensibilibus, non devenimus in Deum nisi procedendo, secundum
quod ista causata sunt et quod omne causatum est ab aliqua causa
agente et quod primum agens non potest esse corpus, et ita in Deum
non devenimus nisi arguendo ; et nullum tale est per se notum. "   *In
I Sent.*, d. 3, q. 1, a. 2 sol.

[21] *In I Sent.*, d. 3, q. 1, a. 2, obj. 4.

[22] " Ad quartum dicendum, quod ratio Anselmi ita intelligenda

reply of St. Thomas will prove to be of no little importance
when the time comes to examine more closely whether, or
with what qualifications, doctrinal development based on the
principle of the *perfectio simplex* has an actual rôle in authentic
Thomist thought.

If, then, God is not *per se notum* to human beings, do
men come to knowledge of Him, St. Thomas asks in the next
article, through creatures? In virtue of what he has said
already, Aquinas can make his solution brief. Unlike the
brute animals, men are capable of reaching God at least in
some way; and unlike the angels, what knowledge men do
have of God in this life begins from creatures and terminates
at the Creator. What makes this knowledge *per creaturas*
radically possible, is the fact that creatures proceed from God
as from their exemplary cause with Whom they stand in the
relationship of analogical likeness.[23]

But what of the Trinity as such? St. Thomas concludes
this *quaestio* by asking, finally, if the philosophers, relying
entirely upon natural reason, came to know even the divine
Trinity through this same knowledge of creatures. Once again
however, he states that it is simply impossible for unaided
reason to attain knowledge of the Trinity of Persons. As he
had explained in the two previous articles, natural reason
knows God only from His creatures, and everything that can
be said of God with respect to creatures pertains, not to the
plurality of Persons, but to the divine essence. Natural reason, then, cannot go beyond knowledge of this essence and its
attributes.

Of course, in knowing the divine power, wisdom and
goodness, it is true that the philosophers would have been
able to know the Persons indirectly, that is, through what is

---

est. Postquam intelligimus Deum, non potest intelligi quod sit Deus,
et possit cogitari non esse; sed tamen ex hoc non sequitur quod aliquis
non possit negare vel cogitare, Deum non esse; potest enim cogitare
nihil hujusmodi esse quo majus cogitari non possit; et ideo ratio
sua procedit ex hac suppositione, quod supponatur aliquid esse quo
majus cogitari non potest. " *In I Sent.*, d. 3, q. 1, a. 2, ad 4m.

[23] " Respondeo dicendum, quod cum creatura exemplariter procedat ab ipso Deo sicut a causa quodammodo simili per analogiam,
ex creaturis potest in Deum deveniri tribus illis modis quibus dictum
est, scilicet per causalitatem, remotionem, eminentiam. " *In I Sent.*,
d. 3, q. 1, a. 3 sol.

appropriated to them.[24] Nevertheless, as Aquinas qualifies almost immediately, this is not proper knowledge of the Persons themselves, nor even, for that matter, knowledge through appropriations precisely as appropriations, but rather as attributes of the divine essence.[25]

Yet, is there not in the human soul an express similitude of the Trinity of Persons, which would provide the philosopher with the necessary starting point in knowledge of God through creaturely effects ? [26] For the moment, St. Thomas answers the objection simply by saying that the likeness of the Trinity shining forth in the human soul is quite imperfect and inadequate, and is called express only in comparison with the inferior likeness of a mere vestige.[27] But this is the problem — *similitudo, vestigium, imago* — to which he will give detailed attention throughout the second, third, fourth and fifth *quaestiones* that follow immediately.

First, St. Thomas explains the theological usage of the similitude that is called vestige. The term, of course, is metaphorical, being drawn from the common footprint, and is used to designate the similitude in which there is true likeness, likeness, however, that is deficient or imperfect, but capable, nevertheless, of leading to some actual knowledge

---

[24] " Respondeo dicendum, quod per naturalem rationem non potest perveniri in cognitione Trinitatis personarum ; et ideo philosophi nihil de hoc sciverunt, nisi forte per revelationem vel auditum ab aliis. Et hujus ratio est, quia naturalis ratio non cognoscit Deum nisi ex creaturis. Omnia autem quae dicuntur de Deo per respectum ad creaturas, pertinent ad essentiam et non ad personas. Et ideo ex naturali ratione non venitur nisi in attributa divinae essentiae. Tamen personas, secundum appropriata eis, philosophi cognoscere potuerunt, cognoscentes potentiam, sapientiam, bonitatem. " *In I Sent.*, d. 3, q. 1, a. 4 sol.

[25] " Ad quartum dicendum, quod philosophi non pervenerunt in cognitionem duarum personarum quantum ad propria, sed solum quantum ad appropriata, non inquantum appropriata sunt, quia sic eorum cognitio dependeret ex propriis, sed inquantum sunt attributa divinae naturae. " *In I Sent.*, d. 3, q. 1, a. 4, ad 4m.

[26] " Praeterea, philosophi potuerunt devenire in cognitionem eorum quae in creaturis relucent. Sed in anima est expressa similitudo Trinitatis personarum. Ergo videtur quod per potentias animae, quas philosophi multum consideraverunt, potuerunt in Trinitatem personarum devenire. " *In I Sent.*, d. 3, q. 1, a. 4, obj. 2.

[27] " Ad secundum dicendum, quod similitudo Trinitatis relucens in anima est omnino imperfecta et deficiens, sicut infra dicet Magister. Sed dicitur expressa per comparationem ad similitudinem vestigii. " *In I Sent.*, d. 3, q. 1, a. 4, ad 2m.

of that whose likeness it is. Thus in creatures, inasmuch as they contain real but imperfect likeness of God leading to His knowledge, there is said to be the vestige of their Creator. This is particularly verified, Aquinas adds, in the instance where the creature becomes the basis of knowledge, not of God's essence, but of the Divine Persons, because the creature is more deficient as representing the distinction of Persons than as representing the essential attributes. It is here, therefore, that the term vestige is used more properly.[28]

Next, St. Thomas discusses at some length the various perspectives from which a triplicity of parts or elements can be discovered in the creaturely vestige, according to the way this or that in the complex perfection of the creature is assigned the formality of *principium*, *media* and *finis*.[29] He concludes his introductory account by noting that such a vestige can be found in all creatures, at least wherever there is a fully actuated individual in the genus of substance, and not merely metaphysical or logical components. For the creature is a vestige of the Trinity only when and inasmuch as it is in full possession of its own existence.[30]

The single article of the third *quaestio* brings St. Thomas from this general discussion of a trinitarian vestige in all creatures to the *imago Trinitatis* discovered in the human intelligence. On the difference between vestige and image, he is most precise. While the vestige is only a confused, imperfect likeness of the thing, the image, on the other hand, represents the thing more determinately according to all its parts and their dispositions, from which something of the interior elements of the thing can be perceived. Where the image of God is concerned, therefore, this image will be found only in those creatures which, in virtue of their special excellence, imitate and represent the divine being in a more perfect manner.[31] In this connection, Aquinas observes how

---

[28] *In I Sent.*, d. 3, q. 2, a. 1 sol.
[29] *In I Sent.*, d. 3, q. 2, a. 2.
[30] *In I Sent.*, d. 3, q. 2, a. 3.
[31] " Respondeo dicendum, quod imago in hoc differt a vestigio ; quod vestigium est confusa similitudo alicujus rei et imperfecta ; imago autem repaesentat rem magis determinate secundum omnes suas partes et dispositiones partium, ex quibus etiam aliquid de interioribus rei percipi potest. Et ideo in illis tantum creaturis dicitur esse imago Dei quae propter sui nobilitatem ipsum perfectius imitantur et reprae-

Augustine had shown a trinitarian similitude in quite a number of things, but found a perfect similitude only in the powers of the mind, where there was consubstantial distinction and equality.[32]

Addressing himself, then, to the first image as described in the *Littera*, St. Thomas indicates the three distinct powers of the soul constituting this representation of the Trinity. First, there is the spiritual memory, the power of retaining species. Secondly, since the soul itself is immaterial and hence intellectual in its nature, there follows the power of understanding, whereby the species retained in the intellectual memory are understood. Thirdly, inasmuch as what is thus understood is grasped as self-agreeable (*conveniens*), there follows finally the power which tends toward the agreeable, or will.[33]

St. Thomas then takes a moment to expose two points of general doctrine concerning the powers of the soul in relation to the soul's essence and to one another. First, the powers are distinct from the essence itself.[34] Secondly, a natural order is to be observed, according to which latter powers are radicated in the essence only mediately through those that are former.[35] Neither of these points is developed, however, in precise relation to the constituents of the trinitarian image. Application is nevertheless implicit, and is presumed

sentant ; et ideo in angelo et homine secundum id quod est in ipso nobilius. Alia autem, quae plus et minus participant de Dei bonitate, magis accedunt ad rationem imaginis. " *In I Sent.*, d. 3, q. 3, a. 1 sol.

[32] " Ad primum ergo dicendum, quod Augustinus in multis ostendit similitudinem Trinitatis esse ; sed in nullo esse perfectam similitudinem, sicut in potentiis mentis, ubi invenitur distinctio consubstantialis et aequalitas. " *In I Sent.*, d. 3, q. 3, a. 1, ad 1m.

[33] " Unde dicitur, III *De anima*, text. 6, quod anima est locus specierum, praeter quam non tota, sed intellectus. Ista ergo virtus retinendi dicitur hic potentia memoriae. Ulterius, quia anima est immunis a materia, et omnis talis natura est intellectualis, consequitur ut id quod in ipsa tenetur ab ea intelligatur, et ita post memoriam sequitur intelligentia. Item, quia id quod intelligitur accipitur ut conveniens intelligenti, ideo consequitur voluntas, quae tendit in ipsum conveniens : nec potest ultra procedere ; quia voluntas est respectu finis, cum ejus objectum sit bonum, et rei perfectio non extendatur ultra finem. Et secundum hoc sunt tres potentiae distinctae ab invicem, memoria, intelligentia et voluntas. " *In I Sent.*, d. 3, q. 4, a. 1 sol.

[34] *In I Sent.*, d. 3, q. 4, a. 2.

[35] *In I Sent.*, d. 3, q. 4, a. 3.

in the article immediately following, at least to the limited
extent that *ordo* will be involved in the discussion of objects.

St. Thomas asks : is the trinitarian image found in the
rational powers irrespective of this or that particular object ?
He notes, first of all, that the image, as an express representation, turns upon five different factors : consubstantiality and
distinction of powers, equality, order, and actual imitation.
The first two mentioned pertain to the soul itself, and here
variation in object is of no account. But the three remaining
factors do involve such variation in object, as he proceeds
to explain.

In matters learned through acquired habits, where the
act of understanding precedes memory, order is not preserved;
nor, consequently, actual imitation. In the same matters,
there is equality between one potency and another, inasmuch
as whatever is comprehended by one potency is somehow
comprehended also by the other : men do not necessarily
will what they understand, of course, but at least they will
to understand this thing. But equality between potency and
object is lacking, inasmuch as corporeal objects have a more
excellent existence in the mind than in their extramental
reality.

In the matter of that particular object which is the soul
itself, however, there is, first, order, because the soul is naturally present to itself, and hence, in this case, understanding
follows conscious awareness (*notitia*). There is, secondly, simple equality between the potencies, for the soul wills and loves
itself to the precise degree it understands itself. There is
also, and obviously, equality between potency and object.
Thirdly and finally, there is actual imitation of the Trinity
itself, inasmuch as the soul is here an image expressly leading
the mind to God.

Yet, St. Thomas concludes his somewhat lengthy exposition, the image is verified still more closely when the particular object of the rational powers is God Himself. First,
there is again actual imitation. Secondly, there is order.
In fact, here order is preserved in the highest degree : understanding proceeds from memory, because God is present in
the soul *per essentiam* as opposed to being retained through
acquisition. As for equality, there is the simple equality between potency and potency, and while equality between potency and object is lacking, due to the superiority of the

divine being over the human soul, nevertheless, Aquinas appends, this latter equality is not especially important among the factors which constitute an image. St. Thomas then summarizes his discussion of the objects : image is present in some degree irrespective of object, but more truly when the object is the soul itself, and most truly of all when the object is God.[36]

Yet, what is to be said of the fact that the powers of the soul are not always in act with respect to those very

---

[36] " Respondeo dicendum, quod, sicut dictum est, imago dicit expressam repraesentationem. Expressa autem repraesentatio est in ipsis potentiis propter quinque. Quorum duo se tenent ex parte ipsius animae, scilicet consubstantialitas et distinctio potentiarum, et ideo se habent indifferenter respectu quorumlibet objectorum ; alia vero tria, scilicet aequalitas, et ordo, et actualis imitatio respiciunt objecta, unde se habent diversimode respectu diversorum objectorum. Potest autem attendi in potentiis animae duplex aequalitas, scilicet potentiae ad potentiam, et potentiae ad objectum. Et haec secunda aequalitas salvatur hic diversimode respectu diversorum objectorum. In illis enim quae per habitum acquisitum discuntur, non servatur ordo, ut dictum est supra, quia intelligendi actus praecedit actum memorandi ; et ideo non est ibi actualis repraesentatio ipsius Trinitatis, secundum quod intendit illis objectis quae non exprimunt Trinitatem. Servatur autem ibi aequalitas quaedam, scilicet potentiae ad potentiam : quia quaecumque comprehenduntur una potentia, comprehenduntur alia : non quod quidquid intelligimus, simpliciter velimus ; sed aliquo modo in voluntate sunt, inquantum volumus nos ea intelligere : sed non servatur aequalitas potentiae ad objectum : quia res corporales sunt in anima nobiliori modo quam in seipsis, cum anima sit nobilior eis, ut dicit Augustinus. Si autem considerentur istae potentiae respectu hujus objecti quod est anima, sic salvatur ordo, cum ipsa anima naturaliter sit sibi praesens ; unde ex notitia procedit intelligere, et oon e converso. Servatur etiam aequalitas potentiae ad potentiam conpliciter : quia quantum se intelligit, tantum se vult et diligit : non sicut in aliis, quod velit se tantum intelligere, sed simpliciter. Servatur etiam ibi aequalitas potentiae ad objectum. Servatur etiam ibi actualis imitatio ipsius Trinitatis, inquantum scilicet ipsa anima est imago expresse ducens in Deum. Si autem considerentur respectu hujus objecti quod est Deus, tunc servatur ibi actualis imitatio. Maxime autem servatur ordo, quia ex memoria procedit intelligentia, eo quod ipse est per essentiam in anima, et tenetur ab ipsa non per acquisitionem. Servatur etiam ibi aequalitas potentiae ad potentiam simpliciter, sed non potentiae ad objectum : quia Deus est altior quam sit anima. Unde dico, quod imago quodammodo attenditur respectu quorumlibet objectorum ; verius autem respectu suiipsius, et verissime respectu hujus objecti, quod est Deus ; nisi tantum quod deest aequalitas potentiae ad objectum, quae etiam non multum facit ad imaginem. " *In I Sent.*, d. 3, q. 4, a. 4 sol.

objects — itself and God — in which the *imago Trinitatis* is found ? Following Augustine, St. Thomas distinguishes between discernment and analytical knowledge, on the one hand, and simple intellectual intuition of that which is present to the mind as intelligible, on the other. Quite obviously, the soul does not always have of either God or itself the analytically reflective and discerning knowledge that requires not only intelligible presence, but presence after the manner of an object. Nonetheless, since intelligence (or understanding, as Aquinas describes it in this particular and early passage) means nothing more than simple intuition requiring only that the intelligible be somehow present to the intellect, in this latter sense it remains true that the soul always understands both itself and God, and that there follows even a certain indeterminate act of love.[37]

Thus St. Thomas concludes his discussion of the *imago Trinitatis* as found in the rational powers of memory, intelligence and will — and with it, his treatment of the divine cognoscibility in what pertains both to the oneness of essence and to the plurality of Persons.[38]

This consideration has enabled him once again to stress the law of analogical continuity, whereby God, as exemplary cause of all creatures, can be known from the knowledge of these same creatures. But it has also afforded him the op-

---

[37] " Respondeo dicendum, quod, secundum Augustinum, *De util. credendi*, cap. XI, differunt cogitare, discernere et intelligere. Discernere est cognoscere rem per differentiam sui ab aliis. Cogitare autem est considerare rem secundum partes et proprietates suas : unde dicitur quasi coagitare. Intelligere autem dicit nihil aliud quam simplicem intuitum intellectus in id quod sibi est praesens intelligibile. Dico ergo, quod anima non semper cogitat et discernit de Deo, nec de se, quia sic quilibet sciret naturaliter totam naturam animae suae, ad quod vix magno studio pervenitur : ad talem enim cognitionem non sufficit praesentia rei quolibet modo ; sed oportet ut sit ibi in ratione objecti, et exigitur intentio cognoscentis. Sed secundum quod intelligere nihil aliud dicit quam intuitum, qui nihil aliud est quam praesentia intelligibilis ad intellectum quocumque modo, sic anima semper intelligit se et Deum, et consequitur quidam amor indeterminatus. " *In I Sent.*, d. 3, q. 4, a. 5 sol.

[38] In a fifth and final *quaestio*, Aquinas turns briefly to the second trinitarian image described in the *Littera*. The parts of this second image — *mens, notitia, amor* — are assigned, he notes, not according to the powers of the soul, but " secundum essentiam et habitus consubstantiales. " This second image is not developed, however. See *In I Sent.*, d. 3, q. 5.

portunity of introducing the extremely important distinction between *per se notum quoad se* and *per se notum etiam quoad nos* : even in what concerns the divine essence, God is not present to the human intellect as an object of direct knowledge where simple intuition into what is perceived through sense would reveal His intelligibility the same way simple perception of the terms ' whole ' and ' part ' would reveal at once the necessary intelligible nexus between them. To say, therefore, that God can be known through the knowledge of creatures, means that God can be known only through some process of discursive reasoning which has its epistemological basis in the knowledge of creatures.

In this new context, St. Thomas then goes on to repeat once more the basic contrast he had previously observed between knowledge of the divine essence and knowledge of the distinct Persons. Though God is not *per se notum quoad nos*, unaided natural reason can nevertheless attain knowledge of His existence and essential perfection from creatures, through a process based upon the metaphysical principles of causality and analogy. But no process of discursive reason is able by itself to penetrate to the plurality of Persons. For knowledge that is so gathered from creatures leads only to the divine essence as their ultimate exemplar.

But this raises the problem — *per modum objectionis*, as it were — of the *imago expressa in creaturis relucens*. First, speaking of vestige in general, St. Thomas notes its representational deficiency. In fact, it is precisely inasmuch as creatures represent the Persons so much less perfectly than the essence, that *vestigium* is used only in connection with knowledge of the Persons.

Yet, one might be tempted to ask, in Aquinas' mind, does the same imperfection attach to that particular vestige which is the image of the Trinity in the powers of the human soul ? In this very passage, has he not distinguished *vestigium* and *imago* precisely on the basis that while the vestige is merely a confused and imperfect representation, the image, on the other hand, is a more perfect likeness, in which the several elements and their organization reveal something of the interior of that which it represents ?

There can be no doubting St. Thomas' own intention, however. Though the difference between vestige and image is of significant degree, it is still just that — a difference of

degree. The text is quite clear on the point. The objection
in the fourth article of the first question — cited above —
referred explicitly to the "expressa similitudo Trinitatis in
anima," and it was with reference to the same image, again
explicitly, that Aquinas remarked: "similitudo Trinitatis relucens in anima est omnino imperfecta et deficiens."

Finally, what is to be concluded from the details of the
memory, intellect, will image as Aquinas here discusses them?
On the positive side, first, arguing from the way these powers
derive from the essence of the soul and as really distinct from
it, St. Thomas provides representational basis for the trinitarian consubstantiality and distinction. Secondly, considering
the additional factors of order in emanation from the soul's
essence and in actual operation, equality between potency and
potency and between potency and object, and lastly actual
imitation, he proceeds to indicate how the initial representation
is elaborated and intensified in connection with two particular objects toward which the rational powers are directed
— to the soul itself, and still more to God.

Nevertheless, there is not a little in this account that is
less than perfectly satisfying. For instance, what is the nature of the distinction between the intellectual memory retaining the species and the intellectual faculty which understands the same species? By what exact token does the
essential (*per essentiam*) presence of God to the soul render
the image more perfect when the powers are turned to God
as object than when they are turned toward the soul's own
self-comprehension? Why is it that at no point in the whole
discussion does St. Thomas draw the lines of comparison between the representation and the represented, to speak of
procession, or of the Persons as such?

Perhaps it is merely the distraction of knowing before-
hand the major rôle a perfectly constructed *imago Trinitatis*
will eventually come to play in Thomist trinitarian theology
that makes the presentation here in the *Sentences* appear half-
hearted. In any case, far from there being the slightest evidence of a development through *imago* that would double back
upon the root existence of the mystery in apologetical corroboration, one might well ask if even such purely explanatory
development as is achieved at this point through use of the
same *imago* should be accorded more than minor doctrinal
significance.

III. ANALYSIS OF THE DIVINE GENERATION

A decidedly more positive impression is given, however, when St. Thomas begins, in the distinction immediately following, to discuss the generation of the Son. For here, as will be seen presently, the Thomist analytical method — first posing the basic supposition on the authority of divine revelation, and then proceeding to see how this same basic supposition must be taken, or understood, by rational theology — is conspicuously in evidence throughout.

That there is in fact generation in God, Aquinas starts off, cannot be proved satisfactorily by rational demonstration, but is simply to be affirmed on the testimony of faith.[39] Nevertheless, he goes on immediately to take the first step toward showing how, in the light of rational principles, the supposition, once its revelation is accepted, will have to be understood.

Perfections found in creatures can be attributed to God, in a proper and not merely symbolic or metaphorical sense, only when and to the extent that every last element of imperfection has been removed. In its generic aspect, generation, as change, involves passage from potency to act, materiality in the one generated, and consequently division of essence — none of which, of course, can be assigned to God. In its specific difference, however, generation designates a certain perfection : passively, the acceptance of essence in perfect likeness ; actively, the communication of the same. But neither of these involves imperfection, inasmuch as communication is in the line of act, and pertains therefore to excellence. Thus, it is only under this aspect of communication that generation can be spoken of in God ; under the same aspect, in fact, generation belongs to God *per prius*, and to creatures only secondarily as imperfect imitators of the divine perfection.[40]

---

[39] " Respondeo dicendum, quod generationem esse in divinis, ratione efficaciter confirmari non potest, sicut supra dictum est, sed auctoritate et fide tenetur : unde simpliciter concedendum est, generationem esse in divinis. " *In I Sent.*, d. 4, q. 1, a. 1 sol, par. 1.

[40] " Sciendum tamen est, quod, cum omnis perfectio sit in Deo et nulla imperfectio, quidquid perfectionis invenitur in creatura, de

The reply to the first objection completes the explanation by stating simply that generation in God is not change (*mutatio*) but operation (*operatio*) of the divine nature. While *mutatio* or *motus*, as *actus imperfecti*, would involve actuation and hence the element of imperfection, *operatio*, on the other hand, as *actus perfecti*, involves not actuation, but only act, and hence, at least *de se*, no element of imperfection at all. [41]

The remaining articles in the same question, plus the two articles of the question following, are concerned with proprieties of expression — "Deus genuit Deum," "Deus genuit alium Deum" — with the radical possibility, but comparative inconvenience, of predicating *persona de essentia*, and with

---

Deo dici potest quantum ad id quod est perfectionis in ispa, omni remota imperfectione. Si autem nomen imponitur ab eo quod imperfectionis est, sicut lapis, vel leo, tunc dicitur de Deo symbolice vel metaphorice. Si autem imponitur ab eo quod est perfectionis, dicitur proprie, quamvis secundum modum eminentiorem. Dicitur autem nomen imponi ab eo quod est quasi differentia constitutiva et non ex ratione generis; et ideo quandocumque aliud secundum suum genus dicit imperfectionem, et secundum differentiam, perfectionem, illud invenitur in Deo quantum ad rationem differentiae, et non quantum ad rationem generis: sicut scientia non est in Deo quantum ad rationem habitus vel qualitatis, quia sic habet rationem accidentis; sed solum secundum id quod complet rationem scientiae, scilicet cognoscitivum certitudinaliter aliquorum. Similiter dico, quod si accipiamus genus generationis, secundum quod invenitur in inferioribus, imperfectionis est: mutatio enim, quae est genus ipsius, ponit exitum de potentia ad actum, et per consequens ponit materialitatem in genito, et per consequens divisionem essentiae: quae omnia divinae generationi non competunt. Si autem consideretur secundum differentiam suam, per quam completur ratio generationis, sic dicit aliquam perfectionem: passive enim accepta dicit acceptationem essentiae in perfecta similitudine; cujus communicationem dicit, si sumatur active: quorum neutrum imperfectionem dicit: communicatio enim consequitur rationem actus: unde omnis forma, quantum est de se, communicabilis est; et ideo communicatio pertinet ad nobilitatem. Et hoc modo accepta generatione est per prius in Deo, et omnis generatio in creaturis descendit ab illa, et imitatur eam quantum potest, quamvis deficiat. Unde ad Ephes., III, 15: 'Ex quo omnis paternitas in caelis et in terra nominatur'." *In I Sent.*, d. 4, q. 1, a. 1 sol, par. 2.

[41] " Et per hoc jam patet solutio ad primum: quia generatio, secundum suum genus, quod est mutatio, in divinis non invenitur; unde in Deo non est mutatio, sed operatio divinae naturae, secundum Damascenum, lib. I *Fid. orth.*, cap. VIII, col. 814, t. I. Differt autem operatio a motu, secundum Philosophum, *Ethic*, V, cap. IV, V et VI, quia operatio est actus perfecti, sed motus est actus imperfecti, quia existentis in potentia. " *In I Sent.*, d. 4, q. 1, a. 1, ad 1m.

the legitimacy of forming compound propositions. [42] As for these latter, St. Thomas asserts that the enunciation is valid in the same measure the apprehension which it expresses is valid, and for the human mind, apprehension of the simple is achieved only through a certain composition. [43]

In the fifth distinction, Aquinas resumes his doctrinal elaboration of the divine generation. First, considering this generation in its relationship to the divine essence, he asks whether it is the essence itself that generates. In creatures, there would be no problem, for in creatures, it is the supposit, not the essence, that acts. Since there is real distinction between supposit and essence, the same act cannot be predicated also of essence, unless insofar as essence is cause. In God, however, since the distinction between supposit and essence is not real, but only rational, it follows that in every instance where this rational distinction does not underlie predication of an act *de supposito*, the same act can be predicated as well *de essentia*. Thus one says that the essence creates, or governs the universe. Wherever, on the other hand, an act is predicated *de supposito* precisely in terms of the rational distinction between supposit and essence, the same act cannot be predicated also *de essentia*.

Divine generation belongs, then, to this second category, because generation is said of the Father precisely as a supposit distinct from the Son, and therefore — this is obviously St. Thomas' meaning — the predication of the act *de supposito Patris* is an instance of predication *de supposito* where the rational distinction between supposit and essence is necessarily and clearly at play. The divine essence, therefore, does not generate, but rather the Father generates in virtue of the divine essence, or nature. [44]

---

[42] *In I Sent.*, d. 4, q. 1, aa. 2 and 3 ; q. 2, aa. 1 and 2.

[43] *In I Sent.*, d. 4, q. 2, a. 1 sol.

[44] " Respondeo dicendum, quod in creaturis actus sunt suppositorum ; et essentia non agit, sed est principium actus in supposito : non enim humanitas generat, sed Socrates virtute suae naturae. In creaturis autem essentia realiter differt a supposito, et ideo nullus actus proprie de essentia praedicatur nisi causaliter. In divinis autem essentia realiter non differt a supposito sed solum ratione, sive quantum ad modum significandi : quia suppositum est distinctum et essentia est communis. Et ideo in divinis quaecumque praedicantur de supposito non secundum modum quo differt ab essentia, praedicantur

Furthermore, St. Thomas rounds off his argument, since
generation is predicated of the supposit as distinct, one observes an order of descending propriety when there is question
of predicating the same act of other divine names. *Pater
generat* is the most proper of all, because here the name is
imposed by the distinguishing personal property. *Persona
generat* would be next in line, inasmuch as the name designates
at least personality as common. *Deus generat*, on the other
hand, is much less appropriate, because here the supposit only
dimly suggested is not distinct, and the name derives from
the common essence rather than from a distinguishing property.
Even *substantia* (*generat*) would be tolerable to the extent that
substance makes some approach to the formality of supposit.
But *essentia*, being entirely cut off from that same formality,
is simply inadmissible. [45]

---

etiam de essentia : dicimus enim, quod essentia creat et gubernat et
hujusmodi. Sed actus qui dicitur de supposito secundum modum secundum quem differt ab essentia, non potest de essentia praedicari ;
et hujusmodi est actus generandi, qui praedicatur de supposito Patris,
secundum quod distinctum est a supposito Filii : unde non est concedendum quod essentia generet, sep quod Pater generat virtute essentiae, vel naturae. Unde etiam dicit Damascenus, lib. I *Fid. orthod.*,
cap. VIII, col. 814, t. I, quod generatio est opus divinae naturae existens. ” *In I Sent.*, d. 5, q. 1, a. 1 sol.

[45] “ Respondeo dicendum, quod, sicut dictum est, generare proprie
convenit supposito inquantum distinctum ;   et ideo quanto magis
appropinquat nomen ad suppositum distinctum, tanto verius potest
praedicari de ipso actus generandi. Unde haec est propriissima, Pater generat, quia imponitur nomen Patris a proprietate distinguente.
Et similiter potest dici, persona generat, quia nomen personae imponitur a proprietate communi, quae dicitur personalitas : et consequen-
tur minus proprie dicitur, Deus generat ; quia, quamvis claudat in se
suppositum, non tamen suppositum distinctum ; nec imponitur nomen a proprietate distinguente, sed ab essentia communi. In omnibus autem abstractis etiam est ordo : quia quaedam ordinem dicunt
ad actum, sicut virtus, bonitas, lux, natura et hujusmodi : et quia
actus sunt suppositorum, ideo in istis invenitur dictum, quod sapientia generat vel natura generat ; tamen hujusmodi locutiones non sunt
extendendae, sed pie intelligendae. Quaedam vero nomina sunt quae
non dicunt ordinem ad operationem, sed tantum imponuntur secundum rationem nominis ab actu substandi, sicut substantia. Unde
hoc nomen substantia adhuc accedit ad rationem suppositi, sed hoc
nomen essentia removetur omnino a ratione suppositi : et ideo mini-
me potest dici, quod essentia generat. Si tamen inveniretur, esset
exponenda, essentia generat, id est Pater, qui est essentia. ” *In I
Sent.*, d. 5, q. 1, a. 2 sol.

In view of the apologetical problem which is the chief concern of the present study, an important question should be asked at this point. Is the actual conclusion of St. Thomas' argument as he puts it in this passage, ' therefore God the Father in virtue of the divine essence generates the Son ', or simply, ' therefore the divine essence as such does not generate ' ? The question posed at the head of the main article was " utrum essentia generet. " But the concluding lines of the same article — to be reinforced with the clarifications on predication in the article immediately following — read : " unde non est concedendum quod essentia generet, sed quod Pater generat virtute essentiae. "

In other words, has Aquinas proceeded from the initial revealed datum ' *datur generatio in divinis* ', which he had affirmed as the doctrine of faith in the fourth distinction, to conclude from this more or less abstract and at least minimal supposition of revelation that it is the Father who, in virtue of the divine essence, generates the Son ? At first sight, it could well appear that, aside from introducing the specific names ' Father ' and ' Son ', this is exactly what Aquinas meant to accomplish. Furthermore, should one look for the *media* through which this doctrinal development was effected, what else would he find except the body of purely rational principles seen here to have been appropriated from the metaphysics of participated being and analogy, act and potency, change and operation, *actus imperfecti* and *actus perfecti*, person or supposit as *principium quod* and essence or nature as *principium quo* — that is to say, the ensemble of philosophical principles upon which the final conclusion, whatever it was, is evidently based ?

If, however, this is exactly what St. Thomas has done, then the general description of his theological elaboration as a substantially philosophical affair constructed upon the barest minimum of positive and revealed data would be all the more valid. In the light of such an interpretation, moreover, the still further presumption of apologetical intent is much more easily made. For when points two, three, four and five are considered as equivalently philosophical conclusions, there is a much more natural and perhaps understandable inclination to presume that point one, irrespective of its revelation, is somehow reestablished as the now philosophical supposition or point of departure within the philosophical synthesis.   There is, therefore, the inclination to look and see if the same supposition has not been, or subsequently will be, verified by the processes of rational demonstration proper to philosophy — or, if this is not altogether possible, at least by their close imitation.

Yet, a more careful examination of the passage shows rather clearly that, on the evidence of the text itself, the actual conclusion Aquinas arrives at is simply ' therefore the divine essence does not generate ' — which is in direct reply to his original question " utrum essentia generet " — and that the ' conclusion ' stated at the end of the same article, ' therefore the Father, in virtue of the divine essence, generates the Son ', is not properly the conclusion at all — or if so, only in some sense that calls for a great deal of clarification.

To prove it was impossible that the essence itself generate, Aquinas argued from the principle that wherever the mode of predication was according to the rational distinction between the divine supposit and the divine essence, acts assigned to the supposit could not be assigned as well to the essence. But such a case is the act of generation assigned to the Father precisely as a supposit or Person distinct from the Son, and hence an act assigned to supposit precisely inasmuch and insofar as rationally distinct from essence. In other words, the instance alleged, no less than the general principle, belongs to the process of argument as premise — the ' minor ' to be exact — and not as conclusion. And the source of the instance is simply Christian revelation.

But if the ' conclusion ' which seems to stand at least as the last point reached in a process of systematic development is not really the conclusion of the argument, what then is its positive value? In the writer's judgment, this value is twofold. First, and one might say superficially, there is the value of a proposition, already established, but now restated and reaffirmed after the dispossession of an adverse claimant. It is impossible that the essence generate because the act of generation assigned to the Father with respect to the Son is shown, on analysis, to be an act attributed to a divine supposit precisely as rationally distinct from, not as really identical with, the divine essence — hence it is to be affirmed once again, this time with added reason, that it is only the Father who, in virtue of the divine essence, generates.

On a further and more profoundly significant level, however, the final assertion ' therefore the Father generates the Son in virtue of the divine essence ' represents a distinct advance in doctrinal development — not as the conclusion of something not already known, and not merely as a conclusion reaffirmed after the dismissal of a sort of alternative, but as substantially the same conclusion transposed to a different level of understanding.

For supposed at the beginning of the discussion, and brought in as the ' minor ' of the argument against " essentia generat, " was the revealed datum : ' The Father generates the Son '. But in the full context of the explanatory elaboration presented in the passage, the same revealed datum now stands theologically transposed : ' The Father (here understood as a supposit, or Person, in the metaphysically refined sense of the *principium quod* to which alone acts can be assigned) in virtue of the divine essence (as rationally distinct from the divine supposit, and as *principium quo* of the latter's acts) generates (as communication in the line of act, designating the *actus perfecti* of operation in opposition to the *actus imperfecti* of change) the Son (as supposit, or Person, corresponding to the Father, and recipient of the Father's communication without any potentiality, actuation or imperfection being involved).

In this qualified sense, then, there is conclusion, even new conclusion, and the *media* through which it has been produced is rational — not, to be sure, the ' rational ' of pure reason or philosophy, but the ' rational ' of *ratio per fidem illustrata de mysterio*. The initial datum supposed from divine revelation has been ' reduced ' — at this stage, at least to some degree — to its causal principles, and the reduction has been accomplished through rational theology's application of the metaphysics of being. The datum itself, therefore, is not new, nor newly verified as a (now) philosophical conclusion, but rather transposed from the level of common, one might say primitive, knowledge — where God's self-communication in His revealed word is first received by men — to the level of strictly scientific understanding, that is to say strictly theological understanding, where the gift of human intelligence allows the believer an obscure but precious glimpse into the revealed mystery.

With the focus still on the divine essence in relation to the act of generation, Aquinas next explains the force of the preposition in the formula *genitus de substantia Patris*. Since *de* signifies consubstantiality as well as source, the Son is *de Patre* as generator, but *de essentia Patris* as principle communicated. [46] In no sense, then, can the Son be said to be *ex nihilo*. [47] St. Thomas concludes the distinction with a brief explanation of how the divine essence may be considered as term of the generation. The one generated, of course, is simply the Son, in perfect personal correspondence to the one generating, which is the Father. But the divine essence is also term, as the reality received by the Son through the act of generation. [48]

In the sixth distinction, immediately following, St. Thomas explains, first, the sense in which the divine generation is absolutely necessary; next, the wholly unconditioned sense which is the only way it can also be considered as object of the divine will; and finally, the sense in which the generation of the Son from the Father is *naturalis*. [49] The formal *ratio* of generation requires that the one generated be produced according to the likeness (*in similitudinem*) of the one generating, and the principle of such production pertains to nature as procreating the like from the like. It is thus, consequently, that the expression *Pater natura generat Filium* must be understood. [50]

Is it correct, then, to speak of a *potentia generativa* mediating between the divine essence or nature and the act of

---

[46] " Sed ' de ', cum notet consubstantialitatem, semper notat vel principium materiale, vel agens consubstantiale, sicut dicimus quod homo filius generatur de patre suo, cum sit generatio per decisionem substantiae. Et secundum istum modum Filius dicitur de Patre et de essentia Patris : tamen de Patre sicut de generante, et de essentia sicut de principio generationis communicatio. " *In I Sent.*, d. 5, q.2, a. 1 sol.

[47] *In I Sent.*, d. 5, q. 2, a. 2.

[48] " ... similiter in divinis terminus generationis, quamvis non sit ibi actio vel mutatio, potest accipi dupliciter : scilicet ipsum generatum, et hoc est Filius ; vel essentia accepta a Filio per generationem. " *In I Sent.*, d. 5, q. 3 sol.

[49] *In I Sent.*, d. 6, q. 1, aa. 1, 2 and 3.

[50] " Et quia de ratione generationis est ut producatur genitum in similitudinem generantis, et hujus productionis principium pertinet ad naturam, quae est ex similibus similia procreans ; ideo dicitur, quod Pater natura generat Filium. " *In I Sent.*, d. 6, q. 1, a. 3 sol.

generation? Aquinas distinguishes two basic types of potency, natural and rational, and indicates how this distinction
obtains in God as well as in creatures. In natural potency,
something is produced after the likeness of the producer's
own nature — a man will generate another man. In rational
potency, on the other hand, what is produced is still after the
likeness of the producer — not, however, according to the
species of the producer's own nature, but according to a species
existing in mind. The generation of the Son, therefore, is
through potency of the first type. For the Son proceeds *in
similitudinem naturae*, receiving from the Father the whole
nature, not only specifically but also numerically one with
the Father's own. In this way, does the generative potency
differ from the divine omnipotence, which is rather in the line
of rational potency, inasmuch as creatures proceed from God
according to species existing in the eternal wisdom. [51]

Two further problems pertaining to the same potency are
then briefly discussed. First, St. Thomas notes that the
generative potency is not mere relation, but something both
absolute and relative at the same time. The divine essence
as really identical with paternity is the *principium quo* of
generation. The generative principle, therefore, is essential,
but under the aspect (*ratio*) of relation, and hence a quasi
medium between the essential and the personal, with the
character of absolute as radicated in the divine essence, and
the character of relation as linked to operation. [52] Secondly,
St. Thomas indicates the priority of the generative potency
over the creative. Insofar as both are rooted in the divine
essence, there is but one potency. If, however, each potency
is considered in immediate relation to its operation, then, as
generation is prior to creation, so must the mind recognize a
corresponding rational priority of the generative potency over
the creative. [53]

With three still further articles explaining that the generative potency, looked at actively, is not shared by the Son,
and that neither the Son nor the Father, respectively, can
bring forth another ' Son ', St. Thomas concludes his treatment of the *potentia generativa*. [54]

---

[51] *In I Sent.*, d. 7, q. 1, a. 1.
[52] *In I Sent.*, d. 7, q. 1, a. 2.
[53] *In I Sent.*, d. 7, q. 1, a. 3.
[54] *In I Sent.*, d. 7, q. 2, aa. 1 and 2 ; quaest. 3.

As Aquinas himself explicitly observes at the beginning of the eighth distinction, and referring to the development in the text of the *Littera*, the Trinity of Persons in the unity of essence that has just been exposed must now be examined in the more particular determination of its main doctrinal elements — the common essence, the distinct Person, and the distinguishing property. The first of these, the common essence, is the subject treated in the questions of the eighth distinction, and need not be reviewed here. [55]

In the ninth distinction, St. Thomas proposes to discuss the distinction of the Son from the Father. Nevertheless, since the treatment as presented makes no significant advance over what has already been seen in the analysis of divine generation, from the viewpoint, at least, of the basic orientation and movement in doctrinal development, the investigation can turn at once to the tenth distinction, where St. Thomas begins to speak of the procession of the Holy Spirit. [56]

IV. ANALYSIS OF THE PROCESSION 'PER MODUM AMORIS'

Whatever else might be said of St. Thomas' analysis of the first procession, the generation of the Son, it was not, quite obviously, an intellectualist or psychological account. Later on, as will be seen in due course, he will attempt to reduce procession *per modum naturae* and procession *per modum intellectus* to one, and then the intellectualist account, though perhaps a not very satisfying one, will be worked out.

In sharp contrast, however, the analysis of the second procession, that of the Holy Spirit, is intellectualist or psychological right from the start.

Inasmuch as the introductory article, " utrum Spiritus sanctus procedat ut amor ", is to some extent transitional, the

---

[55] *In I Sent.*, d. 8, div. prim.

[56] First, Aquinas explains that the Son is " alius ", but not " aliud, " with respect to the Father. The *contra* cites the authority of Augustine, as well as indicating that this follows necessarily from the real distinction already exposed. *In I Sent.*, d. 9, q. 1, a. 1. Next, he clarifies predication of " aeternus " and " coaeternus. " *Ibid.*, a. 2. The perfect simultaneity between Father and Son, even in the order of relation, is then treated. *Ibid.*, q. 2, a. 1. Finally, he discusses predication in the present and past tenses for the eternal nativity — " semper natus " being most suitable. *Ibid.*, a. 2.

terms of this transition deserve to be noted. In the *contra*, St. Thomas approaches the procession of the Holy Spirit *per modum amoris* by drawing a comparison to the procession of the Son *per modum notitiae*. The created image which is the representation of the Trinity in the human soul involves this twofold procession. Since the Son proceeds *per modum notitiae*, the first element in the image is already, so to speak, accounted for. It remains that there will be another Person, therefore, proceeding *per modum amoris* to account for the second element. [57]

A false impression could easily be given here. One might presume, in view of such a transition, that St. Thomas had developed the theme of the Son's generation relying on the so - called psychological analogy : specifically, on *processio per modum notitiae*. Yet, the reader will quickly recall that this was simply not the case. The divine generation was developed as act of the Father in virtue of the divine essence. The psychological analogy that had been outlined in the early part of the *Commentary* was not employed to advance the doctrine on generation.

With this observation in mind, it becomes easier to appreciate the precise focus of St. Thomas' *solutio* in the present article. The procession of creatures involves a twofold source in the Creator : the divine essence whose plenitude and perfection is the agent and exemplar of every perfection in the creature, and the divine will to whose liberality — as opposed now to natural necessity — the actual endowment of the creature is due. But the procession of Persons in the Trinity, which is known only through God's revelation, is the all-perfect reason and cause of the procession of creatures. St. Thomas then goes on to draw the double lines of parallel.

First, then, there is the perfect image of God, containing the divine perfection in all its fulness, which is the Son — this is the perfect image which stands to all the imperfect representations of the divinity to be found in creatures as the ultimate principle to which these latter must be reduced, the

---

[57] " Contra, imago creata, quae est in anima, repraesentat Trinitatem in creatura. Sed in imagine creata procedit aliquid per modum notitiae, et aliquid per modum amoris. Cum igitur in Trinitate increata procedat Filius per modum notitiae, erit alia persona procedens per modum amoris. " *In I Sent.*, d. 10, q. 1, a. 1, contra.

ratio and exemplar of the creature in the order of imitation
of nature.   Secondly, there is the divine love as personal, and
this stands to the liberality of God recognized in the procession
of creatures as the quasi *ratio* of all gratuitous endowment,
and thus, the ultimate principle to which this also must be
reduced in parallel to the natural exemplarity as rooted in the
imago perfecta that is the Son.   This second principle is the
Holy Spirit. [58]

The fact of the second procession, therefore, or the existence of the mystery as such, is unequivocally based on revelation.   Once again, St. Thomas explicitly denies to unaided
reason the ability of undertaking a satisfactory demonstration
of the trinitarian processions.   Nor does the conclusion " et
ideo oportet aliquam personam esse in divinis procedentem
per modum amoris " in any way compromise his initial stand.
For in the very same paragraph (the not too lengthy *solutio*)
in which St. Thomas uses the image of the psychological analogy to describe the procession of the Spirit as *processio per
modum amoris*, he insists, equivalently, that this description
presumes the revelation of the basic datum, which it serves,
therefore, not to verify, but to explain.

Yet, even as explanatory, the psychological analogy constitutes, at this early point, scarcely more than a remote background.   In the *contra*, as seen above, and in the first *respon-*

---

[58] " Respondeo dicendum, quod in processione creaturarum duo est
considerare ex parte ipsius Creatoris : scilicet naturam ex cujus pleni-
tudine et perfectione omnis creaturae perfectio et efficitur et exem-
platur, ut supra dictum est, et voluntatem, ex cujus liberalitate ; non
naturae necessitate, haec omnia creaturae conferuntur.   Supposita autem, secundum fidem nostram, processione divinarum personarum in
unitate essentiae, ad cujus probationem ratio sufficiens non invenitur,
oportet processionem personarum, quae perfecta est, esse rationem et
causam processionis creaturae.   Unde sicut processionem creaturarum
naturae divinae perfectionem imperfecte repraesentatium reducimus in
perfectam imaginem, divinam perfectionem plenissime continentem,
scilicet Filium, tamquam in principium, et quasi naturalis processionis
creaturarum a Deo, secundum scilicet imitationem naturae, exemplar
et rationem ; ita oportet quod, inquantum processio creaturae est ex
liberalitate divinae voluntatis, reducatur in unum principium, quod
sit quasi ratio totius liberalis collationis.   Haec autem est amor, sub
cujus ratione omnia a voluntate conferuntur ; et ideo oportet aliquam
personam esse in divinis procedentem per modum amoris, et haec est
Spiritus sanctus.   Et inde est quod quidam philosophi totius naturae
principium amorem posuerunt. "   *In I Sent.*, d. 10, q. 1, a. 1 sol.

sum — where *amor subsistens* is compared to the equally subsistent *Verbum* — Aquinas makes a general, one might say vague, appeal to a previous intellectual procession *per modum notitiae* to prepare for this volitional procession *per modum amoris*. [59] This suffices for his immediate purpose, which seems to be merely to situate or locate the second procession in the psychological order — in the order of will and love, alongside intellect and word.

The here and now more significant parallel, however, that is to say the explanatory vehicle Aquinas actually introduces to describe the second procession, consists not in the elements of the *imago Trinitatis* in the human soul, but rather in a comparison between the procession of creatures and the procession of Divine Persons, inasmuch as the uncreated procession is the archetype of the created. But in this context, the procession of the Son is not *per modum notitiae*, but simply *per modum naturae*. The creature proceeds from the Creator according to both nature and will : according to nature, inasmuch as the divine essence is cause and exemplar ; according to will, inasmuch as the creature is not necessary, but owes its existence to God's liberality.

The eternal procession is parallel. Corresponding to the imperfect imitation *secundum naturam* in the creature, there is the perfect imitation in the procession of the Son *per modum naturae*. Corresponding to the imperfect endowment of the divine goodness in the love bestowed upon the creature, there is the quasi *ratio* and ultimate principle of every such bestowal, which is the procession of the Spirit *per modum amoris*.

To sum up, then, it can be stated quite simply that, at least at this early stage, Aquinas was so far from using the image in the powers of the human soul in a way that would amount to intentional or unintentional demonstration for the existence of the trinitarian processions, that he does not even make serious use of the same image to further their description in merely explanatory development. This failure, moreover, if failure is the right word, results in a certain unevenness of

---

[59] " Ad primum ergo dicendum, quod licet amor, inquantum amor, non dicat quid perfectum et subsistens ; tamen inquantum est Dei amor, a quo omnis imperfectio removetur, habet quod sit perfectum quid et subsistens ; et simile est de verbo. " *In I Sent.*, d. 10, q. 1, a. 1, ad 1m.

7

treatment in the elaboration upon the procession of the Spirit
which follows immediately.

In the very next article, for instance, Aquinas will find
it necessary to distinguish procession as such from procession
per modum amoris specifically, in order to show that the Spirit
is the love which the Father has for the Son, and the Son for
the Father. By itself, procession would give only that the
Spirit is subsistent ; but the mode of procession, in this
instance love, since the beloved must be understood as the
one in whom love terminates and the lover as the one from
whom it issues, gives that the Spirit can be called the Father's
love for the Son, and the Son's love for the Father. [60] Again,
since love involves the lover's complacence in the beloved, and
thus draws the beloved into union with himself, the Spirit
becomes the bond of union between the Father and the Son. [61]
Again, the notion of love as the first of gifts and the agent of
union in spirit will be appealed to in discussing the propriety
of the very name *Spiritus*. [62]

V. PROCESSION 'PER MODUM NATURAE' AND 'PER MODUM
    INTELLECTUS' IDENTIFIED. SPECIFIC TREATMENT OF THE
    'VERBUM CORDIS'

The largely unfinished state of St. Thomas' trinitarian
analysis as achieved in the *Sentences* shows up quite clearly
when his explanation why there can be only Three Persons in
God encounters the objection of the double formula *per modum
naturae et intellectus*. For unless these two can be identified,
there will be two processions, not one, in addition to the
procession *per modum amoris*, and hence more than three

-----

[60] " Respondeo dicendum, quod in processione Spiritus sancti est
considerare duo : scilicet processionem ipsam, et modum procedendi.
Et quia Spiritus sanctus procedit ut res distincta et per se existens,
non habet ex processione sua, inquantum processio est, quod sit a
Patre in Filium, vel e contrario ; sed quod sit in se subsistens. Si
autem consideretur modus processionis quia procedit ut amor, ut dictum est, cum amatum secundum rationem intelligendi sit id in quod
terminatur amor, et amans a quo exit amor : cum Pater amet Filium,
potest dici amor Patris in Filium ; et cum Filius amet Patrem, amor
Filii in Patrem. " *In I Sent.*, d. 10, q. 1, a. 2, sol.

[61] *In I Sent.*, d. 10, q. 1, a. 3.

[62] *In I Sent.*, d. 10, q. 1, a. 4.

Divine Persons.   It is interesting to note how the problem arises.

As seen above, doctrinal development through analysis, however limited, of a faculty — will — and its immediate object — love — contrasts awkwardly with the treatment of the generative potency as a power so intimate to essence that its distinction from essence is not a little obscure, and whose proper act can be termed by Aquinas *naturalis*. But this same awkwardness carries over into the fifth and last article of the section as St. Thomas seeks to show that there can be only Three Persons in God, and does so without the help of a principle that there can be in a purely spiritual being only two immanent processions, one through intellect, and the other through will. [63]

Here in the *Sentences*, then, St. Thomas confines his exposition to the lines already laid down.   Thus, the sole ground for real distinction within the divine essence is the relation of origin.   It is the relation of origin that constitutes the Person. To do this, however, the relation of origin must signify something proper and determined, not something in common, for its rôle is comparable to that of the constitutive difference. [64]

Also, since person is a designation of excellence, the relation of origin which constitutes the Divine Person must itself be in the order of excellence.   Before beginning his detailed analysis, therefore, St. Thomas observes that there are three elements to be accounted for in what constitutes the Divine Persons, and hence determines their precise number : first, there must be a relation of origin ; secondly, this relation must signify something proper ; and thirdly, it must be in the order of excellence or nobility.

In its common aspect, the relation of origin is satisfied upon verification of the two conditions contained in the for-

---

[63] For a succinct statement of the problem whether more than two processions are possible, as Aquinas will treat it later, see especially *S. T.*, *I*, q. 27, a. 5.

[64] " Respondeo dicendum, quod non sunt nisi tres personae in divinis.   Et ratio hujus est, quia in divinis propter essentiae simplicitatem non potest esse distinctio secundum aliquod absolutum, sed secundum relationem, et tantum secundum relationem originis, quae non potest constituere personam, si significet in communi ; sed oportet quod significet aliquid proprium et determinatum.   Habet enim se loco differentiae constitutivae respectu personae, quam oportet esse propriam. " *In I Sent.*, d. 10, q. 1, a. 5 sol, par. 1.

mula *qui ab alio et a quo alius*. The condition *a quo alius* is, of course, a mark of dignity or excellence, but it is in itself common, and hence can constitute a Divine Person only when and insofar as it is determined or further specified by a particular mode of origin. Aquinas' task, then, is to show how this specification in particular mode of origin is actually achieved.

The double agency found in creatures, he observes — *agens a natura* and *agens a voluntate* — has its cause and exemplar in the divine generation and spiration respectively. Since these two, taken actively, are not mutually opposed, they can be assigned to the one Person who is thus *a quo alius* in both respects, that is to say, the Father.

But to assign *qui est ab alio* is not so simple — first, because the relation of origin described to this extent is common, not proper; and secondly, because it does not automatically imply the excellence or nobility that would have to be present to constitute one of the Divine Persons. *Qui est ab alio*, therefore, must be further specified according to that special mode which will imply personal excellence. In God, only two such modes are possible: *qui est ab alio per generationem* and *qui est ab alio per spirationem*. Nor can these two modes belong to one and the same Person. For a single reality can originate from another in one fashion only, just as originating *a natura* is specifically different from originating *ab arte*. Thus there is one Person issuing from the Father through generation, or the Son; and another Person issuing from the Father through spiration, or the Holy Spirit. And finally, since these relations cannot be numerically multiplied while remaining specifically one, because there is no material division here, it follows that there can be only these three distinct Persons and no others. [65]

---

[65] " Item, quia persona est nomen dignitatis, oportet quod in a relatio sit ad dignitatem pertinens. Sic ergo oportet tria considerare in constituentibus personas, scilicet quod sit relatio originis, quod sit propria, quod sit ad dignitatem pertinens. Relatio autem originis in communi importatur in his duobus, ' qui ab alio et a quo alius '. " Hoc autem quod dico, ' a quo alius ', est quidem ad dignitatem pertinens, sed commune est. Unde oportet, ad hoc quod constituat personam, quod determinetur per specialem modum originis. In divinis autem non potest esse nisi duplex modus originis, secundum quod omne agens dividitur in agens a natura et agens a voluntate : et istae actiones inventae in creaturis, ut supra dictum est, reducuntur, ut in

In the same fifth article, the objection that, in addition to the two processions *per modum naturae*, and *per modum amoris*, a third must be conceded *per modum intellectus* forces St. Thomas to close with the problem created by the two possible alternatives in treating the procession of the Son. [66]

He must show that the processions *per modum naturae* and *per modum intellectus* share a basic similarity in virtue of which they can stand together in opposition to the procession *per modum voluntatis*. Consequently, St. Thomas notes that in natural procession, what proceeds, does so as from a single principle, at least if this be a perfect being. But this is also true in intellectual procession ; two different men are not responsible for a numerically single conception. In volitional procession, on the other hand, inasmuch as will tends to the other, giving rise to reciprocation, there emerges from two principles (*ex duobus*) a single conformity of will that is the bond of union between them — which is why *procedere per*

---

causam et exemplar, in duas processiones in divinis, quarum una est per modum naturae et vocatur generatio, et alia per modum voluntatis et vocatur spiratio, ut supra dictum est. Oportet igitur ita specificare a quo alius per generationem, a quo alius per spirationem. Haec autem duo non habent repugnantiam, quia idem potest esse principium plurium diversis modis. Unde ex hoc non constituentur duae personae, sed una tantum ; quia nihil habet virtutem distinguendi, nisi quod habet aliquam rationem oppositionis. Sic igitur habemus unam personam, a qua est aliquis per generationem et spirationem, sicut Pater. Si autem accipiamus aliud, scilicet, ' qui est ab alio ', quamvis importet relationem originis, tamen non sufficit ad constituendam personam : tum quia commune est, tum quia nihil dignitatis importat. Esse enim ab alio potest aliquid vel nobili vel ignobili modo. Unde oportet ad hoc quod constituatur persona, quod determinetur per specialem modum ad dignitatem pertinentem, et isti sunt tantum duo in divinis, et ideo oportebit ita dicere : ' qui est ab alio ' per generationem, et ' qui est ab alio ' per spirationem. Ista autem duo non possunt uni convenire, quia una res habet tantum unum modum quo oritur ex alio. Non enim idem in specie est a natura et ab arte, nec per putrefactionem et seminationem. Et ideo erit una persona quae est ab alia per generationem, et hic est Filius, et alia quae est ab alia per spirationem, et hic est Spiritus sanctus. Et cum istae relationes non possint multiplicari secundum numerum, ita quod remaneat unitas in specie, eo quod non est ibi aliqua divisio materialis, oportet quod sint tantum tres personae. " *In I Sent.*, d. 10, q. 1, a. 5 sol, par. 2.

[66] *In I Sent.*, d. 10, q. 1, a. 5, obj. 1.

modum voluntatis belongs to the Holy Spirit, Who proceeds
a duobus uniting them as distinct Persons. [67]

The common ground thus found for natural and intellectual procession, however, is a far cry from their simple identification, and it should be noted that in the text itself Aquinas
speaks only of the *quaedam similitudo*. Nor is the picture
substantially clarified in the twenty-seventh distinction, when
Aquinas will devote a separate question to the *Verbum* as
such.

In this later section of the *Commentary*, the introductory
article affirms that God is *Verbum* and in the proper sense of
the word. Moreover, this is exactly how St. Thomas expresses
himself: ' God ', and not specifically ' the Son '. [68] The
strength of the affirmation seems rather clearly to derive from
the citation of John 1 : 1 in the *contra*. [69] The balance of
the lengthy solution is taken up with distinguishing proper
from metaphorical usage, with the conclusion that only *verbum cordis* as found in the operation of intellect can be assigned properly to God. [70]

In the article immediately following, however, which com-
bined with a *quaestiuncula* poses the double question — is
verbum said personally, and if so, only of the Son ? — the

---

[67] " Ad primum igitur dicendum, quod processio intellectus et naturae habent quamdam similitudinem per quam distinguuntur a processione per modum voluntatis. Potest enim procedere aliquid ab uno
vel a pluribus. Quod autem procedit per modum naturae, procedit
ut ab uno, si illud perfectum sit ; et similiter quod procedit per modum intellectus ; non enim plures homines habent unam conceptionem
in numero. Et ita Filio, qui est tantum ab uno, scilicet a Patre, attribuitur uterque modus ; procedit enim per modum naturae ut Filius, et
per modum intellectus ut Verbum. Sed voluntatas tendit in alium,
et potest esse reciprocatio, ut ex duobus una voluntatis procedat con-
formitas, quae est unio utriusque. Et ideo procedere per modum voluntatis convenit Spiritui sancto, qui procedit a duobus, uniens eos,
inquantum sunt distinctae personae. Inquantum enim sunt una essentia, uniuntur per essentiam ; et secundum hoc est inter eos amor
essentialis. " *In I Sent.*, d. 10, q. 1, a. 5, ad 1m.

[68] " Respondeo, absque omni dubio confitendum est, Deum esse
verbum, et proprie verbum dici. " *In I Sent.*, d. 27, q. 2, a. 1 sol,
par. 1.

[69] " Contra, Joan., I, 1 : ' In principio erat Verbum, et Verbum
erat apud Deum, et Deus erat Verbum '. " *In I Sent.*, d. 27, q. 2, a. 1,
contra.

[70] *In I Sent.*, d. 27, q. 2, a. 1 sol, par. 2.

position of St. Thomas points up the comparative uncertainty in his own mind at this time as to the actual and full value of the *verbum* concept to explain, in whatever degree is humanly possible, the formality of the divine generation. The term itself, unlike ' Father ' or ' Son ', does not signify only a relation, but rather something absolute with, at the same time, a relation of origin to the *dicens*. But such a relation of origin could be either real — as *paternitas* or *filiatio* — or merely rational — as the relation between the divine *operatio* and *operans*.

If then, Aquinas continues, the relation involved in *verbum* is merely rational, there is no reason why it cannot be said essentially. Since, moreover, the human *verbum* is simply the *species intellecta*, or possibly *ipsa operatio intelligentis*, the purely rational relation seems to satisfy the proper *ratio* of *verbum* as it will be predicated analogically of God. If, on the other hand, the term involves a relation requiring real distinction, in this case it can be said only personally, inasmuch as personal distinction is the only real distinction possible in God. Thus too, one might speak of *amor essentialis* and *amor personalis* in the same way. Laying aside the consideration of *de se* possibilities, however, Aquinas concludes with the observation that the *Verbum* in traditional Christian usage is the *Verbum Personale*. [71]

---

[71] " Et ideo dicendum est cum aliis, quod hoc nomen ' verbum ' ex virtute vocabuli potest personaliter et essentialiter accipi. Non enim significat tantum relationem sicut hoc nomen ' Pater ', vel ' Filius ', sed imponitur ad significandum rem aliquam absolutam simul cum respectu ... Hujusmodi autem relationes in divinis contingit esse dupliciter : quaedam enim sunt relationes reales, quae requirunt distinctionem realem, sicut paternitas et filiatio, quia nulla res potest esse pater et filius sibi ipsi ; quaedam autem sunt relationes rationis tantum, quae non requirunt distinctionem realem, sed rationis, sicut relatio quae importatur in hoc nomine ' operatio '. Habet enim operatio respectum implicitum ad operatorem a quo est : nec in divinis differunt operans et operatio, nisi ratione tantum. Si igitur relatio importata hoc nomine ' verbum ' sit relatio rationis tantum, sic nihil prohibet quin essentialiter dicatur, et videtur sufficere ad rationem verbi, secundum quod a nobis in Deum transumitur ; quia in nobis, ut dictum est, nihil aliud est verbum nisi species intellecta, vel forte ipsa operatio intelligentis : et neutrum eorum realiter distinguitur ab essentia divina. Si autem importet relationem realem distinctionem exigentem, oportet quod personaliter dicatur, quia non est distinctio realis in divinis nisi personarum. Et est simile de amore, qui secundum eamdem distinc-

In the second half of his solution, Aquinas shows briefly
that if *verbum* is taken in the personal sense, then it can be
predicated of the Son only, and not also of the Holy Spirit.
For the Holy Spirit does not proceed *per modum naturae vel
intellectus*, as the Son, but rather *per modum voluntatis.* [72]

As is already clear, and as will become still more evident
in the section which follows, St. Thomas was able to give,
even in the *Sentences*, a fair explanatory account of the distinction of Persons in terms of the real relations through which
the Persons were actually constituted. But when he attempted
to extend this explanation to the modes of origin upon which
the relations themselves depended, it was quite a different
matter. The methodology is unmistakably analytical — its
intention being not to demonstrate or support the primary
revealed datum, but simply to accept this latter as the ' given '
and offer a coherent account of the same, to whatever degree
is possible, in rational theology. The achievement, on the
other hand, at least when compared with subsequent works,
leaves much to be desired.

Thus, the complex structure introduced to explain how
the relations constitute the distinct Persons — 1) relation of
origin, 2) signifying what is proper, 3) in the order or line
of excellence — is almost patchy. The identification of the
processio per modum naturae with the *processio per modum
intellectus* on the common ground of *processio ab uno*, and the
distinction of this procession from that which is *per modum
voluntatis* as *processio ab uno* from *processio a duobus*, is not
especially satisfying. The analysis of the notion of *verbum*,
and the treatment of the question of personal or essential
predication, is rather hesitant.

Behind all this, in the writer's judgment, would seem to
be two factors. First, at the time St. Thomas was composing

---

tionem essentialiter et personaliter dicitur, ut supra dictum est. Sed
tamen in usu sanctorum et communiter loquentium est hoc nomen
' verbum ' secundum quod relationem realiter distinguentem importat."
In I Sent., d. 27, q.2, a. sol. 1, par. 3.

[72] " Ad id quod ulterius quaeritur, dicendum, quod si verbum
personaliter sumatur, soli Filio convenit, et non Spiritui sancto, quia
Spiritus sanctus procedit per modum voluntatis, et ideo proprie dicitur amor et donum ; sed procedere per modum naturae vel intellectus
convenit Filio ; et ideo ipse proprie et genitus et verbum dicitur. "
In I Sent., d. 27, q. 2, a. 2 sol. 2.

the *Sentences*, his attention was riveted upon the first procession, the generation of the Son, as *processio per modum naturae*. He clearly makes of this the dominant element in the compound formula. Secondly, during this same early period, St. Thomas had not yet recognized the profound psychological and metaphysical implications of the emanation of an inner word in human understanding. When he turned, therefore, to the second element in the compound formula, *per modum intellectus*, he did not yet possess the simple and penetrating rational structure whereby he could effect the perfect adjustment of the intellectualist account to his previous account of generation as such.

VI. Further Doctrinal Development. The Persons and Relations

Since the purpose of the present study is to examine the essential orientation and movement of the Thomist ' *de Trinitate* ' in an effort to prove, or disprove, an element of aprioristic demonstration touching upon the roots of the mystery itself, and not to offer an account of its doctrinal detail, the analysis of what remains to be seen in the first book of the *Sentences* may be swiftly concluded. What Aquinas will have to say in the course of subsequent distinctions will have no substantial effect on determining one way or the other the matter that is being investigated.

In the thirteenth distinction, then, St. Thomas completes his treatment of *processio ab utroque* running through the eleventh and twelfth with an analysis of procession (in the narrow or particular sense of *processio Spiritus*) as distinguished from generation. The basic difference between the two, however, is explained in the context *processio ab uno, processio a duobus*, and according to the description of generation as *processio per modum naturae vel intellectus* and of spiration as *processio per modum voluntatis*. In other words, there is no significant progress in the penetration of causes or formalities over what has been seen already. [73]

In the five distinctions immediately following, St. Thomas discusses the temporal procession of the Spirit. [74] Next, hav-

---

[73] *In I Sent.*, d. 13, q. 1, aa. 1-5.
[74] *In I Sent.*, dd. 14-18.

ing thus completed his treatment of the divine generation
and the divine procession grounding the distinction of Persons,
he will pause, as it were, to explain the equality that obtains
among all Three Persons notwithstanding the difference in
relation of origin. [75]

The twenty-second distinction begins one of the best
ordered and systematic sections of the *Commentary*, in which
St. Thomas treats step by step, first the Persons, then the
relations, finally the notions and properties. Aquinas takes
his point of departure in a reaffirmation of the principle that
the human mind can make proper predications of the divine
being according to the laws of analogy and the removal of
whatever imperfection belongs to the creature as such. [76] This
principle, situated here in the context of the divine names,
but already contained in the early distinctions of the first
book, is then applied to the use of ' person ', in a strictly
proper but eminent sense, to designate the three *subsistentes*
in the divine nature. [77]

Persona, St. Thomas explains, has the same force as the
Greek *hypostasis* except that it specifies one who is subsistent
in a higher, that is to say intellectual, nature. *Pater* specifies
the same Person still further, inasmuch as the name expresses
the particular reason of His distinction, which is the relation
of paternity. [78] In fact, if one should make a mental precision
from this relation, there remains not so much as the underlying reality in which the relation subsists ; for the relation
itself is *res subsistens*. [79]

To clarify this last point, St. Thomas exposes the error
of the *Porretani*, as he refers to Gilbert's followers, who attended only to the formality of the relation and neglected its
real foundation. The trinitarian relations exist really in God ;
they are identified, in virtue of the divine simplicity, with the
Three Persons, and mark, in virtue of the proper formality
of relation, the precise reference of the Person *ad alterum*. [80]
Moreover, it is only relation, the sole genus in which opposition

---

[75] *In I Sent.*, dd. 19-21.
[76] *In I Sent.*, d. 22, q. 1, aa. 1-5.
[77] *In I Sent.*, d. 23, q. 1, aa. 1-3 ; also, on understanding of unity
and plurality, dd. 24, 25ff.
[78] *In I Sent.*, d. 26, q. 1, a. 1.
[79] *In I Sent.*, d. 26, q. 1, a. 2.
[80] *In I Sent.*, d. 26, q. 2, a. 1.

does not involve imperfection, that can account, to this extent, for the plurality of Persons. [81] As Aquinas puts it succinctly in the reply to an objection : relation, *qua* relation, would not distinguish on the level of hypostasis, but when the relation is divine, and the possibility of accidental or non-subsistent inherent form is therefore excluded, the opposition and distinction that belongs to relation as relation cannot, in this case, but be on the level of hypostasis. [82]

Nevertheless, if, even at this early stage, Aquinas had already worked out a clear exposition to account, within the limitations imposed by a revealed mystery, for plurality of Persons in one nature as three real and really distinct relations subsisting in the unity of the divine essence, he had not yet come to the time when he would complement this exposition of the divine relations *in facto esse* with a truly satisfactory formal, or quasi-formal analysis penetrating, as much as possible, to the operations which ground these relations, so to speak, *in fieri*. The discussion of the notions, properties and relations in the remaining article of the twenty-sixth distinction, and first article of the twenty-seventh, clarifies the terminology, assigns proper numbers to each category, and shows exactly which of the properties and relations can be really distinct, but it does not explore the operations of origin beyond the point reached in the earlier sections. [83]

Finally, when in the article immediately following the subject of personal operation is actually introduced — " utrum operatio personalis praecedat secundum rationem relationem personae " — it is interesting to note that if the solution here in the *Commentary* is substantially the same, though much briefer, as that which will be given later in the parallel passage in the *Pars Prima*, the emphasis quite clearly is not.

In the *Sentences*, the solution is constructed as follows. For those who claim that the relations do not distinguish or

---

[81] *In I Sent.*, d. 26, q. 2, a. 2.

[82] " Ad primum igitur dicendum, quod relatio divina habet aliquid inquantum est relatio, et aliquid inquantum est divina ; inquantum enim divina, habet quod sit subsistens hypostasis, quia nihil ibi est accidens, nec aliqua forma inhaerens non subsistens ; unde quamvis ex hoc quod est relatio, non habeat quod distinguat hypostasim, quia sic omnis relatio hoc faceret ; tamen habet hoc inquamtum est relatio divina : sic enim non assequitur substantiam, immo est ipsa substantia. " *In I Sent.*, d. 26, q. 2, a. 2, ad 1m.

[83] *In I Sent.*, d. 26, q. 2, a. 3 ; d. 27, q. 1, a. 1.

constitute the Persons, but merely manifest the Persons as already constituted and distinct, the relation in its understanding (*secundum intellectum*) follows the personal operation absolutely. Yet, since relation in the formality of its opposition is the only thing to be found that can distinguish and constitute the Persons, the relation as thus constituting the Persons must, in its understanding, precede the operation. Consequently, considering relation absolutely, it would not precede, but rather follow, operation — as is seen in creatures. Considering the relation, however, as divine, as constituting the Person, and being the subsistent Person, the relation in its understanding does precede the operation. Finally, taking the relation as the personal operation itself, relation and operation are simultaneous in understanding, one and the same. [84]

In the *Summa*, however, there is a significant change of attitude. Replying to the question — " utrum actus notionales praeintelligantur proprietatibus " — St. Thomas makes basically the same initial observation noted in the *Sentences*. According to those who say that the properties do not distinguish and constitute the Persons, but only manifest such as are already distinguished and constituted, it must be affirmed absolutely that the relations in their mode of understanding follow the notional acts — so that it can be said simply, " quia generat, est pater ". [85]

---

[84] " Respondeo dicendum, quod secundum illos qui dicunt, quod relationes non distinguunt nec constituunt personas, sed tantum manifestant constitutas et distinctas, relatio consequitur operationem personalem absolute secundum intellectum. Sed quia non invenitur aliquid distinguens personas et constituens eas nisi relatio secundum rationem suae oppositionis ; ideo dico, quod relatio, inquantum est constituens personam, praecedit secundum intellectum operationem. Secundum hoc ergo dico, quod ipsa relatio potest tripliciter considerari. Vel inquantum est relatio absolute, et ex hoc non habet quod praecedat operationem, immo magis quod sequatur, sicut patet in creaturis ; vel inquantum est relatio divina quae est constituens personam et ipsa persona subsistens ; et sic praecedit secundum intellectum operationem. Vel inquantum est ipsa operatio personalis ; et sic sunt simul secundum intellectum, et idem. " *In I Sent.*, d. 27, q. 1, a. 2 sol.

[85] " Respondeo. Dicendum quod secundum illos qui dicunt quod proprietates non distinguunt et constituunt hypostases, sed manifestant hypostases distinctas et constitutas, absolute dicendum est quod relationes secundum modum intelligendi consequuntur actus notionales, ut dici possit simpliciter quod quia generat, est Pater. " *S.T., I*, q. 40, a. 4c, par. 1.

Yet, supposing that it is in fact the relations that distinguish and constitute the divine hypostases, one must distinguish. St. Thomas introduces the question of origins. When signified passively — as the Son's nativity and the Spirit's procession — the origins are understood to precede the properties, even personal properties, of the Persons who are thus proceeding without qualification, because the origin, in this passive acceptance, is signified as the way (*via*) toward the Person constituted by the property. In like manner, even when accepted actively — as the generation attributed to the Father, and spiration as the notional act attributed to both the Father and the Son — the origin is still understood as being prior to that relation of the *persona originans* which is not personal — thus, the notional act of spiration is understood as preceding the un-named relative property common to both the Father and the Son.

Finally, as for the personal property of the Father, this can be taken in two respects. First, as relation ; and then once again the notional act is understood as prior, because relation, as such, is founded upon act. Secondly, the same personal property can be taken as constitutive of the Person ; and in this last case the relation is necessarily understood as prior to the notional act, just as a Person acting is understood as prior to the action he will perform. [86]

In both accounts, therefore, St. Thomas states that absolutely speaking, the relations follow the operations. But in

---

[86] " Sed supponendo quod relationes distinguant et constituant hypostases in divinis, oportet distinctione uti. Quia origo significatur in divinis active et passive ; active quidem, sicut generatio attribuitur Patri, et spiratio sumpta pro actu notionali attribuitur Patri et Filio ; passive autem, sicut nativitas attribuitur Filio, et processio Spiritui Sancto. Origines enim passive significatae simpliciter praecedunt secundum intellectlm proprietates personarum procedentium, etiam personales, quia origo passive significata significatur ut via ad personam proprietate constitutam. Similiter et origo active significata prior est secundum intellectum quam relatio personae originantis, quae non est personalis : sicut actus notionalis spirationis secundum intellectum praecedit proprietatem relativam innominatam communem Patri et Filio. Sed proprietas personalis Patris potest considerari dupliciter. Uno modo, ut est relatio, et sic iterum secundum intellectum praesupponit actum notionalem, quia relatio, inquantum huiusmodi, fundatur super actum. Alio modo secundum quod est constitutiva personae; et sic oportet quod praeintelligatur relatio actui notionali, sicut persona agens praeintelligitur actioni. " *S.T.*, *I*, q. 40, a. 4c, par. 2.

the *Sentences*, this observation, first introduced in the context
of an erroneous position, is made concessively ("ex hoc non
habet quod praecedat ... immo magis quod sequatur") with
the whole positive emphasis placed upon the precedence of
the relation over operation when the divine relation is taken
as constitutive of the Person and itself subsistent.

In the *Summa*, on the other hand, this precedence of
relation over operation is stated only briefly, is restricted,
moreover, to the Father's paternity — not precisely as relation, but as personal property constituting the Person — and
appears not before the very end of a fairly lengthy *corpus* in
which all the positive emphasis was placed, this time, rather
upon the precedence or priority of the operations as grounding the relations themselves. For, as will be seen later in
more detail, by the time St. Thomas composed the first part
of his *Summa*, he had discovered a key enabling him to penetrate much more deeply the processional operations, and
thus understand more accurately the character of the trinitarian relations *in fieri*, as it were, or in their causes.

VII. CONCLUSION. THE APOLOGETICAL PROBLEM NOT YET IN QUESTION

In what concerns, then, the problem of apologetical perspective, analysis of the basic orientation and movement of
the earliest Thomist ' *de Trinitate* ', which is contained in the
first book of the *Sentences*, leads to a double conclusion.

On a superficial level, St. Thomas makes it extremely
clear that it is simply not his intention to demonstrate the
primary suppositions. Unaided reason, he explains, can attain
the existence of God and the divine attributes. For while
the nature of God is not *per se notum quoad nos*, there is,
nevertheless, an analogical continuity between God and His
creatures, which makes it possible for the human mind to
advance from knowledge of creatures to knowledge of the
Creator, but only insofar as the divine being is cause and
exemplar, and therefore only in what pertains to the unique
and utterly simple divine essence. Then when he goes on to
introduce the plurality of Persons, the generation of the Son
and the procession of the Spirit, there is a radical change in

approach.   These basic suppositions are revealed ; nor can they also, he emphasizes, be proved by reason.

On a deeper level, however, it would be more correct to say that the real question has not yet arisen. As was seen in the earlier section of this study, when contemporary theological opinion on the subject was under review, the problem is not so much whether or not St. Thomas had the intent to demonstrate, but whether or not, regardless of the contrary intent, some element of *de facto* demonstration of an apologetical nature was involved in doctrinal elaboration. This latter problem becomes a serious consideration, if at all, only when the elaboration actually performed penetrates so deeply in the rational explanation of causes and *rationes* that demonstration of aprioristic necessity might seem to be implicated. St. Thomas has not arrived at such a stage in the *Sentences*.

It is true, of course, and as seen in the foregoing examination of the text, that even here in the *Sentences* he does propose to give some explanatory rational account of the revealed data, to explore, in some limited way, not through essential understanding, but through the vicarious understanding of the *via analogiae, causalitatis, remotionis et eminentiae*, the inner reality of that whose existence is known solely on the authority of Christian faith in divine revelation. On the positive side, therefore, Aquinas has relied on the metaphysics of relation to give systematic structure to the plurality of Persons subsisting in the unity of the divine essence. From the metaphysics of act, of operation as *actus perfecti*, he has been able to provide a similar structure for the generation of the Son as communication without actuation, potency, or any manner of imperfection.

Yet, for the problem of the moment, the negative indications are perhaps still more significant. By itself, the doctrine on relations provides only a general, one might say remote, metaphysical foundation for approaching the trinitarian relations *in facto esse* — admirably suited to confound false or heretical expositions, and even to impart, once revelation is supposed, some obscure understanding of the radical possibility that there could be three distinct supposits subsisting in a single undivided essence — but the same doctrine, precisely because it is limited to the most general metaphysical categories, contributes comparatively little to the understanding of internal procession in a spiritual nature. For it is not directly concerned with this spiritual nature as such, nor with analysis of its specifically spiritual perfections. Also, though the treatment of the divine generation in terms of communication of act without actuation of a potency does involve the explicit contrast between the material and the spiritual, the approach to spirituality here is through the *via remotionis*, and there is still the same preoccupation with only the most general categories.

As a matter of fact, in the *Sentences*, St. Thomas actually turned away from the strictly specific analysis of spiritual being that would later characterize Thomist trinitarian theory.

His treatment of the *imago Trinitatis in anima relucens* was, as already observed, scarcely more than half-hearted. His technique for approaching the divine processions was the comparison of the eternal procession with the temporal, in terms, not of intelligible emanation, but of natural imitation and liberality. His description of the Son's generation was as *processio per modum naturae*, with spiritual nature merely equivalent to the immaterial. Finally, when facing the question whether *verbum* is said personally or essentially, Aquinas was unable, at this time, to accord the *verbum* in God an unequivocally relative and personal status. And when discussing the precedence of relation and notional operation, the point he chose to emphasize was not the priority of the operation as 'cause' of the relation, but rather the priority of the relation itself as constitutive of the Person.

To conclude, therefore, what theological elaboration is present in the *Sentences* takes the purely forward direction of explanatory development. In no sense at all, can it be said to double back upon the fundamental suppositions taken from revelation to demonstrate or verify these suppositions by the rational or philosophical processes of the apologetical a priori. Furthermore, even the possibility of such demonstration is at this stage quite definitely postponed. By the nature of things, any treatment of the trinitarian processions in which proof, rational proof, of a priori necessity might be thought to be implicated would have to expose these processions precisely as causes or modes of origin, and hence as divine acts or operations. But this is exactly what St. Thomas does not do in the *Commentary*.

Chapter Two

IN BOETHII DE TRINITATE: A TREATISE ON THEOLOGICAL METHOD

As a discussion of the Trinity, St. Thomas' commentary *In Boethii de Trinitate* never really got into orbit. It is not, therefore, as yet another presentation of the Thomist ' *de Trinitate* ', falling between the first book of the *Sentences* and the fourth book of the *Contra Gentiles*, that it is being included here.

It remains, nevertheless, that the work is of primary importance for the matter at hand. As was noted in the account of Dom Vagaggini's challenge and the contemporary theological dialogue, the problem of whether or not there is some element of a priori demonstration in Aquinas' trinitarian elaborations becomes, in the final analysis, a problem of scientific intent and perspective — or putting it more simply still, a problem of method. But in the *In Boethii de Trinitate*, this is exactly the attitude seen to have been assumed by St. Thomas himself. For while it is true that the work is a treatise on theological method as such, and in no true sense a treatise on the Blessed Trinity, it does contain, on the other hand, an explicit and clear discussion of the problem of unaided reason's inability to demonstrate the trinitarian processions, and approaches this problem, moreover, from within the precisely methodological context of the human intellect's inability to achieve quidditive knowledge of the divine.

Furthermore, though the treatise dates from sometime between 1255 and 1259 — thus making it at least possible that as little as a single year had separated its composition from that of the first book of the *Sentences* — it stands in fact, if not in design, as the methodological background for the second Thomist ' *de Trinitate* ', which Aquinas will work out, again not in this commentary on Boethius, but in the fourth book of the *Contra Gentiles*. [1]

---

[1] See Bruno Decker, *Sancti Thomae de Aquino Expositio Super Librum Boethii de Trinitate* (ed. altera, Leiden: E. J. Brill, 1959),

Replying, then, to the question whether, to know truth, the human mind needs a new illumination of the divine light, St. Thomas sets up two themes, one positive and the other negative or restrictive, which he will go on to develop simultaneously throughout the rest of the work. There is an order of truths, Aquinas asserts, which lies within the efficacy of the agent intellect, such as principles which man knows naturally, along with whatever can be deduced from these. In this order, no special illumination is necessary. But there is another order of truths to which the principles just mentioned do not extend, such as matters of faith transcending the rational faculty, contingent futures, and the like. In this second order, the human mind is not self-sufficient, but does require a new illumination to be conferred by God in addition to the light of pure reason. [2]

The significance of this distinction is not, of course, that there is a province, the purely natural, in which reason enjoys serene competence, offset by another, that of faith and revealed mystery, in which reason has no place or rôle at all. The point Aquinas wishes to make is rather that the human reason is *per se* capable of attaining to its proportioned truth in general, but requires a special illumination to attain to that truth which lies outside this proportion. The implication, therefore, is that even in the province of faith and mystery, reason, not as ' pure ' but as illustrated by faith, still retains a possible and legitimate function, though one that has to be understood with proper qualification and restriction due to the fundamental disproportion already indicated.

With this brief introduction, St. Thomas can begin immediately to discuss the twofold theme, the restrictive and the positive, which he has thus proposed. First, what precisely are the limitations encountered by reason, enlightened reason

---

Prolegomena, p. 44. Decker indicates the opinions of Grabmann (1257-1258) and Wyser (1255-1259), and accepts Chenu's argument placing the outside limit before 1260. He also assigns 1254 as the date of *In I Sent.* For Père Chenu's own position, see M.-D. CHENU, O.P., " La date du commentaire de saint Thomas sur le De Trinitate de Boèce, " *Les Sciences Philosophiques et Théologiques*, II (1941-1942), pp. 432-434.

[2] *In Boet. de Trin.*, q. 1, a. 1, 3. (Numbers following indication of the article are those of the Decker critical edition, from which all references and citations in the present study have been taken.)

as well as unaided reason, in its exploration of the divine?
Secondly, taking these same limitations into systematic account, what precisely is the nature, scope, and value of illuminated rational inquiry, or theological science, in the area
of revealed mystery?

I. Development of the Restrictive Theme

Turning, therefore, from the mind's natural ability to
know its proportioned truth in general, Aquinas asks if this
capacity extends to the knowledge of God.

Three possibilities are systematically excluded. Since the
human intellect here on earth is conditioned solely to forms
abstracted from sense, it cannot know God through the pure
form which is the divine essence. [3] Nor would any similitude
impressed by God upon the human intellect suffice to make
the divine essence, infinitely exceeding any created form,
known. Nor, here on earth, could this knowledge be achieved
through any purely intelligible forms. It remains, therefore,
that the human mind can know God, but only through the
forms of His effects. Yet, even a further qualification is
necessary. Inasmuch as the effects in question are not proportionate to the power of their cause, they cannot give full
knowledge of the power of the cause, nor, consequently, full
knowledge of its quiddity or essence. The human mind, therefore, in knowing God through His effects, knows, not ' what '
He is, but only ' that ' He is. [4]

---

[3] *In Boet. de Trin.*, q. 1, a. 2, 1.

[4] " Similitudo enim quaecumque impressa ab ipso in intellectum
humanum non sufficeret ad hoc quod faceret eius essentiam cognosci,
cum in infinitum excedat quamlibet formam creatam, ratione cuius
intellectui per formas creatas pervius non potest esse deus, ut Augustinus dicit. Nec etiam in statu huius viae cognoscitur deus a nobis
per formas pure intelligibiles, quae sint aliqua similitudo ipsius propter
connaturalitatem intellectus nostri ad phantasmata, ut dictum est.
Unde relinquitur quod solummodo per effectus formam cognoscatur.
Effectus autem est duplex : quidam, qui adaequatur virtuti suae causae, et per talem effectum cognoscitur plenarie virtus causae, et per
consequens quiditas ipsius : alius effectus est, qui deficit a praedicta
aequalitate, et per talem effectum non potest comprehendi virtus agentis
et per consequens nec essentia eius ; sed cognoscitur tantum de causa
quod est. Et sic se habet cognitio effectus ut principium ad cogno-

This distinction, of course, has to be rightly understood. By opposing knowledge *an sit* to *quid sit*, Aquinas does not intend to deny to human intelligence all knowledge of 'what' God is, but rather such knowledge *quid sit* as would be properly proportionate to the divine object.

To achieve this latter, man would have to know God either through the divine form — St. Thomas has already shown this to be impossible, and he will further explain the reasons why later on — or at least through the form of His effects that would perfectly reproduce His own power and being. For, as Aquinas puts it succinctly in the reply to an objection, when knowledge of a thing cannot be obtained *per formam propriam*, the *forma effectus* supplies. [5] Nevertheless, there is no effect which could possibly measure up to the power and reality of the divine cause. At the same time, however, Aquinas goes on to explain how the knowledge of God — *an est* or *quod est* — that men do achieve through knowledge of His effects admits of varying degrees, according as one may understand more or less perfectly the conformity of the cause to its effect. [6] Also, later on in the treatise, he will remark explicitly that knowledge *an sit* always entails at least some knowledge *quid sit* as well. [7]

Understood, then, with this qualification, it remains nonetheless that St. Thomas' chief concern at the moment is simply to note and emphasize the radical inability of the human intellect to know 'what' God is as He is in Himself. This radical limitation, moreover, is not removed even by the light of faith. [8]

---

scendum de causa an est, sicut se habet quiditas ipsius causae, cum per suam formam cognoscitur. Hoc autem modo se habet omnis effectus ad deum. Et ideo non possumus in statu viae pertingere ad cognoscendum de ipso nisi quia est." *In Boet. de Trin.*, q. 1, a. 2, 2.

[5] "Ad quintum dicendum quod quando aliquid non cognoscitur per formam suam, sed per effectum suum, forma effectus supplet locum formae ipsius rei; nam ex ipso effectu scitur an causa sit." *In Boet. de Trin.*, q. 1, a. 2, ad 5m.

[6] "Et tamen unus cognoscentium quia est alio perfectius cognoscit, quia causa tanto ex effectu perfectius cognoscitur, quanto per effectum magis apprehenditur habitudo causae ad effectum." *In Boet. de Trin.*, q. 1, a. 2, 2 ad fin.

[7] "Et tamen sciendum quod de nulla re potest sciri an est, nisi quoquo modo sciatur de ea quid est vel cognitione perfecta vel saltem cognitione confusa ..." *In Boet., de Trin.*, q. 6, a. 3, 3.

[8] *In Boet. de Trin.*, q. 1, a. 2, 4.

The same negative or restrictive point receives further confirmation when Aquinas passes on to the question whether God is the first known, and replies that, in the light of the human intellect's dependence upon abstraction from the sense phantasm, neither God nor any other separated substances can be the first objects known, but must be understood from knowledge of other things within man's immediate competence. [9] As in the *Sentences*, so again here, he takes Anselm's meaning in the *Proslogion* to be that God is indeed *per se notum*, but not *quoad nos*, inasmuch as human beings do not see His essence. [10]

Finally, in the last section of this treatise, St. Thomas goes into the same question somewhat more fully, asking whether the human intellect is able to look upon (*inspicere*) the divine form. He begins by observing that a thing may be known in two ways : *an est*, or *quid est*. To attain knowledge of 'what' something is, the intellect must be able to reach through to its quiddity or essence, and this, either immediately, or at least through the mediation of other things whose knowledge is sufficient to manifest its quiddity or essence.

But immediately, the human intellect is able to conceive the quiddities only of sensible objects — thus ruling out immediate vision of God or of any other pure intelligible. And mediately, while a certain class of invisible things, such as genus or species, is quite perfectly represented from direct knowledge of sensible objects, the natures of these same sensible objects simply cannot sufficiently represent the divine essence, nor the essence of any other separated substance. For they are not of the same class ; and quiddity and other such terms are used almost equivocally when they are being referred to sensible objects and these higher substances. Thus it is, that neither *per viam similitudinis* — because the similitudes drawn from objects of sense are necessarily deficient — nor *per viam causalitatis* — because effects belonging to

---

[9] *In Boet. de Trin.*, q. 1, a. 3, 3 and 4.

[10] " Ad sextum dicendum quod deum esse, quantum est in se, est per se notum, quia sua essentia est suum esse — et hoc modo loquitur Anselmus — non autem nobis qui eius essentiam non videmus. Sed tamen eius cognitio nobis innata esse dicitur, in quantum per principia nobis innata de facili percipere possumus deum esse. " *In Boet. de Trin.*, q. 1, a. 3, ad 6m.

the same lower order can never be adequate to the power of
their cause — can the human understanding attain quidditive
or essential knowledge of the divine form. [11]

Even when the human mind is elevated, St. Thomas
continues, to knowledge of God *per viam revelationis*, man cannot attain, so long as he is on this earth, quidditive knowledge of God. For the ray of divine revelation reaches man
only in the circumstances and basic limitations of the human
condition. [12] It is precisely at this point, however, that St.
Thomas makes the qualification, already noted above, to the

---

[11] " Dicendum quod dupliciter aliquid cognoscitur : uno modo,
dum scitur de eo an est, alio modo, dum scitur de eo quid est. Ad
hoc autem quod de aliqua re sciamus quid est, oportet quod intellectus
noster feratur in ipsius rei quidditatem sive essentiam vel immediate
vel mediantibus aliquibus quae sufficienter eius quiditatem demonstrent.
Immediate quidem intellectus noster ferri non potest secundum statum
viae in essentiam dei et in alias essentias separatas, quia immediate
extenditur ad phantasmata, ad quae comparatur sicut visus ad colo-
rem, ut dicitur in III De anima. Et sic immediate potest concipere
intellectus quiditatem rei sensibilis, non autem alicuius rei intelligibilis.
Unde dicit Dionysius 2 c. Caelestis hierarchiae quod ' nostra analogia
non valet immediate extendi in invisibiles contemplationes '. Sed
quaedam invisibilia sunt, quorum quiditas et natura perfecte exprimi-
tur ex quiditatibus rerum sensibilium notis. Et de his etiam intelli-
gibilibus possumus scire quid est, sed mediate, sicut ex hoc quod
scitur quid est homo et quid est animal, sufficienter innotescit habitudo
unius ad alterum et ex hoc scitur, quid est genus et quid est species.
Sensibiles autem naturae intellectae non sufficienter exprimunt essentiam divinam neque etiam alias essentias separatas, cum non sint
unius generis naturaliter loquendo et quiditas et omnia huiusmodi nomina fere aequivoce dicantur de sensibilibus et de illis substantiis.
Unde similitudines rerum sensibilium ad substantias immateriales tran-
slatas vocat Dionysius 2 c. Caelestis hierarchiae ' dissimiles similitudines alio modo intellectualibus habentibus quae sensibilibus aliter
distributa sunt '. Et sic per viam similitudinis non sufficienter illae
substantiae ex his innotescunt. Neque etiam per viam causalitatis,
quia ea, quae ab illis substantiis inveniuntur effecta in his inferioribus, non sunt effectus adaequantes earum virtutes, ut sic perveniri
possit ad sciendum quod quid est de causa. " *In Boet. de Trin.*, q. 6,
a. 3, 1.

[12] " Unde de substantiis illis immaterialibus secundum statum viae
nullo modo possumus scire quid est non solum per viam naturalis cognitionis, sed etiam nec per viam revelationis, quia divinae revelationis
radius ad nos pervenit secundum modum nostrum, ut Dionysius dicit.
Unde quamvis per revelationem elevemur ad aliquid cognoscendum,
quod alias esset nobis ignotum, non tamen ad hoc quod alio modo
cognoscamus nisi per sensibilia. " *In Boet. de Trin.*, q. 6, a. 3, 2.

effect that some quidditive (*quid est*) knowledge, however vicarious and imperfect, is necessarily involved in the knowledge *an est*. [13] Yet, this knowledge will not be attained in the ordinary terms of genus, proximate or remote.   For naturally speaking, though God is substance, still, inasmuch as He does not have a *quod quid est* that would be other than *esse*, God does not belong to any generic class. [14]

But if the limited and 'confused' knowledge men can obtain of the separated substances — and Aquinas is obviously speaking here of knowledge in the order *quid est* — is not obtained through knowledge of generic classes and identifying accidents, in what manner, then, is it obtained ?   St. Thomas states that, supplying for the genus, there are the positive negations, whereby such realities are understood to be immaterial, incorporeal, and which, as they become multiplied, lead to a progressively more and more narrowed or refined understanding in much the same way the ultimate genus is contracted and determined through a succession of differences.

Secondly, supplying for the identifying accidents, there are the relationships between the intelligibles and material substances, the order of causality extending from the higher realities to the lower, and the comparison that is to be made in terms of eminence.   In this fashion — *per viam negationis, causalitatis, excessus* — the human intellect knows of the superior substances 'that' they are — *an est* — and has also, supplying for the knowledge 'what' they are — *quid est* — the *triplex via* just explained. [15]

---

[13] *In Boet. de Trin.*, q. 6, a. 3, 3.   (Cited above in note no. 7.)

[14] " Hoc autem non potest esse per cognitionem alicuius generis proximi vel remoti, eo quod deus in nullo genere est, cum non habeat quod quid est aliud a suo esse, quod requiritur in omnibus generibus, ut Avicenna dicit.   Aliae autem substantiae immateriales creatae sunt quidem in genere, et quamvis logice considerando conveniant cum istis substantiis sensibilibus in genere remoto quod est substantia, naturaliter tamen loquendo non conveniunt in eodem genere, sicut nec etiam corpora caelestia cum istis inferioribus. "   *In Boet. de Trin.*, q. 6, a. 3,4.

[15] " Et ideo non possumus dicere quod confusa cognitione cognoscantur a nobis substantiae immateriales per cognitionem generis et apparentium accidentium.   Sed loco cognitionis generis habemus in istis substantiis cognitionem per negationes, ut cum scimus quod huiusmodi substantiae sunt immateriales, incorporeae non habentes figuras et alia huiusmodi.   Et quanto plures negationes de eis cognoscimus, tanto et minus confusa est earum cognitio in nobis, eo quod per nega-

In the article immediately following, the last, as it happens, in the treatise, St. Thomas speaks of the ' conditions ' of such separated substances being grasped by intellect while their quiddity or essence is not, and the formula throws further light on what he means when he says that in this area knowledge *quid est* cannot be had, except to the extent that some knowledge *quid est* is necessarily involved in knowledge *an est.* The question here is whether or not the human mind can attain vision of the divine form through some speculative science. St. Thomas, as he explains himself, is thinking of the scientific process from the previously known to the unknown, and of the ultimate first principles behind any demonstration or definition, which themselves are neither demonstrated nor learned, presuppose no still previous knowledge, and are known naturally.

But no such speculative process, he goes on to show, could ever produce a vision of the divine form. The reason is the same fundamental dependence upon the sense phantasm that Aquinas has insisted on all along. The first principles become manifest to intelligence only through the operation of the agent intellect actualizing the intelligibility of the phantasm. Nothing can be known through the processes of speculative science, therefore, that lies beyond the limitation of the first principles in terms of this dependence upon sense. St. Thomas concludes, then, by noting once more that the quiddities of the separated substances cannot be grasped from what man knows of and through the objects of sense. Man knows only that they do exist, and, Aquinas adds, certain of their con-

---

tiones sequentes prior negatio contrahitur et determinatur, sicut genus remotum per differentias. Unde etiam et corpora caelestia, in quantum sunt alterius generis ab istis inferioribus, a nobis ut plurimum per negationes cognoscuntur, utpote quia neque sunt levia neque gravia neque calida neque frigida. Loco autem accidentium habemus in substantiis praedictis habitudines earum ad substantias sensibiles vel secundum comparationem causae ad effectum vel secundum comparationem excessus. Ita ergo de formis immaterialibus cognoscimus an est et habemus de eius loco cognitionis quid est cognitionem per negationem, per causalitatem et per excessum, quos etiam modos Dionysius ponit in libro De divinis nominibus. Et hoc modo Boethius intelligit esse inspiciendam ipsam divinam formam per remotionem omnium phantasmatum, non ut sciatur de ea quid est. " *In Boet. de Trin.,* q. 6, a. 3, 5.

ditions — as, for instance, that they are immaterial or incorruptible. [16]

It is important to observe at this point that it is the negative or restrictive side of his theme which Aquinas develops first — that is, in the second, third, and, as will be seen presently, fourth articles of the first question. For it is the restrictive considerations taken up in the first question — to which the two last articles of the sixth question are rather complementary, and were included above for the sake of convenience — that lead up to the question whether the human mind left to its own natural resources can attain knowledge of the Trinity.

Aquinas' treatment of this question in the *responsio* is characteristically brief and emphatic. One recalls the similar treatment of such questions in the *Sentences*, as seen earlier. That God is one and three, is something which is believed only, notwithstanding the fact that reasons of a sort may be brought to bear on the point — reasons, however, which are neither necessary nor even, except for the believer, particularly suasive (*nec multum probabiles*).

---

[16] " Dicendum quod in scientiis speculativis semper ex aliquo prius noto proceditur tam in demonstrationibus propositionum quam etiam in inventionibus diffinitionum... Unde omnis consideratio scientiarum speculativarum reducitur in aliqua prima, quae quidem homo non habet necesse addiscere aut invenire, ne oporteat in infinitum procedere, sed eorum notitiam naturaliter habet. Et huiusmodi sunt principia demonstrationum indemonstrabilia, ut ' omne totum est maius sua parte ' et similia, in quae omnes demonstrationes scientiarum reducuntur, et etiam primae conceptiones intellectus, ut entis et unius et huiusmodi, in quae oportet reducere omnes diffinitiones scientiarum praedictarum. Ex quo patet quod nihil potest sciri in scientiis speculativis neque per viam demonstrationis neque per viam diffinitionis nisi ea tantummodo, ad quae praedicta naturaliter cognita se extendunt. Huiusmodi autem naturaliter cognita homini manifestantur ex ipso lumine intellectus agentis, quod est homini naturale, quo quidem lumine nihil manifestatur nobis, nisi in quantum per ipsum phantasmata fiunt intelligibilia in actu ... Phantasmata autem a sensu accipiuntur ... Quiditas autem substantiarum separatarum non potest cognosci per ea quae a sensibus accipimus, ut ex praedictis patet, quamvis per sensibilia possimus devenire ad cognoscendum praedictas substantias esse et aliquas earum condiciones. Et ideo per nullam scientiam speculativam potest sciri de aliqua substantia separata quid est, quamvis per scientias speculativas possimus scire ipsas esse et aliquas earum condiciones, utpote quod sunt intellectuales, incorruptibiles et huiusmodi. " *In Boet. de Trin.*, q. 6, a. 4, 1-3.

This conclusion follows from what has previously been shown ; namely, that here on earth, the human mind knows God only from His effects. Thus, by the light of natural reason, man can know of God only what is perceived of Him from the relation of creaturely effects to their divine cause in terms of causality itself, supereminence, and the negation or removal of all imperfections. But the Trinity of Persons cannot be perceived in this way — not from the divine causality, inasmuch as this causality is common to the whole Trinity, and not from the removal of imperfections, inasmuch as the Trinity is not spoken of according to such removal. Consequently, in no way can it be proved demonstratively that God is three and one. [17]

In the same article, the sixth objection had argued to the contrary. Natural reason can prove that God is intelligent — that is, that God understands. But from the fact that God understands, it follows that He conceives a word (*verbum*), for this is common to every intelligence. Therefore, from natural reason alone, it can be learned that there is in God both the generation of the Son and the procession of love. [18]

St. Thomas replies, however, that in God, the intelligent and the understood are the same. From the mere fact that God understands, therefore, it is not necessary that one postulate in God any concept really distinct from Himself, as there

---

[17] " Dicendum quod deum esse trinum et unum est solum creditum, et nullo modo potest demonstrative probari, quamvis ad hoc aliquales rationes non necessariae nec multum probabiles nisi credenti haberi possint. Quod patet ex hoc quod deum non cognoscimus in statu viae nisi ex effectibus, ut ex praedictis patere potest. Et ideo naturali ratione de deo cognoscere non possumus nisi hoc quod percipitur de ipso ex habitudine effectuum ad ipsum, sicut illa quae designant causalitatem ipsius et eminentiam super causata et quae removent ab ipso imperfectas condiciones effectuum. Trinitas autem personarum non potest percipi ex ipsa causalitate divina, cum causalitas sit communis toti trinitati. Nec etiam dicitur secundum remotionem. Unde nullo modo demonstrative probari potest deum esse trinum et unum. " *In Boet. de Trin.*, q. 1, a. 4c.

[18] " Praeterea, quod deus sit intelligens, ratione naturali haberi potest. Sed ex hoc quod est intelligens sequitur quod verbum concipiat, quia hoc est omni intelligenti commune. Ergo naturali ratione cognosci potest quod sit filii generatio et eadem ratione amoris processio. " *In Boet. de Trin.*, q. 1, a. 4, obj. 6.

is in human beings. But the Trinity of Persons demands real distinction. [19]

In St. Thomas' mind, therefore, at least at the time he was composing this treatise on the nature, scope and method of theological science, psychological or philosophical analysis of the intricacies of human understanding, taken by itself, would not only contribute no support for the a priori necessity of a plurality of Persons, but would serve in fact, when the analogy was extended to the divine understanding, to give still further emphasis to God's unequivocal unity and simplicity. It remains to be seen, then, whether, as Dom Vagaggini suggests, Aquinas would subsequently change his mind on the matter, or would rather change the context in which his original solution had been given.

II. DEVELOPMENT OF THE POSITIVE THEME

In the articles of the second question, to proceed with the Thomist text, Aquinas shifts from the negative or restrictive theme developed in the first question to the positive theme of applying the scientific ideal to such knowledge of the divine as the enlightened human reason can actually achieve.

He notes first of all that the aspiration itself is quite legitimate and praiseworthy. The perfection of man consists in his being drawn into union with God. Hence, every faculty and device man possesses should, so far as possible, further his initiation into divine things — the intellect, therefore, finding time for their contemplation, and the reason for their investigation. [20]

Next, St. Thomas asks if a science of the divine — in the strict sense that, from what is already known, conclusions

---

[19] " Ad sextum dicendum quod in deo idem est intelligens et intellectum, et ideo non oportet quod ex hoc quod intelligit ponatur in ipso aliquid conceptum realiter distinctum ab ipso, sicut est in nobis. Trinitas autem personarum requirit realem distinctionem ' *In Boet. de Trin.*, q. 1, a. 4, ad 6m.

[20] " Dicendum quod cum perfectio hominis consistat in coniunctione ad deum, oportet quod homo ex omnibus quae in ipso sunt, quantum possibile est, ad divina admittatur, ut intellectus contemplationi et ratio inquisitioni divinorum vacet ... " *In Boet. de Trin.*, q. 2, a. 1, 1.

are drawn with necessity — is possible.   After answering the
basic question affirmatively, he begins his explanation of the
nature of theological science with this distinction : knowledge
of the divine can be considered from two different aspects —
from the human side, where divine things can be known by
men only through such knowledge as is derived from creatures;
and from the side of their divine nature, where these same
things are supremely knowable in themselves and known in
their own proper reality to God and the saints. [21]

On the basis of this distinction, St. Thomas goes on,
science of the divine is likewise twofold.   First, there is the
science attaching to the human mode of understanding the
divine, whereby the things of God are made known through
principles drawn from the objects of sense, and in light of
which the *prima philosophia* is also called *scientia divina*.   Secondly, there is the science that looks to the divine as the
things of God exist in their own proper reality.   So long as
men are on this earth, they cannot perfectly grasp the things
of God in this latter fashion ; there is, nevertheless, and even
in this life, a certain participation in such knowledge, an assim-
ilation to divine knowledge, to the extent that the human
mind, through infused faith, clings to the divine truth itself
as its own sufficient reason (*propter se ipsam*). [22]

To elucidate, Aquinas draws a subtle, but very pregnant,
analogy.   As God, in knowing Himself, knows everything else

---

[21] " Dicendum quod cum ratio scientiae consistat in hoc quod ex
aliquibus notis alia necessario concludantur, hoc autem de divinis
contingat, constat quod de divinis potest esse scientia.   Sed divinorum
notitia dupliciter potest aestimari.   Uno modo ex parte nostra, et sic
nobis cognoscibilia non sunt nisi per res creatas, quarum cognitionem
a sensu accipimus.   Alio modo ex natura ipsorum, et sic ipsa sunt ex
se ipsis maxime cognoscibilia, et quamvis secundum modum suum non
cognoscantur a nobis, tamen a deo cognoscuntur et a beatis secundum
modum suum. "   *In Boet. de Trin.*, q. 2, a. 2, 1.

[22] " Et secundum hoc de divinis duplex scientia habetur.   Una
secundum modum ostrum, qui sensibilium principia accipit ad notificandum divina, et sic de divinis philosophi scientiam tradiderunt,
philosophiam primam scientiam divinam dicentes.   Alia secundum
modum ipsorum divinorum, ut ipsa divina secundum se ipsa capiantur,
quae quidem perfecte in statu viae nobis est impossibilis, sed fit nobis
in statu viae quaedam illius cognitionis participatio et assimilatio ad
cognitionem divinam, in quantum per fidem nobis infusam inhaere-
mus ipsi primae veritati propter se ipsam. "   *In Boet. de Trin.*, q. 2,
a. 2, 2.

in His own way, not through discursus, but by a simple intuition, so human beings, from what they learn through faith, relying upon the first or divine truth, come to know other things also, in the human way, however, moving through discursus from principles to conclusions. And thus it is, that what men hold in faith stands in this theological science as its quasi principles, and what they derive from these same principles, as its quasi conclusions. It is clear, moreover, that this science is of a higher order than the merely philosophical, because the principles from which it proceeds are themselves of a higher order. [23]

In replying to the objections contained in the same article, St. Thomas complements his doctrine by restating, now in the rather positive context, the more significant points he had previously stressed discussing the fundamental limitations of human reason, even when enlightened by faith, to attain knowledge of the divine. Thus, it is true that human beings cannot know of God *quid est*. But in order to have a science of the divine, this would not be strictly necessary. In such circumstances, knowledge obtained from the effect can supply for knowledge of the quiddity of the cause, and hence knowledge of the quiddity of a thing is not the indispensable first presupposition in the subsequent elaboration of its science. It may also be said, Aquinas adds, that in the case of God, knowledge *quid non est* takes the place of knowledge *quid est*. [24]

---

[23] " Et sicut deux ex hoc, quod cognoscit se, cognoscit alia modo suo, id est simplici intuitu, non discurrendo, ita nos ex his, quae per fidem capimus primae veritati adhaerendo, venimus in cognitionem aliorum secundum modum nostrum discurrendo de principiis ad conclusiones, ut sic ipsa, quae fide tenemus, sint nobis quasi principia in hac scientia et alia sint quasi conclusiones. Ex quo patet quod haec scientia est altior illa scientia divina, quam philosophi tradiderunt, cum ex altioribus procedat principiis. " *In Boet. de Trin.*, q. 2, a. 2,3.

[24] " Ad secundum dicendum quod, sicut supra dictum est, quando causae cognoscuntur per suos effectus, effectus cognitio supplet locum cognitionis quiditatis causae, quae requiritur in illis scientiis quae sunt de rebus quae per se ipsas cognosci possunt ; et sic non oportet ad hoc quod de divinis scientiam habemus, quod praesciatur de eo quid est. Vel potest dici quod hoc ipsum quod scimus de eo quid non est supplet locum in scientia divina cognitionis quid est ; quia sicut per quid est distinguitur res ab aliis, ita per hoc quod scitur quid non est. " *In Boet. de Trin.*, q. 2, a. 2, ad 2m.

A moment later, answering the objection that a science
of faith would invert the necessary order of reason preceding
and grounding assent, St. Thomas states that the assent to
which reason leads in the scientific process is not the assent
to principles, but rather the assent to conclusions. Assent to
principles, on the other hand, is not the consequence, but the
source, of scientific reasoning.

In the matter at hand, however, the articles of faith,
notwithstanding the fact that they can be defended against
attack, are still not the conclusions of demonstrative process,
but its principles. As such, they become illuminated (*manifestantur*) through certain analogies, but are not themselves
rationally demonstrated. [25]

The significance and importance of Aquinas' reply here
should not be minimized. Whatever might be said of the
scientific ideal as applied to theology by others, at other
times, it was clearly St. Thomas' judgment, at least when
composing this particular treatise devoted explicitly to the problems of theological method, that it was simply not the function of theology as science to demonstrate or verify its primary suppositions. By the same token, therefore, to assess
the orientation and value of the conclusions of St. Thomas'
own theological achievement precisely inasmuch and insofar
as they would prove, or in some way, justify the primary
suppositions — the articles of faith, that is — is simply to
miss the point of what had been St. Thomas' basic intention.

Moreover, as it is not the task of theological science to
demonstrate its principles, neither is it necessary that these
principles be *per se nota* to men. Even in human sciences,
there may be certain principles which are not *per se nota* to
all, but must be supposed from higher sciences. Thus, in
subalternated sciences, some things are supposed and taken

---

[25] " Ad quartum dicendum quod in qualibet scientia sunt aliqua
quasi principia et aliqua quasi conclusiones. Ratio ergo quae inducitur in scientiis praecedit assensum conclusionum, sed sequitur assensum principiorum, cum ex eis procedat. Articuli autem fidei in hac
scientia non sunt quasi conclusiones, sed quasi principia quae etiam
defenduntur ab impugnantibus, sicut Philosophus in IV Metaphysicae
disputat contra negantes principia, et manifestantur per aliquas similitudines, sicut principia naturaliter nota per inductionem, non autem
ratione demonstrativa probantur. " *In Boet. de Trin.*, q. 2, a. 2, ad
4m.

on authority from higher sciences, and are *per se nota* only to those who possess knowledge of the higher order. In what concerns the articles of faith, then, which act as principles of this science leading to knowledge of the divine, what God knows in His own self-knowledge is supposed in human theology, accepted on the authority of God Who has revealed such matters through His messengers, just as the physician accepts from the physicists that there are four elements. [26]

A still further reply reaffirms the point previously made that the science of theology does not seek to demonstrate its principles, this time under the aspect of the manifest or the evident. For science does not make evident its principles, but rather, from the already supposed evidence of the principles, proceeds to make evident its conclusions. [27]

And finally, to the argument against a science derived from faith on the ground that the *intellectus principiorum* is the source or principle for every science, St. Thomas counters that the understanding of principles is indeed the first principle of every science, but not always the proximate principle. For again, even in human sciences, 'faith' or authority is often seen to play this rôle, with scientific conclusions proceeding proximately from acceptance of what is attested to by the higher science, and ultimately from the understanding of the one possessing the superior knowledge, whose certitude of what the other will believe is based upon his own direct understanding.

---

[26] " Ad quintum dicendum quod etiam in scientiis humanitus traditis sunt quaedam principia in quibusdam earum quae non sunt omnibus nota, sed oportet ea supponere a superioribus scientiis, sicut in scientiis subalternatis supponuntur et creduntur aliqua a scientiis superioribus, et illa non sunt per se nota nisi superioribus scientiis. Et hoc modo se habent articuli fidei, qui sunt principia huius scientiae, ad cognitionem divinam, quia ea quae sunt per se nota in scientia, quam deus habet de se ipso, supponuntur in scientia nostra et creduntur ei nobis haec indicanti per suos nuntios, sicut medicus credit physico quattuor esse elementa. " *In Boet. de Trin.*, q. 2, a. 2, ad 5m.

[27] " Ad sextum dicendum quod apparentia scientiae procedit ex apparentia principiorum ; quoniam scientia non facit apparere principia, sed ex hoc, quod apparent principia, facit apparere conclusiones. Et per hunc modum scientia, de qua loquimur, non facit apparere ea de quibus est fides, sed ex eis facit apparere alia per modum quo de primis certitudo habetur. " *In Boet. de Trin.*, q. 2, a. 2, ad 6m.

Similarly, faith is the proximate principle in theological science, but the ultimate principle is the divine understanding in which men place their belief. Yet, for human beings, it is the end of faith that they come to understand what they believe, as when one with inferior knowledge should come to learn that of his superior, and then men will understand or know what previously they had only believed. [28]

In the article immediately following, Aquinas takes up the possible use of philosophy in the science of faith. Since the gifts of divine grace do not destroy nature, but perfect it, the gratuitous light of faith does not impair the natural light of reason. And while the light of reason cannot make known the truths of faith, nevertheless there can be no opposition between what God has revealed and what is known by the innate power of human understanding. The truths of philosophy, moreover, contain certain analogies for the truths of faith, and also certain preambles toward what is revealed in faith, just as nature itself is the preamble for grace.

Sacred doctrine, therefore, can employ philosophy in three ways : first, to demonstrate the preambles of faith, and which are necessary to faith, as God's existence, God's unity, etc. ; secondly, to elucidate through certain analogies what pertains to faith, as the philosophical analogies introduced by Augustine to expose the Trinity ; and thirdly, to reject the challenges that are made against faith, either by showing that these are false or by showing that they are not necessary. [29]   But once

---

[28] " Ad septimum dicendum quod cuiuslibet scientiae principium est intellectus semper quidem primum, sed non semper proximum, immo aliquando est fides proximum principium scientiae. Sicut patet in scientiis subalternatis, quia earum conclusiones sicut ex proximo principio procedunt ex fide eorum quae supponuntur a superiori scientia, sed sicut a principio primo ab intellectu superioris scientis, qui de his creditis certitudinem per intellectum habet. Et similiter huius scientiae principium proximum est fides, sed primum est intellectus divinus, cui nos credimus, sed finis fidei est nobis, ut perveniamus ad intelligendum quae credimus, sicut si inferior sciens addiscat superioris scientis scientiam, et tunc fient ei intellecta vel scita, quae prius erant tantummodo credita. " *In Boet. de Trin.*, q. 2, a. 2, ad 7m.   ,

[29] " Dicendum quod dona gratiarum hoc modo naturae adduntur quod eam non tollunt, sed magis perficiunt ; unde et lumen fidei, quod nobis gratis infunditur, non destruit lumen naturalis rationis divinitus nobis inditum. Et quamvis lumen naturale mentis humanae sit insufficiens ad manifestationem eorum quae manifestantur per fidem, tamen impossibile est quod ea, quae per fidem traduntur nobis

again, St. Thomas emphasizes that it is not on account of such philosophical truths that the truth of faith itself is to be believed. [30]

Strange as it may seem, in the treatise as St. Thomas left it, only one article takes up the matter of trinitarian belief itself from an objectively doctrinal, as opposed to epistemological, viewpoint, and even here, the consideration is rather of heretical attacks against personal equality. It is worth noting, however, that, just as previously in the *Sentences*, and later in the fourth book of the *Contra Gentiles*, here also the practice of Aquinas is in perfect accord with the theory — the certitude of what is true to the authentic confession of Christian Faith being taken solely from the sources of faith, from the scriptures chiefly, together with frequent appeal to the authority of Augustine. [31]

There is not in the treatise, however, any elaboration of trinitarian doctrine in the light of which comparisons could be made with other works. There is, of course, the rejection of the *verbum* argument, if one may call it that, in the fourth article of the first question, and the significance of this rejection in the larger context of St. Thomas' works will be considered in due course.

---

divinitus, sint contraria his quae sunt per naturam nobis indita ... Sicut autem sacra doctrina fundatur supra lumen fidei, ita philosophia fundatur supra lumen naturale rationis ; unde impossibile est quod ea, quae sunt philosophiae, sint contraria his quae sunt fidei, sed deficiunt ab eis. Continent tamen aliquas eorum similitudines et quaedam, ad ea praeambula, sicut natura praeambula est ad gratiam ... Sic ergo in sacra doctrina philosophia possumus tripliciter uti. Primo ad demonstrandum ea quae sunt praeambula fidei, quae necesse est in fide scire, ut ea quae naturalibus rationibus de deo probantur, ut deum esse, deum esse unum et alia huiusmodi vel de deo vel de creaturis in philosophia probata, quae fides supponit. Secundo ad notificandum per aliduas similitudines ea quae sunt fidei, sicut Augustinus in libro De trinitate utitur multis similitudinibus ex doctrinis philosophicis sumptis ad manifestandum trinitatem. Tertio ad resistendum his quae contra fidem dicuntur sive ostendendo ea esse falsa sive ostendendo ea non esse necessaria. " *In Boet. de Trin.*, q. 2, a. 3, 1-3.

[30] *In Boet. de Trin.*, q. 2, a. 3, ad 1m.

[31] " Utrum haec sit verae fidei confessio quod pater et filius et spiritus sanctus singulus est deus et tres sunt unus deus absque omni inaequalitatis distantia. " *In Boet. de Trin.*, q. 3, a. 4.

9

III. CONCLUSION. SIGNIFICANCE AND VALUE OF THE TREA-
      TISE FOR THE PRESENT PROBLEM OF APOLOGETICAL
      PERSPECTIVE

If it is obvious that the pertinence of the *In Boethii de
Trinitate* to the question of the moment is not as a new and
further elaboration of Thomist trinitarian doctrine — for the
simple reason that such an elaboration is not offered in the
text — it should also be clear, from what was observed in
the first part of the present study, when the attempt was
being made to determine exactly the *status quaestionis*, that
the significance and value of the treatise does not lie merely
in its emphatic rejection of a priori rational demonstration for
the revealed processions. By itself, this rejection would be
inconclusive. For the real question here is not whether Aquinas intended to demonstrate, or formally admitted the possibility of demonstration in this area, but whether some element of the same demonstration was automatically involved
in his theological reasoning — particularly, as already seen,
in Aquinas' formulation and use of the universal principle
that procession of inner word was essential to intellectual
nature.

At the same time, however, to say that the rejection is
inconclusive, is not to dismiss a problem as already settled,
but rather to make a valid critical observation which would
have to be taken into account in the course of further investigation. The point that would have to be determined in that
investigation, moreover, is just what place the rejection had
in the context of St. Thomas' own thought. It would be one
thing if the remark, regardless of how often repeated, were
no more than an historical *locus communis* only loosely incorporated into an author's personal text, but quite another thing
if the same remark were clearly radicated in the basic structure
of the author's scientific synthesis.

It is in this light that one of the two important conclusions to be drawn from the *In Boethii de Trinitate* can be
made.

Before discussing the question of whether or not unaided
reason could penetrate to the Trinity of Persons, Aquinas
himself laid the groundwork for that discussion, and thus
established, explicitly moreover, his own context. The human

intelligence, he explained, cannot know God through the pure form which is the divine essence. As the reason for this, he introduced what is one of the most strictly fundamental principles of Thomist thought : the dependence of the human intellect on abstraction from phantasm. In the present life, therefore, man can know God only through the forms of His creaturely effects.

But the restriction is more serious still. Even in the knowledge through effects, St. Thomas continues, since no finite effect is proportionate to the power and reality of the divine cause, and hence cannot give full knowledge of the divine cause, man cannot in this life achieve knowledge of God's quiddity or essence. He will come to know, therefore, not ' what ' God is, but only ' that ' He is. For while Aquinas qualifies this latter statement — some knowledge *quid est* is necessarily involved in the knowledge *an est* — his chief concern at this point is rather to emphasize that the limited knowledge in the order *quid est* which man can acquire is vicarious, through the forms of the effects, and in no sense properly proportionate to the divine object. So radical is this limitation, in fact, that it carries over, as St. Thomas himself insists, even into the illuminated knowledge of faith.

At the end of his treatise, Aquinas returned to the same restrictive theme once again. The knowledge *quid est* must penetrate to quiddity or essence. Where man's knowledge of God is concerned, it is obvious that this particular essence is not immediately accessible to the human mind. For immediately, the human mind can grasp only the quiddities or essences of sensible objects. But the same sensible objects cannot possibly represent perfectly the divine essence, since they pertain to a different ontological order altogether, and since, as Aquinas did not hesitate to express it, quiddity and other such terms are used " almost equivocally " when applied to both God and these inferior realities. Consequently, the divine quiddity or essence is not accessible to the human mind even mediately. For whether it be through the way of causality — since finite effects are not proportionate to the divine cause — or through the way of similitude or analogy — since sensible objects cannot perfectly represent the divine essence — St. Thomas' position is absolutely clear : in the present life, knowledge of God in the order of quiddity or essence is simply inaccessible.

In precisely this context, then, because it is Aquinas' own, his rejection of the mere possibility that unaided reason might demonstrate the trinitarian processions has to be understood.

The human intellect, St. Thomas explains, knows of God only what can be perceived from the relation of created effects to the divine cause according to the *triplex via* of causality, supereminence, and the removal of imperfection. But the Trinity of Persons cannot be perceived in this manner — not through causality, because the causality of creation is common to the entire Trinity; not through removal of imperfection, because this is not in point.

In the same context, though the subject will be discussed more fully in the chapter immediately following, one must also interpret St. Thomas' specific rejection of an argument for trinitarian processions based on the necessity of inner word in the process of understanding. Reason does know from the evidence of created effects that God is intelligent, but reason also has to affirm that in God the one understanding and the one understood are identical, and hence has no basis for postulating with any certainty the procession of a really distinct concept in the divine intellect.

From the negative or restrictive theme of the *In Boethii de Trinitate*, therefore, the conclusion must be drawn that Aquinas' rejection of trinitarian demonstration is not an *obiter dictum*, nor an historical commonplace, nor a 'pious' assertion whose full implications had not been thoroughly integrated into his own ideal of theological science, but a primary and essential consequence of this ideal. For St. Thomas, that unaided reason could penetrate in some fashion to the a priori necessity of the divine processions, would mean that the same unaided reason had achieved quidditive knowledge of the divine being. For the trinitarian processions pertain to the order of 'what' God is in Himself. But this is impossible. Not only is such quidditive knowledge of the divine inaccessible to unaided reason left, so to speak, to its own natural resources, but it is denied as well even to reason illuminated by supernatural faith.

Aquinas anticipates, moreover, a final objection. From created effects and similitudes, it is true, the human mind can achieve a highly qualified, in no sense properly proportionate, but strictly vicarious, knowledge of the divine quiddity derived from knowledge of the sensible. Man can know, therefore, ' that ' God is, and certain ' conditions ' imposed by the *via excessus* and the *via remotionis*, as, for instance, that God is immaterial. But this knowledge of God *per formam effectus* remains just that ; it is not, and in this life never can be, knowledge of God *per formam Dei*. Because similitudes derived from the objects of sense are radically deficient in representing the divine form, and because created effects are not proportionate to the power and reality of the divine cause, the original position is not in any way compromised. For St. Thomas, the properly quidditive knowledge man would have to achieve in order to recognize the a priori necessity of the trinitarian processions is in this life simply and unequivocally impossible.

A second conclusion, however, is also to be drawn from the treatise, this time from the positive theme developed by Aquinas alongside the restrictive.

From what has thus far been seen in the ' *de Trinitate* ' of the first book of the *Sentences*, and from the discussion of theological science in *In Boethii de Trinitate*, there is no evidence at all that some element of aprioristic demonstration had any place in St. Thomas' trinitarian expositions. There remains, of course, the possibility that he would yet change his stand in subsequent works. Nor will this possibility be ruled out until these later works will have been examined in adequate detail.

On the other hand, since all the evidence up to the present moment has been quite negative, it is not premature to ask even now what exactly *was* Aquinas' intention and perspective in approaching these same trinitarian expositions. For in the last analysis, the best, if not solely satisfying, proof of what a thing is not is simply the proof of what it is.

Taking, then, the strictly positive development of theological science and method as contained in the same treatise *In Boethii de Trinitate*, what precisely is it that St. Thomas seems to envision as the proper accomplishment of theological elaboration in the area of revealed mystery ? Moreover, to what extent, if any, would the apologetical intention and perspective being called into question in the present study be compatible, not only with such a concept of theological science, but also, and more pertinently, with the internal principles and processes germane to this concept ?

In coming to the question whether or not there can be a science of the divine, St. Thomas notes that two points must be kept in mind. First of all, there is the human mode of knowledge with its basic dependence on abstraction from the sense phantasm, in the light of which man's knowledge of God is only such as can be derived from the sensible. But there is also the fact that the divine is supremely knowable in itself, and as such known to God and the saints.

Science of the divine, therefore, and in the strict sense of necessary conclusions issuing from what is previously known, is twofold. There is the *prima philosophia* or *scientia divina* attendant upon the human mode of understanding in its dependence on the sensible. There is also the science of the divine according to the transcendent mode which is proper to itself. With regard to this latter, St. Thomas goes on to explain, and in perfect conformity with his restrictive principles previously laid down, man can never achieve the perfection of such knowledge in the present life. Yet even here on earth, man is able to participate in this divine knowledge and become assimilated to it as the human mind clings in faith to the divine truth for its own sake (*propter seipsam*) — as its own sufficient reason, that is, or source.

What God knows of Himself, and also of everything else, is according to the simple intuition that is the mode or manner of divine understanding. Man, on the other hand, is restricted to his own manner of understanding moving from principles to conclusions through intellectual discourse. But what in this context are the principles from which and through which man arrives at further understanding of the divine in theological science? As Aquinas himself explains it, the principles, or quasi principles, are simply that which is held in faith.

Two things should be noted here. First, St. Thomas does not speak of the articles of faith as ' data ', or as the material object, so to speak, upon which rational investigation, or any process of ' philosophizing ', would then be turned, but as the principles, or internal energy, primarily responsible for the generation of subsequent conclusions. For St. Thomas, it is not a matter of simple reason being applied to some given object, in this case articles of faith, but of reason precisely as illuminated by the light of infused faith seeking, to the limited extent possible in this life, the proper and connatural *finis* of faith, which is understanding.

This is exactly the point Aquinas makes a moment later when he faces the objection that a science of the divine should be excluded, inasmuch as understanding of principles is necessarily itself the first principle in every science, but would be lacking to man who must accept the principles of the *scientia divina*, not with understanding, but with faith. Understanding of the principles is necessarily itself the first principle in any science, St. Thomas replies, but not necessarily nor always the proximate principle. For even in profane science, conclusions will often depend immediately upon human authority, upon what is attested to by another. Understanding of the principles, therefore, is indeed possessed by someone, and hence the ultimate source of conclusions, but it is not necessarily possessed by the man of inferior knowledge who must consequently rely for his own certitude upon the understanding of his better. In the matter at hand, therefore, conclusions in theological science will depend immediately or proximately on what is known, not in understanding, but in faith, and only ultimately on understanding of the principles, which in this case is the divine understanding itself. Nevertheless, St. Thomas is quick to add, it is the end of faith that one come to understand what previously one could only believe.

Hence, it is in terms of an eschatological dynamism, to borrow from a recent critique of this element in the *In Boethii de Trinitate*, that Aquinas would have the rôle of faith in rational theology interpreted.[32] The perfect fulfilment of faith is not had, of course, until faith is transformed into understanding of God as He is in Himself in the beatific vision. The tendency toward this precise transformation, however, is the internal finality of faith itself, and in virtue of this noetic energy whereby the reason is attracted or assimilated to the divine understanding, man can achieve, even in this life, a certain participation in that mode of knowledge which is proper to the divine.

Secondly, it must also be noted that in St. Thomas' mind, at least when he composed this particular treatise, demonstration or verification of the principles — the articles of faith — is not only not provided for as the function, or part of the

---

[32] See C. DUMONT, S. J., " La réflexion sur la méthode théologique, II : Le dilemme théologique, " *Nouvelle Revue Théologique*, LXXXIV (1962), pp. 17-35.

function, of theological science, but is even formally excluded. While the articles of faith may and can be defended against error, as Aquinas observes, they are not themselves the conclusions of demonstrative process, but rather its principles. The assent to which scientific reason leads is assent to conclusions ; assent to principles, on the other hand, is not the consequence, but rather the source, of such reasoning. As the scientific process develops, St. Thomas remarks, the principles — the articles of faith — are elucidated (*manifestantur*), but they are not proved or demonstrated (*demonstrantur*).

When the question is asked, therefore, what exactly was it that Aquinas envisioned as the proper accomplishment of theological science, the answer given by Aquinas himself is quite clear. This answer can be summed up in the single word : *understanding.* With the articles of faith presupposed from the very beginning as what is first known, and with faith itself acting as the primary internal energy in the genesis of subsequent conclusions, the nature, scope and value of rational theology is simply to give the limited, obscure, only vicariously quidditive, or ' infraquidditive ', understanding of revealed mystery, which is, in this life, man's remote participation in the mode of knowledge proper to the divine.

Moreover, as St. Thomas himself explicitly indicates, a further, or even subordinate, function which would be to demonstrate in some way, however qualified, the a priori necessity of the revealed mystery is positively excluded from this ideal of understanding. Not only has Aquinas no intention of attempting such demonstration, but he also declares that it would have no place in the processes of theological reasoning whereby he does intend to achieve understanding.

It would be interesting to speculate, perhaps, how in the light of these minutely articulated principles on the nature of theological science and its basic methodology St. Thomas might have gone on to elaborate, at this early period in his career, a new and more personal ' *de Trinitate* ', as contrasted, that is, with the largely uneven and cumbersome exposition found in the first book of the *Sentences*. He does not do this, of course, in the *In Boethii de Trinitate*. He does do it, however, in the fourth book of the *Contra Gentiles*, as will be seen in the chapter immediately following.

UNDERSTANDING — "QUALITER ACCIPI," "QUALITER INTELLIGI" — AS THE IDEAL OF RATIONAL THEOLOGY IN *CONTRA GENTILES IV*

Appearing roughly a decade later than the ' *de Trinitate* ' of the *Sentences*, the parallel treatment contained in the fourth book of the *Contra Gentiles* differs in not a few obvious respects both from the earlier account, and also from that of the *Pars Prima*, which was yet to follow.[1] It is first of all considerably more brief, occupying as it does only the initial twenty-six chapters out of the total ninety-seven which make up the last of the four books in the treatise. Thus, in the *Contra Gentiles*, there is neither the cumbersome theological miscellany which constantly interrupts systematic progression with loosely connected detail in the *Sentences*, nor, at the same time, the minutely elaborated synthesis which structures and integrates every last point thought to be doctrinally significant in the *Pars Prima*.

For the moment, St. Thomas restricts himself by and large to the simple articles of faith, or what one might call the principal formularies of trinitarian belief. These, he proposes to explain and defend against heretical interpretations or distortions, by showing how the latter are false to the clear meaning of Sacred Scripture, and also, in many instances, to certain necessary laws of human understanding.

Nevertheless, as will be seen presently, purely positive exposition is clearly the goal toward which apologetical or po-

---

[1] It has already been observed that the *Sentences* belong to the period 1254-1256. See, for example, CHENU, *Introduction*, pp. 226ff. There is also general acceptance (indicated by Chenu, *ibid,*. p. 251) of Dondaine's argument placing *Contra Gentiles IV* not earlier than 1263. For the latter, see H. DONDAINE, " Le *Contra Errores Graecorum* de S. Thomas et le IVe livre du *Contra Gentiles,* " *Les Sciences Philosophiques et Théologiques*, XXX (1941), pp. 156-162.

lemical passages are ultimately being directed.   Moreover, when
this step is reached, it shall prove interesting to observe that
not only is the exposition positive, but it is also speculative.
For in the *Contra Gentiles*, Aquinas will take his immediate
point of departure for explaining, in whatever degree possible,
the nature of the divine generation in the apparently philosophical notion of the *verbum cordis*.   And at least on the face
of things, the adoption of such a methodological procedure
is going to make the question whether or not Aquinas' presentation involves some measure of apodictic rational proof considerably more pertinent than it was seen to have been in the
Commentary.

In the final paragraphs of the *Prooemium*, which itself
serves as the introduction to the entire fourth book, St. Thomas lays down the purpose, scope and basic plan of development that will direct his treatment of revealed truths, beginning with the Trinity.

What he has covered in the first three books, he notes
here, concerned matters accessible to rational inquiry.[2] As
Père Chenu has observed, however, this remark of Aquinas
does not at all mean that the tracts on God, creation, man's
last end and the morality of human conduct, were essentially
philosophical.   For the truths presented in these earlier sections are always introduced as belonging to the deposit of
faith, and are discussed in a strictly theological order.[3] One
might add to this observation that certain topics, more than
loosely integrated into the central movement of the treatise
— as, for instance, the treatment " *de gratia* " at the end of
the third book — would be out of place in a purely philosophical work as ordinarily accepted.[4] In any case, Aquinas
states quite emphatically that throughout this fourth and
last book, his attention will be given solely to those truths

---

[2] " Competunt autem verba praemissa nostro proposito. Nam in
praecedentibus de divinis sermo est habitus secundum quod ad cognitionem divinorum naturalis ratio per creaturas pervenire potest :
imperfecte tamen, et secundum proprii possibilitatem ingenii ... " *C.G.*,
IV, c. 1, 9. (Numbers following indication of the chapter are according
to the paragraph distribution of the Leonine edition, from which all
the references and citations in the present study are taken.)
[3] See CHENU, *Introduction*, pp. 252-253.
[4] *C. G.*, *III*, cc. 148-164.

which lie beyond the reach of the human intelligence, and have
been revealed by God to be believed.[5]

What is contained, therefore, in the discourses of Sacred
Scripture, St. Thomas continues, will act as the *quasi principia*
for subsequent doctrinal development. The aim will then be
to see how the content of such discourses, where the meaning
is less than clear, must be taken — in the process of defend-
ing the truths of Scripture against infidel aberrations. Perfect
grasp, on the other hand, is never to be presumed. For these
truths are demonstrated upon the authority of Sacred Scripture itself, not by natural reason. It remains, nevertheless,
that how the same truths are not in any way contrary to
natural reason, must still be shown ; that thus the attacks of
unbelievers may be refuted.[6]

In this statement of his immediate objective, it is true,
St. Thomas does not stress, or even mention, an element of
purely positive exposition that would stand outside the context
of defense against error. It will soon be evident, however,
that although more space is given to the details of this defense,
and while the defense itself is apparently the practical or pastoral aim of the theological genre Aquinas has chosen, the method
of development whereby he achieves this goal involves a climactic arrangement, with the forward movement terminating
by evident design in the strictly positive, systematic account
of authentic Christian doctrine for which the polemical passages are then seen to prepare.

---

[5] " Restat autem sermo habendus de his quae nobis revelata sunt
divinitus ut credenda, excendentia intellectum humanum. " *C. G., IV,*
c. 1, 9 ad fin.

[6] " ... erit hic modus servandus, ut ea quae in sermonibus Sacrae
Scripturae sunt tradita, quasi principia sumantur ; et sic ea quae in
sermonibus praedictis occulte nobis traduntur, studeamus utcumque
mente capere, a laceratione infidelium defendendo ; ut tamen prae-
sumptio perfecte cognoscendi non adsit ; probanda enim sunt huiusmodi auctoritate Sacrae Scripturae, non autem ratione naturali. Sed
tamen ostendendum est quod rationi naturali non sunt opposita, ut
ab impugnatione infidelium defendantur. Qui etiam modus in principio huius operis praedeterminatus est. " *C. G., IV,* c. 1, 10.

I. The Mystery of the Divine Generation and its Defense Against the Heretics

St. Thomas begins his treatment by considering the scriptural testimonies proclaiming the divine generation, paternity and sonship. He notes, first of all, that the use of names indicative of paternity and filiation is very frequent in those passages of the New Testament where Jesus Christ is designated as the Son of God, and Son of the Father.[7] He finds similar usage, though more rarely, in the Old Testament also.[8] Moreover, since the names ' Father ' and ' Son ' follow upon some manner of generation, it is likewise natural that in both the Old and New Testament generation as such is occasionally spoken of directly and explicitly.[9]

An early objection is next disposed of. Aquinas observes that in certain biblical texts the notion of fatherhood and generation is introduced figuratively to describe God as Creator — as, for instance, " the father of the rain. " He completes his brief account of the scriptural *auctoritates*, therefore, by citing the explicit and unequivocal testimony of passages in which it is clear that the one being referred to as *filius* and *genitus* is no creature, but God Himself.[10]

In the fourth chapter, St. Thomas takes up the heterodox opinion of those who recognized in the scriptural testimony only the created sonship of such as are justified by divine grace.[11] Cerinthus and Ebion, Paul of Samosata, Photinus and the later Photiniani are mentioned by name.[12] For these, Christ was merely a man, who began to exist only when born

---

[7] " Principium autem considerationis a secreto divinae generationis sumentes, quid de ea secundum Sacrae Scripturae documenta teneri debeat, praemittamus. Dehinc vero ea quae contra veritatem fidei infidelitas adinvenit argumenta ponamus : quorum solutione subiecta, huius considerationis propositum consequemur. Tradit igitur nobis Sacra Scriptura in divinis *paternitatis* et *filiationis* nomina, Iesum Christum *Filium Dei* contestans. Quod in scriptura Novi Testamenti frequentissime invenitur. Dicitur enim *Matth.* XI 27 : *Nemo novit Filium nisi Pater : neque Patrem quis novit nisi Filius ...* " *C. G.*, IV, c. 2, 1 and 2.

[8] *C. G.*, IV, c. 2, 3 and 4.

[9] *C. G.*, IV, c. 2, 5.

[10] *C. G.*, IV, c. 3.

[11] *C. G.*, IV, c. 4, 2.

[12] *C. G.*, IV, c. 4, 9.

of the Virgin Mary, whose title to a special and preeminent, but still adoptive, sonship rested in the holiness of his life.[13]

Aquinas indicates the main biblical passages — as, for example, Mt 28 : 18 : " Data est mihi omnis potestas in coelo et in terra " — to which these heretics had appealed in support of their error.[14] He notes also the presupposition underlying their exegesis : the a priori impossibility, namely, that such human characteristics found in Christ's personal history as being carried in the womb, growing up in age, suffering thirst, bodily fatigue and the like, could ever belong to one who was God *per naturam*.[15] His filiation, therefore, would have to be explained in terms of adoption, *consortium*, and divinization through grace.

But this interpretation, Aquinas argues in rebuttal, cannot stand in the face of a careful reading of what the Scriptures have revealed of the Son of God. For the divine generation spoken of in Scripture is before all time (Pv 8 : 24). It was as God that He descended from heaven Who was later to return to the Father in His ascension (Jn 3: 13).[16] The point made by the Apostle Paul (Phil 2: 6) is not that of the Photiniani — not of a man advancing toward God through the merit of a good life, but of one who was God becoming man.[17] Again, if Christ were called *Filius* in virtue of the grace of adoption, Christ and Moses, or any of the other saints, would deserve the name on a substantially common ground; but the Apostle is rather at pains to distinguish Christ from Moses as " Filius a servo " (Heb 3 : 5), thus making Christ's sonship unique.[18] The titles " unigenitus " and " primogenitus " add still further confirmation to this unique sonship.[19] Moreover, certain of the powers attributed in Scripture to Christ could

---

[13] " Per hunc ergo modum, opinantes Iesum Christum purum hominem esse, et ex Maria Virgine initium sumpsisse, et per beatae vitae meritum divinitatis honorem prae ceteris fuisse adeptum, aestimaverunt eum, similiter aliis hominibus, per adoptionis spiritum Dei filium ; et per gratiam ab eo genitum ; et per quandam assimilationem ad Deum in Scripturis dici Deum, non per naturam, sed per consortium quoddam divinae bonitatis ... " *C. G., IV*, c. 4, 3.

[14] *C. G., IV*, c. 4, 4-7.

[15] *C. G., IV*, c. 4, 8.

[16] *C. G., IV*, c. 4, 10.

[17] *C. G., IV*, c. 4, 11.

[18] *C. G., IV*, c. 4, 12.

[19] *C. G., IV*, c. 4, 13.

not possibly be assigned to anyone else — such as the sanctification of souls, and the remission of sins.[20]

St. Thomas sums up his discussion in a final paragraph.
The scriptural testimonies his adversaries had cited against
the natural sonship of Jesus Christ do not lend any efficacious
support to such a position. For Christian faith professes that
there are in Christ, after His Incarnation, two natures, the
human and the divine. In virtue of the divine nature, therefore, that can be said of Christ which is proper to God alone ;
while in virtue of the human nature, that can also be said
of Him which might appear to lie in the order of imperfection. This latter, Aquinas says he will explain more fully
when he comes (in the twenty-seventh chapter) to treat the
Incarnation as such. For the moment, so he concludes, in
what pertains to the question of the divine generation, it
should be enough to have shown that, according to the usage
of Sacred Scripture, Christ is called Son of God and God, not
merely as a pure man in virtue of the grace of adoptive sonship,
but on account of the divine nature which He possessed.[21]

In the chapters immediately following, Aquinas treats
first the Sabellian, and next the Arian, heresies. Since the
order and method of his presentation is basically the same
as in the section on Photinus, and since the detail of Thomist
exegesis and antiheretical polemic is not immediately pertinent to the scope of the present study, it will suffice to indicate the development in a more general manner.

Thus, just as he had done before, St. Thomas first gives
a summary picture of the Sabellian position. Starting from
the conviction that there cannot be but one who is naturally
(*naturaliter*) God, heretics of this second group accepted from
Scripture that Christ was truly and naturally God, and con-

---

[20] *C. G., IV*, c. 4, 14.

[21] " Illa vero Scripturae testimonia quibus ostendere nitebantur
quod Christus non esset Deus per naturam, efficacia non sunt ad eorum propositum ostendendum. Confitemur enim in Christo Dei Filio,
post Incarnationis mysterium, duas naturas, humanam scilicet et divinam. Unde de eo dicuntur et quae Dei sunt propria, ratione divinae naturae ; et quae ad defectum pertinere videntur, ratione humanae
naturae, ut infra plenius explanabitur. Nunc autem, ad praesentem
considerationem de divina generatione, hoc sufficiat monstratum esse
secundum Scripturas quod Christus Dei Filius et Deus dicitur non solum sicut purus homo per gratiam adoptionis, sed propter divinitatis
naturam. " *C. G., IV*, c. 4, 15.

fessed that there was only one God, Christ the Son of God
and God the Father — not, however, with the understanding
that this God be called Son according to His nature or from
all eternity, but that He would have received the title of
sonship only when born of the Virgin Mary through the mystery
of His Incarnation. From this, they went on to attribute to
God the Father everything Christ Himself sustained — conception, birth, passion, death and resurrection — in His flesh.[22]

St. Thomas then points out the special biblical texts
which the Sabellians and *Patripassiani* claimed for substantiation of their view, and next proceeds to show how the doctrine is in manifest contradiction to the authority of Scripture.[23] He postpones a more detailed refutation of the theological assumption that, since God is one, since the Father is
in the Son and the Son in the Father, Father and Son must
be one in supposit to a later chapter, when he will have completed his discussion of Arianism.[24]

This, then, brings St. Thomas to the opinion of Arius on
the Son of God. Here, his treatment will be considerably
longer, with three distinct and successive chapters devoted to
the objective statement of the position, its refutation, and
a solution to the tendentious supporting exegesis, respectively.
The basic plan, however, remains the same.

First, the position is outlined clearly and succinctly, and
in terms of its contrast to the two positions previously treated. Since one cannot reconcile with the teaching of Scripture,
either the opinion (Photinus) that the Son of God owed His
initial existence to the Virgin Mary, or the further opinion
(Sabellius) that He Who was God from all eternity and is the
Father would begin to be Son only through His Incarnation,
there were yet others who held that the Son of God did exist
before the Incarnation and before the creation of the world.
But because this Son was distinct from the Father, they could
not allow that he would be of the same nature as the Father.

---

[22] *C. G., IV*, c. 5, 1.

[23] *C. G., IV*, c. 5, 2-11.

[24] " Ea vero quibus Sabellius suam positionem nititur confirmare,
id quod intendit non ostendunt, ut infra plenius ostendentur. Non
enim per hoc quod *Deus est unus*, vel quod *Pater est in Filio et Filius
in Patre*, habetur quod Filius et Pater sit unum supposito : potest enim
et duorum supposito distinctorum aliqua unitas esse. " *C. G., IV*, c.
5, 12.

His nature, therefore, could not be eternal, but only the first of all creatures, Himself created from nothing.[25] Nevertheless, forced by the authority of Scripture to call Him Son of God, they conceived His unity with the Father, not as unity of nature, but as unity of 'consensus', and participation of the divine likeness — the first and noblest of creatures, through whom God the Father created all others.

Next, following the plan already observed, Aquinas lists the biblical passages used by the Arians in the attempt to demonstrate the orthodoxy of their stand.[26] He follows this with a brief account of the emanation theories of the Platonici, which he refers to as the apparent (" videtur ") origin of the heresy.[27]   Then, in the somewhat lengthy seventh chapter, St. Thomas proceeds to refute the Arian position by demonstrating on the authority of Sacred Scripture the unequivocal divinity of Christ as the natural Son of the Father, paying particular attention in the course of several paragraphs to the impossibility of assigning to the Son of God the excellent, but still creaturely, status of angelic being.[28]   Finally, in the even more lengthy eighth chapter, he concludes his formal discussion of Arianism with solutions to the erroneous points of Arian exegesis along with its metaphysical sophisms.[29]

The matter covered in the three chapters on the Arian heresy, where St. Thomas had larger scope to develop in detail the theme of the eternal and divine Son of God as revealed in the Sacred Scriptures, has made it easier for him to reexamine and, this time, solve the problems posed in the earlier exegesis of the Photinians and Sabellians.[30]   Thus, to take only his first text (Mt 28 : 18), when Christ announced after His Resurrection, that all power was given to Him in heaven and on earth, His meaning was not that He had only now received such power, but simply that the power received by the Son of God from eternity now began to shine forth in the same Son of God made man, through the great victory of His Resurrection.[31]

---

[25] *C. G.*, *IV*, c. 6, 1.
[26] *C. G.*, *IV*, c. 6, 2-12.
[27] *C. G.*, *IV*, c. 6, 13 and 14.
[28] *C. G.*, *IV*, c. 7.
[29] *C. G.*, *IV*, c. 8.
[30] *C. G.*, *IV*, c. 9.
[31] *C. G.*, *IV*, c. 9, 2.

This concludes St. Thomas' discussion of the divine generation, paternity and natural sonship from the exegetical and historical point of view. In the tenth chapter immediately following, he will turn to the basic rational or philosophical problems which he had noted previously as motivating heterodox exegesis, but whose treatment he had postponed to consider more extensively once he had completed his biblical apologetic.

Before taking up this passage, however — and it is the chapter leading immediately into the lengthy positive and systematic exposition of chapter eleven — an observation should first be made with regard to the biblical apologetic itself. It is apt to seem strange that, in a study explicitly devoted to the question whether or to what extent there is an apologetical perspective in the trinitarian theology of St. Thomas, the writer will find as directly pertinent to his subject, not the foregoing nine chapters, which were obviously — at least in some sense of the word — 'apologetical', but rather the section which is to follow and which is taken up with positive and systematic exposition.

It is necessary, therefore, to recall once again the distinctions made in the introduction and first part of the present study. The 'apologetical perspective' to be examined in this investigation of the Thomist text is not such as could accurately qualify or describe any defense of Christian doctrine, or even any defense in which purely rational and philosophical principles would play a significant rôle, but only such as could truly characterize that particular species of apologetic which aims to demonstrate or verify, at least in some manner, and on the ground of purely rational intelligence, the primary elements of the revealed mystery.

In this extremely precise sense, however, the nine chapters treating of the generation of the Son of God in Scripture and in heretical exegesis are not in the least apologetical. As already seen — and the purpose of analyzing these passages was to make quite certain that it would be seen — St. Thomas remains true to his declared intent. Throughout, his focus is not at all on the a priori necessity, or even *convenientia*, of the divine generation, but exclusively upon its revelation in Sacred Scripture. The rebuttal addressed to the Photinians, Sabellians and Arians is addressed at every stage in the argument, not to those who do not know or refuse to accept

10

the word of God contained in the documents of Scripture, but to those who most emphatically do accept it while erring, albeit through bad will, in their interpretation of it.

The question remains, however, whether in subsequent passages, where rational principles and structure are going to contribute so much to the development of Aquinas' positive exposition, there will be preserved this same neat enclosure within the testimony, authority and light of revelation.

II. SYSTEMATIC EXPOSITION IN TERMS OF INTELLECTUAL EMANATION

The tenth chapter outlines St. Thomas' transition. In view of all that has thus far been considered, he continues, the unmistakably clear teaching of Sacred Scripture on the divine generation is that the Father and Son, though two distinct Persons, are nevertheless but one God, with but one essence or nature in common. Yet, since the idea of two distinct supposits sharing the same single essence is extremely remote from anything discovered in the nature of creatures, the human reason, taking its start from what is proper to creatures, encounters many difficulties with regard to this mystery.[32]

St. Thomas enumerates several of these. Since human experience knows generation only as a species of change, how can the notion be applied to the Son of God, immutable and eternal, pure act without any vestige of potentiality?[33] How is it possible that the nature received in generation by the Son from the Father be specifically and numerically the same nature as the Father's?[34] Would this not involve a composition in the Son — of *recipiens* and *natura recepta* — which could not be true in a divine being?[35] If, on the other hand, the Son is simply identified with the divine essence, as the

---

[32] " Omnibus igitur diligenter consideratis, manifeste apparet hoc nobis de generatione divina in Sacris Scripturis proponi credendum, quod Pater et Filius, etsi personis distinguantur, sunt tamen unus Deus, et unam habent essentiam seu naturam. Quia vero a creaturarum natura hoc invenitur valde remotum, ut aliqua duo supposito distinguantur et tamen eorum sit una essentia ; humana ratio, ex creaturarum proprietatibus procedens, multipliciter in hoc secreto divinae generationis patitur difficultatem." *C. G.*, *IV*, c. 10, 1.

[33] *C. G.*, *IV*, c. 10, 2 and 3.
[34] *C. G.*, *IV*, c. 10, 4.
[35] *C. G.*, *IV*, c. 10, 5.

Father is also, it would seem to follow of necessity, since the same divine nature is itself subsistent, that the Father and the Son are fused in one subsistent reality — therefore, in one Person.[36] The list continues with further problems derived from the metaphysics of individuation, person and personal distinguishing principle, the inadequacy of a doctrine of relations to explain away the contradiction, and finally the logic of predication.[37]

Not, however, until the fourteenth chapter, will St. Thomas offer a solution to the difficulties he has just indicated. Instead, he turns immediately to his positive exposition : " Quomodo accipienda sit generatio in divinis, et quae de Filio Dei dicuntur in Scripturis. " [38]

Aquinas first lays down a twofold general principle : the difference in the mode of emanation discovered in things is proportioned to the difference in natures ; the more excellent the nature, so much the more intimate to this nature will be whatever emanates from it.[39]

He proceeds to examine the deployment of this principle throughout the universe of being. In inanimate bodies, emanation is restricted to the action of one body upon another, as in ignition.[40] In plants, where emanation proceeds from the interior (the internal humor converted into seed), the entity moves itself, not merely something external to itself, unto action. Yet, though this is truly an instance of life, it is an imperfect instance. For what emanates from the interior becomes eventually quite external. In fact, even the first principle of vegetative emanation, its ultimate source, is from the outside, inasmuch as the plant draws its internal humor from the soil through its roots.[41]

---

[36] *C. G.*, *IV*, c. 10, 6.

[37] *C. G.*, *IV*, c. 10, 7-14.

[38] *C. G.*, *IV*, c. 11.

[39] " Principium autem huius intentionis hinc sumere oportet, quod secundum diversitatem naturarum diversus emanationis modus invenitur in rebus : et quanto aliqua natura est altior, tanto id quod ex ea emanat, magis ei est intimum. " *C. G.*, *IV*, c. 11, 1.

[40] " In rebus enim omnibus inanimata corpora infimum locum tenent : in quibus emanationes aliter esse non possunt nisi per actionem unius eorum in aliquod alterum. Sic enim ex igne generatur ignis, dum ab igne corpus exstraneum alteraur, et ab qualitatem et speciem ignis perducitur. " *C. G.*, *IV*, c. 11, 2.

[41] " Inter animata vero corpora proximum locum tenent plantae, in quibus iam emanatio ex interiori procedit : inquantum scilicet hu-

A higher grade of life attaches to the sensitive soul, whose proper emanation, while originating from the outside as the sensible object impresses its form upon the external senses, terminates nevertheless internally as the impressed species proceeds into the imagination and memory. Sensory life, then, is all the more excellent than plant life to the degree that its proper operation is contained within its own recesses. Throughout the sensory process, however, principle and term remain different entities — for it is not upon itself that the sense faculty reflects — and the emanation is from one to the other (*ex uno in alterum*). Sense life, consequently, though superior, is still not altogether perfect.[42]

So it is, Aquinas goes on, that the supreme and perfect mode of life is found only in intellect ; for intellect reflects upon itself, and is capable of understanding itself. Yet, there are levels of perfection even within intellectual life. Thus, the human intellect, dependent as it is upon the sense phantasm, draws the beginning of its processes from what is outside itself, even though it is capable of knowing itself.

---

mor plantae intraneus in semen convertitur, et illud semen, terrae mandatum, crescit in plantam. Iam ergo hic primus gradus vitae invenitur : nam viventia sunt quae seipsa movent ad agendum ; illa vero quae non nisi exteriora movere possunt, omnino sunt vita carentia. In plantis vero hoc inditium vitae est, quod id quod in ipsis est, movet ad aliquam formam. — Est tamen vita plantarum imperfecta : quia emanatio in eis licet ab interiori procedat, tamen paulatim ab interioribus exiens quod emanat, finaliter omnino extrinsecum invenitur. Humor enim arboris primo ab arbore egrediens fit flos ; et tandem fructus ab arboris cortice discretus, sed ei colligatus ; perfecto autem fructu, omnino ab arbore separatur, et in terra cadens, sementina virtute producit aliam plantam. — Si quis etiam diligenter consideret, primum huius emanationis principium ab exteriori sumitur : nam humor intrinsecus arboris per radices a terra sumitur, de qua planta suscipit nutrimentum. " *C. G., IV*, c. 11, 3.   .

[42] " Ultra plantarum vero vitam, altior gradus vitae invenitur, qui est secundum animam sensitivam : cuius emantio propria, etsi ab exteriori incipiat, in interiori terminatur ; et quanto emanatio magis processerit, tanto magis ad intima devenitur. Sensibile enim exterius formam suam exterioribus sensibus ingerit ; a quibus procedit in imaginationem ; et ulterius in memoriae thesaurum. In quolibet tamen huius emanationis processu, principium et terminus pertinent ad diversa : non enim aliqua potentia sensitiva in seipsam reflectitur. Est ergo hic gradus vitae tanto altior quam vita plantarum, quanto operatio huius vitae magis in intimis continetur : non tamen est omnino vita perfecta, cum emanatio semper fiat ex uno in alterum. " *C. G., IV*, c. 11, 4.

The intellectual life of the angels, then, is still more perfect, inasmuch as the angelic intellect, in achieving self-knowledge, does not proceed from something external to itself, but knows itself through itself.   Nevertheless, the highest level of intellectual life has not yet been reached.   In angels, the *intentio intellecta* is wholly intrinsic to the angelic intelligence.   The same *intentio intellecta*, however, is not identical with the angelic substance ; for in the angels, knowing and being are still distinct.

It is only in God, consequently, that the ultimate perfection of intellectual life is found.   In God, ' to know ' and ' to be ' are one ; in God, the *intentio intellecta* must be one with the divine essence.[43]

At this point, St. Thomas defines the *intentio intellecta* which he has just introduced to designate the proper emanation of intellectual life, and then goes on to explain the notion more fully.   The *intentio intellecta* is what the intellect conceives in itself of the reality being understood.   In human beings, this conception is neither the object of understanding nor the substance of the intellect, but rather that likeness conceived by intellect of the thing which is understood.   It is that which is (immediately) signified by the external word, therefore ; and hence is given the name ' word ' (*verbum*).

Next, Aquinas offers proof for the two distinctions previously mentioned.   That the intention, or conception, is not the same as the thing understood, is shown from the fact that it is one matter to understand the thing itself, and quite another — as when intellect reflects upon its own operation

---

[43] " Est igitur supremus et perfectus gradus vitae qui est secundum intellectum : nam intellectus in seipsum reflectitur, et seipsum intelligere potest.   Sed et in intellectuali vita diversi gradus inveniuntur.   Nam intellectus humanus, etsi seipsum cognoscere possit, tamen primum suae cognitionis initium ab extrinseco sumit : quia non est intelligere sine phantasmate, ut ex superioribus patet. — Perfectior igitur est intellectualis vita in angelis, in quibus intellectus ad sui cognitionem non procedit ex aliquo exteriori, sed per se cognoscit seipsum.   Nondum tamen ad ultimam perfectionem vita ipsorum pertingit : quia, licet intentio intellecta sit eis omnino intrinseca, non tamen ipsa intentio intellecta est eorum substantia ; quia non est idem in eis intelligere et esse, ut ex superioribus patet. — Ultima igitur perfectio vitae competit Deo, in quo non est aliud intelligere et aliud esse, ut supra ostensum est, et ita oportet quod intentio intellecta in Deo sit ipsa divina essentia. "   *C. G.*, *IV*, c. 11, 5.

— to understand the intention. That the intention is not the same as the intellect itself, is shown from the fact that the *esse* of the intention also is a matter of intellect, while the *esse* of the human intellectual faculty — whose *esse* is not simply its *intelligere* — is not.[44]

But in God, Aquinas continues, it is quite otherwise. In God, since *esse* and *intelligere* are identical, intention and intellect are identical. In God, what is understood and intellect are likewise identical; for it is by understanding Himself, that He understands everything else. It remains, then, that in God's act of self-understanding, there is complete identification of intellect, thing understood, and *intentio intellecta*.[45]

After having completed his analysis of emanation as vital self-communication, and the progressively increasing intimacy of the communicated to its principle — until in God perfect identity between the two is at last attained — St. Thomas proceeds to show how, in the light of this frame of analysis, it is possible to conceive in some manner the meaning of the divine generation.

Obviously, the data of revelation do not allow that the generation of the utterly immaterial and divine Son of God be assimilated to the generation of inanimate objects consisting in the impression of a species upon exterior matter. Again, since God is indivisible and since the begotten Son of God

---

[44] " Dico autem *intentionem intellectam* ip quod intellectus in seipso concipit de re intellecta. Quae quidem in nobis neque est ipsa res quae intelligitur ; neque est ipsa substantia intellectus ; sed est quaedam similitudo concepta in intellectu de re intellecta, quam voces exteriores significant ; unde et ipsa intentio *verbum interius* nominatur, quod est exteriori verbo significatum. Et quidem quod praedicta intentio non sit in nobis res intellecta, inde apparet quod aliud est intelligere rem, et aliud est intelligere ipsam intentionem intellectam, quod intellectus facit dum super suum opus reflectitur : unde et aliae scientiae sunt de rebus, et aliae de intentionibus intellectis. Quod autem intentio intellecta non sit ipse intellectus in nobis, ex hoc patet quod esse intentionis intellectae in ipso intelligi consistit : non autem esse intellectus nostri, cuius esse non est suum intelligere. " *C. G.*, *IV*, c. 11, 6.

[45] " Cum ergo in Deo sit idem esse et intelligere, intentio intellecta in ipso est ipse eius intellectus. Et quia intellectus in eo est res intellecta, intelligendo enim se intelligit omnia alia, ut in Primo ostensum est ; relinquitur quod in Deo intelligente seipsum sit idem intellectus, et res quae intelligitur, et intentio intellecta. " *C. G.*, *IV*, c. 11, 7.

does not exist outside the Father in a state of separation, but rather in the Father, it is likewise clear that the divine generation cannot be attracted to the generation of plants or, on the same level, of animals. Finally, inasmuch as God is both first agent and incorporeal, it is also impossible to understand the divine generation in terms of the generation attendant upon the sensitive soul, whose operations require the instrumentality of the body and whose generation depends upon receiving from outside itself the ultimate source of its influx into some other. It remains, therefore, that the divine generation would have to be understood in terms of such emanation as is strictly intellectual.[46]

St. Thomas then proposes to elucidate specifically. It is taken as already demonstrated from what he had written in earlier parts of his treatise on the essence, attributes and operations of God, that God understands Himself. But whatever is understood, precisely inasmuch as it is understood, must be in the one who understands. For this is the meaning of understanding : apprehension of what is understood through intellect.

Thus even the human intellect, when it understands itself, is in itself — not only as essentially one with itself, but

---

[46] " His igitur consideratis, utcumque concipere possumus qualiter sit divina generatio accipienda. Patet enim quod non est possibile sic accipi generationem divina, sicut in rebus inanimatis generatio invenitur, in quibus generans imprimit suam speciem in exteriorem materiam. Oportet enim, secundum positionem fidei, quod Filius a Deo genitus veram habeat deitatem, et sit verus Deus. Ipsa autem deitas non est forma materiae inhaerens ; neque Deus est ex materia existens ; ut in Primo probatum est. — Similiter autem non potest accipi divina generatio ad modum generationis quae in plantis invenitur, et etiam in animalibus, quae communicant cum plantis in nutritiva et generativa virtute. Separatur enim aliquid quod erat in planta vel animali, ad generationem similis in specie, quod in fine generationis est omnino extra generantem. A Deo autem, cum indivisibilis sit, non potest aliquid separari. Ipse etiam Filius a Deo genitus non est extra Patrem generantem, sed in eo : sicut ex superioribus auctoritatibus patet. — Neque etiam potest generatio divina intelligi secundum modum emanationis quae invenitur in anima sensitiva. Non enim Deus ab aliquo exteriori accipit ut in alterum influere possit : non enim esset primum agens. Operationes etiam animae sensitivae non complentur sine corporalibus instrumentis : Deum autem manifestum est incorporeum esse. — Relinquitur igitur quod generatio divina secundum intellectualem emanationem sit intelligenda. " *C. G.*, *IV*, c. 11, 8.

also, now, as apprehended by itself in the process of understanding. God, therefore, must be in Himself as the understood in the one understanding, or, that is to say, as the
word — *intentio intellecta, verbum.* Aquinas appeals to Jn
1 : 1 : " Verbum erat apud Deum. " In God's act of self-
understanding, then, there exists in ' God understanding ' the
Word of God, which is ' God understood '.[47]

Moreover, since the divine intellect does not pass from
potency to act, God's act of self-understanding is eternal, and
hence the Word existing in God is co-eternal with God. Once
more Aquinas appeals to Jn 1 : 1 : " In principio erat Verbum. " [48] Also, since the divine intellect is pure act, there
is necessarily identity between the substance of the divine
intellect and the act of understanding. Therefore, in God
there is likewise identity between the *esse* of the Word and
the *esse* of the intellect, inasmuch as the *esse* of an interior
word is one with its being understood. The argument here
is simply : *substantia intellectus* (in God) = *actus intellectus* ;
but *verbum = actus intellectus.* But the divine intellect is
identical with God-Himself — with His existence, essence,
nature. Therefore, the Divine Word is likewise identical with
His existence, essence, nature — that is to say, is truly God.[49]

---

[47] " Hoc autem sic manifestari oportet. Manifestum est enim ex
his quae in Primo declarata sunt, quod Deus seipsum intelligit. Omne
autem intellectum, inquantum intellectum, oportet esse in intelligente : significat enim ipsum intelligere apprehensionem eius quod intelligitur per intellectum ; unde etiam intellectum noster, seipsum intelligens, est in seipso ; non solum ut idem sibi per essentiam, sed etiam ut
a se apprehensum intelligendo. Oportet igitur quod Deus in seipso
sit ut intellectum in intelligente. Intellectum autem in intelligente est
intentio intellecta et verbum. Est igitur in Deo intelligente seipsum
Verbum Dei quasi Deus intellectus : sicut verbum lapidis in intellectu
est lapis intellectus. Hinc est quod *Ioan.* I 1 dicitur : *Verbum erat
apud Deum.*" *C. G., IV,* c. 11, 9.

[48] " Quia vero intellectus divinus non exit de potentia in actum,
sed semper est actu existens, ut in Primo probatum est ; ex necessitate oportet quod semper seipsum intellexerit. Ex hoc autem quod
se intelligit, oportet quod Verbum ipsius in ipso sit, ut ostensum est.
Necesse est igitur semper Verbum eius in Deo extitisse. Est igitur
coaeternum Deo Verbum ipsius, nec accedit ei ex tempore, sicut intellectui nostro accedit ex tempore verbum interius conceptum, quod est
intentio intellecta. Hinc est quod *Ioan.* I 1 dicitur : *In principio
erat Verbum.*" *C. G., IV,* c. 11, 10.

[49] " Cum autem intellectus divinus non solum sit semper in actu,
sed etiam sit ipse actus purus, ut in Primo probatum est : oportet quod

Next, after having distinguished carefully between conception of the word in human beings — where intellect and act are not identical, nor, therefore, intellect and word — and the Divine Word, Aquinas proceeds to show that the Word of God possesses the divine nature as not only specifically, but also numerically, the same. For such numerical division is impossible in a purely spiritual being.[50]

Now thus far in his exposition, St. Thomas has not discussed the Word of God as in any way distinct from the principle of its emanation, but solely as identical with the existence and nature of God, co-eternal and divine. In the paragraph immediately following, however, the question of distinction is at last introduced.

He had remarked just before that in creatures essence and existence are distinct, and in certain creatures at least, that which subsists in its essence and the essence or nature itself are also distinct. Thus, this particular man is neither his humanity nor his existence. God, on the other hand, is both His essence and His existence.[51]

Nevertheless, Aquinas continues, though in God these components of being are unequivocally identical, there is still

---

substantia intellectus divini sit ipsum suum intelligere, quod est actus intellectus ; esse autem Verbi interius concepti, sive intentionis intellectae, est ipsum suum intelligi. Idem ergo esse est Verbi divini, et intellectus divini ; et per consequens ipsius Dei, qui est suus intellectus. Esse autem Dei est eius essentia vel natura, quae idem est quod ipse Deus, ut in Primo ostensum est. Verbum igitur Dei est ipsum esse divinum et essentia eius, et ipse verus Deus. — Non autem sic est de verbo intellectus humani ... ” *C. G.*, *IV*, c. 11, 11.

[50] “ Non sic autem natura Dei est in Verbo ut sit una specie et numero differens. Sic enim Verbum habet naturam Dei sicut intelligere Dei est ipsum esse eius, ut dictum est. Intelligere autem est ipsum esse divinum. Verbum igitur habet ipsam essentiam divinam non solum specie, sed numero eandem. — Item, natura quae est una secundum speciem, non dividitur in plura secundum numerum nisi propter materiam. Divina autem natura omnino immaterialis est. Impossibile est igitur quod natura divina sit una specie et numero differens. Verbum igitur Dei in eadem natura numero communicat cum Deo. ” *C. G.*, *IV*, c. 11, 12.

[51] “ Ostensum est autem in primo libro ea quae in creaturis divisa sunt, in Deo simpliciter unum esse : sicut in creatura aliud est essentia et esse ; et in quibusdam est etiam aliud quod subsistit in sua essentia, et eius essentia sive natura, nam hic homo non est sua humanitas nec suum esse ; sed Deus est sua essentia et suum esse. ” *C. G.*, *IV*, c. 11, 12 ad fin.

in God whatever pertains to the proper reality (*ratio*), whether
it be of subsistence, or essence, or existence itself. Thus it
belongs to God as subsistent, not to be in others; as essence,
to be something; as existence, to be in act. It is necessary,
then, since in God the one understanding, the act of understanding, and the Word are likewise identical, that there should
also and most truly be in God whatever pertains to the proper
reality of the one understanding, the act of understanding,
and the Word. But it is of the proper reality (*de ratione*)
of internal word, or *intentio intellecta*, that it proceed from
the one understanding upon the act of understanding. For
the interior word is the quasi term of intellectual operation,
inasmuch as the intellect in its act of understanding conceives
and forms this intention, or *ratio intellecta*, which is the word.
The Word of God, therefore, is referred to God understanding,
Whose Word this is, as to the one from whom it has its being
("comparatur ... sicut ad eum a quo est"). For this pertains
to the proper reality of interior word.

Since, therefore, in God the one understanding, the act
of understanding, and the Word, are essentially one, and
since, consequently, it is necessary that each of these be simply
God, there remains only the distinction of relation, insofar as
the Word is referred to the one conceiving it as to the one
from whom it has its being (*a quo est*). Hence it is, that John
the Evangelist, having said: "Deus erat Verbum," added,
so that distinction of the Word from God conceiving this
Word would not be entirely removed: "Hoc erat in principio apud Deum" — as though to say: This Word that I
have called God is somehow distinct from God Who utters
it, and thus could be said to be "apud Deum".[52]

---

[52] " Et quamvis haec in Deo unum sint verissime, tamen in Deo
est quicquid pertinet ad rationem vel subsistentis, vel essentiae, vel
ipsius esse : convenit enim ei non esse in aliquo, inquantum est subsistens ; esse quid, inquantum est essentia ; et esse in actu, ratione
ipsius esse. Oportet igitur, cum in Deo sit idem intelligens, et intelligere, et intentio intellecta, quod est Verbum ipsius ; quod verissime
in Deo sit et quod pertinet ad rationem intelligentis ; et quod pertinet
ad rationem eius quod est intelligere ; et quod pertinet ad rationem
intentionis intellectae, sive Verbi. Est autem de ratione interioris
verbi, quod est intentio intellecta, quod procedat ab intelligente secundum suum intelligere, cum sit quasi terminus intellectualis operationis : intellectus enim intelligendo concipit et format intentionem
sive rationem intellectam, quae est interius verbum. Oportet igitur

The objective of the present study will make it necessary to examine this passage just cited more closely in the attempt to determine whether, or in what sense, the procession of the Divine Word, and as somehow distinct from God Who utters it, amounts to a conclusion from the metaphysical principles of intellectual emanation. For the moment, however, so that the presentation of Aquinas might subsequently be evaluated in the fulness of its own proper perspective, the further doctrinal points which he goes on to make in the remaining passages of the eleventh chapter, and in the three chapters following, should first be noted, at least briefly.

St. Thomas next considers the Word from the aspect of similitude or likeness of the thing understood. When God understands things other than Himself, His understanding stands as principle in the order of cause, and His Word is exemplar. But when God understands Himself, it is rather the divine intelligible that stands as principle to His act of understanding, and His Word is image — " imago invisibilis Dei " (Coloss 1 : 15).[53]

Again, since the similitude proper to intellectual knowledge is of the essence or substance of the thing understood, and not merely of externals as in sense, the Word of God as image is image according to the divine essence or substance " figura substantiae Dei " (Hebr 1 : 3).[54] Moreover, since the Word of God is not only substantial image, but also communicates of the same nature with the one uttering the Word, the Word of God is not only image, but Son. For to be image in the sense of having the same nature is not found in such as could not be called son — at least not in living beings,

---

quod a Deo secundum ipsum suum intelligere procedat Verbum ipsius. Comparatur igitur Verbum Dei ad Deum intelligentem, cuius est Verbum, sicut ad eum a quo est : hoc enim est de ratione verbi. Cum igitur in Deo intelligens, intelligere, et intentio intellecta, sive Verbum, sint per essentiam unum, et per hoc necesse sit quod quodlibet horum sit Deus ; remanet tamen sola distinctio relationis, prout Verbum refertur ad concipientem ut a quo est. Hinc est quod Evangelista, quia dixerat, *Deus erat Verbum* ; ne omnino distinctio sublata intelligeretur Verbi a Deo dicente sive concipiente Verbum, subiunxit : *Hoc erat in principio apud Deum* : quasi dicat : Hoc Verbum, quod Deum esse dixi, aliquo modo distinctum est a Deo dicente, ut sic possit dici *apud Deum esse.* " *C. G., IV*, c. 11, 13.

[53] *C. G., IV*, c. 11, 14.
[54] *C. G., IV*, c. 11, 15.

inasmuch as what proceeds from the living being unto specific likeness is called son. Thus it was said: "Dominus dixit ad me: Filius meus es tu" (Ps 2 : 7).[55]

Also, against the Arians who made the divine generation voluntary, it is clear that the procession of the Word must be natural. For in every nature, the procession of son from father is natural. But at this point, St. Thomas takes a moment to show how such a fact is not in any way out of harmony with the intellectualist description of divine generation, but rather in support of it, and this gives him the opportunity to emphasize the identity between generation and procession of the Word.

In human intelligence, of course, some things are known naturally, as the first intelligible principles, and other things known only through process and acquisition. Only the interior words pertaining to the first class could be called natural processions. In God, however, being and understanding are one, and hence God's self-understanding is purely natural, and the Word proceeding from this understanding proceeds in a purely natural manner.

Finally, since the Word is of the same nature as God Who utters it, and also the likeness of the divine nature, it follows that the natural procession of the Word of God is unto the likeness of Him from Whom the procession originates, along with identity in nature. The proper reality of generation in living beings is thus verified. The Word of God, therefore, is truly begotten of God uttering the Word, and His procession can rightly be called generation or nativity — "Ego hodie genui te" (Ps 2 : 7).[56] The lengthy exposition

---

[55] *C. G., IV*, c. 11, 16.

[56] " Rursus considerandum est quod, cum in qualibet natura processio filii a patre sit naturalis, ex quo Verbum Dei Filius Dei dicitur, oportet quod naturaliter a Patre procedat. Et hoc quidem supra dictis convenit : ut ex his quae in intellectu nostro accidunt, perspici potest. Intellectus enim noster aliqua naturaliter cognoscit : sicut prima intelligibilium principia, quorum intelligibiles conceptiones, quae verba interiora dicuntur, naturaliter in ipso existunt et ex eo procedunt. Sunt etiam quaedam intelligibilia quae non naturaliter intellectus noster cognoscit, sed in eorum cognitionem ratiocinando pertingit : et horum conceptiones in intellectu nostro naturaliter non existunt, sed cum studio quaeruntur. Manifestum est autem quod Deus seipsum naturaliter intelligit, sicut et naturaliter est : suum enim intelligere est suum esse, ut in Primo probatum est. Verbum igitur Dei

concludes with a brief treatment of the problems arising from
the distinction between conception and birth in creatures,
and the idea of active and passive virtues in the medieval
theory of genetics.[57]

The short twelfth chapter that follows, where Aquinas
explains how the Son of God is also called Wisdom, adds
still further confirmation to his by now exclusively intellectualist interpretation of the Son's generation. In men, wisdom
is the habit directing knowledge of divine things, according
to which the human mind forms concepts or interior words
of the same. Hence, since it is customary to assign acts the
names of the virtues or habits from which they proceed, words
conceived of divine things will themselves be called wisdom.
In God likewise, though the divine Wisdom is not a habit,
but one with the divine essence, the Word of God proceeding
in Wisdom from God's self-understanding will itself be called
Wisdom — thus designating, not the essential Wisdom common to the Father and Son alike, but the personal Wisdom
that is a proper name of the Son as such.[58]

The same total identification between generation of the
Son and conception of the Word, Aquinas drives home still
more forcefully as he takes up the problem of there being
not more than one Son. In one simple intuition, he writes,
God understands Himself, and everything outside Himself as
well. Since, then, God's understanding is one with His being,
it follows necessarily that the Word of God be utterly unique.
But there is absolutely no difference between the generation
of the Son and the conception of the Word. Therefore, there
can be but one generation in God, and only one Son born of

---

seipsum intelligentis naturaliter ab ipso procedit. Et cum Verbum
Dei sit eiusdem naturae cum Deo dicente, et sit similitudo ipsius ;
sequitur quod hic naturalis processus sit in similitudinem eius a quo
est processio cum identitate naturae. Haec est autem verae generationis ratio in rebus viventibus, quod id quod generatur, a generante
procedat ut similitudo ipsius et eiusdem naturae cum ipso. Est ergo
Verbum Dei *genitum* vere a Deo dicente : et eius processio *generatio*
vel *nativitas* dici potest. Hinc est quod in Psalmo dicitur : *Ego hodie genui te* : idest, in aeternitate, quae semper est praesens, et nulla
est in ea ratio praeteriti et futuri. — Unde patet falsum esse quod
Ariani dixerunt, quod Pater genuit Filium voluntate. Quae enim voluntate sunt, non naturalia sunt. ” *C. G., IV*, c. 11, 17.

[57] *C. G., IV*, c. 11, 18 and 19.
[58] *C. G., IV*, c. 12.

the Father — "Vidimus eum quasi Unigenitum a Patre."
(Jn 1 : 14) ; "Unigenitus, qui est in sinu Patris, ipse nobis
enarravit." (1 : 18).[59]

St. Thomas recognizes the objection, however. If God
must understand Himself, and thus generate the Divine Word,
and if this same Divine Word is truly God, why should not
the Word generate a second Son, the second Son still another,
and so on ? [60] But Aquinas observes that what was demonstrated earlier in his exposition was not that the Son was
'another God', but the one true God. He is not, therefore,
another intellect, nor another act of understanding from which
there would proceed another Word. For He is distinct solely
as proceeding Word. Everything must be attributed to the
Father and Son together, except what is strictly proper to
this procession : that is, it belongs to the Father alone that
He conceive the Divine Word, and to the Divine Word alone
that He proceed from the Father's utterance.[61]

There is no question, then, of an inequality in power.
For it is in virtue of the one and commonly shared divine
power, both that the Father conceive, and that the Son be
conceived — the only distinction being the purely relative
distinction, that the Father has this power in the order of
generating, while the Son has the same power in the order
of being generated.[62]

Next, Aquinas goes on to explain that, though the one
indivisible Word of God is Word of all else as well, this is not
to be taken in the sense of procession, but in the sense of
exemplar, form, *ratio*, through which, on analogy with the
idea in the mind of the artificer, God creates.[63] Unlike the
artist's conception, however, which is merely the principle
through which another and subsistent being acts, the Divine

---

[59] " Quia vero Deus, intelligendo seipsum omnia alia intelligit, ut
in Primo ostensum est ; seipsum autem uno et simplici intuitu intelligit, cum suum intelligere sit suum esse : necesse est Verbum Dei
esse unicum tantum. Cum autem in divinis nihil aliud sit Filii generatio quam Verbi, conceptio sequitur quod una sola sit generatio in
divinis, et unicus Filius solus a Patre genitus. Unde *Ioan.* I 14 dicitur : *Vidimus eum quasi Unigenitum a Patre* ; et iterum ; *Unigenitus,
qui est in sinu Patris, ipse nobis enarravit.* " *C. G., IV*, c. 13, 1.

[60] *C. G., IV*, c. 13, 2.
[61] *C. G., IV*, c. 13, 3.
[62] *C. G., IV*, c. 13, 4.
[63] *C. G., IV*, c. 13, 6 and 7.

Word, being itself subsistent, is a true agent.[64] But like the artist's conception, the Word of God pre-exists the artifact, all creatures being contained in the Divine Word from eternity and according to the perfectly simple mode of the divine life.[65] Finally, the Word of God is not only exemplar (*ratio*) for all that exists naturally in the created universe, but also, as " Lux hominum," the source of all human and finite thought.[66]

At this point, St. Thomas feels that he has completed his exposition on the generation of the Son of God. In the chapter immediately following, the fourteenth, he will merely return to the rational objections posed in the tenth chapter, that he may reply to these in terms of the principles substantiated and developed in the course of his positive treatment. As Aquinas disposes of these objections, moreover, it will be his minutely articulated theory of intellectual emanation and word that will exercise the rather decisive rôle in showing that the divine generation involves neither change, nor actuation or passage from potency to act, nor duality within the Divine Word between *recipiens* and *natura recepta*.[67]

That done, he will then go on to discuss the procession of the Holy Spirit. Since, then, St. Thomas' positive treatment of the divine generation finishes with the thirteenth chapter, it is interesting to note the exact words with which he concludes this passage on the unique Son, and with it, his entire discussion of the divinely conceived Word on analogy with the inner word of human understanding. Aquinas writes : So much there is, then, that we are able somehow to conceive, on the basis of what we have been taught by the Sacred Scriptures, of the divine generation and the power of God's Only-begotten Son.[68]

As he completes his long systematic exposition, therefore, St. Thomas points out once more, and quite explicitly, that everything he has been saying in this exposition, no less than what he had said earlier in direct exegesis of the biblical testimonies and in refutation of heretical opinions, has been

---

[64] *C. G., IV*, c. 13, 9.
[65] *C. G., IV*, c. 13, 10.
[66] *C. G., IV*, c. 13, 11.
[67] *C. G., IV*, c. 14, 2-5.
[68] " Haec igitur sunt quae de generatione divina, et ˉde virtute Unigeniti Filii Dei, ex Sacris Scripturis edocti, utcumque concipere possumus. " *C. G., IV*, c. 13, 12.

said, and must be interpreted as having been said, strictly
within the authoritative context of Christian faith.

But now that the doctrinal elaboration on the divine
generation has been reviewed in full, it is time to return to
the problematical eleventh chapter, to discuss in detail the
nature and significance of the 'argument from emanation
of the inner word', which appears to play the decisive rôle
in St. Thomas' exposition.

III. The 'Verbum Argument' of "Contra Gentiles IV" from the Perspective of the Progressive Development of Aquinas' Thought

It is Dom Vagaggini's contention, the reader will recall
from the first part of the present study, that here in the fourth
book of the *Contra Gentiles* St. Thomas reaches the summit of
a personal evolution — beginning with the flat denial in the
Sentences that unaided reason could devise, in Anselmian fashion, apodictic proofs for the a priori necessity of the trinitarian
processions, and culminating with what has at least every
appearance of being an apodictic demonstration of his own
in the eleventh and nineteenth chapters of the *Contra Gentiles*,
book four.[69]

As has already been mentioned, it is not in line with the
object and scope of this study to engage in controversy — all
the less so since, as previously remarked, Dom Vagaggini's
contentions seem to have been set down on paper rather to
stimulate a fresh examination of a yet unsettled problem,
that to offer its definitive solution. Nevertheless, the two
points scored by Vagaggini apropos of *Contra Gentiles IV*
supply a pertinent frame of reference for trying to determine
what was the precise theological perspective and methodology
of St. Thomas as he composed the passages on the conception of the Word that have just been reviewed.

First, that there was at least a great personal evolution
of some sort in this matter, can hardly be denied. In his
Commentary on the Sentences, St. Thomas not only emphasized
his conviction that the divine processions lay quite outside
the reach of human reason left to its own resources, but also

---

[69] See Vagaggini, " La hantise, " pp. 124ff.

failed to include in his theological explanation *post factum revelatum* any really penetrating account of the trinitarian relations *in fieri*, such as might have tempted him to look for some sort of a priori necessity in assigning causes, or inclined him to move in that direction, perhaps without even averting to it.

For in the *Commentary*, Aquinas had already worked out, it is true, the doctrine of relations as the cornerstone for his positive and polemical treatment of the Divine Persons *in facto esse*. But he had not as yet discovered any adequate key for probing into the causes, or quasi causes, of these same relations, and thus to treat the Persons, as it were, *in fieri*.

The first Thomist ' *de Trinitate* ', therefore, did not contain any profound analysis of the processions as divine operations, much less strictly intellectual operations. Undoubtedly, Aquinas' preoccupation with the uneven formula *per modum naturae et intellectus* to characterize the generation of the Son held him back from the moment when he could seek his explanation solely in the order of spiritual operation. Then too, his notion of the inner word in human intellect, which he could not yet distinguish with real confidence from the act of understanding, was at best in the very earliest stages of its development, with the net result, as already noted, that Aquinas' handling of the Augustinian analogy was scarcely more than halfhearted. Not having as yet recognized, or at least fully appreciated, the distinction of the inner word from its corresponding and source principle in the act of understanding, Aquinas was willing to speak of the Word of God in an essential, as well as strictly personal, sense.

In summary, then, at the time St. Thomas composed the *Sentences*, he was still far from the day when the analogical law of intellectual conception, with which, in God, the divine generation was to be unequivocally identified, would make it possible for him to probe, obscurely but nevertheless in terms of a proper proportionality, the *fieri*, the coming into being, as it were, of the Second Person — and, *mutatis mutandis*, of the Third Person as well. By the same token, he was also far from the day when such causal, or quasi causal, penetration might give rise to the question whether or not a demonstration of a priori necessity was somehow implicated in his analysis.

But here in the *Contra Gentiles*, the picture has obviously changed. The problem of the moment, however, is to deter-

mine accurately just what has changed, and to just what extent it has changed.   For, in the writer's judgment, there
are three essentially different questions here, which might
nonetheless quite easily become confused unless strict attention is paid to proximate and remote literary context in the
works that are involved.

Thus, it would be one thing if Aquinas had in fact ex-
perienced a significant personal evolution in his idea — one
might say psychological and metaphysical idea — of the inner
word in human understanding.   It would be another thing if,
dependent upon such progress achieved in the areas of human
psychology and general metaphysics, there could be shown to
have taken place in St. Thomas' larger thought a parallel
evolution in his strictly theological account of the divine
generation.   It would be still another and third thing if this
latter development could also be proved to have involved
some change of position on the question of a priori demonstration — that is, on the precisely apologetical question which
is being investigated in the present study.

These are three different questions, therefore, and logical
presentation suggests that each of them be treated separately.

1.   *Evolution in the concept of the human* verbum cordis

On the first point, then, that a far-reaching evolution had
certainly taken place in St. Thomas' understanding of the human inner word, the matter is clear.   One need only study
the contrast in positions between the *Sentences* and the *Contra
Gentiles*.

In the *Sentences*, as already seen, Aquinas appears to have
been uncertain whether or not the word in human understanding was distinct from the operation of intellect.   Also,
while he could and did discuss the Divine Word in terms of
that which proceeded *per modum notitiae*, thus assigning this
Word a certain relative quality, this relative quality did not
automatically impose itself, in St. Thomas' mind, at this time,
on the basis of any philosophical conviction that the inner
word as such was essentially relative.   This serves to bring
out the fact that, while he saw the inner word in human
understanding as proceeding somehow in the overall activity
of intelligence, he had not as yet settled upon the immediate

source principle with any real precision.   Such is the position
of the *Sentences*.

In the eleventh chapter of the fourth book *Contra Gentiles*,
on the other hand, it is quite evident that Aquinas' concept
of the inner word has undergone a radical development.   In
men, the inner word is to be identified neither with the object
understood, nor with the substance of intellect, nor, as it seems
to be his position now, with the operation of intellect.

The inner word, as St. Thomas explains, does not itself
proceed from potency to act, but rather exists in intellect
when and inasmuch as the intellect is in act.[70]   By implication, the human *verbum* is likewise one in the class of real
relations Aquinas describes as following upon the proper operation of a thing — in this case, attending to the larger context
of the passage, of the human intellect.[71]   Finally, Aquinas
states explicitly that it is of the very formality (*de ratione*)
of the inner word as such that it proceed from the one understanding upon the act of intellect, since it is the quasi term
of the intellectual operation.[72]   It is in the same passage,
moreover, and as noted at the time, that to elucidate the
distinction of the Divine Word from its principle of utterance,
St. Thomas argued that it was of the very nature of inner
word to be related to the intellectual operation from which
it proceeds as term.

Contrasted, then, with the rather nebulous and undefined
doctrine of the *Sentences*, the description Aquinas gives of the
inner word in the *Contra Gentiles*, book four, represents a fairly
decisive advance in his psychological and metaphysical understanding of the matter.

This evolution, presumably, did not take place overnight.
From the preceding chapter, moreover, the reader will recall
that something had been said by St. Thomas with regard to

---

[70] " Similiter etiam verbum quod in mente nostra concipitur, non
exit de potentia in actum nisi quatenus intellectus noster procedit
de potentia in actum. " *C. G., IV*, c. 14, 3.

[71] " Omnis enim relatio quae consequitur propriam operationem
alicuius rei, aut potentiam aut quantitatem aut aliquid huiusmodi,
realiter in eo existit ... "   *C. G., IV*, c. 14, 11.

[72] " Est autem de ratione interioris verbi, quod est intentio intellecta, quod procedat ab intelligente secundum suum intelligere, cum
sit quasi terminus intellectualis operationis : intellectus enim intelligendo concipit et format intentionem sive rationem intellectam, quae
est interius verbum. "   *C. G., IV*, c. 11, 13.

the inner word in the methodological treatise *In Boethii de Trinitate*. Consequently, what exactly is the place to be accorded the *In Boethii de Trinitate* in the same line of development?

In the writer's judgment, however, the answer is simply: no place at all. It is not on this particular question — that is to say, the strictly psychological and metaphysical question — that the remarks of *In Boethii de Trinitate* have any significance. Perhaps the point should be clarified.

In the entire treatise *In Boethii de Trinitate*, the *verbum*, it will be recalled, is mentioned only once. The question of the moment was whether the human intellect left to its own devices could attain to knowledge of the Trinity of Persons. An objection had argued that, since God understands, He must conceive a word. For this is common to every instance of intellect. To this, Aquinas replied that, in God, the intelligent and the understood were the same. Therefore, one cannot argue a priori that there must be in God some concept really distinct from Himself — as there is in human beings — and the Trinity of Persons requires a real distinction. [73]

This passing reference to a real distinction in the human inner word, however, is hardly conclusive of any change in position from what had been seen in the *Sentences*. On the face of things, such an inner word would not have to be really distinct from anything more than the substantial reality of the person conceiving it. Hence, the text seems to offer no suitable evidence in either direction — either toward a change of mind from what he had said about the inner word in the *Sentences*, or toward persistence in that same earlier mentality.

Should one choose to look outside the text of *In Boethii de Trinitate*, however, but keeping as close as possible to the same time period, the *Quaestio Disputata de Verbo*, the fourth in the *De Veritate* series, does give some indication as to what Aquinas' idea of the inner word must have been around the time he composed his commentary on Boethius. This part of the *De Veritate* dates most likely from 1256. [74] It is interesting to observe here the progress that has been made at least over the *Sentences*.

---

[73] *In Boet. de Trin.*, q. 1, a. 4, obj. 6 and ad 6m.
[74] See CHENU, *Introduction*, pp. 241 and 242.

In the introductory article, St. Thomas disposes of the question of proper predication. Since the *verbum cordis*, as opposed to external and imaginary words, is completely free from materiality and defect, its usage with reference to the divine is not metaphorical, but strictly proper.[75]

Next, just as previously in the *Sentences*, he asks the further question, whether ' word ' is said of God essentially or personally. At first sight, Aquinas remarks, this would appear to be a simple enough problem. For the inner word implied a certain origin ; and it is by origins that the Divine Persons are distinguished. But this is not quite satisfactory. Operation likewise implies origin from the one operating, but in God, the procession of operation is merely rational and hence not capable of being the ground of real distinction. The question, therefore, is more difficult than would appear. St. Thomas puts it quite succinctly : does the |word *Verbum* imply a real procession, just as the word *Filius*, or a merely rational procession, as the word *operatio* ? [76]

Continuing his analysis, then, he notes first of all that the inner word in human understanding, which stands as the root of the divine analogy, is that in which intellectual operation terminates — what is understood, therefore, or the conception of intellect.[77] But everything thus understood is something really proceeding from another — whether this be conceptual procession of conclusions from principles, or of posterior quiddities from those that are prior, or at least the

---

[75] *De Ver.*, q. 4, a. 1c.

[76] " Quaestio autem ista in superficie videtur esse planissima, propter hoc quia verbum originem quamdam importat secundum quam in divinis personae distinguuntur. Sed, interius considerata, difficilior invenitur, eo quod in divinis invenimus quaedam quae originem important non secundum rem, sed secundum rationem tantum ; sicut hoc nomen *operatio,* quae proculdubio importat aliquid procedens ab operante : tamen iste processus non est nisi secundum rationem tantum ; unde operatio in divinis non personaliter, sed essentialiter dicitur ... " *De Ver.*, q. 4, a. 2c, 2. (Paragraph divisions within the *corpus* or *responsio* are indicated according to the distribution of the Marietti edition, from which all citations and references from the *Quaestiones Disputatae* in the present study are taken.)

[77] " Unde, ad huius notitiam, sciendum est, quod verbum intellectus nostri, secundum cuius similitudinem loqui possumus de verbo in divinis, est id ad quod operatio intellectus nostri terminatur, quod est ipsum intellectum, quod dicitur conceptio intellectus ... " *De Ver.*, q. 4, a. 2c., 3.

actual conception proceeding from habitual knowledge. For
the conception itself is effect of the act of understanding.
Hence, when the mind understands itself, its conception is
not identical with the faculty, but rather something expressed
by its act of knowledge.[78]

The inner word of human understanding, therefore, has
two properties attaching to its formal perfection (*de sua ratione*). It is what is understood; and it is expressed by the
other.[79] If, in the divine analogy, both properties are taken
together, the procession involved in the inner word is strictly
real.[80] If, on the other hand, only the one property — *quod
est intellectum* — be considered, the divine inner word would
imply a merely rational distinction, as does the divine intellect.
But this usage amounts to taking terms in a sense that is
not proper, inasmuch as one of the essential properties has
been omitted. It remains, therefore, that so long as the
inner word is applied to God in its proper sense, the usage
is strictly and exclusively personal; though if it were taken
commonly, the usage might also be essential.[81]

In the lengthy reply to the seventh objection, St. Thomas
complements his analysis in terms of the distinction between
processio operationis and *processio operati*. The procession of

---

[78] " Omne autem intellectum in nobis est aliquid realiter progrediens ab altero; vel sicut progrediuntur a principiis conceptiones conclusionum, vel sicut conceptiones quidditatem [sic — apparently for
' quidditatum '] rerum posteriorum a quidditatibus priorum; vel saltem sicut conceptio actualis progreditur ab habituali cognitione ...
Ipsa enim conceptio est effectus actus intelligendi; unde etiam quando
mens intelligit seipsam, eius conceptio non est ipsa mens, sed aliquid
expressum a notitia mentis. " *De Ver.*, q. 4, a. 2c., 4.

[79] " Ita ergo verbum intellectus in nobis *duo* habet de sua ratione;
scilicet quod est intellectum, et quod est ab alio expressum. " *De
Ver.*, q. 4, a. ac., 5.

[80] " Si ergo secundum utriusque similitudinem verbum dicatur in
divinis, tunc non solum importabitur per verbum divinum processus
rationis, sed etiam rei. " *De Ver.*, q. 4, a. 2c, 6.

[81] " Si autem secundum similitudinem alterius tantum, scilicet
quod est intellectum, sic hoc nomen *verbum* in divinis non importabit
processum realem, sed rationis tantum, sicut et hoc nomen *intellectum*. Sed hoc non erit secundum propriam verbi acceptionem, quia si
aliquid eorum quae sunt de ratione alicuius auferatur, iam non erit
propria acceptio. Unde si verbum proprie accipiatur in divinis, non
dicitur nisi personaliter; si autem accipiatur communiter, poterit
etiam dici essentialiter. " *De Ver.*, q. 4, a. 2c, 7. See also *ibid.*, ad
4m, and ad 5m.

operation does not distinguish a thing existing *per se* from another thing existing *per se*, but only the perfection from the thing perfected — for operation is the perfection of the one operating. The procession of 'the operated', on the other hand, distinguishes one reality from another. In God, then, where there can be no real distinction between perfection and perfectible, the procession of operation is only rational. But to ground the real distinction that must be affirmed between the Divine Persons, there is discovered the further mode of procession, that of a reality from its principle. [82]

What is the significance of this *Quaestio de Verbo* for the gradual evolution of St. Thomas' thought on the inner word as such ? Two things must be considered here. First, with regard to the rôle played by the *De Veritate* itself, what precise progress has been made since the composition of the *Sentences ?* Secondly, how much positive light can be thrown by the *De Veritate* on what was probably St. Thomas' mind on the same subject at the time he would have written his commentary *In Boethii de Trinitate ?*

With regard, then, to the *De Veritate* itself, progress over the *Sentences* may be noted at the following points. In the earlier discussion, Aquinas had argued that the inner word was not something purely relative, but rather something absolute entailing, at the same time, a relation of origin to the one uttering the inner word. This relation, moreover, could be merely rational — like the relation between God's operation and the one operating. In fact, inasmuch as the word is simply the understood species, or perhaps the very operation of intellect, such a merely rational relation would seem to satisfy the proper formality (*ratio*) of the inner word.

---

[82] " Ad septimum dicendum, quod *dupliciter* potest aliquid procedere ab altero : *uno modo* sicut actio ab agente, vel operatio ab operante ; *alio modo* sicut operatum ab operante. Processus ergo operationis ab operante non distinguit rem per se existentem ab alia re per se existente, sed distinguit perfectionem a perfecto, quia operatio est perfectio operantis. Sed processus operati distinguit unam rem ab alia. In divinis autem non potest esse secundum rem distinctio perfectionis a perfectibili. Inveniuntur tamen in Deo res ab invicem distinctae, scilicet tres personae ; et ideo processus qui significatur in divinis ut operationis ab operante, non est nisi rationis tantum ; sed processus qui significatur ut rei a principio, potest in Deo realiter inveniri. " *De Ver.*, q. 4, a. 2, ad 7m.

Finally, when speaking of the opposite possibility, St. Thomas had expressed himself rather hypothetically : if the inner word does involve a relation requiring real, not merely rational, distinction, then use of the term *Verbum* is necessarily personal, not essential. He had concluded by observing that it is, of course, the personal usage that is found throughout the Christian tradition. What is to be noted, however, is that at least in the *Sentences*, St. Thomas was not at all prepared to base the necessity for this personal usage upon a real relation belonging to the inner word as such.

In the *Quaestio de Verbo* of the *De Veritate*, on the other hand, Aquinas' description of the inner word is no longer the somewhat crude picture of something basically absolute — almost static ? — with a relation of origin hardly more than tagged on. Here, whatever he will say about the inner word, will at least be phrased in the vocabulary of origin and procession. He repeats, nonetheless, his earlier misgivings to the extent of noting that the origin implied in the inner word of God could not be presumed to be more than merely rational automatically. For there is origin in the divine operation, but the procession involved is not real. A much deeper analysis, therefore, is necessary.

It is now that the points of difference in comparison with the *Sentences* show up quite clearly. The inner word is not given the loose designation of being simply the understood species or perhaps the operation of intellect as previously, but is now much more sharply defined as the term of the intellectual operation, and therefore, as that which really proceeds from another (*ab altero*). Again, whereas in the *Sentences* Aquinas could not see why a merely rational relation would not satisfy the formal perfection of the inner word, here in the *De Veritate* he is rather at pains to insist that two properties attach to the inner word — to be that which is understood ; but also to be expressed by the other — and that both of these properties pertain to the formal perfection of the inner word as such.

Yet, a word of qualification might be introduced in passing. In the judgment of the writer, it would be a mistake to overlook the measure of vagueness and lack of perfect precision that continues to be found even in the *De Veritate*. On the one side, Aquinas speaks of the inner word as " realiter progrediens ab altero, " as " id ad quod operatio intellectus nostri

terminatur, " and even, in one place, as " effectus actus intelligendi. "   On the other side, in describing the " realiter
progrediens ab altero, " St. Thomas does not explain the terms
of origin and destination in the basic, one might say mechan-
ical, dynamics of intellect, but rather according to the more
logical or intentional categories : " sicut progrediuntur a principiis conceptiones conclusionum, vel sicut conceptiones quidditatum rerum posteriorum a quidditatibus priorum. "

He adds in the same place, as the third instance, " vel
saltem sicut conceptio actualis progreditur ab habituali cognitione, " but one may well ask if this does not tend to soften
the apparent precision of the inner word as " id ad quod operatio intellectus nostri terminatur ? "   Immediately after having described the conception as " effectus actus intelligendi, "
he refers to the same conception as " aliquid expressum a
notitia mentis, " where " notitia " seems to be a comprehensive
term, or perhaps, as " habitualis cognitio " above, a residue
from the preoccupation with the spiritual memory as ultimate
source in the *Sentences*.

In other words, while in the *De Veritate* the inner word
is clearly described as the *realiter progrediens ab altero*, as
term, and even as effect, of understanding, and while at least
in one place understanding is explicitly designated as the
act of understanding, there is still some reason to doubt that
Aquinas was altogether clear in his own mind at this time
just what precisely, in terms of the basic mechanics of intellect, the *alterum*, from which the inner word proceeded, actually
was.

In any case, what can be deduced from the degree of
progress that most certainly had been achieved by the time
of the *De Veritate* with regard to what had most probably
been St. Thomas' thought on the same point — the inner
word as such — at the time he would have composed his
commentary *In Boethii de Trinitate?*

As shown already, the single reference to the inner word
in the article taken up with the possibility of demonstrating
the Trinity from the light and principles of pure reason does
not yield any satisfactory conclusion. It would be a clear
case of forcing a test, therefore, to argue from the rejection
in this passage of the inner word as an instrument of apodictic
demonstration to the hypothesis that St. Thomas maintained
at this time such or such a position on the essential properties

of the inner word itself — for example, that he must also
have rejected during this period the procession of an inner word,
really distinct from its principle, as pertaining to the formal
perfection of intellect.

On the positive side, since the composition of the *In Boethii de Trinitate*, if it preceded this first collection of *Quaestiones Disputatae De Veritate* at all, could not very likely
have done so by more than a year, the rather natural supposition would seem to be that Aquinas was at least moving
in the direction he is seen actually to have taken in the *De
Veritate*. But the position he assumes in the *De Veritate* is
that to be *expressum ab alio* — to be, therefore, at least in
some way really proceeding from the activity of intellect —
is one of the essential properties of inner word as such.

In any case, it is not until the fourth book of the *Contra
Gentiles* that St. Thomas will complete the development of his
own thought transforming the still vague ' procession from
the activity of intellect ', where ' activity ' seems to be meant
comprehensively, to the precisely defined ' procession from the
act of understanding' (*actus intelligendi*), to characterize with
greater psychological and metaphysical exactness the emanation of the inner word.

So much, then, for the evolution of Aquinas' thought on
the doctrine of the *verbum cordis* considered in itself.

2. *Evolution in the intellectualist analysis of the divine gener-
    ation through application of the notion of* verbum cordis

The next question that must be treated is that of the
parallel evolution in Aquinas' thought, not specifically on the
inner word as such, but on the application of the psychological
and metaphysical analysis to his theological account of the
divine generation.

As for the *Sentences*, it has already been observed more
than once that the use St. Thomas made of the *verbum* notion
in his first ' de Trinitate ' was very negligible. Unconvinced,
at the time, that a real relation had to be assigned to the
proper formality of the *verbum cordis*, Aquinas could not see,
on this ground, why the Word of God should be spoken personally any more than essentially. It is rather Christian tradition that imposes the personal use.

And so it was, that in attempting to unite the two terms of the double formula *per modum naturae et intellectus*, Aquinas could speak of intellectual conception less as merely a " quaedam similitudo " of the divine generation, and could explain the identity involved on the basis that, like generation, but unlike the procession *per modum voluntatis* from which both were distinguished, intellectual conception was *ab uno principio* — two different men do not produce the numerically same concept !

On the other end of the evolutionary process, there is the stately exposition of *Contra Gentiles IV* in which the divine generation is at last perfectly reduced to the conception of the Divine Word. But what of the *De Veritate*. And what of the *In Boethii de Trinitate*.

In the *De Veritate*, Aquinas still admits that an essential use of the Word would be possible. But this would be a truncated use, for it would mean eliminating one of the two essential properties of the inner word to give exclusive place to the other. His position is no longer that of the *Sentences*, where he argued that, to the extent the inner word might involve a relation requiring real distinction, then it would have to be employed of God in only a personal sense, but rather that it is essential to the inner word to carry such a real relation inasmuch as it must be *expressum ab alio*. In the *De Veritate*, therefore, St. Thomas will countenance the essential use, but only as improper. For proper use, in the very nature of things, demands that whatever is of the essential properties of a thing be left intact.

As for the *In Boethii de Trinitate*, it is necessary to repeat the caution mentioned just a moment ago. The single reply to an objection in the fourth article of the first question amounts only to rejection of the inner word as an instrument for the philosophical demonstration of the first procession, and *per se* implies nothing whatsoever for the use of the *verbum* principle in the quite different context of doctrinal elaboration, in which, and according to the emphatically declared position of the treatise itself, faith in divine revelation is necessarily presupposed — presupposed, moreover, not merely as the matter to be treated and the starting point in the discussion, but as the primary internal energy generating all subsequent conclusions.

For the rest, on the basis of what was noted above with regard to the first question — St. Thomas' idea of the inner word as such — the more reasonable supposition is that with regard to the second question also — St. Thomas' mind on the rôle of the inner word in positive theological exposition — what Aquinas thought on the matter at the time he composed the *In Boethii de Trinitate* was in all probability close to what he actually wrote down in *De Veritate*.

In any case, so far as the second question is concerned, the profound evolution that had taken place in St. Thomas' theological conception of the divine generation, and precisely because of the analytical key provided by a new and carefully developed theory of intellectual emanation, can only be appreciated in its full perspective by comparing the account in the fourth book of the *Contra Gentiles* with that in the first book of the *Sentences*, written about ten years earlier. The further significance of this evolution, and the true nature of the *Contra Gentiles* presentation as theological understanding achieved through the process of illuminated rational analysis, will be brought out more completely and more clearly in the following sections of the present study — beginning immediately with its *pari passu* treatment in the course of the third and last question.

3. *The problem of a still further evolution in St. Thomas' thought, which would touch directly on the matter of apologetical demonstration*

There remains, then, the third question, the one most important for the purposes of the present study, but whose solution, in the mind of the writer, could not be undertaken until the two previous questions had been carefully distinguished and handled apart.

The development through which Aquinas' notion of the inner word passed — from the *Sentences* on into the *In Boethii de Trinitate* and *De Veritate*, and up to the fourth book *Contra Gentiles* — has already been traced. The parallel process of development through which his theological doctrine on the divine generation as built around this notion of the inner word passed, during the same period, has also been traced. But what is to be said on the point of the strictly apologetical question ?

As St. Thomas' position on the *verbum cordis* developed, and with it, his theological exposition upon the divine generation, was there also a progressive and parallel change of attitude toward the problem of a priori demonstration of the first trinitarian procession ? Still more particularly, was the general rejection of such philosophical attempts in the *Sentences*, and the specific rejection of the argument derived from the inner word in the *In Boethii de Trinitate*, set aside, at least *ipso facto*, by the treatment given to the divine generation in the eleventh chapter of *Contra Gentiles IV* ?

In the *Sentences*, speaking of whether the philosophers could have attained knowledge of the Trinity of Persons, St. Thomas asserted that such knowledge lay quite beyond the competence of unaided reason. He explained that natural reason knows God only through the knowledge it can obtain from His creatures, and this knowledge from creatures manifests only the divine essence, not the plurality of Persons.

The reach of unaided human reason, therefore, does not extend beyond God's nature and attributes. But is there not in the human soul a clear image (*imago expressa*) of the Trinity ? Even in the *Sentences*, St. Thomas confronted this objection. His reply, however, was that this image, whatever its merits, was at least wholly inadequate to the task of an a priori demonstration. This image is called express only in comparison with the inferior likeness of a mere vestige. At the same time, it should be kept in mind that, when writing the *Sentences*, Aquinas had not yet developed his doctrine of the inner word, nor, consequently, his explanation of the divine generation precisely in terms of the analogy this doctrine would later afford him. In this sense, therefore, the crucial problem had not yet arisen.

What, then, of the more specific rejection in the commentary *In Boethii de Trinitate?* In the text itself — for the sake of clarity, it is worth repeating — the objection reads as follows : the fact that God is intelligent, is accessible to natural reason. But from this it follows that God should conceive an inner word, for this is common to every intelligent being.[83] To this argument, Aquinas replies : in God, the

---

[83] " Praeterea, quod deus sit intelligens, ratione naturali haberi potest. Sed ex hoc quod est intelligens sequitur quod verbum concipiat, quia hoc est omni intelligenti commune. Ergo naturali ratione cognosci potest quod sit filii generatio et eadem ratione amoris processio. " *In Boet. de Trin.*, q. 1, a. 4, obj. 6.

intelligent and the understood is the same. It is not necessary, therefore, from the mere fact that God is intelligent,
to postulate in God some concept really distinct from Himself,
as there is in us. But the Trinity of Persons requires real
distinction. [84]

The seriousness of the problem which a too hasty reading of
this objection with its reply might well occasion can be appreciated from the following transposition. Is not St. Thomas saying
here, that is equivalently : it is not essential to intellect that
there proceed in intellect a concept really distinct from intellect ? And later, in the fourth book *Contra Gentiles*, will he
not affirm precisely the opposite, saying, again equivalently :
it is essential to intellect as such that there proceed in intellect a concept really distinct from intellect ?

From such a transposition, one could easily argue that,
in his later works, St. Thomas came to reverse his original
position and offered, if not a strictly apodictic proof for the
first procession, at least its very close imitation — and all
this revealing a cast of mind in which the ideal of Anselm's
rationes necessariae had eventually triumphed.

In the writer's judgment, however, the proposed transposition fails to take note of the fact that the rejection in
the commentary *In Boethii de Trinitate* had been made in the
terms and larger context of an explicitly stated apologetical
question, whereas the acceptance of the really distinct inner
word as a universal or transcendental law of spiritual being
in the fourth book *Contra Gentiles* was made in the non-apol-
ogetical terms and context of explanatory theology. In the
first instance, the point of view, both in the objection and
in St. Thomas' reply, was what could or could not be attained
by the light of pure reason ; in the second, the point of view
was rather what could be attained by theological reason in a
scientific process whose first principles were taken from Christian faith in the divine revelation, and, more significantly
still, according to a doctrine so far from having been as yet
undiscovered or ignored in the *In Boethii de Trinitate*, that
it was the main positive conclusion of the treatise.

---

[84] " Ad sextum dicendum quod in deo idem est intelligens et
intellectum, et ideo non oportet quod ex hoc quod intelligit ponatur
in ipso aliquid conceptum realiter distinctum ab ipso, sicut est in nobis. Trinitas autem personarum requirit realem distinctionem. " *In
Boet. de Trin.*, q. 1, a. 4, ad 6m.

The precise subject under discussion in the fourth article of the first question in the Boethius commentary was whether the human mind, left to its own resources, could attain to the knowledge of the Trinity — "utrum ad divinae trinitatis cognitionem mens humana pervenire per se sufficiat." The sixth objection did not contend that, since God understood, He must conceive a word, inasmuch as this is common to all understanding, but rather that, from the fact of God's understanding, which is accessible to natural reason, the same natural reason could know that God must conceive a word, since natural reason sees that this is common to all understanding.

Actually, when St. Thomas wrote "quia hoc est omni intelligenti commune," he did not add, in this particular six word phrase, something to the effect 'uti naturali ratione cognoscitur'. But this is unmistakably his meaning ; the words with which he began his conclusion immediately following, "ergo naturali ratione cognosci potest," were clearly intended to situate the entire argument of the objection, and therefore each of its essential component parts, in the framework of a purely rational process. Otherwise, considering the apologetical question of the article in which the objection appears, the objection itself would have been simply without point.

But the style of St. Thomas' reply has to be examined even more closely. As a Christian who accepted the mystery of the Divine Trinity, Aquinas does not say, of course, that God does not conceive a Word ! Nor does he say that, from the fact God understands, it follows that He conceives — even must conceive — an inner word. Nor finally does he say that, from the fact God understands, it follows that He conceives an inner word really distinct from God understanding. But someone will object : that is *exactly* what he says !

The distinction here is a lot less subtle than might appear. Aquinas certainly intends his reply to meet the objection. It will not meet the objection, however, unless the " ideo non oportet ex hoc " is meant to be understood of purely natural reason. Moreover, if the " ideo non oportet " were meant to include what was known from revelation as well, the reply would be clearly erroneous, and even, at least in large part, heretical.

Even in the *Sentences*, as already seen, St. Thomas accepted that the intellectual word — granted his precision of thought did not then go much beyond such a generic notion — was a proper description of the Son of God. Further, if to this evidence from the *Sentences* that from the *De Veritate* be added as well, it is highly probable that at the time he composed his *In Boethii de Trinitate*, St. Thomas already considered each and every negation he attaches here to " ideo non oportet " a matter of faith. What St. Thomas is saying, therefore, is simply that unaided natural reason cannot argue to the existence in God of a really distinct concept from the fact — which is accessible to natural reason — that God understands. And he gives the reason : because in God the intelligent and the understood are the same — " in deo idem est intelligens et intellectum. "

This, of course, is true even in the light of revelation : God the Son and God the Father are the same, not in Person, but in essence. But as Aquinas never failed to insist, right from the first pages of the *Sentences*, unaided reason can attain knowledge of God only as He is in His essence. The point he makes in his reply, therefore, is that unaided reason considering God's intelligence is forced by every principle to which it has access to affirm the perfect unity and simplicity of the divine understanding.

It will have been noticed, too, that in his reply St. Thomas does not say precisely that pure reason is incompetent to posit a word in God — which was the mode of expression used in the objection — but rather that pure reason is incompetent to posit in God a word, or concept, really distinct from God understanding. It seems this is a case of going immediately to the heart of the matter. Theoretically, Aquinas might have constructed his answer in two steps. In the first, he might have said that reason could postulate the existence of a word as synonymous with ' God understood '. In the second, he might have gone on to say that such a word would be purely essential therefore, in no way distinct, so far as unaided reason could see, from ' God understanding '.

Though the writer has no wish to urge the matter, perhaps the fact Aquinas did not construct his reply in this fashion can be taken as a sort of confirmatory argument against separating the *verbum* doctrine actually found in the *De Veritate* from what was most likely St. Thomas' thought on the same point while composing the *In Boethii de Trinitate*. For there is the suggestion that even here in the *In Boethii de*

Trinitate, he would have accepted the really distinct procession as at least one of the essential properties of the inner word as such — as he has already been seen to have done in the *De Veritate*.

The conclusions drawn from the analysis of this objection with its reply, however, rest on a much more solid foundation than the uncertain inference just mentioned. It is not a question of arguing : the Boethius commentary must have been close in time to *De Veritate* ; but, far from there being, in *De Veritate*, a rejection of the really distinct procession of the inner word as such, this point is rather positively and explicitly declared ; therefore, a substantially similar attitude may be presumed for the unstated background of *In Boethii de Trinitate*. In confirmation, there is also the fact that Aquinas passed immediately to the problem of real distinction in constructing the reply to the sixth objection.

In the writer's opinion, this argument would actually possess considerable value. Nevertheless, the more important and more certain proof that the passage was never intended to reject really distinct procession as essential to the inner word as such — a rejection that would then be neatly reversed in *Contra Gentiles IV* — lies in the context of the *In Boethii de Trinitate* itself.

The treatise is methodological. St. Thomas' deliberate intention is to discuss the positive and negative, or restrictive, aspects of human knowledge of the divine. As for the latter, he is at great pains, not merely to state and emphasize the fact of these restrictions, but to explain in minute detail the reasons why. The human mind cannot know God *per formam propriam*, nor even through the *forma effectus* adequate to express the power and reality of the divine cause.

In fact, in this life, because of the human intellect's dependence on phantasm, it can never look upon the divine form — not even when elevated through the gift of infused faith. Man can know, therefore, only 'that' God is, not 'what' He is. And even in the very fruitful knowledge man can achieve through philosophical principles and strictly scientific discourse — wherein the *quod est Deus* that cannot be known directly and *per se* this side of the beatific vision is to some remote, but nonetheless very real extent, supplied for through the *via causalitatis, remotionis, et excessus* — such rational processes never become the reason on account of which man at-

12

tains to the certainty of the *articuli fidei*, but remain always only the instrument for imperfect understanding with faith and divine revelation necessarily presupposed, and with faith and divine revelation the dominant energy in generating subsequent theological conclusions.

It is in this context, and precisely at the moment when St. Thomas is preoccupied, not with the positive, but with the restrictive, theme, that he poses the question whether unaided reason can penetrate to the Trinity of Persons, and, in the course of the very same article, proceeds to reject the proof or demonstration of the first procession based, not on what is actually essential to the inner word as such, but on what purely natural reason knows to be essential to the inner word as such. For this is the only point of view taken up in the immediate and larger context in which the rejection is found, and the only point of view in which St. Thomas' negative reply would have any force or meaning against the objection precisely as he himself had proposed it.

Unfortunately, Aquinas did not include in his Boethius commentary the systematic and scientific theological elaboration of trinitarian doctrine for which the positive theme developed concurrently in the same treatise had so well prepared. Nevertheless, it is interesting to see how the discussion in the fourth book *Contra Gentiles*, in which St. Thomas elucidates the mystery of the divine generation on analogy from the inner word of human understanding, follows out the methodological principles set down in the *In Boethii de Trinitate*, and does so without contradicting in the slightest degree the negative or restrictive laws that had been established in the very same treatise.

As seen earlier, the purpose and scope of the *Contra Gentiles* caused St. Thomas to limit his treatment of the Trinity to the primary formularies, those, moreover, that had figured prominently in the trinitarian and christological heresies, and later, when speaking of the *Summa*, there will be occasion to explain how this limitation would make the *Contra Gentiles* fall rather short of the *Summa* as an achievement of theological science — not merely from the point of view of detail, but also, and more significantly, from the point of view of order and synthesis. At the same time, however, even in the *Contra Gentiles*, the overall orientation and movement of doctrinal development represents the working-out in practice of the theological ideal espoused and defined in the *In Boethii de Trinitate.*

In the introductory chapter to the fourth book, St. Thomas proposed to treat of the mystery of the Trinity, among others, according as God had revealed Himself in the Sacred Scriptures, and to defend these articles of Christian faith, relying on the same testimony of the Scriptures as well as appealing to the fundamental principles of reason which at least could not be contradicted, against false and heretical doctrines. He observes, moreover, in fact emphasizes, that what he is discussing now, is that which can be known exclusively through God's revelation. Thus, Aquinas adds, repeating the positive theme of the *In Boethii de Trinitate,* it is the Sacred Scriptures themselves that will stand as the quasi-principles throughout the process of systematic development.

He begins, then, with a concise statement of the divine paternity, sonship and generation as contained in the clear message of Scripture. Next, he proceeds to list the more important heresies — the Photinian, Sabellian, and Arian — which grew out of an erroneous interpretation of Scripture, but which in turn stemmed from certain rational or philosophical assumptions imposing forced and tendentious exegesis. Finally, Aquinas goes on to refute this exegesis and restate orthodox Christian belief — relying throughout on what he considers the authentic message of the biblical text, confirmed by Christian tradition — by the Fathers, Augustine mostly, and by the rejection on the part of the Church — for this is at least implicit in the opposed terms of his dialogue — of the doctrines of the heretics.

In the tenth chapter, Aquinas summarizes what he has shown thus far. It is the unmistakable testimony of Sacred Scripture upon the divine generation that the Father and Son, while two distinct Persons, are still one and the same God, with the same identical nature or essence. He goes on to explain, nevertheless, how such an idea is quite remote from anything in the realm of nature that is immediately accessible to human reason. He then enumerates several of the particular difficulties reason might have in attempting to reconcile the complex notion of two supposits in a single, undivided nature. But he postpones a solution to these difficulties until after he has completed the lengthy positive exposition in chapter eleven.

St. Thomas begins this positive exposition from a point that appears at first sight to be quite far afield — with a discussion of different modes and grades of emanation as varying directly with the status different classes of things are seen to enjoy in the hierarchical universe of being. He even introduces this discussion with the words " principium hujus intentionis hinc sumere oportet. "

To understand these words, however, as meaning that in this eleventh chapter there will be a radical change of approach or that what had previously been treated in the light of faith on the testimony of the Sacred Scriptures would now be treated anew, from a completely different focus, from the light of pure reason and the principles of philosophy, is at best a serious oversimplification.

The *principium*, the starting point, in this passage is the point of origin or remote source only in the methodological sense of what first must be understood, defined, clarified, as the necessary background for the ensuing discussion. It may also be 'first', if the whole passage is taken in its ensemble, as indicating the *priora quoad se*, in the sense that the ultimate radix of the Son's generation from the Father is, by theological reduction, proved to be simply emanation within the divinity. In the writer's judgment, however, this latter is not perfectly clear from the construction of the passage in the text, and would more profitably be discussed later when the build-up of the exposition in the *Contra Gentiles* can be compared with the parallel, but more mature, build-up in the *Pars Prima*.

For the immediate purpose, the point that must be brought out with all possible clarity is that in no sense of the idea can Aquinas' style of speaking in this introductory expression be taken to mean that the philosophical account of emanation will here and now supplant the *principia fidei* as the first principles, understood epistemologically, for the theological exposition that is to follow. For not only were the *principia fidei*, exclusively moreover, assigned the rôle of first principles in scientific theology in the *In Boethii de Trinitate*, but they were explicitly confirmed in this same rôle in the *Contra Gentiles* as well.

Throughout the earlier portions of the fourth book, Aquinas has repeated again and again that the only source of human knowledge of divine mysteries is the authority of God's

revelation. Again, once he has outlined his doctrine of emanation in the first seven paragraphs of chapter eleven, he
does not proceed to deduce from these rational principles the
existence in God of a distinct Divine Word, but announces
that this philosophical structure will now serve to elucidate
how the divine generation — whose certainty is presupposed
from some other source, being the obvious implication — is
to be understood, to the degree that such understanding is
possible — " His igitur consideratis, utcumque concipere possumus qualiter sit divina generatio accipienda. " Again, at
the very end of chapter thirteen, when he has completely
finished his positive exposition, St. Thomas will sum up his
treatment with the words : so much there is, then, that we
are able somehow to conceive, on the basis of what we have
been taught by the Sacred Scriptures, of the divine generation
and the power of God's only-begotten Son — " Haec igitur
sunt quae de generatione divina, et de virtute Unigeniti Filii
Dei, ex Sacris Scripturis edocti, utcumque concipere possumus. "

The philosophical medium St. Thomas employs in this
passage, therefore, is introduced in strict accordance with the
principles laid down on the matter in the *In Boethii de Trinitate*. Philosophy, he had affirmed in the earlier treatise,
may exercise a valuable rôle in theology : not that articles
of faith will owe their certainty to the findings of philosophy,
but that philosophy may be used either to demonstrate the
preambles to faith, or to elucidate what is already believed
(*ad notificandum*), or to refute errors brought against the faith.
It is the second use, *ad notificandum*, that Aquinas has applied
here to the divine generation.

Accepting the testimony of Scripture on the divine generation, St. Thomas proceeds to see how this generation would
have to be understood. He follows the method of systematic
exclusion : obviously not in the sense that inanimate bodies
act one upon the other ; nor in the sense of vegetative or
animal generation ; nor in the sense of sensory cognition —
for all these modes of emanation involve manifest potency and
imperfection. There remains, then, only intellectual or spiritual emanation. But this also has degrees. In human beings,
the origin of intellectual activity is in sense. In angels, at
least the known intention is not drawn into perfect fusion
with the angelic substance. But in God, whatever intellectual

emanation there would be, the understood would be utterly
one with the divine essence — for in God, to know and to
be are the same.

As a medium towards the understanding of the divine
generation, therefore, the theory of intellectual emanation
will at least not prove offensive to God's utter unity and simplicity — and, recalling, no doubt, the trend observed in the
great heresies he has been refuting, it is the same divine unity
Aquinas is first careful to protect.

But what is this presence of the understood in the one
understanding? In human beings, St. Thomas continues, the
intentio intellecta is that which intellect conceives in itself of
the reality being understood. It is distinct from both the
object of understanding and the substance of intellect. It is
the likeness conceived in intellect of what which is known.
It is what external words immediately signify; and hence it
is called ' inner word '.

In God, of course, there cannot be these distinctions:
in God, to be, to understand, to be understood, must all be
identified with God Himself. Yet, it is of the nature of understanding as such, that the understood be in the one understanding. In God's self-understanding, therefore, there exists
in God understanding the Word of God, or God understood.

It should be noted, however, that at this point St. Thomas
is not at least demonstrating the existence of the Divine Word.
The question of real distinction has not yet been introduced,
and even as far back as the *De Veritate*, he had determined
that use of inner word without this real distinction was not
proper usage at all. For the moment, St. Thomas focuses
rather on the element of unequivocal identity, and from this
perspective proceeds to integrate into his intellectualist structure the truths that the Word must be eternal, consubstantial,
in every respect truly God. Natural reason itself, of course,
could prove that whatever emanated within the divine nature
would have to be eternal, consubstantial, God. But even
here, St. Thomas situates his conclusions in the scriptural
frame of citations from St. John's Gospel.

At last, the real distinction is introduced. In God, St.
Thomas goes on, the components of being are not distinct.
Nevertheless, whatever truly pertains to the formal perfections of these realities must be assigned to God. God as subsistent does not exist in others; as essence, is something;

as existence, is in act.   So also, while in God, the intelligent,
the act of understanding and the understood, must be absolutely identical, still, whatever pertains strictly to the formal
perfections of these realities too must be assigned to Him.
But it pertains to the formal perfection of the inner word as
such (*de ratione eius*) that it proceed from the intelligent
upon the act of understanding. This is true, because the inner
word is the quasi-term of intellectual operation, what the
intellect conceives or forms in itself of what is understood.
In God, therefore, the Word of God must be referred or related to God understanding as to Him from Whom it is (" sicut ad eum a quo est ").

But is this not a rational demonstration of the first trinitarian procession ?

In the writer's judgment, the difficulty presented by St.
Thomas' manner of approach in this passage is far more apparent than real.   A more serious problem of interpretation
could arise, perhaps, in the *Summa*, where there is at least
the semblance of deduction from two principles of pure reason.
For at that later point in his teaching career, St. Thomas'
approach will be as follows : whoever understands, by this
fact alone that he does understand, there proceeds something
within him that is the conception of the thing understood.[85]

From the immediate context of the same article in the
Summa, one could easily supply the ' minor ' : but God understands.   In such a case, one of the premises is certainly a
principle accessible to pure reason :   that God understands.
If the other premise — in every act of understanding there
is procession of concept or word — is also taken to be a principle accessible to pure reason, one might well ask why such an
approach did not involve, automatically, some sort of proof
or demonstration for the a priori philosophical necessity of the
Divine Word.

In the present passage, however, in the text of the fourth
book *Contra Gentiles*, Aquinas does not argue, or even seem
to argue, from what is proper or essential to understanding

---

[85] " Quicumque enim intelligit, ex hoc ipso quod intelligit, in eo
procedit aliquid intra ipsum, quod est conceptio rei intellectae, ex eius
notitia procedens. "   *S. T.*, *I*, q. 27, a. 1c, par. 3 ad fin. (The paragraph is indicated according to the Geyer critical edition, which co-
vers questions 27 through 32 of the ' *de Trinitate* ' in *Pars Prima*.)

as such, but rather from what is proper or essential to the inner word as such. The distinction here is of no small moment, as failure to observe it might lead someone who had already concluded that there was rational demonstration from the nature of intellect in the *Summa* to look a bit too hastily for adumbrations of the same general approach in the *Contra Gentiles*.

Pure reason knows, or at least can know, that in God there is intellect and understanding. If, then, it should be claimed that reason can also know that procession of a really distinct inner word is essential to intellect and understanding as such, it would certainly seem that the first trinitarian procession had been demonstrated. The existence of the Divine Word would have been concluded from the existence and essential properties of intellect. The approach, on the other hand, that argues, not from what is necessary to intellect, but from what is necessary to inner word, does not attempt to prove the existence of this inner word in a given case, but rather what must pertain to this inner word once its existence is presupposed. Logically, therefore, the question whether or not existence of the inner word is presupposed in fact, and if so, on what grounds, would be a matter still to be determined.

The issue, however, is decided on the basis of more positive evidence than logical consistency. Throughout this tract on the divine generation, Aquinas has been speaking explicitly of a mystery of faith which man knows, not from any exercise of rational inquiry, but solely from the revealed word of God. He has pointed out the chief passages of Sacred Scripture giving formal testimony to these particular articles of Christian belief — generation, fatherhood and sonship in the Divinity. He has discussed, in some detail, the great heresies touching upon the same doctrine in the attempt to distort and corrupt the certitude of faith, and he has rejected these false claims by appealing to the authentic message of Sacred Scripture, the authority of the Fathers, and, at least implicitly, the authority of the Church as such in its condemnations of the heresiarchs.

This done, Aquinas then went on to present a lengthy and purely positive doctrinal account. The immediate occasion was, of course, the desire to create an organized, systematic background against which he could give a more satisfac-

tory reply to the rational objections proposed in the tenth
chapter. In the writer's judgment, however, it was Aquinas'
further and deeper purpose to give this positive account also
for its own sake. The exposition contained in the eleventh
chapter, taken together with the complementary material in
the two chapters immediately following, makes up roughly
a third of the entire tract on the generation of the Son. Its
position, moreover, is climactic — structured around the ideal
of that *veritas* against which there can be no successful challenge, the ideal explicitly set in focus by the concluding words
of chapter ten and the opening words of chapter fourteen.[86]

Nevertheless, far from losing sight of the utter dependence
upon divine revelation and the authority of Christian faith
that had dominated his treatment of the biblical testimonies
and the trinitarian heresies, the systematic theological exposition itself preserved, as already seen, the same strict enclosure
within the *principia fidei*, as being the limited understanding
of this mystery that human reason, not as left to its own
resources, but precisely as instructed by the Sacred Scriptures,
can achieve.

Precisely what this meant for St. Thomas, moreover, and
the clear proof that his exposition in no way entailed any attempt, however qualified, to demonstrate the existence of the
Divine Word, is seen in the manner he executes his transition
from the philosophical discussion of emanation in general to
the use and application he plans to make of this doctrine in
theological understanding of the divine generation.

On the basis of what has just been considered, St. Thomas
begins, we are able in some fashion to conceive how the divine
generation is to be taken — " qualiter sit divina generatio
accipienda. " He does not say : on the basis of what we
have just considered, we can now ask ' utrum in divinis generatio sit ponenda ', and much less ' quamobrem in divinis generatio sit ponenda '. He says simply : on the basis of what

---

[86] " Haec igitur et similia sunt ex quibus aliqui, divinorum my-
steria propria ratione metiri volentes, divinam generationem impu-
gnare nituntur. Sed quia veritas in seipsa fortis est, et nulla impugnatione convellitur, oportet intendere ad ostendendum quod veritas
fidei ratione superari non possit. " *C. G.*, *IV*, c. 10, 14. " Quia vero
veritas omnem falsitatem excludit et dubietatem dissolvit, in promptu
iam fit ea dissolvere quae circa generationem divinam difficultatem
afferre videbantur. " *ibid.*, c. 14, 1.

we have seen, we are able to understand to some degree how the divine generation, whose existence we know with the certitude, not of reason, but of faith, must be taken. If there is generation in God, this is how we should have to understand that generation.

The rest of the development confirms that this is exactly St. Thomas' point of view : quite clearly, he continues, the divine generation could not possibly be understood in terms of what is proper to the action of one body upon another in inanimate creation, nor in terms of what is proper to generation in plants and animals, nor in terms of what is proper to sensory cognition.

Finally, when he has observed that generation in God could only be understood on analogy from what is proper to strictly intellectual emanation in the higher creatures, he first explains carefully that the altereity or otherness involved in divine intelligence, could not, and must not, diminish the unequivocal oneness and simplicity of God's being — the *intentio* thus emanating must remain identical, on the absolute level, with intellect, act of intellect, nature and existence. Only then does St. Thomas begin to consider the real distinction of this *intentio*, or, to use the synonym he now introduces, this *verbum*.

But what is his approach at this last and crucial point ? That some sort of real distinction between inner word and its corresponding intelligible source is demanded by rational or philosophical analysis of intellect ? Not in the least. St. Thomas does not begin from what is required of intellect as such, much less on purely rational or philosophical grounds. His approach is rather that of the already confirmed hypothesis, thus continuing in strictest parallel the same methodological focus he has maintained throughout the previous stages of his exposition.

Earlier, when Aquinas concluded his discussion or analysis of emanation in general, and began to treat of its application to the theological understanding of the divine generation, he effected his transition in the manner noted above, saying, equivalently : with this philosophical analysis as vehicle for scientific theological explanation, we can now see to some extent how generation in God, if such exists, would have to be understood. Right now, he preserves exactly the same focus, inserting only the term of generation — the Word — for

the act : extending our explanatory structure, we can now
see that the Word of God, should such exist, and be Word
in the proper sense, must possess or include whatever is truly
essential (*de ratione*) to inner word as such, and therefore
must proceed from ' God understanding ' upon the divine act
of understanding as ' God understood '.

But the double hypothesis is already verified. That there
is in God generation of the Son from the Father, has been
supposed throughout as the authentic message of Christian
revelation. And Word of God is simply another name for
the Son of God. Though the formula ' eo Filius quo verbum ;
eo Verbum quo Filius ' is not employed, the immediate context,
the successive citations from St. John's Gospel, and the way
the doctrine *de Verbo* is developed in the passages immediately
following, leave no doubt as to the complete identification
St. Thomas wishes to be presumed at this point between Word
and Son.

But no less clearly does St. Thomas also wish it to be
assumed that Word, when spoken of God, is intended in the
strict or proper sense. For the Word is personal as identified
with the Son. This, moreover, has been St. Thomas' supposition since as far back as the fourth question *De Veritate*, and is
implied in the very nature of the argument constructed on
what pertains to the formal perfection of inner word as such.
Finally, it is the only possible inference to be drawn from the
strictly formal interpretation St. Thomas makes of the use
of the term in the first chapter of St. John. Thus, in St.
Thomas' mind, not only the existence of a Word in God, but
also that this Word is to be taken in the proper, not metaphorical, sense of the term, is a matter of Christian faith
rooted in the clear testimony of the Sacred Scriptures.

Since, then, Christian faith bears witness to the Word
of God, and Word as used in the proper sense, it follows —
this is St. Thomas' actual approach — that Christian theology
must assign or attribute to the Word of God whatever is
essential to the formal perfection of inner word as such. But
it is essential to inner word that it proceed upon the act of
understanding from the principle of understanding as from its
correspondent source : " sicuti ab eo a quo est. " In brief,
therefore, it is not the existence of the Divine Word, nor its
proper predication, that is the object of St. Thomas' demonstration, but rather the manner of its procession, to be conclud-

ed from what is essential to inner word as such, once the
existence and proper predication of the Divine Word is already supposed — supposed, moreover, not from any principles of rational or philosophical origin, but exclusively from
divine revelation.

In the period, therefore, extending from the first book
of the *Sentences* through the fourth book of the *Contra Gentiles*, it is certainly true that St. Thomas developed his notion
of the *verbum cordis*, or inner word, and also, relying on this
newly developed theory, his strictly theological and analytical
exposition of the divine generation. But it is not true that
he consequently changed his formerly negative stand on the
question of apologetical demonstration of a priori necessity.

The use of the *verbum* analogy in *Contra Gentiles IV* is
in perfect, point by point accord with the teaching on the
nature, scope and method of theological science in *In Boethii
de Trinitate*. Thus, with the revealed mystery clearly and
explicitly presupposed, and with infused faith guiding illuminated rational analysis throughout, St. Thomas' sole intent
and preoccupation in the lengthy positive exposition beginning
in chapter eleven is simply to see how what has *de facto* been
revealed might, in some limited but real way, be understood.
Man does not enjoy in this life knowledge of God *per formam
Dei*. He can know God, therefore, only in the substitutional,
or vicarious, manner *per formam effectus*. Nevertheless, drawing in his understanding from created similitudes and analogies
— in this instance, of the *verbum cordis*, or inner word — he is
able to conceive in some limited degree — again, not through
pure reason, or purely philosophical analysis, but through
enlightened reason, and strictly theological analysis — how
the mystery itself, the generation of the Son of God, has to
be ' taken ' (*accipi, accipienda*) or ' understood ' (*intelligi, intelligenda*).

In this process of theological analysis, moreover, there
is simply no question of proving or demonstrating the original mystery. Nor is there the slightest evidence in the
text that such proof or demonstration, even if not intended,
was to some extent nevertheless automatically involved in
the rational structure employed by St. Thomas in the course
of his theological exposition.

It might be objected, of course : but what of the rational, or at least apparently rational, demonstration which is

ipso facto involved in Aquinas' use of the principle that procession of inner word is essential to intellectual being as such ? As was shown above, however, this objection would be premature with regard to the account of the divine generation as given in *Contra Gentiles IV*. The principle in question will be introduced only in the *Pars Prima*, the *Compendium Theologiae*, and in passages of the *Quaestiones Disputatae De Potentia* belonging to this somewhat later period. When it is introduced, as will be seen in the third part of the present study, it must be interpreted, on the strict evidence of the text itself, not as a purely rational or philosophical principle, but as an unequivocally theological principle taking its place in the ' argument' according to the explicit intention and design of the *ordo doctrinae*, the order of understanding in synthesis. This latter problem has not yet arisen, however, in the text of *Contra Gentiles IV*.

IV. The Parallel Treatment of the Procession of the Holy Spirit

It remains, then, to indicate at least in more summary form, how Aquinas maintains the same explanatory perspective as he goes on to treat the second trinitarian procession, the procession of the Holy Spirit.

St. Thomas begins with a concise basic statement of the mystery : according to the authoritative message of Sacred Scripture, there is in the divinity, not only the Father and the Son, but also the Holy Spirit. With regard to this same Spirit, Scripture also speaks in terms of a certain ' procession '.[87] Then there is a slight change from the order followed in discussing the generation of the Son. Instead of exposing

---

[87] " Divinae autem Scripturae auctoritas non solum nobis in divinis Patrem et Filium annuntiat, sed his duobus Spiritum Sanctum connumerat. Dicit enim Dominus, *Matthaei* ult. : *Euntes docete omnes gentes, baptizantes eos in nomine Patris et Filii et Spiritus Sancti* ; et *I Ioannis* V 7 : *Tres sunt qui testimonium dant in caelo, Pater, Verbum et Spiritus Sanctus*. Huius etiam Spiritus Sancti processionem quandam Sacra Scriptura commemorat. Dicit enim *Ioannis* XV 26 : *Cum venerit Paraclitus, quem ego, mittam vobis a Patre, Spiritum veritatis, qui a Patre procedit, ille testimonium perhibebit de me.* " *C. G.*, *IV*, c. 15. The entire chapter consists in these few lines.

right away the revealed doctrine of the Spirit's divine nature, St. Thomas interposes a brief account of the Arian and Macedonian heresies.[88]

Some there were, he notes, who considered the Holy Spirit a creature, though higher than other creatures. In support of such a notion, they made appeal to various passages of both the Old and New Testament, where the Spirit seems to be understood as inferior to, and subject to, God. He will speak what He has heard from another. He will be sent, given, by the Father. He will ask on behalf of men. In still other passages, when Christ is speaking of His own life and relations with the Father, the Spirit appears left out or excluded.[89]

Then there is the dilemma of theological inference. If the Spirit is truly God, He must have the divine nature. As proceeding from the Father, He would, moreover, receive this divine nature from the Father. But this would mean the Spirit was generated, and therefore Himself Son — which is contrary to faith.[90] If, on the other hand, the Spirit is not generated, it follows that there must be two modes of communication of the divine nature. But it is incompatible with any known nature that it be communicated in more than one way. If, therefore, the Spirit does not receive the divine nature through generation, He does not receive it at all, and consequently is not truly God.[91]

Nevertheless, St. Thomas begins his reply, it is the unmistakable testimony of Sacred Scripture that the Holy Spirit is in fact God.[92] For it is to the Holy Spirit, that the human temple is dedicated, and the fulness of latreutic worship paid.[93] He is the source of human sanctification, justice and restored life.[94] He is the Spirit who comprehends all things, the secrets of God and men ; Who speaks through the prophets, reveals the mysteries of God, inspires and instructs the hearts

---

[88] *C. G.*, *IV*, c. 16.
[89] *C. G.*, *IV*, c. 16, 1-10.
[90] *C. G.*, *IV*, c. 16, 12.
[91] *C. G.*, *IV*, c. 16, 13.
[92] " Ostenditur autem evidentibus Scripturae testimoniis quod Spiritus Sanctus sit Deus.. " *C. G.*, *IV*, c. 17, 1.
[93] *C. G.*, *IV*, c. 17, 1 and 2.
[94] *C. G.*, *IV*, c. 17, 3-5.

of men.[95] He it is Who dwells in the souls of the just, and is the cause of adoptive sonship.[96]

Finally, anticipating the objection that such *opera Dei* would be assigned to the Holy Spirit, not as to God acting in His own right, but as to His creaturely minister, St. Thomas concludes with the text of St. Paul (I Cor 12 : 6) : " Divisiones operationum sunt, idem vero Deus qui operatur omnia in omnibus . . . . Haec omnia operatur unus atque idem Spiritus, dividens singulis prout vult. " Aquinas notes that the Apostle not only attributes to the Spirit the operation he had just a moment before attributed to God, but characterizes this operation of the Spirit as " pro suae voluntatis arbitrio." [97]

One further point, however, has to be treated before St. Thomas will propose the doctrine of the *processio Spiritus* in systematic form. Some did not deny the reality or divine nature of the Spirit, but rather His subsistent personality. For such as these, Aquinas notes, the Holy Spirit is either the very divinity of the Father and Son, or even some created accidental perfection wherewith God would endow the human mind — wisdom perhaps, or charity.[98]

The latter notion, he dismisses briefly. Accidental forms do not properly operate, but rather the one possessing them, who operates in virtue of these forms according to his pleasure. One could not say of such forms what must be said of the Holy Spirit, Whom Scripture describes as operating " pro suae arbitrio voluntatis, " and also as being Himself the cause of the accidental perfections in question.[99] But it is no less repugnant to the scriptural tradition that the name Holy Spirit should be used to designate the essence of the Father and Son, and thus be personally distinguished from neither of them. For one could never say of the divine essence what is said of the Holy Spirit : that He proceeds from the Father, and receives from the Son, and is, moreover, one with both the Father and Son in essence or nature.[100]

St. Thomas concludes this chapter with a brief rejection of the attempt to separate from the *Spiritus Sanctus* the *Spi-*

---

[95] *C. G., IV*, c. 17, 7-14, 18 and 19.
[96] *C. G., IV*, c. 17, 15 and 21.
[97] *C. G., IV*, c. 17, 23.
[98] *C. G., IV*, c. 18, 1.
[99] *C. G., IV*, c. 18, 2 and 3.
[100] *C. G., IV*, c. 18, 4-6.

ritus Dei, and the further attempt to attract the inhabitation of the divine Spirit to the purely finite mode of possession or indwelling spoken of in Scripture with reference to the devil.[101]

With this, Aquinas feels that the existence, true divinity and subsistent personality of the Holy Spirit as revealed by God and contained in the authoritative testimonies of the Sacred Scriptures has been sufficiently manifested. It remains to see, then — so St. Thomas introduces his theological exposition — how both the divinely subsistent Person of the Spirit, and His real distinction from the Father and Son, known to us from the teaching of Scripture (" Scripturarum testimoniis edocti "), is to be taken or understood (" qualiter accipi debeat "), that thus this belief might be defended against the challenge of infidels.[102] The perfect parallelism between the " qualiter accipi debeat " of this transition and the " qualiter sit accipienda " introducing the systematic doctrinal account of the divine generation in chapter eleven must be carefully observed.[103]

Aquinas does not leave the slightest suggestion that he is now going to complement his biblical presentation of the revealed doctrine with a rational, philosophical, or apologetical, demonstration to support, much less to verify, the revealed doctrine. The revealed doctrine is clearly being presupposed, and from two points of view: as the 'given', to which explanatory process will now be applied — " qualiter accipi " — and as the basic energy on which the process itself will move forward — " ex sacris Scripturis edocti. "[104]

In no case, is the revealed doctrine the *quid demonstrandum*, not even in the qualified sense of a subsidiary argument.

---

[101] *C. G., IV*, c. 18, 7-9.

[102] " Sanctarum igitur Scripturarum testimoniis edocti, hoc firmiter de Spiritu Sancto tenemus, quod verus sit Deus, subsistens, et personaliter distinctus a Patre et Filio. Oportet autem considerare qualiter huiusmodi veritas utcumque accipi debeat, ut ab impugnationibus infidelium defendatur. " *C. G., IV*, c. 19, 1.

[103] In the earlier passage, it should be noted, the *accipienda, accipi* formula recurs twice again in the course of the discussion, and is identified with *intelligenda, intelligi*. See *C. G., IV*, c. 11, 8.

[104] In view of the clear overall parallelism, the corresponding phrase *Scripturarum testimoniis edocti* in chapter nineteen, though belonging to the sentence preceding that which contains the formula *qualiter accipi debeat*, must be accorded precisely the same force. For the comparison, see *C. G., IV*, c. 13, 12.

In terms of the pastoral focus of the *Contra Gentiles*, St. Thomas states that his systematic exposition will serve as a basis to answer the false claims of the heretics. Thus he assigns to it this particular species of apologetical function. But he does not state, or so much as imply, that the same systematic exposition will itself constitute an apologetical process of the radically different sort that would consist in the rational or philosophical demonstration of aprioristic necessity.

The further question could still be asked, of course, whether, quite regardless of Aquinas' contrary intention, the theological exposition put forth, making, as it does, such extensive use of philosophical principles and structure, would not *ipso facto* at least lay the basis for this other type of apologetic. Thus, as in the eleventh chapter it was necessary to examine very carefully the successive steps in St. Thomas' presentation, in order to determine whether or not he had demonstrated in some equivalent fashion the procession of the Divine Word as a deduction from the essential properties of intellect, so here in the nineteenth chapter it will be necessary to make a similar analysis, in order to see whether or not Aquinas has demonstrated the procession of the Spirit as a deduction from the essential properties of love.

In chapter eleven, St. Thomas had taken his point of departure (" principium sumere ") in the metaphysics of emanation. It was shown at the time how this methodological, one might perhaps say pedagogical, starting point could not be taken as the ultimate source, epistemologically, for the certainty of the several propositions that would follow, but had rather been intended by Aquinas himself as the necessary background, or perhaps more correctly as the underlying frame of analysis, for giving structure to his explanatory process. That such is, in fact, St. Thomas' approach, is brought out even more explicitly in the present passage. For the parallel theological exposition in chapter nineteen begins by setting down the basic metaphysics of will and love as what must be prefaced, or in this sense presupposed (" praemitti oportet "), to make the ensuing discussion meaningful.

To explain how the revealed procession of the Holy Spirit is to be understood, St. Thomas begins, it must first be noted that in every intellectual nature there is to be found will. For as natural bodies are in act through their proper forms, so is intellect in act through the intelligible form. But the natural

13

body through the same form that establishes it in its specific perfection has an inclination toward such operations as are proper to itself, and toward the proper finis or end which is achieved through these operations. It follows, therefore, that in intellectual beings also, there should be, in virtue of the intelligible form, an inclination toward the operations and end proper to this form. And this inclination found to exist in intellectual nature is what is known as will — in man, the principle of those human operations which intellect performs for the sake of the end. For it is the end or the good that is the object of will.[105]

The first step in St. Thomas' exposition, therefore, is to prove that will is to be found wherever there is intellect, and to do so precisely on the grounds that such is an essential consequence of intellectual nature.

Next, St. Thomas shows that, while several acts seem to belong to will, nevertheless the one principle and common radix of all of these is simply love. For, as in natural bodies the natural appetite has its source in the affinity and proportion dependent upon the natural form, so in intellectual beings every inclination of the will has its source in the proportion and affection apprehended through the intelligible form. But to be affected toward a thing, is, as such, to love the thing. Thus, it is out of love, that men will desire what they have not, rejoice in what they have, experience sorrow when they are held back from what they wish, react with hatred and anger against whatever restrains them from the object that they love.[106]

---

[105] " Ad cuius evidentiam praemitti oportet quod in qualibet in-tellectuali natura oportet inveniri voluntatem. Intellectus enim fit in actu per formam intelligibilem inquantum est intelligens, sicut res naturalis fit actu in esse naturali per propriam formam. Res autem naturalis per formam qua perficitur in sua specie, habet inclinationem in proprias operationes et proprium finem, quem per operationes conse-quitur : *quale enim est unumquodque, talia operatur*, et in sibi con-venientia tendit. Unde etiam oportet quod ex forma intelligibili con-sequatur in intelligente inclinatio ad proprias operationes et proprium finem. Haec autem inclinatio in intellectuali natura voluntas est, quae est principium operationum quae in nobis sunt, quibus intelligens propter finem operatur : finis enim et bonum est voluntatis obiectum. Oportet igitur in quolibet intelligente inveniri etiam voluntatem. " *C.G.*, *IV*, c. 19, 2.

[106] " Cum autem ad voluntatem plures actus pertinere videantur, ut desiderare, delectari, odire, et huiusmodi, omnium tamen amor et

What is loved, then, Aquinas continues, exists not only in the intellect, but also, though differently, in the will, of the lover. The existence of the beloved in the intellect is according to the likeness of its species. The beloved exists in the will, on the other hand, rather as the term of motion in the moving principle, which latter is proportioned to the object of love through the affinity it has for it. To illustrate, Aquinas appeals to the example of fire's natural attraction to rise. The 'place above' (*locus sursum*) thus somehow exists in fire by reason of the levity which gives to fire a certain propensity for this place ; whereas, on the other hand, fire that has been transmitted from the original fire exists in the original through the likeness of its form.[107]

Up to the moment, St. Thomas has said nothing explicitly of God. But now he draws the pertinent conclusions. Since there is will in every intellectual nature, and since God Himself is intelligent or understanding, there must be will in God — not, of course, as superadded to the divine essence, but as one with the divine essence, just as intellect is one with this essence, and therefore also one with intellect.[108] Further,

---

unum principium et communis radix invenitur. Quod ex his accipi potest. Voluntas enim, ut dictum est, sic se habet in rebus intellectualibus sicut naturalis inclinatio in rebus naturalibus, quae et naturalis appetitus dicitur. Ex hoc autem oritur inclinatio naturalis, quod res naturalis habet affinitatem et convenientiam secundum formam, quam diximus esse inclinationis principium, cum eo ad quod movetur, sicut grave cum loco inferiori. Unde etiam hinc oritur omnis inclinatio voluntatis, quod per formam intelligibilem aliquid apprehenditur ut conveniens vel afficiens. Affici autem ad aliquid, inquantum huiusmodi, est amare ipsum. Omnis igitur inclinatio voluntatis, et etiam appetitus sensibilis, ex amore originem habet. Ex hoc enim quod aliquid amamus, desideramus illud si absit, gaudemus autem cum adest, et tristamur cum ab eo impedimur, et odimus quae nos ab amato impediunt, et irascimur contra ea. " *C. G.*, *IV*, c. 19, 3.

[107] " Sic igitur quod amatur non solum est in intellectu amantis sed etiam in voluntate ipsius : aliter tamen et aliter. In intellectu enim est secundum similitudinem suae speciei : in voluntate autem amantis est sicut terminus motus in principio motivo proportionato per convenientiam et proportionem quam habet ad ipsum. Sicut in igne quodammodo est locus sursum ratione levitatis, secundum quam habet proportionem et convenientiam ad talem locum : ignis vero generatus est in igne generante per similitudinem suae formae. " *C. G.*, *IV*, c. 19, 4.

[108] " Quia igitur ostensum est quod in omni natura intellectuali est voluntas ; Deus autem intelligens est, ut in Primo ostensum est :

since every act of will is radicated in love, and since, in God,
will can be attended neither as potency nor habit, but exclusively as act, there must likewise be love in God.[109]

St. Thomas then considers the primary object of this
divine love. Since the proper object of the divine will is His
own goodness, it follows necessarily that God must first and
foremost love His own goodness and being. But inasmuch as
the beloved must exist somehow in the will of the lover, it
follows that God, as He loves Himself, must exist in His own
will *ut amatum in amante*. This divine act of love or will,
however, according to which God is in Himself as the beloved
in the lover, can only be essential, substantial. The existence
of God in His own will, therefore, is truly and substantially
God Himself.[110]

The reader will have noticed how closely Aquinas' exposition in this passage parallels that on the divine generation
in chapter eleven. In both presentations, he turns from having established the existence of the mystery on the authoritative testimony of Sacred Scripture to explain how what
has actually been revealed must be taken, or understood (*accipi, intelligi*), by human reason — to the limited extent
scientific theology, drawing its first principles from revelation
and Christian faith is capable of achieving such understanding.

---

oportet quod in ipso sit voluntas : non quidem quod voluntas Dei
sit aliquid eius essentiae superveniens, sicut nec intellectus, ut supra
ostensum est, sed voluntas Dei est ipsa eius substantia. Et cum intellectus etiam Dei sit ipsa eius substantia, sequitur quod una res
sint in Deo intellectus et voluntas. " *C. G., IV*, c. 19, 5.

[109] " Et quia ostensum est in Primo quod operatio Dei sit ipsa eius
essentia ; et essentia Dei sit eius voluntas : sequitur quod in Deo non
est voluntas secundum potentiam vel habitum, sed secundum actum.
Ostensum est autem quod omnis actus voluntatis in amore radicatur.
Unde oportet quod in Deo sit amor. " *C. G., IV*, c. 19, 6.

[110] " Et quia, ut in Primo ostensum est, proprium obiectum divinae
voluntatis est eius bonitas, necesse est quod Deus primo et princi-
paliter suam bonitatem et seipsum amet. Cum autem ostensum sit
quod amatum necesse est aliqualiter esse in voluntate amantis ; ipse
autem Deus seipsum amat : necesse est quod ipse Deus sit in sua voluntate ut amatum in amante. Est autem amatum in amante secundum quod amatur ; amare autem quoddam velle est ; velle autem
Dei est eius esse, sicut et voluntas eius est eius esse ; esse igitur Dei
in voluntate sua per modum amoris, non est esse accidentale, sicut
in nobis, sed essentiale. Unde oportet quod Deus, secundum quod
consideratur ut in sua voluntate existens, sit vere et substantialiter
Deus. " *C. G., IV*, c. 19, 7.

In both accounts, first for the Word and now for the
Holy Spirit, he begins by creating a rational basis or structure
of understanding, at once both psychological and metaphysical, and derived, not from an analysis of terms or notions,
but from a deep penetration into the nature of spiritual reality
rooted, ultimately, in personal introspection.   From this basic
frame of reference, again in both passages, St. Thomas draws
the respective principles : 1) the existence of ' the understood ' in ' the intelligent ', 2) the existence of the beloved
in the lover — and, by analogy, extends these principles to
include the divine.   But once he has done this, first in the
case of God's self-understanding, and then in the case of God's
self-love, his immediate concern is not to introduce any matter of real procession or real distinction, but rather to bring
out, and still quite within the frame of rational analysis, the
unequivocal *absolute* identity between ' God understood ' and
' God understanding ', ' God loved ' and ' God loving '.

Only when this identification has been scored, stressed
in fact, will Aquinas pass on, in both accounts, to consider
the matter of real procession and, therefore, real distinction.
In the earlier account, devoted to the generation of the Son
as procession of the Word, it has already been shown how
this first trinitarian procession was not itself the object of
proof or demonstration, in no sense the rational conclusion
from philosophical principles, but rather what was being presupposed from divine revelation, to be understood, so far as
this is possible, by the inquiring human intelligence seeking
its way through psychological and metaphysical analogy in
the light of Christian faith.   The question at the moment,
then, is whether in this second account, devoted to the procession of the Spirit, and perfectly parallel to the first account
in every other significant respect, St. Thomas holds fast to
the same methodological perspective.

After having concluded, therefore, that there is will in
God, and consequently love, and the existence, in substantial
identity, of God beloved in God loving, Aquinas goes on as
follows.   That something should be present in the will *ut
amatum in amante*, means that it bears a certain order or
ordination both to the conception whereby it is conceived
through intellect, and to the thing itself of which the conception is the expressed inner word.   For nothing would be loved
unless it were somehow known.   Nor is it only the knowl-

edge of the beloved that is loved, but the thing itself according
to its own goodness.   It is necessary, therefore, that the love
whereby God exists in the divine will as beloved in the lover
should proceed both from the Word of God and from God
Who utters the Word.[111]

This second procession, however, since it is not procession
in intellect according to likeness of species, is not generation,
nor can God proceeding *per modum amoris* be called ' Son '.[112]
Rather is it proper that He be called ' Spirit ', inasmuch as
the beloved existing in the will draws the lover from within
toward that which he loves, and in living beings, such internal
driving force is pertinent to spirit.[113]

St. Thomas completes his exposition with two citations
from St. Paul bringing out the aspect of this *impulsus* to characterize the Spirit, along with the final observation that,
since it is customary to speak of what belongs to God as holy,
the full name of God proceeding as love is *Spiritus Sanctus.*[114]

---

[111] " Quod autem aliquid sit in voluntate ut amatum in amante,
ordinem quendam habet ad conceptionem qua ab intellectu concipitur,
et ad ipsam rem cuius intellectualis conceptio dicitur verbum : non
enim amaretur aliquid nisi aliquo modo cognosceretur ;   nec solum
amati cognitio amatur, sed secundum quod in se bonum est.   Necesse est igitur quod amor quo Deus est in voluntate divina ut amatum
in amante, et a Verbo Dei, et a Deo cuius est Verbum, procedat. " *C. G.
IV*, c. 19, 8.

[112] " Cum autem ostensum sit quod amatum in amante non est se-
cumdum similitudinem speciei, sicut intellectum in intelligente ; omne
autem quod procedit ab altero per modum geniti, procedit secundum
similitudinem speciei a generante : relinquitur quod processus rei ad
hoc quod sit in voluntate sicut amatum in amante, non sit per modum
generationis, sicut processus rei ad hoc quod sit in intellectu habet
rationem generationis, ut supra ostensum est.   Deus igitur procedens
per modum amoris, non procedit ut genitus.   Neque igitur filius dici
potest. "   *C. G., IV*, c. 19, 9.

[113] " Sed quia amatum in voluntate existit ut inclinans, et quodammodo impellens intrinsecus amantem in ipsam rem amatam ; impulsus autem rei viventis ab interiori ad spiritum pertinet : convenit
Deo per modum amoris procedenti ut *spiritus* dicatur eius, quasi quadam spiratione existente. "   *C. G., IV*, c. 19, 10.

[114] " Hinc est quod Apostolus Spiritui et Amori impulsum quendam attribuit : dicit enim, *Rom.* VIII 14 : *Qui Spiritu Dei aguntur,
hi filii Dei sunt* ; et *II ad Cor.* V 14 : " *Caritas Christi urget nos.*   Quia
vero omnis intellectualis motus a termino denominatur ;   amor autem
praedictus est quo Deus ipse amatur : convenienter Deus per modum
amoris procedens dicitur *Spiritus Sanctus* ;   ea enim quae Deo dicata
sunt, *sancta* dici consueverunt. "   *C. G., IV*, c. 19, 11 and 12.

In the remaining chapters of his treatise on the divine processions, Aquinas will treat of the work assigned to the Holy Spirit in Sacred Scripture with respect to all creation, to the rational creature in particular, and in the process of personal sanctification.[115] After that, he will discuss the historical problem of *processio ab utroque*, and finally conclude his treatise with a brief demonstration why there can be in God only the Three Persons actually revealed, and no others.[116]

For the purposes of the present study, however, these later passages can be left aside and attention concentrated upon the final section in the theological exposition of chapter nineteen at the point where St. Thomas introduces the element of real procession and real distinction.

Reduced to its essentials, the argument of St. Thomas, briefly enough stated — seventy-five words ! — as it is, comes down to this : the existence of the beloved in the lover implies that the ' thing loved ' have a relationship or order both to the ' thing understood ' and the ' thing ' of which the concept or word is the intelligible expression. Aquinas gives his reason for this : nothing can be loved except inasmuch and insofar as it is known : and also — thus he accounts for the double relationship — what is loved is not only the ' thing as understood ', but also the ' thing itself ' for its own goodness. He draws his conclusion : it is necessary, therefore, that the love whereby God exists in the divine will as the ' one loved ' in the ' one loving ' should proceed both from the Word of God and from God as uttering this Word.

On the face of things, then, the passage bears at least the superficial lineaments of a rational argument for the existence of the second procession. But is this really true ? Even superficially ? Or does the concession, however academic or provisional, tend to accept an extremely literalist approach to a given text, almost completely isolating this text from its context, immediate as well as general, and in so doing, even distort the actual thrust and force of the argument taken precisely in this imposed isolation ?

Aside from the fact that here in chapter nineteen, as previously in chapter eleven, St. Thomas explicitly attributes the certitude of the processional mystery to the authority of

---

[115] *C. G., IV,* cc. 20-22.
[116] *C. G., IV,* cc. 24-26.

God revealing, and announces, moreover, not that he will verify, reaffirm or even support this certitude with rational argument, but rather seek to explain how the mystery once presupposed should be taken or understood (*accipi, intelligi*), aside, finally, from the obvious and detailed parallelism between the two accounts — and it has already been shown how demonstration of this sort was quite absent in the first account — aside, then, from all considerations of remote and proximate literary and didactic context, the argument, even if totally removed from its actual setting and restricted to the seventy-five words of all that would thus remain, can be accepted as a rational demonstration for the second procession, or even as a very close imitation of such a demonstration, only with no small measure of disregard for the laws and form of rational argument itself.

One would be justified in saying that in St. Thomas' own mind, the existence of the divine will, and of the act of love substantially identified with God's essence and being, the fact that God's own goodness must be the first object of this love, and even, therefore, the presence of ' God loved ' in ' God loving ', were all principles *per se* accessible to the unaided human intelligence. But that there should be an order or relationship — at least real relationship, involving real distinction — between the divine *amatum*, on the one hand, and both the divine *Verbum* and the divine *Dicens*, on the other hand, could not possibly have been considered by Aquinas himself as accessible to pure reason, for the simple fact that, in Aquinas' mind, and as seen in the text of chapter eleven, the prior relationship or order existing between the *Verbum* and the *Dicens*, and upon which, here in chapter nineteen, St. Thomas makes the further relationship or order between the *amatum* and both the *Verbum* and the *Dicens* depend, is not so accessible.

For the existence of something — here, the second trinitarian procession — to be demonstrated by pure reason, at least in some qualified, suasive or merely corroborative sense, each of the essential elements comprising the process of argumentation would have to be themselves principles of reason. But in the passage at hand, St. Thomas clearly presupposes the real procession of the Word as grounding the real procession of the divine Beloved. The existence of the *amatum in amante*, he affirms, involves that the *amatum* be ordered both to the inner word whereby it is conceived and to the principle uttering, this inner word as well. Hence it is, he continues, that the love according to which God exists in the divine will as *amatum in amante* must proceed from both the *Verbum* and *Deus Dicens Verbum*. The order that is thus involved, and the procession that is thus involved, are clearly presupposed to be real — but presupposed, not proved.

So far as proof is in question, Aquinas' conclusion actually moved, so to speak, in precisely the opposite direction. Since there is will and love in God, and since this love must have the divine goodness as its first and foremost object, God must be present in His own will as *amatum in amante*. But since there is no real distinction in God between will, act of love, nature and existence, this presence can only be as essentially and substantially identical with the divine being. Then St. Thomas introduces the order that is also involved.

Theoretically, one might be justified in saying that from the mere presence of the *amatum in amante*, Aquinas was able to conclude to a purely rational order or relationship between the *amatum* and the *amans*, or more completely, between the *amatum*, on one side, and *Deus intellectus* and *Deus intelligens*, on the other. But in the writer's judgment, there is no support from the text that St. Thomas wishes to insert this preliminary step, or to assume this particular point of view. For in the text itself, he introduces the order or relationship as applying to the inner word and its principle of utterance — understanding this word according to its real procession. That the order involved in the *amatum*, therefore, when it is introduced at this point, was meant to be taken as strictly real, is not what Aquinas intended to prove, but rather what he was presupposing.

One might ask : presupposing from where, or on what grounds ? In the context of chapter nineteen, St. Thomas is presupposing this real order or relationship on the simple grounds that the second trinitarian procession, the procession of the Holy Spirit, real procession, moreover, and implying real distinction, is an article of Christian faith.

As a point of logical reasoning, therefore, the reality of the order existing between the divine *amatum* and both the divine *Verbum* and the divine *Dicens*, and the reality of the procession of the Holy Spirit, could not possibly have been introduced by Aquinas as purely rational conclusions unless the reality of the procession of the Word, upon which Aquinas makes these further conclusions depend — or would make them depend, if he had actually assumed such an approach — had previously been introduced as itself a purely rational conclusion. Consequently, any attempt to discover in the presentation of chapter nineteen either apodictic demonstration or at least its close imitation could be successful only to the extent the same demonstration or its approximation had already been shown in the earlier and parallel presentation in chapter eleven. In the writer's judgment, the precise contrary has already been proved.

Nevertheless, the writer would not be misunderstood. Attention has here been given to the form and technicalities of logical process in order to show that the academic concession on the point of appearances should not be too quickly made, or allowed to stand without comment. For it is often customary in matters of this sort to grant that, yes indeed, the style and idiom of the author might well give rise to such and such an interpretation. At the same time, however, the larger and more significant aspects of the issue must not be lost sight of.

The ultimate question here is one of theological method. If one presumes that the sole use a theologian will make of rational or philosophical principles is such as would lend additional verification or confirmation to the certitude of the revealed mystery, he will naturally incline, in his analysis of a given text, to look rather exclusively for some species of apologetical conclusion, when it is a matter of articles of faith, or for conclusions belonging to the luxury of pure ' speculation ', when it is a matter of derivatives. For in either instance, as he sees it, the object in view is determination or certitude or verification of the fact, not its understanding.

But it is the initial methodological presumption itself that must be questioned. Otherwise, the attitude of the historian is apt to be: oh yes, admittedly St. Thomas starts off by showing that the trinitarian processions have been revealed by God ; admittedly, he encloses his subsequent doctrinal elaboration within the testimonies of Sacred Scripture ; but in this particular text, at least, do we not see him giving way to the Anselmian ideal triumphant in his own day, and applying the full weight of his purely rational philosophy to show that what has in fact been revealed is also strongly suggested by the principles and argument of a well-disciplined human reason ?

That this, however, was not the attitude or point of view assumed by St. Thomas himself, stands squarely on the evidence of a closer examination of his personal methodology. *Qualiter accipi, qualiter intelligi* — this is the key to what that methodology was. The mysteries themselves, he never tires of saying, are revealed by God. They cannot be demonstrated by the unaided human reason. But once they are presupposed on the authority of Christian faith, the Christian theologian can and should apply the principles and processes of reason — not, it should be noted, in the effort to see what other facts or data, not revealed, might be deduced or inferred, but rather in the effort to see how the facts and data that have been revealed, the articles of faith in the strictest sense of the word, should be taken (*accipi*) or understood (*intelligi*).

In the fourth book of the *Contra Gentiles*, the broad outlines of this methodology as pivoting essentially on understanding are already developed. The specifically Thomist ideal of theological science presented, but not implemented, in the commentary *In Boethii de Trinitate* has already received its first systematic expression, and this, without the slightest compromise to the negative or restrictive principles that had been set down confining the exercise and scope of scientific reasoning in the same treatise.

In the *Contra Gentiles*, however, St. Thomas limited himself more or less to the primary elements of what Christian faith knows of the Blessed Trinity. In the *Summa Theologiae*, he will go far beyond this, and construct from the same *principia fidei* a massive and minutely articulated synthesis of theological understanding. Moreover, since the use Aquinas will make of rational principles and rational structure in the *Summa* will be far greater than here in the *Contra Gentiles*, it will be only through a careful study of the text precisely as a synthesis of theological understanding, that a satisfactory reply to the challenge of apologetical perspective will be able to be given.

PART THREE

FINAL ACHIEVEMENT IN THE IDEAL
OF THEOLOGICAL SYNTHESIS

CHAPTER ONE

"ORDO DOCTRINAE"
IN THE *SUMMA THEOLOGIAE*

Though not more than a comparatively few years separate the composition of the *Pars Prima* from that of the fourth book *Contra Gentiles*, it will be noticed right from the very beginning that in its scope and detail of coverage, and still more significantly in its plan and order of treatment, the '*de Trinitate*' of the *Summa* is quite a different theological conception. [1]

The basic methodological ideal — *qualiter accipi, qualiter intelligi* — already firmly established in the earlier work perdures, but the particular manner in which it is now applied, developed and perfected introduces a specifically new dimension in the Thomist understanding of theological science.   Moreover, this awareness of a specifically new approach is impressed upon the reader immediately.

St. Thomas begins his treatise noting that, having completed his discussion of what pertains to the unity of the divine essence, he has now to pass on to the discussion of what pertains to the Trinity of Persons.   Since the Divine Persons, then, are distinguished according to relations of origin, the first point he must consider, following the plan or

---

[1] On the dating of the *Pars Prima*, see P. GLORIEUX, " Pour la chronologie de la Somme," *Mélanges de Science Religieuse*, II (1945), pp. 59-98.   Resuming the results of his investigation in table form (p. 85, n. 1), Glorieux places the *Pars Prima* between 1267, certainly not earlier, and 1268.   As previously noted in the present study, *Contra Gentiles IV* would not antedate 1263.

order of doctrinal development (" ordo doctrinae "), is that
of origin or procession, secondly that of the relations of origin,
thirdly and lastly that of the Persons. [2]

Two things will strike the reader as peculiar here, at least
if the present approach of St. Thomas be compared with what
had previously been observed both in the *Sentences* and the
Contra Gentiles. On the one hand, Aquinas does not propose
to introduce his theme by substantiating, on the authority of
Christian revelation, what might be called the basic facts, or
data, of trinitarian belief. In the *Sentences*, it will be recalled,
he had begun by showing that there was in God a plurality of
Persons and that this plurality was real. In the *Contra Gentiles*, his initial step was to present a lengthy and detailed
scriptural account of the divine generation, paternity, and
filiation. On the other hand, the point Aquinas does choose
to begin with here in the *Summa* — origin or procession
(" de origine sive processione ") — he proposes to introduce
in the first place, not, as it were, arbitrarily, but on the
assumption that origin or procession is truly ' first ' according
to a certain order of doctrine. He indicates, moreover, even
here in his briefly stated *prooemium*, the precise source of this
primacy or priority.

The reason why he must first treat of origin or procession,
St. Thomas explicitly states, is because it is through relations
of origin that the Divine Persons are distinguished. The
Persons, therefore, which he says he will discuss only in the
third place, are in some manner and from some point of view
dependent upon the relations, and the relations in turn somehow dependent upon procession or origin. But what is the
nature of this dependence? At the moment, St. Thomas
does not give a full explanation. Yet, he does indicate, and

---

[2] " Consideratis autem his quae ad unitatem divinae essentiae
pertinent, restat consideratio de his quae pertinent ad trinitatem personarum in divinis. Et quia personae divinae secundum relationes
originis distinguuntur, secundum ordinem doctrinae prius considerandum est de origine sive processione, secundo de relationibus originis,
tertio de personis. " *S. T.*, *I*, q. 27, proem. All citations and references in the present study are taken from the critical edition of B.
GEYER (*Florilegium Patristicum*, fasc. XXXVII) covering qq. 27 through
32 for the entire portion of the ' *de Trinitate* ' of the *Pars Prima* that
is thus reproduced in this edition. All remaining citations and references — i. e., previous to q. 27 or subsequent to q. 32 are taken
from the Ottawa edition.

quite clearly, at least the general area to which this dependence pertains : the area of internal cause.

The expression here, as might be expected in a brief introduction, is highly compact.   In the crucial part of his sentence, Aquinas does not speak separately of origin, first, and then relations, but simply of relations of origin.   Origin (or procession) will be treated first, because the relations of origin distinguish, in some way, therefore — as human understanding would endeavor to approach the matter — ' cause ' the Persons.   But by describing the relations as relations of origin, Aquinas clearly, though implicitly, assigns a further, or more intimate, causal proportion as obtaining between the relations themselves and origin.

It is quite the same as if he had said, in a somewhat fuller expression : origin or procession must be taken up first, because the Persons are distinguished by the relations, and the relations themselves depend upon — or are ' caused ' by — origin.   For, as will become clearer and more explicit once St. Thomas gets into the twenty-seventh question, a relation of origin is a relation that has its source or foundation in origin, just as a relation of quantity is one that has its source or foundation in quantity.

The priority, therefore, that Aquinas assigns here to origin or procession is the priority of cause — in this case, of the internal cause found within the divine being itself. Recognition of this priority, moreover, is of the highest importance to the scope and purpose of the present study.

The point St. Thomas proposes to discuss first is not that which is actually first in the order of what is known to man on the authority of God revealing — this would be the activity, interrelationships, and personal character of the Father, Son and Holy Spirit — but rather what is first in the order of what pertains to God in His own existence, to the extent that theological understanding penetrates in some obscure way the mysteries of the divine, and does so only in virtue of interior faith and as having presupposed from revelation the existence and distinction of the Three Persons, the generation of the Son and the procession of the Holy Spirit.

It is not, consequently, this primordial content of the revealed mystery that St. Thomas proposes to demonstrate. His intention is rather to expose in theological understanding, and to the limited extent that this is possible, the ' cause ' or

ultimate *ratio* whose ' effect ' or consequence has been revealed
— and precisely inasmuch as it has been revealed, not in any
academic abstraction from the fact.

That, where the Trinity is concerned, no such abstraction,
amounting, as it would, to a rational demonstration of the
mystery, is possible, is what Aquinas had insisted upon in
the *Sentences* and in the *In Boethii de Trinitate*, had clearly
taken for granted in the *Contra Gentiles*, and will insist upon
again, formally and explicitly, even here in the *Summa*, where,
moreover, once again he will give his reasons why. [3]   Of course,
the question may be posed : granting these assertions of a
contrary intention, does not Aquinas at least lay the basis
for some sort of philosophical proof as *ipso facto* implicated
in his use of philosophical principles and rational structure ?

The challenge cannot be dismissed simply on the ground
that it would point up an inconsistency in St. Thomas' clearly
stated position.   On the other hand, the observation is not
out of place, and should be made, that a tendency to treat too
lightly the clear statement of methodological intention and
perspective, such as St. Thomas offers here in the *prooemium*
to his trinitarian exposition in the *Summa*, plus the failure
to recognize its full implications — particularly in the order
of development here chosen — can easily lead to the critical
error of imposing upon selected texts a point of view, and
hence a meaning, rather foreign to the author's own.

The pertinence of this caution will be seen in the textual
analysis of the all-important first article of the twenty-seventh
question, which follows immediately.

I.   *Q. 27, a. 1* : Exposition of Trinitarian Procession in
the Context of What Is Essential to Intellect

It has already been seen in the course of the present study
that the first elaboration of the Thomist ' *de Trinitate* ', that
contained in the *Sentences*, does not offer any realistic problem
in the matter of aprioristic rational or philosophical demonstration. For in the *Sentences*, Aquinas not only explicitly
rejects such a demonstration, but also omits from his strictly
explanatory exposition the causal, or quasi causal, account

---

[3] *S. T.*, *I*, q. 32, a. 1.

of the Persons and subsistent relations ' *in fieri* ' which alone could seriously give rise to the question whether or not, and despite any protestations to the contrary, a measure of *de facto* demonstration is nonetheless involved.

But it has also been shown that even in the second elaboration, that contained in *Contra Gentiles IV*, the precisely apologetical question would still be premature. For in the theological analyses characteristic of this later presentation St. Thomas takes his point of departure throughout from the revealed mystery as such. If there is procession of the Word in God, and if Word must be interpreted, on the basis of revelation, in its proper sense, then rational theology must assign to this Divine Word whatever is essential to the formality, or *ratio*, of inner word considered in itself. As was observed in the preceding chapter, however, such a process of reasoning clearly presupposes the existence of the Divine Word and its procession, and in no way provides a rational or philosophical basis, however unintentional, for demonstrating this initial datum — the revealed mystery.

Yet here in the introductory article to the ' *de Trinitate* ' of the *Pars Prima*, as also in passages of the *De Potentia* and *Compendium* to be taken up later, the apologetical problem comes at last into full focus. For it will soon be apparent that, at least if these texts are examined in relative isolation, some ground could actually be found for the criticism that St. Thomas is concluding, not to what must be said of the procession of the Divine Word from what is essential to the proper formality of inner word as such, but rather to the very existence of this first trinitarian procession from what is essential to the proper formality of intellect.

The difference, moreover, is decisive. The theological elaboration in *Contra Gentiles IV* moves out from the existence of the Divine Word as known exclusively through its revelation. But the theological elaboration in *Pars Prima* moves out from the existence in God of intellect, and knowledge of this latter fact is accessible to natural reason.

The question of the moment, therefore — and the reader will recall that it is precisely the *status quaestionis* determined at the end of the first part of the present study — is simply this : is it possible to account for this procedure, at least on superficial analysis quite at odds with Aquinas' protestations against a priori demonstration, of commencing the theological

14

exposition with the seemingly rational or philosophical principle attributing procession of inner word to the *ratio formalis*
of intellect as such? Furthermore, is it possible to do this,
not by making appeal to some argumentative hypothesis which
would continue to be embarrassed by the idiom and structure
of the text, but by establishing the solution to the problem
quite solidly on the textual evidence of what St. Thomas himself actually wrote?

The subject of this first article in the twenty-seventh question is given in the *rubrica*: "Utrum sit processio in divinis."
Three a priori objections are listed: it seems that procession
could not be found to exist in God, since it would imply
external motion, diversity, and the subordination repugnant
to the notion of first principle.[4] But the *contra* cites Jn 8:
42 — "Ego ex Deo processi" — and the *corpus* begins with
the brief general observation that, in speaking of God, the
Sacred Scriptures use words indicating procession.[5]

In the course of history, however, St. Thomas continues,
different ones have taken or understood ("acceperunt") this
procession in different ways. For Arius, it was the procession
of effect from cause, thus denying, in manifest contradiction
to the testimony of Sacred Scripture the truly divine nature
of both the Son and the Holy Spirit. For Sabellius, it was
again a procession from cause to effect, but in the sense that
the cause would move its effect, or impress its similitude
upon it. Thus Sabellius claimed that God the Father was
called Son inasmuch as He assumed flesh from the Virgin
Mary, and Holy Spirit inasmuch as He sanctifies the rational
creature and moves him toward life. But this understanding
("acceptio") too is contrary to the teaching of Scripture.[6]

St. Thomas remarks that both Arius and Sabellius understood the divine procession as somehow external to God Himself. This raises the question of the distinction between internal and external procession. Aquinas states first the general rule that every procession is consequent to some action.

---

[4] *S. T.*, *I*, q. 27, a. 1, obj. 1-3.

[5] *S. T.*, *I*, q. 27, a. 1, contra, and a. 1c.

[6] *S. T.*, *I*, q. 27, a. 1c, 1 and 2. For the sake of convenience, the
paragraph divisions of the Geyer critical edition will be indicated in
this way wherever a more lengthy *corpus articuli* is being treated in
detail.

Thus, just as there is a certain external procession (*processio ad extra*) following upon the action that is directed into external matter, so too is there a certain internal procession (*processio ad intra*) following upon the action that remains within the agent.

This latter is especially clear in the case of intellect, whose action, understanding, remains in the one who understands. For whoever understands, by this fact alone that he does understand, there proceeds something within him that is the conception of the thing understood, emerging from the power of intelligence and proceeding from its activity of knowing. This conception is what is immediately signified by external words (*vox*) and is called, therefore, inner word — *verbum cordis*. [7]

Now since God is the supreme being, St. Thomas continues, whatever is said of God is to be understood, not in comparison with bodies, which are the lowest of His creatures, but on analogy rather with the highest of His creatures, that is with the intellectual substances, though even analogy of this latter sort is incapable of perfectly representing the divine. In the light of this principle, then, procession in God has to be taken ("accipienda"), not on the basis of the local movement or purely external influence found in material beings, but rather according to the mode of procession seen in intelligible emanation — that is, according to the inner word that emanates from the one who speaks or utters it while remaining within him. It is on this basis, then, that catholic faith recognizes procession in the divinity. [8]

---

[7] " Si quis autem diligenter consideret, uterque accepit processionem, secundum quod est ad aliquid extra. Unde neuter posuit processionem in ipso Deo. Sed cum omnis processio sit secundum aliquam actionem, sicut secundum actionem quae tendit in exteriorem materiam, est aliqua processio ad extra, ita secundum actionem quae manet in ipso agente, attenditur quaedam processio ad intra. Et hoc maxime patet in intellectu, cuius actio, scilicet intelligere, manet in intelligente. Quicumque enim intelligit, ex hoc ipso quod intelligit, in eo procedit aliquid intra ipsum, quod est conceptio rei intellectae, ex eius notitia procedens. Quam quidem conceptionem vox significat ; et dicitur verbum cordis, significatum verbo vocis. " *S. T.*, *I*, q. 27, a. 1c, 3.

[8] " Cum autem Deus sit super omnia, ea quae in Deo dicuntur, non sunt intelligenda secundum modum infimarum creaturarum, quae sunt corpora, sed secundum similitudinem supremarum creaturarum,

To explain the divine procession, therefore, St. Thomas introduces at this point the emanation of the inner word. Moreover, in doing so, he seems to go quite beyond the position he had assumed in the eleventh chapter of *Contra Gentiles IV*. For in that earlier account of the matter, Aquinas was content with affirming what was essential to the inner word as such, rather than what might be essential to intellect as such.

Concretely, his argument at that time had been substantially this : granted, in God, the existence of the Word, and the fact that Word is spoken of God in the strict or proper sense, the Divine Word must proceed from God Who utters it according to the divine act of understanding. For it is of the essence of inner word as such ("de ratione eius "), that it proceed in this manner. In the fourth book *Contra Gentiles*, therefore, even the approach and style of presentation in the immediate passage show Aquinas arguing, not to the existence of the Divine Word, but to the way in which this Divine Word would have to be understood, once its existence were presupposed.

Here in the *Pars Prima*, on the other hand, the language of the text seems to affirm, not only what is essential to the proper reality of the inner word, but also, at least in some sense, the necessary connection between inner word and intellect as such : " Quicumque enim intelligit, ex hoc ipso quod intelligit, in eo procedit aliquid intra ipsum ... verbum cordis. " Moreover, from the context of the paragraph in which this universal formula appears, along with the final paragraph immediately following, is not one expected to supply the second, or minor, premise : ' Atqui Deus intelligit ' ? And is not the conclusion, when all is said and done : ' Ergo procedit intra Deum Verbum Divinum ' ?

It is not difficult to prove, however, that to construct such an argument from the text at hand, it would be necessary to assume two facts : first, that it is the existence of

---

quae sunt intellectuales substantiae, a quibus etiam similitudo accepta deficit a repraesentatione divinorum. Non ergo est accipienda processio, secundum quod est in corporalibus vel per motum localem vel per actionem alicuius causae in exteriorem effectum, ut calor a calefaciente in calefactum, sed secundum emanationem intelligibilem, utpote verbi intelligibilis a dicente, quod manet in ipso. Et sic fides catholica ponit processionem in divinis. " *S. T.*, *I*, q. 27, a. 1c, 4.

divine procession in general, or procession of the Word in
particular, that Aquinas intends to demonstrate — for the
conclusion would have to read : ' Ergo procedit intra Deum
Verbum Divinum ' — and secondly, that the argument itself,
regardless of intention, was at least *per se* capable of giving
such a conclusion.   But neither of these assumptions is
valid.

Though the article is entitled " utrum sit processio in divinis, " it is clear from the treatment which St. Thomas gives
to this question that his intention is not to demonstrate the
existence of procession, but rather to explain how the divine
procession, once presupposed from revelation, should be taken
or understood.   One could say, of course, that Aquinas first
' proves ' the existence of procession by an appeal to Scripture,
and then goes on to offer his explanation.

Yet, even this is misleading. For the simple, twelve-
word assertion that Sacred Scripture in speaking of God uses
language indicative of procession is hardly ' proof ' in the
sense of the literary and didactic effort normally applied by
a careful and systematic author who considers verification of
a certain fact the primary task in treating the subject he
has assigned himself for discussion. In the writer's judgment,
then, it would be more accurate and more faithful to the
text to say simply that the summary appeal to the generic
biblical *auctoritas* serves merely to indicate, almost in passing
fashion, the ground upon which the existence of procession in
God is legitimately being presupposed.

In either case, however, whether the existence of procession is presupposed throughout, and authority for doing so
only briefly mentioned, or whether the existence of procession
is first proved — from Scripture — and then expounded in
theological analysis, this much is certainly evident : not the
proof for the existence of procession, but solely the manner
in which it is to be taken or understood, with the problem
of existence now completely laid aside, is that with which
St. Thomas concerns himself at least in everything he says
following the brief first sentence.

For he turns immediately to the question of false or heretical understanding on the part of those, moreover, who did
not contest the existence of procession, next points out the
common error in these opinions — taking the divine procession to be *processio ad extra* — and then goes on to explain

in a positive exposition of immanent procession the only true
way that procession in God can be understood.

It should be noted also that in the course of this discussion,
Aquinas restricts himself exclusively to the terms *accipere* (eight
times) and *intelligere* (once, and in perfect parallelism) each
and every time he makes reference to both heretical and orthodox understanding of the mystery. As previously in the
expositions of *Contra Gentiles IV*, so too, and if anything even
more so, here in the *Summa*, St. Thomas makes it extremely
clear that the focus of his discussion is not upon the existence
of the revealed mystery — in the sense that this is what he
wants to prove or confirm — but upon its theological understanding.

Beyond the matter of Aquinas' intention, however, there
is also the fact that the argument for procession, or more
specifically for the procession of the Word, that one might
perhaps attempt to isolate from this first article in question
twenty-seven is not even *per se* capable of leading to an apodictic purely rational demonstration. In fact, it does not so
much as correctly imitate the proper form of such an argument.

The pertinent generalization — from this alone that one
understands, there proceeds within him an inner word —
could be taken in three different ways : 1) as a merely comprehensive universal ; 2) as an essential universal in the
strictly philosophical sense, where the connection between the
two terms ' understanding ' and ' inner word ' is the necessary
connection of causal dependence, and causal dependence as
rationally understood ; 3) as an essential universal in the
somewhat wider sense, where the connection between the two
terms may *de facto* be necessary and absolute, but on some
other epistemological basis than that purely rational intelligence has grasped the causal dependence.

If taken, then, as a comprehensive universal, the generalization would have to include God : from this alone that anyone
understands, God included, there proceeds within Him an
inner word. So constructed, however, it is obvious that such
a premise could not be used to demonstrate the procession
of the Divine Word. For it would presuppose that the divine
procession were already known. Yet, to interpret the text
in this fashion, would be to suppress the force of the insertion
" ex hoc ipso quod intelligit. " Aquinas does not simply
make the general observation : wherever there is understand-

ing, there is procession of inner word, but he affirms as well, at least in some manner, a relationship of dependence or source: wherever there is understanding, by this alone, or from this alone, there is procession of inner word.

This raises the question, then, whether the generalization is to be taken in the second sense, that is as an essential universal in the strictly philosophical meaning. One must consider carefully just what this would imply.

Aquinas' intention would have to be the following : wherever there is understanding, there is necessarily procession of inner word, precisely because intellect is, and is known by unaided human reason to be, the cause of inner word essentially and absolutely. It would not be enough if Aquinas meant only that there existed this essential and absolute causal dependence between inner word and intellect. For whatever exists in God is necessary — including, therefore, the procession of the Divine Word.

When St. Thomas asserts — not only here in the *Pars Prima*, but elsewhere, as for instance in *Contra Gentiles IV* — that the Divine Word proceeds from the Divine *Dicens* upon the divine act of understanding, he is saying, equivalently, that this procession of the Divine Word is necessary and essential to the very nature of God's understanding and being. Since, then, an analogous procession of inner word is likewise necessary and essential to the very nature of human understanding, there is nothing whatever to prevent St. Thomas from making the generalization that procession of inner word is of the essence of understanding as such, or *de ipsa ratione intellectus*.

Thus, the writer has no desire to argue that the strictly causal force of Aquinas' insertion " ex hoc ipso quod intelligit " might be less compelling than such a phrase as *de ipsa ratione eius*. The difference is not especially significant. Moreover, as will be seen presently, the ' stronger ' expression, should one want to consider it that, is actually used in a passage of the *De Potentia*, that very likely belongs to the same period as the *Pars Prima*.

The far more significant point which the writer does wish to make is the profound difference between the two ways in which the generalization, even as an essential universal expressing the necessary relationship of an effect to its proportionate cause, could be taken.

The statement is made : inner word accompanies intellect as such, or more strongly : inner word is of the very essence of intellect as such (*de ipsa ratione eius*). But in what precise sense is the statement intended ? Does Aquinas simply assert what he considers something that happens to be true : that inner word is essential to intellect ? Or does Aquinas intend to express in this assertion the purely rational ground upon which he was able to make it : inner word is essential to intellect because this is involved in human understanding's grasp of the nature of the cause ?

Of course, someone might counter with an observation that such a difference is not normally attended to in the examination of rational argument. Nevertheless, whatever might be said in reply to the objection where rational argument is at least being supposed, it must be maintained that the objection is quite out of order where the existence of rational argument itself is exactly what is being called into question.

The legitimacy of the question, moreover, rests squarely upon the text of Aquinas. Having made clear time and again his intention, not to propose some purely rational or philosophical analysis, but rather to seek in the light of faith and divine revelation for such strictly theological understanding of divine mysteries as the human intelligence might achieve on this earth, the prevailing and absolutely valid supposition throughout is that Aquinas would not have any of his arguments taken in an exclusively rational or philosophical meaning. For while it may well be true that some, perhaps several, of St. Thomas' reasonings on this or that particular matter could be transposed, intact one might say, from the theological to the philosophical context, it is also true that the context St. Thomas himself has actually chosen is, nevertheless, theological.

With this in mind, then, the generalization on inner word as an essential consequence of intellect as such must be examined more closely. The decisive question comes down to this : as St. Thomas saw it, is the unaided human reason capable of so understanding intellectual nature as to be able to affirm, on this rational basis alone, that procession of the inner word is essentially and necessarily involved in intellectual nature as in its adequately understood proportionate cause ? But it is clear that Aquinas' own view of the matter is quite the contrary.

As he had insisted in his methodological treatise *In Boethii de Trinitate*, and as he insisted again in the methodological introduction to his *Summa Theologiae*, unaided human reason cannot know *quid sit Deus*, and on this earth, even when illumined by supernatural faith and possessed of God's revealed self-manifestation, human reason does not and cannot *understand* the divine essence — for this is the beatific vision — but can know *quid sit Deus* only in the obscure, imperfect and, so to speak, vicarious manner whereby, through causality, negation and eminence, systematic or scientific theology achieves some limited and humanly proportioned understanding of the revealed mysteries.[9] Such is Aquinas' constant and unchanging position.

If, however, the unaided human reason could so penetrate in understanding the nature of intellectual being as to see that procession of inner word was essentially and absolutely involved as a necessary consequence in all intelligences, including therefore the divine, it would have to follow that the unaided human reason had grasped in understanding the causal nexus between the divine intellect and the Divine Word. And since the divine intellect is identical with the divine essence and being, it would likewise have to follow that human reason knew *quid sit Deus*. But this is precisely what St. Thomas claims is impossible.

When he says, therefore, that whoever understands, from this alone that he does understand, there proceeds within him the inner word, he simply affirms what is *de facto* universally true — that procession of inner word is proper to all intelligences, and that there exists this causal nexus whereby such procession can be stated to be essential to intellect as such, but not that human reason has grasped this causal nexus in its own understanding.

---

[9] The pertinent sections of *In Boet. de Trin.* were discussed extensively in chapter two of the second part of this study. In the early passages of the *Pars Prima*, treating the question " utrum Deum esse sit per se notum, " St. Thomas concludes : " Dico ergo quod haec propositio : Deus est, quantum in se est, per se nota est, quia praedicatum est idem cum subiecto ; Deus enim est suum esse, ut infra patebit. Sed quia nos non scimus de Deo quid est, non est nobis per se nota, sed indiget demonstrari per ea quae sunt magis nota quoad nos et minus nota quoad naturam, scilicet per effectus. " *S. T.*, I, q. 2, a. 1c.

Nor is it permissible to argue that, just as man's understanding of finite being, his own included, allows him a certain analogical understanding of being as such, and hence of the divine being, so too, and according to the soundest principles of Thomist thought, man's understanding of his own intellectual nature can lead him to analogical understanding of intellectual being as such, and therefore as involving the necessary procession of inner word. For knowledge of God derived in analogy from finite being is knowledge of God as supreme cause, of such being and attributes that must exist (*an sit*) in God to account for the being and perfections of creatures, but not knowledge of what the divine being or essence, or the divine intelligence, is in itself (*quid sit*).

Man can demonstrate from a consideration of the created universe and of his own intellectual power, therefore, that there is knowledge and intellect in God.[10] But man cannot demonstrate in this way the interior nature, or what Aquinas sometimes calls 'mode', of the divine intellect.[11] For this nature or mode is quite beyond what man can understand of the divine intellect through its effects.

There is, then, a gratuitous and false assumption in the objection as it stands. Man does know that there is inner word in his own intellectual operation, and he is capable of understanding the necessity for this immanent procession in his own nature, but man does not know, through purely rational inquiry, the transcendental quality of intellectual procession, nor is he able to demonstrate that procession of inner word is an essential and necessary property of intellectual being as such. For to do this, man would have to be able to demonstrate it of God, and to demonstrate it of God, he would first have to understand the nature of the divine intellect, and, since in God intellect, essence and being are identi-

---

[10] For Aquinas' own demonstration in the *Summa*, see the body of questions beginning with *S. T., I*, q. 14; and especially q. 14, aa. 1 and 2.

[11] " Ad duodecimum dicendum, quod licet ratio naturalis possit pervenire ad ostendendum quod Deus sit intellectus, modum tamen intelligendi non potest invenire sufficienter. Sicut enim de Deo scire possumus quod est, sed non quid est; ita de Deo scire possumus quod intelligit, sed non quo modo intelligit. Habere autem conceptionem verbi in intelligendo, pertinet ad modum intelligendi: unde ratio haec sufficienter probare non potest; sed ex eo quod est in nobis aliqualiter per simile coniecturare. " *De Pot.*, q. 8, a. 1, ad 12m.

fied, the nature of God Himself. But for St. Thomas, this would mean having the beatific vision.

It is interesting to note, moreover, that in the ninth of the *Quaestiones Disputatae de Potentia*, where the 'stronger' expression "est absolute de ratione eius quod est intelligere" is explicitly introduced, and where, also, there is at least a greater superficial appearance of some sort of argument from 'pure perfections', Aquinas not only repeats his assertion that a priori demonstration in this matter is simply impossible, but reaffirms as well what is his ultimate reason for this impossibility : the principle, namely, that in this life the human mind does not and cannot know *quid est Deus*.

It is necessary at this point, therefore, to complement the foregoing discussion of *S. T.*, *I*, q. 27, a. 1, with a more brief, but still sufficiently detailed, analysis of *De Pot.*, q. 9, a. 5.

II.   De Pot., q. 9, a. 5 :   Similar Approach to the First Trinitarian Procession From What Is Essential to Intellectual Nature As Such

In this more or less parallel passage of the *De Potentia*, the subject being treated is "utrum numerus personarum sit in divinis." It should be noted from the start, moreover, that this particular section of the *Quaestiones Disputatae* belongs, in all probability, to the same period of time as the *Pars Prima*.[12]

---

[12] *De Pot.*, q. 9, a. 5. For the dating of this group of *Quaestiones Disputatae*, including both *De Pot.*, q. 9, and *De Pot.*, q. 8 cited in the previous note, there is the summary opinion of P.-A. Walz — 1265-1267. See the article : "Thomas d'Aquin. Ecrits," *Dictionnaire de théologie catholique*, XV — 1 (Paris : Librairie Letouzey et Ané, 1946), col. 639. In P. Synave's scheme, both of these questions from the *De Potentia* would have been composed in 1268, or about the same time as the *Pars Prima* itself. See "Le problème chronologique des Questions Disputées de S. Thomas d'Aquin," *Revue Thomiste*, XXXI (1926), pp. 154-159. The same eighth and ninth questions, together with the tenth, are assigned to a rather earlier period, however, in the criticism of C. Vagaggini, who places them around 1263, and is quite insistent that they are at least prior to the composition of *Contra Gentiles IV*. See "La hantise," p. 119 and p. 124. In the writer's judgment, if he might be allowed to anticipate certain conclusions to be drawn from this third part of the present study, evidence is strong that at least the passage *De Pot.*, q. 9, a. 5, must

In the body of the article, St. Thomas begins with the now familiar statement that the plurality of Persons is a matter of faith, which can be neither investigated nor sufficiently understood ("nec investigari nec sufficienter intelligi") by the natural human reason, but will be understood in the life hereafter as the beatific vision succeeds upon faith and God is seen in His essence. Nevertheless, he goes on, a modest investigation of the divine mysteries is suggested and supported by the example of the holy fathers, and is of service in the refutation of errors.[13]

With this, Aquinas takes up his positive exposition. To explain this question, then, in the degree that is possible ("ad manifestationem aliqualem"), and particularly to follow the explanation set down by St. Augustine, the first point to consider is that whatever is perfect in creatures must be attributed to God — not according to the manner in which the perfection might exist in this or that creature, but according to the very essence of the perfection taken absolutely.[14] But there is nothing in the created universe more perfect and more excellent than understanding, and so it follows that one must attribute to God understanding and whatever pertains to its formal or essential perfection ("de ratione eius").[15]

---

be taken as later than *Contra Gentiles IV*. For the presentation here is strictly in accord with that of the *ordo doctrinae*, the order of understanding in synthesis, which does not seem to be found earlier than the *Compendium* and *Pars Prima*, and is furthermore conspicuously absent, certainly in its finished form, in the corresponding passages, particularly chapters eleven and twelve, of *Contra Gentiles IV*.

[13] "Respondeo. Dicendum quod pluralitas personarum in divinis est de his quae fidei subiacent, et naturali ratione humana nec investigari nec sufficienter intelligi potest; sed in patria intelligendum expectatur, cum Deus per essentiam videbitur visione fidei succedente. Sed tamen sancti patres proter instantiam eorum qui fidei contradicunt, coacti sunt et de hoc disserere, et de aliis quae spectant ad fidem .." *De Pot.*, q. 9, a. 5c, 1. (Paragraph distribution within the *corpus articuli* is according to the Marietti edition.)

[14] "Ad manifestationem ergo aliqualem huius quaestionis, et praecipue secundum quod Augustinus eam manifestat, considerandum est quod omne quod est perfectum in creaturis oportet Deo attribui, secundum id quod est de ratione illius perfectionis absolute; non secundum modum quo est in hoc vel in illo. Non enim bonitas est in Deo vel sapientia secundum aliquod accidens sicut in nobis, quamvis in eo sit summa bonitas et sapientia perfecta." *De Pot.*, q. 9, a. 5c, 2.

[15] "Nihil autem nobilius et perfectius in creaturis invenitur quam intelligere; cuius signum est quod inter ceteras creaturas, intellec-

Attending, therefore, to the absolute or essential properties of understanding as such (" de ratione eius quod est intelligere "), St. Thomas notes first that there must be both the intelligent (" intelligens ") and the understood (" intellectum "). Now the thing which is *per se* understood is not the object whose knowledge is obtained through understanding. For the understood must be in the one understanding and one with him, but the object of knowledge exists outside the one understanding, and is sometimes known or understood only in potency. Nor is the thing which is *per se* understood the similitude of the known object in virtue of which the intellect itself is informed. For this similitude is rather the actuating principle of understanding, not its term.[16]

The thing, then, that is primarily and *per se* understood is what the intellect conceives in itself of the object which it understands — either, that is, the definitio or the enunciation, depending on whether the conception attends the first or second operation of intellect respectively. And that which the intellect conceives in this way is called inner word (" verbum cordis "), the reality immediately signified by the external words of human speech.[17]

---

tuales substantiae sunt nobiliores, et secundum intellectum ad Dei imaginem factae dicuntur. Oportet ergo quod intelligere Deo conveniat et omnia quae sunt de ratione eius, licet alio modo conveniat sibi quam creaturis. " *De Pot.*, q. 9, a. 5c, 3.

[16] " De ratione autem eius quod est intelligere, est quod sit intelligens et intellectum. Id autem quod est per se intellectum non est res illa cuius notitia per intellectum habetur, cum illa quandoque sit intellecta in potentia tantum, et sit extra intelligentem, sicut cum homo intelligit res materiales, ut lapidem vel animal aut aliud huiusmodi : cum tamen oporteat quod intellectum sit in intelligente, et unum cum ipso. Neque etiam intellectum per se est similitudo rei intellectae, per quam informatur intellectus ad intelligendum : Intellectus enim non potest intelligere nisi secundum quod fit in actu per hanc similitudinem, sicut nihil aliud potest operari secundum quod est in potentia, sed secundum quod fit actu per aliquam formam. Haec ergo similitudo se habet in intelligendo sicut intelligendi principium, ut calor est principium calefactionis, non sicut intelligendi terminus. " *De Pot.*, q. 9, a. 5c, 4.

[17] " *Hoc ergo est primo et per se intellectum, quod intellectus in seipso concipit de re intellecta*, sive illud sit definitio, sive enuntiatio, secundum quod ponuntur duae operationes intellectus, in *III de Anima* (comment. 12). Hoc autem sic ab intellectu conceptum dicitur *verbum interius*, hoc enim est quod significatur per vocem ; non enim vox exterior significat ipsum intellectum, aut formam ipsius intelligibilem,

This brings Aquinas to the main point of his exposition. Thus far, he has shown that whatever is of the order of absolute perfection in the world of creatures, along with whatever pertains to the very essence or nature of such perfections, must be attributed to God Himself. This will certainly mean that intellect is to be attributed to God, and therefore also that there be in God both the 'intelligent' and the 'understood' — for this is of the very essence of intellect as such. Furthermore, the 'understood' must be taken as that which is understood primarily and *per se* — not the object of knowledge, therefore, nor the intelligible species, but, as St. Thomas explains, the thing which the intellect conceives within itself of what it understands, or simply the inner word.

But Aquinas continues. Since, then, there is understanding in God, and since in understanding Himself God understands all else, it is necessary to affirm in God the existence of the conception of intellect, which pertains absolutely to the formal or essential perfection of understanding as such (" est absolute de ratione eius quod est intelligere "). If we were able to grasp the divine understanding, its *quid* and *quomodo*, just as we grasp our own understanding, St. Thomas goes on without any interruption, the conception of the Divine Word would not be inaccessible to reason, just as the conception of the inner word of human understanding is not inaccessible to reason.[18]

But we can know the *quid non sit* and *quomodo non sit* of the divine understanding, and thus we can appreciate the difference between the Divine Word and the inner word of human understanding.[19] And with this, Aquinas proceeds to explain this difference in detail.[20] The rest of the exposition, however, need not delay the present analysis.

The point to be stressed in this passage of the *De Potentia* — and it is all the more telling insofar as Aquinas has

aut ipsum intelligere, sed conceptum intellectus quo mediante significat rem : ut cum dico, ' homo ' vel ' homo est animal '... " *De Pot.*, q. 9, a. 5c, 5.

[18] " Cum ergo in Deo sit intelligere, et intelligendo seipsum intelligat omnia alia, oportet quod ponatur in ipso esse conceptio intellectus, quae est absolute de ratione eius quod est intelligere. Si autem possemus comprehendere intelligere divinum quid et quomodo est sicut comprehendimus intelligere nostrum, non esset supra rationem conceptio verbi divini, sicut neque conceptio verbi humani. " *De Pot.*, q. 9, a. 5c, 6.

used here the strong and quite technical expression *de ratione eius quod est intelligere* — is that to interpret the exposition as some sort of rational demonstration, or at least a close imitation of this latter, is simply to involve St. Thomas, not merely in a contradiction, but in a very special type of contradiction.

St. Thomas, after all, was not infallible. It could be argued, if the critical historian felt he had evidence for the fact, or even if only for the scholar's hypothesis, that Aquinas had made in one place, possibly even within the same work, a statement whose consequences he then failed to recognize in another place. But it is certainly more difficult to support such a criticism when the original statement is being repeated right in the very passage where it is thought to be contradicted.

Nor is this all. In an age when literary depth analysis has scored its mark, one could perhaps continue to argue that a statement made because the author considered it proper, or accepted it on more or less external authority, or grasped its implications personally only in a superficial manner, is not by itself sufficient proof against the well-articulated reasoning process that stands in apparent contradiction.

But the very opposite is true of the present instance. St. Thomas not only reaffirms his constant teaching that natural reason cannot penetrate to the plurality of Persons, or to the procession of the Divine Word, and reaffirms it, moreover, both at the beginning and at the end of his exposition, but also introduces once again his basic reason for the impossibility : the human mind cannot know in this life *quid sit Deus*. And this reason draws from the heart of his whole theological synthesis.

For it was the compound principle that human understanding cannot know *quid sit Deus*, but must seek, under the light of faith and positive revelation, to understand the divine through the obscure and vicarious *quid non sit Deus*, that gave comprehensive expression to the Thomist ideal of theological science in his methodological treatise *In Boethii*

---

[19] " Posumus tamen scire *quid non sit* et quomodo non sit illud intelligere ; per quod possumus scire differentiam verbi concepti a Deo, et verbi concepti ab intellectu nostro ... '" *De Pot.*, q. 9, a. 5c, 7.
[20] *De Pot.*, q. 9, a. 5c, 7-10.

de Trinitate. This same ideal, rooted in the same principle, was then seen to have been implemented in *Contra Gentiles IV*, and will presently be seen to have been brought to its full perfection in the *Summa.*

III. Correct Understanding of the Thomist Generalization that Procession of Inner Word Is "de Ratione eius quod Est Intelligere"

Since the matter touches squarely on the *status quaestionis* of the present study, it will be useful at this time to draw at least certain provisional conclusions with regard to the nature and function of St. Thomas' seemingly rational or philosophical principle that procession of inner word is essential to intellect as such.

In the writer's judgment, what renders difficult the interpretation of passages such as *S. T., I*, q. 27, a. 1, and *De Pot.*, q. 9, a. 5, already seen — to which can be added *In Ioan.*, c. 1, lect. 1, and *Comp.* c. 52, which will be discussed later — is the presumption that *certitude*, not *understanding*, was necessarily Aquinas' intention and preoccupation.

Thus, if St. Thomas asserts in the preamble to the exposition in the *De Potentia*, q. 9, a. 5, that natural human reason cannot investigate nor sufficiently understand the plurality of Persons, but then goes on to explain the question as *aliqualis manifestatio*, it is simply presumed that this *aliqualis manifestatio*, is intended by St. Thomas to be an argument at least in the direction of certitude, if certitude in the stricter sense is being ruled out. The argument, therefore, will not prove or demonstrate in the normal sense of the term, but it will attain a degree of probability or suasiveness, and this inferior certitude will be considered its sole measure and sole value. Once this presumption has taken over, the rest follows quite naturally. As a good Christian, Aquinas knows that he cannot demonstrate the plurality of Persons, but as a human being obsessed by the ideal of rational proof and rational certitude, he will show how the existence of the mystery that has actually been revealed is at the same time strongly suggested by rational process.

In the same view, the Thomist generalization that whoever understands, from the simple fact that he does understand, there must proceed within him an inner word, is automatically taken as an exclusively rational principle, as a strictly philosophical law, that is to say, though one of somehow diminished certitude. For if rational certitude, albeit less than perfect or absolute, is the ideal, nothing but purely rational principles can possibly be admitted into the argument. As for the generalization itself, moreover, the mere recognition that it is expressed, in fact, as an essential universal suffices to remove all further doubt. For it is presumed that in any system of thought, the assigning of necessary causal dependence, in terms of what is absolutely essential to the very nature of things, is a purely rational or philosophical affair from start to finish.

From the text itself, however, it is quite clear that Aquinas did not see the problem in this perspective. On the one hand, he did not hesitate, at least from the time of the *Pars Prima* and the more or less contemporary questions of the *De Potentia*, not only to affirm in the manner af a comprehensive universal that procession of the inner word was *de facto* discoverable in every instance of understanding, but even to state as well that such procession was of the very essence or nature of understanding.

On the other hand, he also did not hesitate to affirm most explicitly — in the very same article of the *De Potentia* in which the generalization is employed, and also in the methodological passage of the *Pars Prima* (q. 2, a. 1) preceding its appearance in the ‘ *de Trinitate* ’ of the *Summa* — that that alone in virtue of which the generalization would be product of natural human reason was entirely outside the limits of reason’s competence. Since reason does not, and in this life cannot, know *quid sit Deus*, nor therefore the *quid sit* or *quomodo sit* of God’s knowledge, reason simply cannot grasp the causal nexus between the divine understanding and the procession of the Divine Word.

Moreover, it was shown above, apropos of the argument in *S. T.*, *I*, q. 27, a. 1, that for the generalization to be even *per se* capable of grounding a demonstration of the first trinitarian procession, it would have to be interpreted, not merely as a strictly essential universal principle, but as a strictly essential universal principle whose universal or transcendental quality was known to natural reason. But this is precisely the interpretation St. Thomas himself rules out. To be able to generalize in this fashion — to be able to affirm on purely rational evidence that in intellectual nature as such, including therefore the divine, procession of inner word was a necessary and absolute property of intellect itself — reason, once again, would have to grasp the causal nexus between the divine intelligence and procession of the Divine Word. Reason, then, would have to know *quid est Deus*. But in the present life, Aquinas insists, this is simply impossible — impossible, as a matter of fact, not only for unaided reason, but even for reason illuminated by supernatural faith.

It remains, therefore, that for St. Thomas himself, the generalization was not a purely rational, or purely philosophical, principle, but a compound principle, or better still: a theological principle — if it is Aquinas' own theological ideal and perspective that is being considered — in the strictest sense of the word.

In one of its dimensions, the principle would be rational, based upon rational analysis of the procession of inner word in human understanding, the necessity for this procession, and the manner in which what was exclusively in the order of act and perfection in this human procession could be isolated from what pertained rather to the potency and imperfection of the human creature. But in another of its dimensions, the same principle would be indebted for its ultimate formulation and its transcendental quality to the divine revelation of the first trinitarian procession.

Nevertheless, while it is important to point out this genetic dualism in the origin of the principle, it is perhaps still more important to note that this element of composition cannot be emphasized to the damage of the element of synthesis. In the mind of St. Thomas himself, the dimension of reason goes further and deeper than that for which reason would be responsible in the introduction of components ; and so too, as a matter of fact, does the dimension of faith. For the very structure of the principle, the integration of its components, is itself a matter of rational understanding, but yet, as described so clearly and so profoundly in the *In Boethii de Trinitate*, of that rational understanding whose principles and basic energy are Christian faith and the revealed word of God.

To be sure, this integration of rational explanatory structure with faith and revelation would have no proper place in the apologetic of a priori demonstration. Moreover, it is perhaps to be conceded that those for whom the only possible or at least worthwhile ideal of scientific theology is certitude of fact and data rather than its understanding are forced to the apologetical interpretation, for the very good reason that they have left themselves little else to look for.

The interpretation would be the more creditable, however, if the theological ideal of St. Thomas, and the true character of his methodology, had not been so often and so clearly indicated by the author himself. Thus, in the absence of any internal evidence that Aquinas had radically transformed what had presumably been the actual mentality and objective of St. Anselm, the historian might justly assume, at least as a working hypothesis, based both on what is now known of Anselm's influence during that two-century interval, and also on superficial resemblances in the texts, that St. Thomas as well must have allowed himself to be drawn in pretty much the same general direction. [21]

For in the lengthy doctrinal expositions of Aquinas, just as in the dialectical apologetics of Anselm, there is at least a well-articulated rational structure. But what other purpose could a man of this age, or for that matter any age, have in mind as the *raison d'être* of such a rational structure, unless it be the attempt to achieve some degree of certitude in demonstrating the a priori necessity of the revealed mystery?

Yet, whatever merit the assumption might have if St. Thomas had left to be surmised his own idea of the place and function of rational structure in integrated theology, it cannot be allowed to stand against the weighty evidence from the text itself that he was introducing this rational structure for quite a different purpose — not to confirm or in some way support the certitude of faith in the revealed mystery with an inferior, subordinate, less perfect certitude of reason,

---

[21] For the position of St. Anselm, see J. BAYART, S. J., " The Concept of Mystery According to St. Anselm of Canterbury, " *Recherches de théologie ancienne et médiévale*, IX (1927), pp. 125-126. While not pretending to give a personal judgment on Anselm, the writer would call attention to Fr. Bayart's overall reserve in attributing an unqualified apologetical intent, in the sense of demonstrating apriori necessity *post factum revelatum*, even to Anselm. Cf. also P. Bouillard's incisive contribution, "La preuve de Dieu dans le *Proslogion* et son interprétation par Karl Barth," in the *Spicilegium Beccense* volume itself (pp. 191-207).

but rather to achieve a positive, however limited, understanding of the revealed mystery, whose certitude, moreover,
would play the rôle, not of the *quod erat demonstrandum*, but
of the basic energy in its own partial understanding.

This is precisely the goal St. Thomas has set himself
here in the *Summa*, in the *prooemium* to the twenty-seventh
question. He proposes to treat the divine procession, the
trinitarian relations, and the Three Persons. He proposes
to treat them in just this order, and the reason why he
will treat first of the divine procession is because procession
stands in the place, so to speak, of internal cause with
respect to the relations, and ultimately the distinct Persons.
But to treat of procession or origin in the context of cause,
is to treat of it from the aspect of how it should be taken
or somehow understood, and not in any sense to demonstrate
or confirm the certitude of its existence.

Thus, as already seen, when in the very first article following this *prooemium* Aquinas begins to discuss procession
as such, the point of his discussion is not at all the existence
of procession as element in the revealed mystery, but simply
how procession is to be understood (*accipere*, *intelligere*), its
existence and the perfect certitude of its existence presupposed. Furthermore, the very order St. Thomas chooses confirms this intention.

To begin with procession, and pass on, first to the relations, and then to the Persons, is simply to reverse the order
of analysis and follow the order of synthesis. But this is to
move in the order, not of what is first known, and could lead
in this way to knowledge of what would be known subsequently, but of what is first in reality, and is known only
through analysis or reduction from what is first in knowledge.

In God, of course, there is no strict priority, not even
natural priority, of relations with respect to Persons, or of
procession with respect to relations. There is no strict causality within the divinity, as Aquinas himself notes in his refutation of Arianism and Sabellianism. Nevertheless, according
to the human way of understanding, the legitimate and only
possible way in which the revealed mysteries can to some
extent be penetrated through reason enlightened and directed
by faith, there is the analogical order of dependence derived
from the necessity of attributing to God whatever pertains
to the proper reality of that which is known to exist in God,

whether from reason, as in the case of the attributes strictly so called, or, and more especially, on the authority of His revealed self-manifestation, in the case not only of the attributes and essential perfections, but also of what belongs to the inner life of the Divine Trinity.

It is according to this qualified priority, then, that St. Thomas begins his treatment with procession. For it is by or through procession, that there are relations, and through relations, distinction of Persons.

The true nature and consequences of this order of synthesis, and the clear proof it offers that the apologetical perspective and intent — in the sense of establishing some sort of a priori necessity with respect to the existence of the mystery — had no part whatsoever in the theological ideal and method of the *Summa*, will be more fully appreciated when the main course of development in subsequent questions has been studied in some detail. As this is being done, it will likewise become more evident why it is in the nature of the *Summa* as St. Thomas constructed the work, that the apologetical problem under discussion in the present investigation would pose itself, if at all, in the very beginning of the treatise, and would have to be handled then before going on, even though the larger view of St. Thomas' trinitarian synthesis in its ultimate expansion would also be needed to make the solution to this problem adequate and complete.

It is in this connection, moreover, that the conclusions which have just been drawn with regard to the correct understanding of Aquinas' generalization on procession of the inner word as essential to intellectual nature are to some extent provisional.

That St. Thomas himself did not intend this universal principle to be understood as a purely rational generalization, or philosophical law, is already clear. For in his own mind, the ultimate formulation of the principle and its truly transcendental quality depended on the revelation of the first trinitarian procession.

On the further question, however, as to why exactly Aquinas introduced this same principle at the very beginning of his theological exposition, and in the position normally accorded the major premise in syllogistic argument, the solution is at the present juncture necessarily incomplete. For it requires an accurate appreciation of the synthetic order of theological development — the *ordo doctrinae* defined and out-lined by St. Thomas in the *prooemium* in the twenty-seventh question — and up to the moment the major steps in this development, though legitimately anticipated from their ex-plicit indication in the *prooemium*, have nevertheless not yet been sufficiently studied in the full perspective of the ensuing text.

At the moment, therefore, the solution stands as follows. Right at the beginning of his ' *de Trinitate* ' of the *Summa*, in the first article of question twenty-seven, Aquinas introduces the general or transcendental principle that procession of inner word is essential to intellect. This procedure, for some interpreters, raises immediately a question of apologetical in-tent. For it seems that St. Thomas will go on to deduce from this purely philosophical law the a priori necessity for the procession of the Divine Word. Or, since this unqualified assessment would do obvious violence to the constantly repeat-ed assertion that rational demonstration in this area is impos-sible, it seems at least that St. Thomas has made his own the apologetical ideal of imitating such purely rational process as closely as possible — giving reasons that are suasive if not actually conclusive — but still with the theological objec-tive of confirming or supporting the certitude of the revealed mystery in its root existence.

In the attempt to solve the problem thus raised, it has already been shown that St. Thomas' theological objective was not the certitude of the mystery, but rather its partial under-standing once certitude was unequivocally presupposed from positive revelation, and that the principle calling for universal procession of an inner word in intellectual activity was not a philosophical law, but rather a strictly theological general-ization dependent for its ultimate formulation on knowledge of the first trinitarian procession precisely as revealed.[22] Left at this, however, the proposed solution, whatever its merits,

---

[22] The writer should perhaps make it clear at this point that he is not unaware of the existence of a somewhat different approach. The solution is sometimes offered that when Aquinas says intellectual con-ception is " absolute de ratione eius quod est intelligere, " he is speak-ing *ex sola ratione*, but is not thereby demonstrating the real proces-sion of the Divine Word, inasmuch as he says nothing of the *mode* in which this intellectual conception exists in God. On strictly lo-gical grounds, the solution is quite satisfying. On more historical grounds, however, and if one accepts the exegesis that in this and in parallel texts " conceptio intellectus " is meant to be taken in the

belongs to the class of such as address themselves to a difficulty that is actually inherent in a given text without taking the further step of showing that, if the literary genre employed by the author had been correctly understood in the first place, the difficulty itself would never have arisen.

It remains to be seen, then, whether in its more complete form the solution could not only solve the problem, but even dismiss it, as it were, from the text.

The intimation that this is really the case in the present instance has already been given by examining what exactly is implied in the words of the *prooemium*. Presupposing the existence of the trinitarian mystery in all its fulness, St. Thomas does not plan to structure his theological exposition according to the order of things as known to men, but rather according to the order of things as they are in themselves. Thus, he begins, not with the salvific activity, interrelationships and personal character of the Three Persons as described in Sacred Scripture and christian faith, but rather with the divine procession as such, and as reduced, moreover — this is brought out in the first article — to its ultimate cause or *ratio* in the internal procession that is proper to intellectual being.

Quite clearly, therefore, Aquinas has elected to follow a pattern or design of exposition in which the starting point is not the first element in man's own knowledge, but rather what man knows — once his knowledge has been completed through scientific analysis, and extended in this same analysis to the furthest possible limit of causal penetration — to be the first element, so to speak, in reality. But in the light of such a pattern or design of exposition, to introduce at the very beginning of the process the universal or transcendental principle that procession of inner word is an essential property of intellect, far from being unusual or in need of explanation, is quite normal, in a sense even necessary.

Consequently, what is left for the present study is simply to examine the rest of the ' *de Trinitate* ' of the *Pars Prima* in sufficient detail so that the true nature of its synthetic order, the *ordo doctrinae*, will become evident from the text itself, and the foregoing provisional conclusion thus all the more fully substantiated.

---

proper sense from the onset, and that ever since the fourth question *De Veritate* Aquinas considered real procession as essential to the proper notion, it seems that the solution is less applicable.

IV. CONTINUATION AND COMPLETION OF THE DOCTRINE ON
THE DIVINE ORIGIN OR PROCESSION AS PRESENTED IN
QUESTION 27

It is time, then, to resume the reading of the text for the
purpose of determining its structure.

In the opening article of the twenty-seventh question,
Aquinas discussed divine procession in general, and reached
the conclusion that, once the existence of this procession was
known, not from reason but from revelation, rational theology
could see that it had to be taken or understood as the purely
internal, immanent procession of spiritual emanation — beginning, that is, with the emanation of inner word, which is
an essential and absolute consequence of intellectual being.

In the second article, St. Thomas goes on to show that
the procession of the Divine Word is properly called generation, and the Word itself, Son.[23] The intention here is not
to prove the generation of the Son, nor even to substantiate
the actual revelation of this article of faith by indicating, as
in *Contra Gentiles IV*, its biblical sources. The brief appeal
to Ps 2 : 7 in the *contra* suffices to recall the existence and
authenticity of the revealed mystery.[24] With this presupposed, St. Thomas' declared and sole intention is to show how
the procession of the Divine Word, when understood as rational theology would have to understand it, verifies the formal
perfection or reality (*ratio*) of generation.

The procession of the Divine Word, Aquinas begins, is
called generation. The fact, then, is accepted without further
discussion. But to explain this fact (" ad cuius evidentiam "),
St. Thomas adds immediately, one must consider that the
term generation is used in two different ways : first, in the
improper sense, where it is merely a synonym for the change
from non-being to being in material things ; secondly, and
properly, as signifying the origin of a living thing from a conjoined living principle.

Furthermore, generation in the strict sense obtains only
when the generated proceeds from the generator according to

---

[23] *S. T.*, *I*, q. 27, a. 2.

[24] " Sed contra est, quod dicitur in Psalmo (II, 7) : *Ego hodie
genui te.* " *S. T.*, *I*, q. 27, a. 2, contra.

the likeness or similitude of the latter, the likeness or similitude, moreover, of identity in specific nature. Now in human beings, Aquinas notes, since human life passes from potency into act, there is improper, as well as proper, generation
to be accounted for. If, on the other hand, there should be
some living being wholly without such potency and imperfection, any procession to be found in this being could satisfy
the formal essence only of that mode of generation which is
strictly proper to living things.[25]

Against this background, St. Thomas goes on to show
how precisely the procession of the Divine Word is generation
in the proper and strict sense of the term. It is a matter of
life and origin of the living, inasmuch as intellectual emanation
is vital operation. The procession is from a conjoined principle, as brought out by its perfect immanence. The Word
of God proceeds in likeness or similitude, for it is the nature
of the intellectual conception to be the likeness or similitude
of the thing understood. This likeness, finally, is that of
existing in the same nature, since in God, being and understanding are to be identified. Hence it is, St. Thomas concludes, that the procession of the Divine Word is called generation, and the Divine Word so proceeding is called Son.[26]

---

[25] " Respondeo : Dicendum quod processio verbi in divinis dicitur generatio. Ad cuius evidentiam sciendum est quod nomine generationis dupliciter utimur. Uno modo communiter ad omnia genera-
bilia et corruptibilia : et sic generatio nihil aliud est quam mutatio
de non esse ad esse. Alio modo proprie in viventibus : et sic generatio significat originem alicuius viventis a principio vivente coniuncto;
et haec proprie dicitur nativitas. Non tamen omne huiusmodi dicitur
genitum, sed proprie quod procedit secundum rationem similitudinis.
Unde pilus vel capillus non habet rationem geniti et filii, sed solum
quod procedit secundum rationem similitudinis ; non cuiuscumque,
nam vermes qui generantur in animalibus, non habent rationem generationis et filiationis, licet sit similitudo secundum genus, sed requiritur ad rationem talis generationis, quod procedat secundum rationem
similitudinis in natura eiusdem speciei, sicut homo procedit ab homine
et equus ab equo. In viventibus igitur, quae de potentia in actum
vitae procedunt, sicut sunt homines et animalia, generatio utramque
generationem includit. Si autem sit aliquod vivens cuius vita non
exeat de potentia in actum, processio, si qua in tali vivente invenitur, excludit omnino primam rationem generationis, sed potest habere
rationem generationis, quae est propria viventium ." *S. T.*, *I*, q. 27,
a. 2c, a and 2.
[26] " Sic igitur processio verbi in divinis habet rationem generationis. Procedit enim per modum intelligibilis actionis, quae est operatio

In its narrower aspect, therefore, the argument develops according to the principle often set down, as for example in the *De Potentia* passage (q. 9, a. 5) seen a short time ago, that the formal realities that must be attributed to God inasmuch and insofar as what is utterly of the order of perfection in the creature has been divested of all accompanying potency, are to be attributed, not only in the simple essence of the formal reality — generation in this case — but also in everything that necessarily and absolutely pertains to this simple essence. Thus, if there is generation in God, as Aquinas supposes, and if generation is referred to God in a strictly proper sense, as Aquinas likewise supposes, everything that is essential and necessary to the *ratio* of generation must also be found in God.

In its larger aspect, the exposition has the form of the argument, not from cause to effect — which will be the case, though not without qualifications, when Aquinas takes up the divine relations as dependent on procession in the next question — but from the general or abstract to the particular. In a sense, therefore, the development at this point is horizontal rather than vertical. In the first article, St. Thomas had treated the divine procession in general, and in explaining its immanent character was led naturally to introduce the procession of the Divine Word as emanation of the intelligible.

But in God, the first procession, or procession of the inner word in intellect, is also properly called generation, and the Divine Word so proceeding is properly called Son. Consequently, Aquinas is faced with the task of explaining, to the limited extent this can be done, both the intelligible emanation and the Son's generation, one in terms of the other. For it is clear that they are to be identified as one and the same procession. He absolves this task in the manner just seen.

Aquinas moves, therefore, from procession or origin in general, unspecified at first in either mode or number, to the

---

vitae; et a principio coniuncto, ut supra iam dictum est; et secundum rationem similitudinis, quia conceptio intellectus est similitudo rei intellectae; et ineadem natura existens, quia in Deo idem est intelligere et esse, ut supra ostensum est. Unde processio verbi in divinis dicitur generatio, et ipsum verbum procedens dicitur Filius. " *S. T., I,* q. 27, a. 2c, 3.

procession of the Word, which is likewise the generation of
the Son, in particular. In so doing, moreover, he brings out
in emergent detail that essential consequence of the *ordo doctrinae* he has chosen which was already implicit in his *prooemium* : namely, development, not from the prior to the posterior in the order of knowledge, but from the prior to the
posterior in the order of reality. For it is clear that what
is prior in knowledge, from divine revelation and the testimonies of Scripture, is not ' procession ' or ' origin ' in general,
much less in the abstract, but this or that procession in particular. Procession or origin in general, in the *ratio* of cause
or that which in God is rather *ad instar causae*, is, according
to the human way of understanding the divine, prior in reality.

Moreover, it is also clear that, while the procession of
the Divine Word is utterly identical with the generation of
the Son, and both descriptions explicitly contained in the
testimony of Scripture, nevertheless in the explanatory structure of rational theology, the intellectual account of the first
procession enjoys the precedence of being more immediate to
the general account of divine procession as internal cause of
the relations, and hence of the distinct Persons, and is therefore the basis, so to speak, to which the description as generation must conform, and in terms of which it must be understood.

In the third and fourth articles immediately following,
St. Thomas adheres to the same method in introducing the
second trinitarian procession, the procession *per modum amoris*. Once again, he begins with a flat statement of fact to
indicate what is being presupposed : in God, he says, there
are two processions, the procession of the Word, and a certain
other (" quaedam alia ").

He goes on to explain this second procession (" ad cuius
evidentiam ") just as he had the first. One must consider,
St. Thomas begins, that there is no procession in the divinity
except that which follows upon immanent operation. But in
intellectual nature, such operation is either the action of intellect or the action of will. It is the first, action of intellect,
that gives procession of the inner word. In human beings,
however, there is a further procession, procession of love, that
is attendant upon the operation of will, and whereby the beloved exists in the lover, just as through conception of inner

word, the thing ' spoken ' (" res dicta ") or the thing understood (" res intellecta ") exists in the one understanding.   And
thus, there is attributed to God, besides procession of the
Word, a further procession, which is the procession of love.[27]

In his reply to the third objection, answering the difficulty
that, since intellect and will in God are one, the procession of
love would coincide with the procession of the Word, St. Thomas takes occasion to explain the order of the two divine
processions in terms of the necessary structure of intellectual
nature and operation.   Though the divine will is not something
other than the divine intellect, still it is of the essence of
will and intellect that the processions following upon the operations of each should be related to each other according to
a certain order.   For the procession of love exists only in order
to the procession of the word, inasmuch as nothing can be
loved in will unless it is conceived in intellect.   Consequently,
just as, notwithstanding the substantial identity between God's
intellect and the conception of intellect, the Divine Word is
ordered to the principle from which it proceeds, so too, notwithstanding the identity in God of intellect and will, nevertheless, inasmuch as it is of the essence of love that it not
proceed except from the conception of intellect, the procession of love in God is distinct from, and ordered to, the procession of the Word.[28]

---

[27] " Respondeo : Dicendum quod in divinis sunt duae processiones,
scilicet processio verbi et quaedam alia.   Ad cuius evidentiam considerandum est quod in divinis non est processio nisi secundum actionem
quae non tendit in aliquid extrinsecum, sed manet in ipso agente.
Huiusmodi autem actio in intellectuali natura est actio intellectus et
actio voluntatis.   Processio autem verbi attenditur secundum actionem intelligibilem.   Secundum autem operationem voluntatis invenitur in nobis quaedam alia processio, scilicet processio amoris, secundum
quam amatum est in amante, sicut est per conceptionem verbi res
dicta vel intellecta in intelligente.   Unde et praeter processionem verbi ponitur alia processio in divinis, quae est processio amoris. "   *S. T.*,
I, q. 27, a. 3c.

[28] " Ad tertium dicendum, quod licet in Deo non sit aliud voluntas et intellectus, tamen de ratione voluntatis et intellectus est, quod
processiones quae sunt secundum actionem utriusque, se habeant secundum quendam ordinem ; non enim est processio amoris nisi in
ordine ad processionem verbi, nihil enim potest voluntate amari, nisi
sit in intellectu conceptum.   Sicut igitur attenditur quidam ordo verbi
ad principium a quo procedit, licet in divinis sit eadem substantia intellectus et conceptio intellectus ; ita, licet in Deo sit ipem voluntas

In the fourth article, Aquinas completes his exposition of the second procession by explaining its specific nature in contradistinction to the procession of inner word in order to show why it is that the procession of love is not and cannot be called generation. There is a fundamental difference between intellect and will. Intellect is in act inasmuch as the thing understood exists in intellect according to its similitude. Will is in act, on the other hand, not inasmuch as some such similitude of the thing willed exists in the will, but rather inasmuch as the will is inclined or drawn unto the thing willed.

Intellectual procession, therefore, is a matter of similitude and to this extent can have the character of generation. For the generator begets that which is like himself. Volitional procession, to the contrary, is not a matter of similitude, but rather of being drawn or attracted toward something. Hence, what proceeds in God according to will proceeds, not as the begotten or son, but as ' spirit ', since the word ' spirit ' designates that vital motion and force whereby someone is said to be moved or drawn to do something.[29]

As Aquinas himself observes, the second trinitarian procession, unlike the first, has no special or proper name.[30] But the Person Who proceeds in this manner is, of course, and as explicitly indicated in the *contra*, the Holy Spirit.[31] Thus

---

et intellectus, tamen, quia de ratione amoris est, quod non procedat nisi a conceptione intellectus, habet ordinis distinctionem processio amoris a processione verbi in divinis. '' *S. T.*, I, q. 27, a. 3, ad 3m.

[29] '' Respondeo : Dicendum quod processio amoris in divinis non debet dici generatio. Ad cuius evidentiam considerandum est quod haec est differentia inter intellectum et voluntatem, quod intellectus fit in actu per hoc quod res intellecta est in intellectu secundum suam similitudinem : voluntas autem fit in actu, non per hoc quod aliqua similitudo voliti sit in volente, sed ex hoc quod voluntas habet quandam inclinationem in rem volitam. Processio igitur quae attenditur secundum rationem intellectus, est secundum rationem similitudinis ; et intantum potest habere rationem generationis, quia omne generans generat sibi simile. Processio autem quae attenditur secundum actionem voluntatis, non consideratur secundum rationem similitudinis, sed magis secundum rationem impellentis et moventis in aliquid ; et ideo quod procedit in divinis per modum amoris, non procedit ut genitum vel ut filius, sed magis procedit ut spiritus. Quo nomine quaedam vitalis motio et impulsio designatur, prout aliquis ex amore dicitur moveri vel impelli ad aliquid faciendum. '' *S. T.*, I, q. 27, a. 4c.

[30] *S. T.*, I, q. 27, a. 4, ad 3m.

[31] *S. T.*, I, q. 27, a. 4, contra.

it is that St. Thomas does not conclude his treatment of the procession of love until he has explained, from within the structure of intelligible and volitional emanation, the propriety of the word ' spirit ' to describe the Person Who proceeds *per modum amoris.*

For the purposes of the present study, however, the more significant point is that St. Thomas quite clearly understands the second procession in terms of its dependence, quasi-causal moreover, upon the first. The procession of love in the will is from the inner word in intellect, and Aquinas makes use of this consideration later on when he has to explain why the Holy Spirit proceeds from the Son as well as from the Father.[32] Even at the moment, however, the fact that St. Thomas thus anticipates here what is, in the order of reality or of the *priora quoad se*, the ultimate internal reason for the procession *ab utroque*, and discovers this reason in what rational theology — but not pure philosophy — knows to be essential to intellectual nature, helps to bring out more clearly the meaning and significance of the *ordo doctrinae.*

In a fifth and final article, St. Thomas explains briefly why there can be only these two processions in God. The only way in which divine processions can be understood is according to immanent operations. But in intellectual nature, including therefore the divine nature, such operations are only two — the one of understanding, and the other of will.[33]

V. From the Processions to the Relations

Having thus completed his treatment of the two processions, Aquinas begins, in the twenty-eighth question, to take up the trinitarian relations.

A preliminary observation, however, might not be out of place at this juncture. As listed in the *rubricae*, the first of the four articles comprising this next question bears the

---

[32] *S. T., I,* q. 36, a. 2.

[33] " Respondeo : Dicendum quod processiones in divinis accipi non possunt nisi secundum actiones quae in agente manent. Huiusmodi autem actiones in natura intellectuali et divina non sunt nisi duae, scilicet intelligere et velle. Relinquitur igitur quod nulla alia processio possit esse in divinis nisi verbi et amoris. " *S. T., I,* q. 27, a. 5c.

title : " Utrum in Deo sint aliquae relationes. " From the
wording, it might be presumed that St. Thomas proposed to
discuss whether or not these relations existed. On closer
look, it turns out that it is the ' reality ' of these relations
which is really in point. For in the concluding and summational lines of his positive exposition, the final " igitur " is
directed, not to the existence of relations in God, but to their
reality, or, one might be inclined to say, to the existence of
real relations.

Yet, even this correction is misleading. For on still closer
examination, it will turn out that Aquinas' preoccupation in
the passage is not with the ' whether ' of the divine relations,
nor even with the ' whether ' of their reality, but rather with
the ' why '. It was quite the same in the preceding body
of articles concerned with procession or origin.

When the title read : " Utrum sit processio in divinis, "
St. Thomas was clearly presupposing the positive ' answer ',
and his aim, already seen, was to discuss the nature of the
divine procession, or in this sense, the ' why '. In the remaining articles also : " Utrum aliqua processio in divinis generatio dici possit " gave, not the answer ' whether or no ', but
the explanation ' why ' and ' how ' ; " Utrum praeter generationem possit esse aliqua alia processio in divinis " supposed
that there could be and was, and went on to understand ' why'
this could be ; " Utrum illa alia processio possit dici generatio " actually explained the nature of the second procession
in contradistinction from the first ; and the last, " Utrum
sint plures processiones in divinis quam duae, " was less bothered with the fact, than with the reason for the fact, impossibility as derived from the nature of intellectual being.

The point is of some importance — not, of course, the
rather pedantic point that Aquinas might have discovered
titles more in keeping with the actual thrust of his discussions, but the more methodological point that the titles as
they stand, whatever their merits or demerits, must not be
allowed to obscure the basic intention and significance of what
is really being treated, particularly as viewed from within the
larger context and design of the entire treatise.

In other words, the literary or pedagogical device of setting up a problem in the conventional formulation of the *utrum
sit* is not much of an argument that the ' whether or no ' of
existence is what St. Thomas is out to prove, not even when

there is the summary echo of the original *utrum* in the wording of the 'conclusion'.   For as was clear in the procession
articles, often enough these literary conclusions mark, not
what was proved or explained in the article, but rather what
was presupposed throughout.

In the opening article of the twenty-eighth question,
then, Aquinas does, in fact, discuss the reality of the divine
relations.   He begins with the simple statement of fact that
there are in God certain real relations.   The problem here,
he notes, could actually arise only in the case of relations.
For while the proper perfection of any other category implies
real inherence, the proper perfection of relation does not,
but *per se* signifies only the *respectus ad aliud*.   When, however, the *respectus* itself belongs to the very nature of things,
the relation is real.[34]

Next, after having explained at some length the peculiar
difficulty attendant upon relations, and the question that can
always be raised as to the reality of a particular relation,
Aquinas returns to the trinitarian relations as such.   When
something proceeds from a principle of the same nature, he
continues, it is necessary that both the reality so proceeding
and its principle coexist in the same order, and that thus
each should bear to the other a real respect or relation.   But
the divine processions take place in perfect identity of nature,
and hence the relations that follow upon these divine processions are necessarily real.[35]

---

[34] " Respondeo : Dicendum quod relationes quaedam sunt in divinis realiter.   Ad cuius evidentiam considerandum est quod solum
in his quae dicuntur ad aliquid, inveniuntur aliqua secundum rationem
tantum et non secundum rem, non autem in aliis generibus, quia alia
genera, ut qualitas, quantitas, secundum propriam rationem significant
aliquid alicui inhaerens ; ea vero quae dicuntur ad aliquid, secundum
propriam rationem significant solum respectum ad aliud.   Qui quidem
respectus aliquando est in ipsa natura rerum ; utpote quando aliquae
res secundum suam naturam ad invicem ordinatae sunt et invicem inclinationem habent.   Et huiusmodi relationes oportet esse reales ...
S. T., *I*, q. 28, a. 1c, 1.

[35] " Cum autem aliquid procedit a principio eiusdem naturae, necesse est quod ambo, scilicet et procedens et id a quo procedit, in eodem ordine conveniant ; et sic oportet quod habeant reales respectus
ad invicem.   Cum igitur processiones in divinis sint in identitate naturae, ut ostensum est, necesse est quod relationes, quae secundum
processiones divinas accipiuntur, sint relationes reales. " *S. T.*, *I*,
q. 28, a. 1c, 2.

Thus, beyond the problem of the existence of the relations as real with which it is integrated in the course of the exposition, there is the simple and clear prolongation of the central theme as St. Thomas shows that the first and immediate consequence of the processions — in the order of the *priora quoad se* — is the relations, necessarily real relations, which depend upon the processions as upon their quasi-cause.

The reply to the fourth objection, in which Aquinas treats specifically of the divine paternity and filiation as following upon the first procession, brings out the fundamental consistency and progress of theme a bit more clearly. To show that the relations directly dependent upon intellectual operation, between the inner word, that is, and its principle, must be real, St. Thomas notes that the intellect itself is a reality, and is referred in a real manner to that which proceeds from itself in intelligible emanation.[36]

Continuing his discussion of the trinitarian relations, Aquinas next explains, in connection with the extrinsically attached relation and the controversy occasioned by Gilbert de la Porrée, that if perfections which have in creatures the character of accident must be attributed or in this sense transferred to God, such perfections must be attributed to God as identified with His substantial existence. Hence, the divine relations are not distinct in their existence from the unique and simple existence of God.[37]

Nevertheless, he goes on in the article following, these same real relations, which are to be identified with God's substantial existence, are most certainly distinct, and really distinct, one from the other. For once real relations are attributed to God, whatever is essential to the formal perfection of relation must also be affirmed of God, and hence the *respectus unius ad alterum*, the opposition or distinction that

---

[36] " Sed relationes quae consequuntur operationes intellectus, quae sunt inter verbum intellectualiter procedens et id a quo procedit, non sunt relationes rationis tantum, sed rei ; quia et ipse intellectus et ratio res quaedam est ; et comparatur realiter ad id quod procedit intelligibiliter, sicut res corporalis ad id quod procedit corporaliter. Et sic paternitas et filiatio sunt relationes reales in divinis. " *S. T.*, *I*, q. 28, a. 1, ad 4m.

[37] *S. T.*, *I*, q. 28, a. 2c.

is of the very nature of relation, and which, in the case of real relations, cannot but be real.[38]

In the fourth and last article of the section, St. Thomas takes up the matter of the four real relations by name — paternity, filiation, 'spiration', and procession — and explains why there must be just these four, but no others.

The passage becomes at the same time a neat synthetic summary of his treatment of the divine relations as immediately dependent upon the two processions. For relations in God can be grounded solely upon the immanent operations which constitute the processions *ad intra*. But these processions are only two : procession of the Word in intellect, and procession of the beloved in will. And each of these processions grounds two opposite or corresponding relations, the one of what proceeds from its principle, and the other of the principle itself.

Since the procession of the Word is properly also generation, in the first instance, the relation of the principle itself is called paternity, and the relation of what proceeds from this principle is called filiation or sonship. The procession of love, on the other hand, has no proper name ; hence, neither have its two corresponding relations. But in this second instance, the name 'spiration' is given to the relation of the principle itself, and the simple name procession is retained for what proceeds from this principle.[39]

---

[38] " Respondeo : Dicendum quod ex eo quod aliquid alicui attribuitur, oportet quod attribuantur ei omnia illa quae sunt de ratione illius : sicut cuicumque attribuitur homo, oportet quod attribuatur ei rationale. De ratione autem relationis est respectus ad alterum, secundum quem aliquid alteri opponitur relative. Cum igitur in Deo sit realiter relatio, ut dictum est, oportet quod realiter sit ibi oppositio. Relativa autem oppositio in sui ratione includit distinctionem. Unde oportet quod in Deo sit realis distinctio, non quidem secundum rem absolutam, quae est essentia, in qua est summa unitas et simplicitas, sed secundum rem relativam. " *S. T.*, *I*, q. 28, a. 3c.

[39] After showing, in the first paragraph, that of the two possible grounds for relation, that is to say quantity and action (and ' passion '), only action could ground real relation in God, and only such action, moreover, as is strictly immanent, St. Thomas continues : " Huiusmodi autem processiones sunt duae tantum, ut supra dictum est, quarum una accipitur secundum actionem intellectus, quae est processio verbi ; alia secundum actionem voluntatis, quae est processio amoris. Secundum quamlibet autem processionem oportet accipere duas relationes oppositas, quarum una sit procedentis a principio

Thus St. Thomas completes his discussion of the divine relations. In the *prooemium* to the twenty-seventh question, which served as the introduction to the entire treatise ' *de Trinitate* ' in the *Summa*, he had proposed to treat of the processions, the relations, and the Persons, in this order. St. Thomas has come, then, to the third and last point to be taken up, namely the Three Divine Persons as such.

VI.   FROM THE RELATIONS TO THE THREE PERSONS

As one would naturally expect, the exposition now expands considerably. For within this single division ' *de Personis* ', Aquinas will discuss almost everything he has left to say about the Trinity — with, in fact, only the eight articles of the concluding forty-third question on the trinitarian missions still remaining. In terms of the purpose and range of the present study, much of this material is less than directly pertinent, and to comment upon such detail in more than summary fashion, might tend even to obscure the central and immediate issue of apologetical perspective.

So far as this particular problem of apologetical perspective is concerned, the matter would have been substantially disposed of above, where St. Thomas introduced at the very beginning of his treatise the processions or origins as quasi-cause of the relations, and hence of the distinction of Persons, and what was yet to follow, including even the discussion of the Trinity as inaccessible to purely natural reason in the thirty-second question, would have been simply confirmatory, had it not been for the fact, noted at the time, that the best, if not only, way to show what the theological intention and basic perspective of the *Summa* was not, was to show what it was. For, as already remarked, unless the ideal of understanding, in the light of which the question of procession was

---

et alia ipsius principii.   Processio autem verbi dicitur generatio secundum propriam rationem qua competit rebus viventibus.   Relatio autem principii generationis in viventibus perfectis dicitur paternitas ; relatio vero procedentis a principio dicitur filiatio.   Processio autem amoris non habet nomen proprium, ut supra dictum est ;   unde neque relationes quae secundum ipsam accipiuntur.   Sed vocetur relatio principii huius processionis spiratio ;   relatio autem procedentis processio ; quamvis haec duo nomina ad ipsas processiones vel origines pertineant, et non ad relationes. "   *S. T.*, *I*, q. 28, a. 4c, 1 and 2.

the first to be treated, were sufficiently recognized, and its methodological implications and consequences accurately grasped, the historian would be more apt to be seen presuming an ideal of certitude that was not at all what Aquinas himself had in view.

Furthermore, the Thomist ideal, one might call it generic ideal, of understanding, that had been outlined years previously and on a theoretical basis in the *In Boethii de Trinitate*, then translated into actual performance in the fourth book of the *Contra Gentiles*, became in the *Pars Prima* the very much more specific ideal of understanding which is understanding through synthesis. Again as already observed at the time, what St. Thomas proposed to treat in his own explicit declaration of intention and approach in the introduction to this particular '*de Trinitate*' in his *Summa Theologiae*, was not simply the Trinity, nor the Trinity according to some other design and arrangement, but the Trinity according to the *ordo doctrinae*, the order of the *priora quoad se*.

The decision, then, to continue with the *Summa* text into the body of the treatise, to study next Aquinas' presentation of the relations, and now his presentation of the distinct Persons, was taken, not for the sake of being able to incorporate successive proofs that understanding, not certitude, was in fact the perduring intention — for such further proofs, at this stage, would be somewhat superfluous — but solely for the purpose of substantiating the nature of the *ordo doctrinae* and its necessary consequences.

To complete this task, there will be no need of examining the detail of subsequent questions and articles, in which St. Thomas handles from within the structure of his trinitarian synthesis the sundry problems and problematics of definition, legitimate predication, and the like, or where he proposes his own solution to several of the controversies — on relations mostly — that occupied the systematic theologians of the thirteenth century. Rather, it will be sufficient to concentrate upon the synthetic development itself.

Having finished, then, his treatment of the trinitarian relations as immediately dependent upon the two divine processions, St. Thomas goes on to speak of the Persons as immediately dependent upon the relations.[40]

---

[40] " Praemissis autem his quae de processionibus et relationibus

Actually, the four articles comprising the first question of this new section, the twenty-ninth, serve more as a background introduction, than as the first step in organic exposition. Aquinas accepts and explains the definition of person, attributed to Boethius, as the individual or singular in the genus of substance in rational beings.[41] Next, he discusses the respect of person to hypostasis, subsistence, and essence.[42] In the third article, he observes that, inasmuch as the rational subsistent is the most perfect reality in all nature, the designation 'person' is to be attributed to God in an eminent manner.[43] The consideration here is quite general, and the element of relation in the concept of person is not as yet incorporated.

St. Thomas takes up the relative aspect of divine personality in the next and last article of this introductory question. The common notion of person does not involve, it is true, the respect *ad aliquid* proper to relation as such. At the same time, and strictly on the strength of its own formal intent, person signifies the distinct individual in rational nature. But since in God there can be no distinction within the divine essence except such as is founded upon the opposite or corresponding relations, it follows necessarily that the particular notion of person as applied to the divinity will signify relation — not relation precisely inasmuch as it is relation, but more exactly, relation as subsistent hypostasis in the divine nature.[44]

The foregoing consideration, however, is strictly preliminary. Thus far, Aquinas has introduced the plurality of Persons only in passing and with a degree of anticipation, in order that what is necessary for the proper and correct understanding of the Divine Person can be presumed. It is rather in the first two articles of the thirtieth question immediately following, that he approaches the plurality of Persons in the full focus of the *ordo doctrinae*, as directly dependent, therefore, upon the relations of origin.

Thus, in the first article, St. Thomas refers his reader back to the discussion on the relations in the twenty-eighth

---

cognoscenda videbantur, necessarium est aggredi de personis ... " *S.T.* I, q. 29, proem.

[41] *S. T., I*, q. 29, a. 1.
[42] *S. T., I*, q. 29, a. 2.
[43] *S. T., I*, q. 29, a. 3.
[44] *S. T., I*, q. 29, a. 4.

question, and notes that he has already shown how there is a plurality of real relations in God. Hence it follows, that there is likewise in God a plurality of entities subsisting in the one divine nature, or simply a plurality of Persons. For the term person, when used of God, necessarily signifies relation as reality subsisting in the divine nature. [45]

A somewhat more detailed account is supplied in the very next article, as Aquinas explains that, notwithstanding the presence of four real relations, there can be only three distinct Persons. The plurality of Persons is a plurality of really distinct subsistent relations. But there can be real distinction in the divine relations only to the extent that there is relative opposition or correspondence. It follows, therefore, that any two mutually opposed relations must belong to two distinct Persons, and that any relations which are not mutually opposed must belong to the same Person.

Application is immediate in the case of fatherhood and sonship, since these two relations are clearly corresponding or mutually opposed. Subsistent paternity, therefore, is the Person of the Father, and subsistent filiation, the Person of the Son.

The two remaining relations, however, spiration and procession, are opposed to each other, but not to either of the first two, paternity and filiation. Yet, since they are in fact opposed to each other, it is impossible that both spiration and procession should belong to one Person. One of the relations, then, would have to belong to two of the Persons together, or one to one, and the other to another.

As for procession, then, it is clear that this relation cannot belong to the Father and Son together, or to either the Father or the Son separately. For this would reverse the actual and necessary order of origin and made the procession in intellect dependent upon the procession in will. It remains, therefore, that spiration must belong to both the Father and Son together, inasmuch as this relation is not opposed either to

---

[45] " Respondeo : Dicendum quod plures personas esse in divinis, sequitur ex praemissis. Ostensum est enim supra quod hoc nomen persona in divinis significat relationem ut rem subsistentem in natura divina. Supra autem habitum est quod sunt plures relationes reales in divinis. Unde sequitur quod sint plures res subsistentes in divina natura ; et hoc est esse plures personas in divinis. " *S. T.*, I, q. 30, a. 1c.

paternity or to filiation. As a final consequence, the relation of procession must belong to another Person — to the Holy Spirit, that is, Who proceeds *per modum amoris*. [46]

A question might conceivably be asked at this point. Granting for the sake of argument that St. Thomas had not intended to demonstrate through rational process the existence of either the divine processions or the divine relations, has he not at least concluded or deduced the plurality and distinction of Persons from the relations of origin? And if so, should not the evidence of demonstration of this latter sort incline the interpreter to be a bit more wary in dismissing demonstration from St. Thomas' purpose in other and perhaps more serious contexts — the apologetical, for instance — as well?

To support this caution, one could note the fact that Aquinas does not make in the *corpus* of either of the two articles just considered the same flat statement attributing certitude of the mystery to divine revelation that he had made when he was introducing first the divine procession, and next the divine relations. One might also level an accusing

---

[46] " Respondeo : Dicendum quod secundum praemissa necesse est ponere tantum tres personas in divinis. Ostensum enim est quod plures personae sunt plures relationes subsistentes ad invicem realiter distinctae. Realis autem distinctio inter relationes divinas non est nisi ratione oppositionis relativae. Oportet igitur duas relationes oppositas ad duas personas pertinere. Si quae autem relationes oppositae non sunt, ad eamdem personam necesse est eas pertinere. Paternitas igitur et filiatio, cum sint oppositae relationes, ad duas personae ex necessitate pertinent. Paternitas igitur subsistens est persona Patris, et filiatio subsistens est persona Filii. Aliae autem duae relationes ad neutram harum oppositionem habent, sed sibi invicem opponuntur. Impossibile est igitur quod ambae uni personae conveniant. Oportet ergo quod vel una earum conveniat utrique dictarum personarum aut quod una uni et alia alii. Non autem potest esse quod processio conveniat Patri et Filio vel alteri eorum ; quia sic sequeretur quod processio intellectus, quae est generatio in divinis, secundum quam accipitur paternitas et filiatio, prodiret ex processione amorio secundum quam accipitur spiratio et processio, si persona generans et genita procederent a spirante : quod est contra praemissa. Relinquitur igitur quod spiratio conveniat et personae Patris et personae Filii, utpote habens nullam oppositionem relativam neque ad paternitatem neque ad filiationem. Et per consequens oportet quod processio conveniat alteri personae, quae dicitur persona Spiritus Sancti, quae procedit per modum amoris, ut habitum est. Relinquitur igitur tantum tres personas esse in divinis, scilicet Patrem et Filium et Spiritum Sanctum. " *S. T.*, *I*, q. 30, a. 2c.

finger at the formulas " sequitur ex praemissis, " " secundum praemissa ", recurring in both passages.

In the writer's judgment, the solution to such a problem rests simply with a correct understanding of the *ordo doctrinae*. Before taking up this point, however, and to avoid the charge of a cavalier rebuttal, one or two *ad hoc* observations may not be without pertinence.

Turning, then, from what St. Thomas actually intended to do to what he might have done, or what would be possible for anyone to do according to the laws of logical inference, there does not seem to be anything that would prevent a theologian from concluding — *per modum conclusionis theologicae*, one might say — to the plurality of Persons, once the processions of origin and the real relations had been presupposed.

That Aquinas himself, however, was not concerned with such a theological demonstration, but intended that his doctrinal exposition on the plurality of Persons be understood as developing strictly under the light of faith and the authority of revelation, is indicated in various ways, and apart from any direct appeal to the *ordo doctrinae*.

First, it should be noted that the frequent reference to the Three Divine Persons throughout the discussion of procession and relations in the twenty-seventh and twenty-eighth questions would make formal repetition of revealed origin again in the discussion of the Persons rather superfluous. Secondly, there is also to be considered the fact that in the two articles introducing the personal plurality, there is at least an open mention of revealed origin in the *contra*.[47] Finally, there is the added fact, previously commented upon, that not one question — as in the case of procession and relations — but several successive questions are being devoted to the Persons, even to the Persons as taken absolutely and in common.

---

[47] " Sed contra est, quod dicit Athanasius: Alia est persona Patris, alia Filii, alia Spiritus Sancti. Ergo Pater et Filius et Spiritus Sanctus sunt plures personae. " *S. T.*, *I*, q. 30, a. 1, contra. " Sed contra est, quod dicitur I. Joh. ult. (v. 7): *Tres sunt qui testimonium dant in caelo*: Pater, Verbum, et Spiritus Sanctus. Quaerentibus autem: Quid tres? respondetur: Tres personae, ut Augustinus dicit in VII° de Trinitate. Sunt igitur tres personae tantum in divinis. " *ibid.*, a. 2, contra.

After treating the term person as such and in its general
application to God (q. 29), St. Thomas goes on to treat next
the fact of plurality and the limitation to Three Persons (q. 30),
then the specific determination of the plurality as ' Trinity '
(q. 31), and finally the problem of man's knowledge of the
Trinity (q. 32).

It is precisely in the opening article of the same thirty-
second question, that Aquinas discusses natural reason's fundamental incompetence to penetrate beyond the unity of the
divine essence as principle and end of all creatures to the
Trinity of Persons. But according to his explicitly stated
design, this article belongs to the treatment of the divine
plurality precisely under that formality.[48] The four questions,
therefore, comprise a doctrinal ensemble which is strictly parallel
to the single questions on procession and relations respectively.

Inasmuch, then, as St. Thomas planned to introduce the
Trinity of Persons as such, not in a single question, all the
less in a single article, but through a series of four integrated
questions, one of which would be devoted entirely to the matter of cognoscibility, there is no reason why his neglect to
mention, in the two articles just seen, that the plurality of
Persons was known solely from revelation should be considered
an omission. Nor, and this is the more significant point, is
there any reason why the nature of the presentation in the
passages on the Persons should be judged to differ in any
substantial way from what it had been in the earlier passages
on procession and relations. Or to put it concretely, there is
no evidence in the text itself that St. Thomas is introducing
the plurality of Persons in the manner of a theological conclusion as previously described.

When all is said and done, however, the real and adequate
solution to this problem lies less with such *ad hoc* considerations, than with a proper understanding of the *ordo doctrinae*.
The transitional ' therefore ' marking the main steps in the

---

[48] In the introduction to his discussion of the Persons as such,
Aquinas situates this article under the heading ' Person in general ',
and indicates its rôle in the integrated scheme : " Ad communem autem considerationem personarum quatuor pertinere videntur : primo
quidem significatio huius nominis persona, secundo vero numerus personarum, tertio ea quae sequuntur numerum personarum vel ei opponuntur, ut diversitas et solitudo et huiusmodi, quarto vero, ea quae
pertinent ad notitiam personarum. " *S. T.*, *I*, q. 29, proem., par. 2.

strictly vertical development — processions in intellect and
will, ' therefore ' real relations ; real relations, ' therefore ' plurality and distinction of Persons — represent ' conclusions '
in the order of what is prior in reality, not in the order of
what is prior in knowledge. In other words, as the human
intelligence attempts in some limited but salutary way to
understand the divine, it is because there are the two immanent processions, that there are real relations, and because
there are real relations, that there is plurality of Persons.
But this is to assign cause, or in the case of God quasi-cause,
knowledge of the existence of the effect presupposed.

It is entirely in accord with the exigencies of this *ordo
doctrinae*, moreover, that St. Thomas simply stated how the
existence of divine procession and the existence of divine relations depended upon positive revelation, and reserved his
formal and detailed handling of the problem whether natural
reason could know the Trinity of Persons until after he had
reached the discussion of the Persons as such. For the Persons, last in the order of the *priora quoad se*, unless one
includes the missions, as will be clarified in due course, are
first in the order of the *priora quoad nos*. Hence, the proper
place in the Thomist doctrinal synthesis for taking up the
problem whether unaided reason can penetrate to the Trinity of Persons is precisely at that point where, in the very
nature of things, the problem must be posed : that is to say,
where what is being considered is what is first in the order
of human knowledge, and upon which, in the same order of
human knowledge, knowledge of the relations and ultimately
of the divine procession depends.

Thus, after having introduced in the thirty-first question
the ' Trinity ' of Persons as signifying in a determinate way
what ' plurality ' of Persons had already signified indetermi-
nately, St. Thomas begins in the thirty-second question immediately following to treat of the Divine Persons from the
aspect of cognoscibility.[49] In the opening article, he asks
whether the natural human reason can know the Trinity of

---

[49] " Respondeo : Dicendum quod nomen Trinitatis in divinis significat determinatum numerum personarum. Sicut igitur ponitur pluralitas personarum in divinis, ita utendum est nomine Trinitatis : quia
hoc idem quod significat pluralitas indeterminate, significat hoc nomen
Trinitas determinate. " *S. T.*, *I*, q. 31, a. 1c.

Divine Persons, and asserts from the outset of his exposition that this is impossible.

Through natural reason, Aquinas explains, man comes to knowledge of God only from creatures, and hence from that which leads to knowledge of God as effect to knowledge of its cause. The most that natural reason can know of God, therefore, is what necessarily must be affirmed of God as the ultimate source or cause (*principium*) of all being. But the creative power of God, which is attained in this way, is common to the entire Trinity, and thus pertains to the unity of essence, not to the distinction of Persons. Consequently, it is only what pertains to the unity of essence, and not to the distinction of Persons, that man can know of God through natural reason.[50]

St. Thomas appends a somewhat lengthy admonition. Those who attempt to demonstrate (" probare ") the Trinity of Persons through natural reason offend Christian faith in two respects. First, their effort involves an indignity to faith itself, since faith is of the indemonstrable and hidden mysteries of God, which by their very nature exceed the light of simple reason. Secondly, what is tried in this fashion becomes a positive hindrance to the conversion of the unbeliever, for whom the appeal to reasons that do not prove is a matter of ridicule, inasmuch as he is given the impression that it is on account of such reasons that Christians are moved to believe. What belongs to faith, therefore, one must not attempt to prove, except on the strength of the authentic

---

[50] " Respondeo : Dicendum quod impossibile est per rationem naturalem ad cognitionem Trinitatis divinarum personarum pervenire. Ostensum est enim supra quod homo per rationem naturalem in cognitionem Dei pervenire non potest nisi ex creaturis. Creaturae autem ducunt in Dei cognitionem sicut effectus in causam. Hoc igitur solum ratione naturali de Deo cognosci potest, quod competere ei necesse est secundum quod est omnium entium principium ; et hoc fundamento sumus usi supra in consideratione Dei. Virtus autem creativa Dei est communis toti Trinitati ; unde pertinet ad unitatem essentiae, non ad distinctionem personarum. Per rationem igitur naturalem cognosci possunt de Deo ea quae pertinent ad unitatem essentiae, non autem ea quae pertinent ad distinctionem personarum. " *S. T.*, *I*, q. 32, a. 1c, 1. Aquinas is referring here to his discussion, earlier in the *Pars Prima*, of the more general topic " utrum per rationem naturalem Deum in hac vita cognoscere possimus, " in *S. T.*, *I*, q. 12, a. 12.

Christian testimonials ("auctoritates") — in the case, that is, of those who accept these testimonials. And for others, it is enough to show in defense of what faith teaches that what is taught is not impossible.[51]

The long and detailed reply to the second objection also calls for a rather close examination. For in the writer's judgment, the precise point St. Thomas is making in this passage is apt to be missed. The objection had cited Richard of St. Victor to the effect that not only probable, but even necessary, arguments were at hand to complement faith. Thus it is, the objection had continued, that certain individuals argued from the communication of infinite goodness, or from the principle of necessary companionship in the perfect possession of the good, to the existence of the trinitarian processions. Augustine, on the other hand, elucidated the Trinity of Persons from the same procession of inner word and love in the human mind that Aquinas himself has developed here in the *Pars Prima*.[52]

---

[51] " Qui autem probare nititur Trinitatem personarum naturali ratione, fidei dupliciter derogat. Primo quidem quantum ad dignitatem ipsius fidei, quae est, ut sit de rebus invisibilibus, quae rationem humanam excedunt ; unde Apostolus dicit ad Heb. 11 (v. 1) quod *fides est de non apparentibus.* Secundo, quantum ad utilitatem trahendi aliquos ad fidem. Cum enim aliquis ad probandam fidem inducit rationes quae non sunt cogentes, cedit in irrisionem infidelium ; credunt enim quod huiusmodi rationibus innitamur et propter eas credamus. Ea igitur quae fidei sunt, non sunt tentanda probare nisi per auctoritates his qui auctoritates suscipiunt. Apud alios vero sufficit defendere non esse impossibile quod praedicat fides ... "   *S. T.*, I, q. 32, a. 1c, 2.

[52] " Praeterea, Ricardus de sancto Victore dicit in libro de Trinitate : ' Credo sine dubio quod ad quamcumque explanationem veritatis non modo probabilia, imo et necessaria argumenta non desint '. Unde etiam ad probandum Trinitatem personarum aliqui induxerunt rationem ex infinitate bonitatis divinae, quae seipsam infinite communicat in processione divinarum personarum. Quidam vero per hoc quod nullius boni sine consortio potest esse iucunda possessio. Augustinus vero procedit ad manifestandum Trinitatem personarum ex processione verbi et amoris in mente nostra ; quam viam supra secuti sumus. Ergo per rationem naturalem potest cognosci Trinitas personarum. "   *S. T.*, I, q. 32, a. 1, obj. 2. In the writer's judgment, there is an ellipsis of sorts in Aquinas' formulation of the third argument, that connected with the name of Augustine. Two points should be kept in mind. First, St. Thomas does not include this last argument under the heading ' *probatio* ' ("ad probandum Trinitatem personarum"), which did embrace the two other arguments, but turns rather to a different designation, ' *manifestatio* ' (" ad manifestandum Trinitatem ").

Beginning his reply, then, St. Thomas notes that reason can be brought to bear upon a particular matter in either one of two ways. In the first instance, it is to demonstrate sufficiently a particular radix, as when in natural science, there is introduced the reason sufficient to prove that celestial motion is of uniform velocity. In the second instance, the reason introduced is not sufficient to demonstrate the particular radix in question, but is capable of showing that consequent effects are congruent with such a radix once the radix itself is supposed.

In astrology, for example, the eccentricities and epicycles are introduced or supposed in explanation, in the sense that,

---

In light of what has been seen elsewhere in the present study (as, e. g., the passage from *De Pot.*, q. 9, a. 5, cited above in note no. 14), the change cannot be considered accidental. *Manifestatio* is one of the words Aquinas uses to designate the reasoning processes whereby rational theology seeks to show how a revealed mystery has to be taken or understood, as opposed to the apologetical processes seeking to prove or demonstrate (' *probatio* ') the existence of the mystery itself. Secondly, on the other hand, it is clear from the context of the objection that the challenger, so to speak, is envisioned here as making some kind of appeal to this *manifestatio*, not precisely according to its explanatory rôle — the rôle it has *de facto* in Aquinas' own theological expositions, and as he at least implies here, in Augustine's as well — but according to its possible or claimed value in apologetical proof, just as previously in a parallel objection in *In Boet. de Trin.*, q. 1, a. 4, obj. 6. Removing the ellipsis, therefore, the writer would suggest the following as a correct paraphrase to bring out St. Thomas' meaning in this objection : ' In an attempt to prove the Trinity of Persons from natural reason, some have argued from the infinity of the divine goodness, and others from the necessity of companionship for complacency in the good possessed. There is also Augustine's elucidation of the revealed mystery through analogy from the procession of word and love in the human spirit, the same analogy I myself have developed here in the *Pars Prima* (" quam viam upra secuti sumus "), and some might look for similar proof or demonstration in this analogy'. The writer believes that such a paraphrase is necessary to point up both the distinction between " ad probandum " and " ad manifestandum, " on the one hand, and the inclusion of the this third member within the context of the objection, apologetical objection, on the other. For immediately after referring to the psychological analogy, St. Thomas has his challenger conclude : " Ergo per rationem naturalem potest cognosci Trinitas personarum. " But that in speaking of *his own use* of the analogy Aquinas wishes this understood in terms of his technical distinction between ' proof ' and ' manifestation ', is clear from the juxtaposition and contrast of the two notions in the reply itself (q. v.).

once this supposition is made, certain sensible phenomena observed in celestial motion can be accounted for. Such a reason or explanation, however, is not sufficient to demonstrate the supposition, because it could well be that the same sensible phenomena could also be accounted for on the basis of some other supposition.

Reasons of the first type, therefore, can be introduced to demonstrate that God is one and the like. But reasons that are introduced in explanation (" ad manifestationem ") of the Trinity are reasons of the second type. Once the Trinity is supposed, these reasons are congruent, but not in the sense that through these reasons the Trinity of Persons would be sufficiently demonstrated.

Since, then, God's infinite goodness is manifested also in the production of creatures, inasmuch as creation from nothing is indicative of infinite power, one does not have sufficient grounds for postulating from a consideration of this goodness an infinite procession. In like manner, the argument that full contentment in the possession of the good demands companionship would have pertinence only in the case of one in whom perfect goodness was not already found. Finally, since intellect does not exist univocally in God and men, the " similitudo intellectus " is not sufficient to prove something of God. And thus it is, St. Thomas concludes, that through faith, as Augustine has remarked, one comes to knowledge, not from knowledge to faith.[53]

---

[53] " Ad secundum dicendum quod ad aliquam rem dupliciter inducitur ratio. Uno modo ad probandum sufficienter aliquam radicam : sicut in scientia naturali inducitur ratio sufficiens ad probandum quod motus caeli sit semper uniformis velocitatis. Alio modo inducitur ratio quae non sufficienter probet radicem, sed quae radici iam positae ostendat congruere consequentes effectus ; sicut in astrologia ponitur ratio excentricorum et epicyclorum ex hoc quod hac positione facta salvari possunt apparentia sensibilia circa motus caelestes : non tamen ratio haec est sufficienter probans, quia forte etiam alia positione facta salvari possent. Primo ergo modo induci potest ratio ad probandum Deum esse unum et similia ; sed secundo modo se habet ratio quae inducitur ad manifestationem Trinitatis ; quia scilicet, Trinitate posita, congruunt huiusmodi rationes ; non tamen ita quod per has rationes sufficienter probetur Trinitas personarum. Et hoc patet per singula. Bonitas enim infinita Dei manifestatur etiam in productione creaturarum, quia infinitae virtutis est ex nihilo producere. Non enim oportet, si infinita bonitate se communicat, quod aliquid infinitum a Deo procedat, sed quod secundum modum suum recipiet divinam boni-

The reader will have recognized here a favorite text among
Thomist theologians, and in the first part of the present study
it was already seen to what extent an interpretation of this
same text played a fairly conspicuous rôle in comments made
on the apologetical problem by Penido, Paissac, and Vagaggini.
Yet, in the writer's opinion, and also as the divergent views
among the authors just mentioned would seem to confirm,
the text of the famous reply itself is open to a certain
ambiguity.

It will soon be apparent that the ambiguous element is
the precise meaning St. Thomas wishes to give the concept
of ' congruence ' (taken from the two verb forms " congruere "
and " congruunt " used in the text) in the description of his
own trinitarian exposition as based upon the psychological
analogy. The measure of uncertainty that may exist on this
latter point, however, does not substantially affect one way
or the other the basic and much more important points Aquinas is clearly making here. For in the writer's judgment,
either of the two interpretations which could be accorded
the idea of ' congruence ' as introduced in this text necessarily
lead to the same ultimate conclusion.

Putting aside, for the moment, the expressions which
might actually be ambiguous, and beginning with what seems,
on the other hand, to be quite certain, the essential elements
in St. Thomas' reply can be listed as follows. Two species
of ' argument ', or rational process, must be distinguished.
In the first process, reason is employed to prove or demonstrate a basic fact — such as in the proof that God is one —
and the reason so employed is capable of engendering certitude. In the second process, the basic fact is already supposed, and reason is now employed with the objective of explaining or understanding the fact. This explanatory process, moreover, would not suffice to prove the existence of the fact
itself, and the psychological analogy employed in trinitarian

---

tatem. Similiter etiam quod dicitur, quod sine consortio non potest
esse iucunda possessio alicuius boni, locum habet quando in una persona non invenitur perfecta bonitas ; unde indiget ad plenam bonitatem iucunditatis bono alicuius alterius consociati sibi. Similitudo
etiam nostri intellectus non sufficienter probat aliquid de Deo propter
hoc quod intellectus non univoce invenitur in Deo et nobis. Et inde
est quod Augustinus dicit super Ioh. quod per fidem venitur ad cognitionem, et non e converso. " *S. T.*, *I*, q. 32, a. 1, ad 2m.

theology would be a case in point. Nevertheless, the same
second species of argument, or rational process, 'would yield',
or 'does yield' — this is where the ambiguity comes in —
a certain 'congruence'.

Before turning to the last point, however, where there
appears to be at least an ellipsis in St. Thomas' expression,
just as there was in his formulation of the objection to which
the present passage stands in reply, a number of observations
should first be made in order to bring out the full implications
of that part of the reply which seems to be quite clear.

It should be noted, then, that both in the objection and
in the reply, Aquinas characterizes the rational process which
employs the *verbum* analogy as elucidation, or manifestation
("ad manifestandum Trinitatem," "ad manifestationem Trinitatis"), and this description — obviously technical, inasmuch as it is explicitly distinguished from proof, or demonstration ("ad probandum Trinitatem," "sufficienter probetur Trinitas," "non sufficienter probat") — is in strict accord with the manner in which he has described his own use
of the same process elsewhere. There is, for example, the
"aliqualis manifestatio" of *De Pot.*, q. 9, a. 5, already studied
in the second section of the present chapter. There is the
equivalent "ad cuius evidentiam" formula seen used by St.
Thomas throughout the discussion on procession and relations
in the twenty-seventh and twenty-eighth questions of the
Pars Prima itself. There is the "sic manifestari oportet"
introducing the heart of the argument for the intellectualist
understanding of the divine generation in *C. G.*, *IV*, c. 11, 9.

At this juncture, moreover, it should be legitimate to
presume as already substantiated from the textual analyses
of the Thomist 'de Trinitate' as contained in the *Sentences*,
in the *Contra Gentiles*, and in the *Pars Prima* itself, that the
authentic Thomist ideal of rational theology turns upon the
objective, not of proof or demonstration, however qualified
or restricted, of the revealed mystery, but solely of its partial
understanding.

It is precisely against the background of such weighty
textual evidence, then, that Aquinas' introduction here of the
notion of 'congruence' has to be examined. The question
may be put simply. Does St. Thomas introduce this idea of
congruence : 1) to describe the formal intention of his personal theological processes ? or 2) to describe at least one

function of which these same theological processes would be *per se* capable ? or 3) to describe exclusively the theological processes — more accurately, the apologetical processes, and perhaps still more accurately, the *corrected* apologetical processes — of the challenger who speaks in the objection ?

If the first interpretation is correct, that is to say if St. Thomas introduces this notion of congruence to describe the formal intention of his own theological processes, then the notion itself must be identified with the notion of *manifestatio*. It is clear from the text that Aquinas certainly intends to describe his own processes as manifestation : " Augustinus vero procedit ad manifestandum Trinitatem personarum ex processione verbi et amoris in mente nostra ; quam viam supra secuti sumus, " from the objection ; " ratio quae inducitur ad manifestationem Trinitatis, " from the reply. If, then, the phrase immediately following in the reply, " quia scilicet, Trinitate posita, congruunt huiusmodi rationes, " is also taken as a description of these same processes, it follows necessarily that the two concepts, manifestation and congruence, are meant to be identified, at least substantially.

In such a view, however, the notion of congruence, or as some authors, making what they consider a valid transposition, prefer, the notion of ' convenience ', must be accorded the full implications of the parallel notion, manifestation. If and when St. Thomas refers to his own theological reasoning as congruence, or convenience, therefore, this is in no sense the congruence or convenience that would represent ' lesser certitude ', or a degree of probability, in the order of confirming the fact or existence of the revealed mystery. For as has been seen throughout the textual analysis of the present study, such confirmation is simply not Aquinas' own objective in rational theology.[54]

---

[54] This seems to be the position of H. PAISSAC. See *Théologie du Verbe*, pp. 222-223, cited above on p. 46, note no. 8. For a similar approach, see also CHENU, *Introduction*, pp. 154-155. In the writer's opinion, Paissac is rather more successful than Chenu in recognizing that if the notion of congruence as introduced here by St. Thomas was intended to describe his own theological processes, it would have to be interpreted in the order of understanding as opposed to certitude. Where Chenu is quick to transpose the notion into the Aristotelian " arguments de convenance, " Paissac, on the other hand, maintains (p. 224) that " convenance " (*convenientia*) is used by Aquinas himself only in the case of the contingent mysteries. The writer

If the second interpretation is the correct one, that is to say if St. Thomas wishes to describe at least one function of which his theological processes would be *per se* capable, there is certainly no contradiction involved, and it might even be argued that the interpretation itself has more explicit regard for the actual context, apologetical context, of the article, and makes a somewhat better adjustment between the structure of the reply and that of the objection, than the first interpretation. For while Aquinas' remarks on the apologetical argument as such are few and far between, it can be shown, on the other hand, that he does not deny to this argument *all* legitimacy, or *all* value. He himself, of course, employed the *verbum* analogy for quite another purpose — theological understanding. When speaking *nomine proprio*, he never bothered to develop, or for that matter even introduce, an apologetical process in which the *verbum* analogy might be used, *post factum revelatum*, to show, not with any certitude, but with a degree of probability and suasiveness, the a priori 'necessity' for trinitarian procession. But he did admit, *per transennam* one might say, that such a process was possible. In treating the apologetical problem in the *In Boethii de Trinitate*, for example, St. Thomas affirmed flatly that there could be no demonstrative rational proof for the Trinity of Persons, although, he went on to say, certain reasons might be brought to bear on the point, which would be neither necessary, nor, except for the believer, very probable.[55]

According to the second interpretation, then, Aquinas would be saying much the same thing here in the *Summa*. The pertinent phrases of the reply might be paraphrased as follows. 'In the second type of rational process, reason is introduced which would not sufficiently prove the basic fact, but which would show, once this basic fact were supposed, how consequent effects are in agreement. Thus, the reason which is introduced to manifest the Trinity (Aquinas' description of his own theological process) could not produce (in another employment, the apologetical) a demonstrative proof, but could produce (in the same apologetical employment, now

---

feels this last point is confirmed from a study of the ' *de Trinitate* ' in *Pars Prima*. So far as the writer has been able to determine, the word (*convenientia*) appears only in the forty-third question, when Aquinas is treating the missions.

[55] *In Boet. de Trin.*, q. 1, a. 4c.

' corrected ' or reduced to its inherent limitations) a measure
of probability.   For once the Trinity is supposed, such reasons
show congruence '.

The important thing to observe in this second view is
that congruence (or convenience) no longer has the same meaning as it had in the first interpretation.   It is no longer to be
identified with manifestation.   It no longer describes St. Thomas' own theological objective, but simply notes, in the context
of the apologetical objection, that the *verbum* analogy employed
by Aquinas himself exclusively for the purposes of theological
understanding, is at least *per se* capable of serving a quite
different and apologetical function, where it would have an
extremely limited value in the line of probability.

Or thirdly, and finally, does St. Thomas merely describe
here the apologetical processes of his adversary, correcting
these to the extent that they are clearly erroneous, but quite
without intending any direct reference to his own position on
the *per se* apologetical value of the psychological analogy?
As is clear, this third interpretation differs from the second
only in one point.   Aquinas replies to his challenger that no
process of rational argument could demonstrate the Trinity
of Persons, and the argument someone might wish to construct from the analogous procession in the human mind is
no exception.   The most such an argument could ever yield
would be the probability here described in terms of congruence.[56]

The difference between these last two views, therefore,
is comparatively slight.   In the one, St. Thomas would at
least be making a positive reference to the highly restricted
apologetical value of an argument drawn from the *verbum*
analogy, employed by himself exclusively for the purposes of
understanding, if someone were to make the apologetical his
objective.   In the other, St. Thomas' reply would be rather
negative throughout.   Assuming the *status quaestionis* of his
adversary, he denies that such an argument would be necessary or certain, and goes on to show, one might say conces-

---

[56] This is clearly PENIDO's position. See the article " La valeur
de la théorie ' psychologique ', " p. 12, cited above on p. 84, note no.
42.   Though Penido also transposes the notion of congruence into " convenance, " it is his contention that the desire of St. Thomas in this
passage is not to describe his own theological processes at all, but
exclusively the apologetical arguments of his adversaries.

sively, that the most it could achieve was a degree of probability, or, but in the same line of certitude as to fact, 'congruence'.

In what is of more serious significance, then, the three interpretations reduce to two. Either St. Thomas introduces the notion of ' congruence ' in this passage as part of the description of his own employment of the verbum analogy exclusively within the theological ideal of understanding, or else as a characterization of the use someone other than himself might make of the same analogy in the quite different and apologetical context of certitude, with or without the addition of a positive, personal statement as to the worth of such a procedure. In either view, however, the more important conclusions for the present study remain fundamentally unchanged. For in either view, Aquinas quite clearly disassociates himself from the ideal of demonstration and certitude, however qualified, as the objective of rational theology.

Thus, in the opening article of this thirty-second question, St. Thomas takes up the matter of cognoscibility, and discusses first the problem of whether or not natural reason can know the Trinity of Persons. In the *corpus* of the article, he states unequivocally that this is impossible, and he explains why. What man knows of God through natural reason, he knows only from creatures. But such knowledge leads only to the creative power of God that is identified with the divine essence, and common to all Three Persons.

In the reply to the second objection, Aquinas discusses certain arguments or proofs that would seem to except from this rule, in particular the argument that could be construed from the so-called psychological analogy. But such arguments, he answers, could never yield demonstrative proof. The most they could give, therefore, would be some measure of probability or suasiveness. It may be just this probability or suasiveness that St. Thomas refers to here in terms of ' congruence ', which would mean that he was using the notion of ' congruence ' in the line of certitude. Or it may be that he introduces ' congruence ' to describe his own processes leading to understanding, and this would mean that he was using the notion of ' congruence ' itself in the same line of understanding. But in either case, the main point to be noted is that St. Thomas wishes his own theological objective to be recognized, not as certitude, not even the diminished certitude of probability or suasiveness, but simply as understanding.

Moreover, as noted earlier, it is precisely in this section
of his treatise where Aquinas has begun to speak of the plurality of Trinity of Persons as such, that the epistemological
question of how the Trinity is known, and what may be the
rôle of natural reason in this regard, has its proper place.
For according to the *ordo doctrinae*, the order of understanding
in synthesis, which he is following, St. Thomas began with what
was first, not in knowledge, but in reality, and has consequently
only now come to what is first in knowledge — what had
been, that is, the starting point in the process of theological
analysis, which is the implicit background of the treatise
though not explicitly recorded in the text of *Pars Prima*,
whereby from what was first in knowledge the passage to
what was first in reality had originally been effected.

Thus, while Aquinas did in fact indicate the revealed
source for both the divine procession and the relations, he
was also and necessarily presuming knowledge of the procession and relations as dependent upon the prior knowledge of
the Persons. It was right here, therefore, in his treatment
of the Persons as such, that he had to discuss the problem of
cognoscibility, explain in some detail that natural reason could
not attain this knowledge, and in this way make it abundantly clear that his entire trinitarian synthesis was first and last
a matter, not of merely rational inquiry, but of theological
understanding enlightened by supernatural faith.

In the articles remaining of the thirty-second question,
St. Thomas proceeds to introduce the ' notions ' as the abstract
qualities, so to speak, in virtue of which the specific distinction and peculiar character of the Three Persons can, in some
limited manner, be understood.[57] This done, he will then begin
his treatment of each of the Persons considered individually.[58]
Next, he will discuss the Persons in respect to the divine essence, the properties or relations, the notional acts, and finally to one another.[59] He will conclude his treatise with an
exposition of the trinitarian missions.[60]

For the purpose of the present study, however, it will
not be necessary to review this material, since now that the

---

[57] *S. T.*, *I*, q. 32, aa. 2-4.
[58] *S. T.*, *I*, qq. 33-38.
[59] *S. T.*, *I*, qq. 39-42.
[60] *S. T.*, *I*, q. 43.

treatment of the plurality of Persons has been completed, and
allowing for a qualification on the missions still to be made,
the essential movement and development of the *ordo doctrinae* is already set in focus. It was for this reason, moreover, that
the investigation of the treatise was extended beyond the exposition of the divine procession in the twenty-seventh question.

For where the theology of the Trinity is concerned, the
problem of a possibly apologetical intention on the part of
St. Thomas resolves, as Vagaggini has made evident, into the
more particular problem of what might be involved in Aquinas' use of the psychological analogy to give a seemingly
rational account of the trinitarian procession. But in the ' *de
Trinitate* ' of the *Summa*, this problem arises in the very first
question of the treatise. To give an adequate solution to this
problem, however, it was necessary to bring out in more conspicuous relief the actual nature and significance of the *ordo
doctrinae*.

For in terms of the formally declared order and methodology of the treatise itself, the ultimate reason why certainty or knowledge of the existence of the divine procession
was not in any sense whatsoever the object to be demonstrated, or conclusion to be reached, or point to be established, was
the simple fact that the existence of the divine procession
was being presupposed as already known — not only was
being presupposed as known in fact, but was necessarily being
presupposed as known because of the very nature of the *ordo
doctrinae*, the order of understanding through synthesis.

In the introduction to his treatise, the *prooemium* to question twenty-seven, St. Thomas had proposed to treat, first
the divine procession, next the relations of origin, and lastly
the Persons. Moreover, he would follow precisely this order
because, as he had stated explicitly in the same introduction,
it is according to the relations of origin, that the Persons are
distinguished — or, as the three-fold division immediately following makes clear, because the Persons in some way depend
upon the relations, and the relations in turn depend in some
way upon procession. The order, therefore, is an order of
dependence, or in an indetermined general sense and allowing for the qualifications that must be made with respect to
God's infinity and simplicity, an order of internal cause.

Furthermore, the order of dependence or internal cause
is in the line of reality or *priora quoad se*, not in the line of

knowledge or *priora quoad nos*. St. Thomas had proposed to
treat successively the immanent processions, the relations, and
the Persons, because according to the legitimate and necessary human mode of understanding, this order of dependence
is affirmed to exist in God Himself, objectively, though without
the slightest compromise to the infinity and simplicity of the
divine essence. But this is clearly to presuppose an initial
process of analysis, whereby the relations became known as
internal reason or explanation of the Persons, and procession
became known as the internal reason or explanation of the
relations, according to the way in which the *prius notum* is
reduced to its principles through analytical understanding.

In the *Summa*, as also in the *Compendium*, the analytical
process itself is not developed, but is rather implicit as the
necessary reverse correlative of the *ordo doctrinae*. In both
works, it stands as the necessary presupposition to the synthetic process, in which procession is introduced at the beginning
as foundation in the order of *priora quoad se* of what is consequent in the same order, the relations, that is to say, and
then the Persons. But procession is not and cannot even be
known in precisely this context of foundation or internal reason, and hence is not and cannot be supposed in this context
— as Aquinas has nevertheless been seen to suppose it —
except inasmuch and insofar as there has previously been a
process of analysis, at least implicit, beginning from what is
already known in the order of *priora quoad nos*, which in this
case is simply the Three Divine Persons, as portrayed in character, intimate association, and terrestrial salvific activity in
the testimonies of Sacred Scripture.

An observation should be made here, however, with regard
to the trinitarian missions. In his general introduction, the
prooemium to question twenty-seven, St. Thomas had not mentioned the missions. Yet, when at length he introduces the
missions in the forty-third and last question of his treatise,
he does so as a prolongation of the same internal dependence
that had been basic to the *ordo doctrinae* throughout his entire
exposition on the processions, relations, and Persons.

VII. From the Three Persons to the Trinitarian Missions

Though the forty-third question devoted to the salvific missions of the Trinity is rich in theological detail, the immediate purpose and scope of the present study makes it necessary to restrict the consideration here to that aspect of the exposition which is directly pertinent to the order and structure of the ' de Trinitate ' of the *Pars Prima*.

The mission of one of the Three Persons, Aquinas explains, requires not only a new mode of existence in some other, but also such a new mode of existence as is dependent for its coming into being on the habitude of the Person sent to be so sent by either or both of the two Persons remaining. But this habitude within the Trinity itself can only be the procession of origin.

In this light, then, it is suitable that the Son, Who proceeds from the Father eternally, should be sent into the world by the Father in the course of time.[61] In the same way, the Holy Spirit, Who proceeds from both the Father and the Son, is likewise sent into the world by both the Father and the Son together.[62] On the other hand, since the Father Himself does not proceed eternally from either the Son or the Holy Spirit, it is not suitable that the Father should be sent into the world by one or both of the other Persons.[63]

Thus, as the relations and hence the Persons derive, in the order of *priora quoad se*, from procession, so in the same order, and as the final moment, so to speak, in the trinitarian succession, do the missions. Moreover, in the reversely correlative order of analysis, the order, that is, of the *priora*

---

[61] " Missio igitur divinae Personae convenire potest, secundum cundum quod importat ex una parte processionem originis a mittente ; et secundum quod importat ex alia parte novum modum existendi in alio. Sicut Filius dicitur esse missus a Patre in mundum, secundum quod incoepit in mundo esse per carnem assumptam : et tamen ante ' in mundo erat ', ut dicitur *Ioann.* I 10. " *S. T.*, *I*, q. 43, a. 1c, 2.

[62] *S. T.*, *I*, q. 43, a. 7.

[63] " Respondeo. Dicendum quod missio in sui ratione importat processionem ab alio ; et in divinis secundum originem, ut supra dictum est. Unde cum Pater non sit ab alio, nullo modo convenit sibi mitti, sed solum Filio et Spiritui Sancto, quibus convenit esse ab alio. " *S. T.*, *I*, q. 43, a. 4c.

quoad nos, it is really the Divine Persons as ' sent ', that is the first known, inasmuch as the full manifestation of the Trinity was made by the Eternal Son of God, sent into this world by the Father for just this purpose.

To have treated of the missions, therefore, at the very end of his exposition, and to have done so precisely in this focus, throws even more light on St. Thomas' understanding of the *ordo doctrinae*. At the same time, it might be pointed out, there is no inconsistency in the fact that Aquinas failed to include the missions in the division of his *prooemium*.

For it is only the ' convenience ' or suitability of the missions of the Son and Holy Spirit as involved in the processions of origin that pertains to the interiority of the Trinity itself, and not the actual missions in the course of time inasmuch as these latter depend quite obviously on the contingencies of creation and man's supernatural vocation. In what concerns the Trinity itself, therefore, the order of *priora quoad se* extends simply from procession to the relations and finally to the Persons. Further extension to the missions presupposes the communication of trinitarian life to the human creature. By the same token, it is of no special significance that the treatment of the Trinity in the *Compendium*, as will be seen in the next chapter, concludes without any discussion of the missions, though the basic structure of the *Compendium* is the same *ordo doctrinae* as in the *Pars Prima*.

VIII.   THE RÔLE OF THE ' VIA ANALYTICA ' WHICH IS YET TC BE STUDIED

In this chapter on the ' *de Trinitate* ' of the *Summa Theologiae*, it has been seen how the apologetical question as posed by Dom Vagaggini comes at least into clear focus. For when Aquinas begins here to develop a systematic exposition of trinitarian doctrine, his point of departure is not an account of the revealed mystery as contained in the testimonies of Sacred Scripture, but an account of the divine procession precisely as ' cause ' or ultimate *ratio* of the plurality of Persons. Moreover, while human certitude as to the existence of procession in the complex of the mystery is explicitly affirmed to derive solely from revelation, nevertheless it is also true that the first point in organic development is not only the divine procession considered in general, but the same divine procession as the primordial instance of spiritual or intellectual emanation.

Whoever understands, by this alone that he does understand, there proceeds within him a distinct inner word. Such is St. Thomas' beginning. And if this beginning, and the passage in which it occurs, is studied in relative isolation from the larger context of the complete ' *de Trinitate* ' of the *Pars Prima*, it is not surprising that someone might wonder why this procedure does not constitute, if not exactly an apodictic demonstration, at least its close imitation.

In the effort to come to grips with this question, it had been shown in the first part of the present investigation that an adequate solution could most likely only be found in a careful reexamination of the text to determine what precisely was Aquinas' own theological ideal and fundamental methodology. Either the seemingly strange procedure of beginning with an apparently rational or philosophical generalization, from which revealed mysteries would then appear to be concluded, would have a clearly demonstrable, one might even say simple, explanation in the very nature and composition of the particular theological process St. Thomas himself had elected to follow, or the interpreter would be reduced to the sort of appeal against literary inconsistencies and other modes of inferential defense that somehow tend to remain less than perfectly satisfying.

On the evidence of the text itself, however, starting with the brief but highly significant words of the *prooemium*, it was shown that Aquinas did in fact propose to follow an order of exposition whose very nature required that he begin, not with what is first in the order of human knowledge, but with what is known, on prior understanding of what is first known, to be first in reality. St. Thomas, therefore, was not going to conclude to the existence of the first trinitarian procession, or to the relations, or to the Three Divine Persons from the universal or transcendental properties of intellectual being, but rather had already concluded to these universal or transcendental properties of intellectual being — certainly the transcendental necessity of spiritual emanation — from analysis of the revealed mystery.

The only purpose, then, so far as the present study was concerned, for continuing the examination of the text into the subsequent development and detail of the Thomist '*de Trinitate*' was simply to substantiate what had already been seen in the beginning when the *ordo doctrinae* was first proposed. And this examination proved, as the writer believes, that Aquinas remained constant to his original plan, and thereby left no doubt as to the seriousness with which he had proposed it. Procession was treated first, because procession is the ultimate ' cause ' or *ratio* of personal distinction. The trinitarian relations were treated next, because these relations depend immediately on the processions. The Persons were treated finally, because the Persons are constituted by the subsistent relations. At this point, St. Thomas had returned through the order of synthesis to what had been first in the order of human knowledge, and on analysis from which the first elements of synthesis had originally been determined.

There is, then, as the necessary *praesuppositum* of the trinitarian exposition as contained in the *Pars Prima*, the prior analysis of rational theology in virtue of which Aquinas was able to begin his treatment, not from what is first known, but from what is first in reality. Or perhaps it would be more proper to say that, at the moment, this is at least a valid inference.

In the writer's judgment, however, the matter is much too important to leave at mere inference. For the question is apt to be asked : if St. Thomas began from what was ultimate ' cause ' or *ratio* in the order of reality, if this was actually his supposition, on just what grounds had he made it ? And it is doubtful that one asking this question would be satisfied by an appeal, if not summary, at least not elaborated, to inference.

Consequently, the examination of the *ordo doctrinae* in the ' *de Trinitate* ' of the *Summa* will not be considered as completed until in the final chapter of this third part of the present study an opportunity will have been taken to determine more accurately the *via analytica* which is its necessary presupposition. Moreover, since the structure of the ' *de Trinitate* ' contained in the *Compendium Theologiae* reveals what is basically the same *ordo doctrinae* — though, in the writer's judgment, not only briefer, but also rather less perfect in form — it is more logical to postpone consideration of the implied *via analytica* until the tract in the *Compendium* has also been seen.

CHAPTER TWO

SIMILAR " ORDO DOCTRINAE " IN THE *COMPENDIUM THEOLOGIAE*

There can be no doubt that the ' *de Trinitate* ' of the *Pars Prima*, the most complete and most perfectly worked out expression of the Thomist *ordo doctrinae* as the ultimate goal of rational theology, is Aquinas' masterpiece. Nevertheless, a cursory examination of the roughly parallel, though much shorter and much less expertly modulated, presentation in the *Compendium* might well be inserted at this point.

It will soon be seen that the abbreviated treatise of the *Compendium* is structured on the same broad lines of understanding through synthesis, and thus conforms to basically the same ideal of theological science, as already recognized in the ' *de Trinitate* ' of the *Summa*. In the writer's judgment, moreover, there is considerable evidence from the text itself that the exposition as developed in the *Compendium* marks the intermediate stage in the growth of St. Thomas' own thought between the analytical treatise of *Contra Gentiles IV* and the final perfection of synthesis in the *ordo doctrinae* of the *Pars Prima*.[1]

---

[1] The dating of the *Compendium* has long been problematical. For the present purposes, it will suffice to note Chenu's complete rejection of Mandonnet's argument assigning the work to the very last period of St. Thomas' life. As Chenu himself assesses the the available evidence, the *Compendium* belongs to the period 1265-1267 — hence, almost certainly antedating the *Pars Prima*, which, as observed in the preceding chapter, should be placed between 1267 and 1268, but in no case earlier than 1267. See CHENU, *Introduction*, p. 283. In the writer's opinion, a comparison between the *Compendium* and the *Pars Prima* respectively with *Contra Gentiles IV* from the precise viewpoint of structure, specifically of the *ordo doctrinae*, rather strengthens the evidence placing the *Compendium* itself before the *Pars Prima*. Anticipating what will be seen in the present chapter, the significant data can be summarized as follows. 1) As the exposi-

In the thirty-sixth chapter of the *Compendium*, then, St. Thomas concludes this discussion of what pertains to the existence of God in the unity and simplicity of the divine essence. He notes that even the pagan philosophers had attained a certain knowledge of God in this regard.

But there are other matters, he goes on to say, that lie beyond the reach of human experience and are known only through the revelation of christian faith : that while God is one and simple, there is nevertheless God the Father, God the Son, and God the Holy Spirit, and that these Three are still but one God.   St. Thomas proposes, therefore, to ' consider ' this divine revelation, to the extent that this is possible.[2]

_____

tion commences in *Comp.*, c. 37, and continues through the remainder of the tract, it is clear that Aquinas' basic design is the synthetic presentation.   2) Nevertheless, the detailed development of elemental sections within this synthetic structure, particularly in c. 52, shows, on the one hand, striking similarities to the ' parallel ' passage in *C. G.*, *IV*, c. 11, and, on the other hand, stands as a less mature and finished presentation, but still one that is taking the same methodological direction, when compared with the further ' parallel ' in *S. T.*, *I*, q. 27. 3) As will be seen more clearly in the last chapter of this study, the order of *C. G. IV* is analytic, not synthetic, but with 4) some tendency toward the synthetic ideal already appearing in c. 11.   5) In the *Compendium*, the synthetic ideal is formally accepted, but with 6) a certain trend toward retaining, in the central chapter 52, a good deal of the idiom, formulae, and argumentational pattern of *C. G.*, *IV*, c. 11. 7) But in the *Pars Prima*, where the synthetic ideal is again formally accepted, one of the most telling marks of its greater perfection is precisely the total abandonment of this residue, so to speak, from *C. G. IV*.   The argument would have less weight, to be sure, if it could be shown that on the point of basic structure the *Compendium* was a different conception from the *Pars Prima*.   But the considerable differences that do characterize the *Compendium*, as its relative brevity and handbook style, do not, in the writer's view, alter substantially the here and now more decisive fact that the formal objective intrinsic to the exposition of this particular ' *de Trinitate* ' is synthesis.   In this clearly defined context, then, the theological ideal of the two works is the same, and the *Compendium* in the same context, takes the place of an intermediate stage between the fourth book *Contra Gentiles* and the *Pars Prima* in the development of the ideal of understanding through synthesis as the final achievement of Thomist rational theology.

[2] " Sunt autem et alia nobis de Deo tradita in doctrina christianae religionis, ad quam pervenire non potuerunt, circa quae secundum christianam fidem ultra humanum sensum instruimur.   Est autem hoc : quod cum sit Deus unus et simplex, ut ostensum est, est tamen

While the expression "considerare intendimus" lacks the technical precision of the more familiar "qualiter accipere", or "qualiter intelligere," the style of approach assumed by St. Thomas when he begins his exposition in the chapter immediately following makes it clear that the prevailing intention is to explain, to understand, what is already presumed to be known. The process of understanding, moreover, is basically that of understanding through synthesis, just as in the more elaborate *ordo doctrinae* of the *Pars Prima*, but with certain specific differences.

In the *Summa*, Aquinas begins with divine procession in general, or one might even say in the abstract — the very last point reached in analytical reduction, and hence the very first to be introduced in a perfect scheme of synthesis. Here in the *Compendium*, on the other hand, he begins with the first procession concretely, the procession of the Divine Word, and in a manner more reminiscent of the treatment in the eleventh chapter of *Contra Gentiles IV*.

From what he has said in earlier sections of the *Compendium*, St. Thomas is able to presuppose that God understands Himself and loves Himself, and that both understanding and love in God are identified with the divine being. But 'the understood' exists in 'the intelligent' or the one understanding. As God understands Himself, therefore, it follows that God must exist in Himself as the understood in the one understanding, or as the inner word of intellect. It is necessary, then, to recognize in God His Divine Word.[3]

Aquinas next goes on to explain that the inner word

_____

Deus Pater, et Deus Filius, et Deus Spiritus Sanctus, et ii tres non tres Dii, sed unus Deus est : quod quidem, quantum possibile nobis est, considerare intendimus. " *Comp.*, c. 36, 70. (The numbers following those of the chapters are as given in the Marietti edition of the *Opuscula Theologica*, Vol. I, from which all the citations and references here are being taken.)

[3] " Accipiendum autem est ex his quae supra dicta sunt, quod Deus se ipsum intelligit et diligit. Item quod intelligere in ipso et velle non sit aliud quam eius esse. Quia vero Deus se ipsum intelligit, omne autem intellectum in intelligente est, oportet Deum in se ipso esse sicut intellectum in intelligente. Intellectum autem prout est in intelligente, est verbum quoddam intellectus : hoc enim exteriori verbo significamus quod interius in intellectu comprehendimus. Sunt enim, secundum Philosophum, voces signa intellectuum. Oportet igitur in Deo ponere Verbum ipsius. " *Comp.*, c. 37, 71.

is rightly thought of as the conception of intellect.[4] Furthermore, when intellect understands, not something else, but itself, the word that is conceived is related to the one understanding as offspring to father. Hence the Divine Word that is attended to in God's self-understanding, is related to God from Whom it issues as Son to Father.[5] It is thus that catholic faith confesses in God the Father and the Son : " *Credo in Deum Patrem et Filium eius,* " and rather than have anyone hearing this think of it in terms of carnal generation, John the Evangelist, to whom the divine mysteries were revealed, used ' Word ' in place of ' Son ', to make certain that intellectual generation would be understood.[6]

In succeeding chapters, St. Thomas notes the profound differences between the Divine Word and the inner word of human understanding, and following closely the same symbol of faith, proceeds to treat the identity in essence and nature, the eternal nativity, and consubstantiality of the Son of God.[7]

Next, Aquinas treats the second procession on a parallel with the first. Just as the understood, inasmuch as it is understood, exists in the one understanding, so too must the beloved, inasmuch as it is loved, exist in the lover. For he who loves is somehow moved internally by the beloved. Thus, since the mover contacts that which is moved, it is necessary that the beloved, as mover, be internal to the lover. But God in understanding Himself must likewise love Himself. For the good comprehended in understanding is as such lovable. God, therefore, exists in Himself as the beloved in the lover.[8]

---

[4] *Comp.,* c. 38, 72.

[5] " Quando vero intellectus intelligit seipsum, verbum conceptum comparatur ad intelligentem sicut proles ad patrem. Cum igitur de Verbo loquamur secundum quod Deus se ipsum intelligit, oportet quod ipsum Verbum comparetur ad Deum, cuius est Verbum, sicut Filius ad Patrem. " *Comp.,* c. 39, 73, ad fin.

[6] " Hinc est quod in regula catholicae fidei, Patrem et Filium in divinis confiteri docemur, cum dicitur : *Credo in Deum Patrem et Filium eius.* Et ne aliquis audiens nomen Patris et Filii, carnalem generationem suspicaretur, secundum quam apud nos pater dicitur et filius, Ioannes Evangelista, cui revelata sunt secreta caelestia, loco *Filii* ponit *Verbum,* ut generationem intelligibilem cognoscamus. " *Comp.,* c. 40, 74.

[7] *Comp.,* cc. 41-44.

[8] " Sicut autem intellectum est in intelligente inquantum intelligitur, ita et amatum esse debet in amante inquantum amatur. Mo-

Once again, however, St. Thomas explains that the existence of the beloved in the one loving is not according to similitude, as is the existence of the understood in the one understanding, and hence not generation, but rather according to the attraction the beloved exerts upon the lover, and hence is named in Christian faith Spirit, or Holy Spirit.[9] He then shows how the Spirit, no less or otherwise than the Son, is essentially and substantially God.[10] Aquinas completes his discussion of the Spirit with a brief account of the procession *ab utroque*.[11]

At this point, instead of going immediately into the relations, as he does in the more rigorously synthetic development of the *Pars Prima*, St. Thomas observes that, on the basis of what has been said thus far, it should be gathered that Christian faith recognizes a certain ' *trinarium* ' in the divinity, which, nevertheless, does not in any way contradict the unity and simplicity of the divine essence. It is, however, this latter precaution, that accounts for the anticipation. The immediate object of the chapter is simply to explain that what proceeds in God as ' God understood ' and ' God beloved ' is not distinct from God's substantial being, as the understood and the beloved in men are distinct from man's substantial being. At the same time, on the other hand, St. Thomas extends his explanation, even here, to include the specific introduction of the Three Divine Persons as such.

In God, he affirms, being, understanding, and love, are the same. Hence, God as He exists in His natural being, God as He exists in understanding, and God as He exists in love, are one. Yet, each of these Three is subsistent, and therefore given the name that is proper to subsistent reality in intellectual nature — *personae* for the Latins, *hypostases* for the Greeks. There are, then, the Three Divine Persons : Father, Son, and Holy Spirit.[12]

---

vetur enim quodammodo amans ab amato quadam intrinseca motione. Unde cum movens contingat id quod movetur, necesse est amatum intrinsecum esse amanti. Deus autem sicut intelligit seipsum, ita necesse est quod seipsum amet : bonum enim intellectum secundum se amabile est. Est igitur Deus in seipso tanquam amatum in amante." *Comp.*, c. 45, 82.

[9] *Comp.*, cc. 46, 47.

[10] *Comp.*, c. 48, 85.

[11] *Comp.*, c. 49, 86.

[12] " Ex omnibus autem quae dicta sunt, colligi oportet, quod in Divinitate quendam trinarium ponimus, qui tamen unitati et simpli-

Only now, does Aquinas take up the matter of the divine relations, and in the manner of offering a solution to an *argumentum in contrarium* at that. Notwithstanding, however, the above anticipated introduction of the Persons as such, it will presently become clear that St. Thomas is still adhering basically to the order of synthesis, in which the essential dependence is of relations upon processions, and of Persons upon relations.

He poses two correlative objections against his own exposition. First, if there is this ' *trinarium* ' in God, there is number, and hence some species of division and difference to account for the distinction of Persons. But such a difference cannot be admitted in the face of the divine simplicity.[13] Secondly, on the other hand, if it is necessary to maintain that God is one, it seems impossible that God could be begotten or proceeding as love. For no one thing originates or proceeds from itself.[14]

It is in the focus of this problematic, then, that St. Thomas begins to treat systematically of the divine relations. But he does considerably more than this. The passage, as will be seen presently, serves also to recapitulate what Aquinas had said up to now about the two processions, and to do so in terms of the spiritual emanation and *processio ad intra* which is, by reduction, the ultimate formality involved.

As the reader will observe, the style and approach here is extremely similar to that of *Contra Gentiles IV*, chapter eleven — in places, such as the introductions to the two ac-

---

citati essentiae non repugnat. Oportet enim concedi Deum ut existentem in sua natura, et intellectum et amatum a seipso. Aliter autem hoc accidit in Deo et in nobis. Quia enim in sua natura homo substantia est, intelligere autem et amare eius non sunt eius substantia, homo quidem, secundum quod in natura sua consideratur, quaedam res subsistens est ; secundum autem quod est in suo intellectu, non est res subsistens, sed intentio quaedam rei subsistentis, et similiter secundum quod est in seipso ut amatum in amante ... In Deo autem idem est esse, intelligere, et amare. Deus ergo in esse suo naturali existens, et Deus existens in intellectu, et Deus existens in amore suo, unum sunt; unusquisque tamen eorum est subsistens. Et quia res subsistentes in intellectuali natura *personas* Latini nominare consueverunt, Graeci vero *hypostases*, propter hoc in divinis Latini dicunt tres personas, Graeci vero tres hypostases, Patrem scilicet, et Filium, et Spiritum sanctum. " *Comp.*, c .50, 87.

13 *Comp.*, c. 51, 88.

14 *Comp.*, c. 51, 89.

counts, the difference is hardly more than the substitution of
an occasional word or phrase. When the relations are ush-
ered in, it is precisely as the internal consequence of immanent
procession within the divine being. Nor will the lengthy
discussion terminate until Aquinas has once again arrived at
the Three distinct Persons, but this time, precisely as the
further internal consequence of the subsistent relations. Thus,
will St. Thomas complete his trinitarian exposition in the
Compendium according to the basic structure and progression
of the *ordo doctrinae*.

First, Aquinas lays down the general principle, that diversity in mode of origin or procession is proportionate to diversity in nature. Where there is no life, one thing can proceed from another only in the purely extrinsic sense of being
altered or changed in some way by this other. In living things,
on the other hand, where the chief and proper characteristic
is self-movement, something is brought forth, or generated,
within the very generator, according to the diverse potencies
of the particular living beings in question.

The potencies of the vegatative soul, therefore, are restricted in their operations to the corporeal and the material
as such. What proceeds here is merely corporeal, and corporeally distinct from its principle, though yet in some way
conjoined to this same principle. The potencies of the sensitive soul are likewise basically material, but nevertheless
capable of operations extending to the 'species' of bodies
inasmuch as these species are received without matter. Hence,
the reception is to some extent immaterial. On the other
hand, it is made only through use of the bodily organ. What
proceeds in sensitive life, therefore, like the formations of
imagination, is somehow immaterial itself, in some fashion
immaterially distinct from, while yet conjoined to, its principle.

Perfect immateriality of procession, however, is attained only in the potencies of the intellectual soul. Thus, the
inner word which proceeds upon the corporeally transcendent
operation of intellect proceeds internally within the intellect
of the one who utters it according to the order of origin.
Similarly, what proceeds in the will proceeds in the same
internal manner.[15]

---

[15] " Principium autem ad dissolvendum hanc dubitationem, hinc
sumere oportet, quia secundum diversitatem naturarum est in diver-

It is common to every intellect, then, that what is conceived in intellect must proceed in some way from the one
understanding, inasmuch as he is understanding, and be, in
virtue of its procession, distinct from the one understanding
according to the way in which the conception of intellect, or
' intention understood ', is distinct from ' intellect understanding '.   By the same token, the affection of the one loving, whereby the beloved exists in the one loving, must proceed from
the will of the one loving inasmuch as he is loving.

In the divine intellect, however, since being and understanding are identified, the conception of intellect, or ' the
understood ', must be God's own substance, as also must be
the affection of will.   It remains, therefore, that the Divine

sis rebus diversus modus aliquid ex alio oriendi vel procedendi.   In
rebus enim vita carentibus, quia non sunt seipsa moventia, sed solum
extrinsecus possunt moveri, oritur unum ex altero quasi exterius al-
teratum et immutatum, sicut ab igne generatur ignis, et ab aëre aër.
In rebus vero viventibus, quarum proprietas est ut seipsas moveant,
generatur aliquid in ipso generante, sicut foetus animalium et fructus
plantarum.   Est autem considerare *diversum modum* processionis secundum diversas vires et processiones earumdem.   1) Sunt enim quaedam vires in eis, quarum operationes non se extendunt nisi ad corpora,
secundum quod materialia sunt, sicut patet de viribus animae vegeta-
bilis ... et secundum hoc genus virium animae non procedit nisi aliquid
corporale corporaliter distinctum, et tamen aliquo modo coniunctum
in viventibus ei a quo procedit.   2) Sunt autem quaedam vires, quarum
operationes etsi corpora non transcendant, tamen se extendunt ad
species corporum, sine materia eas recipiendo, sicut est in omnibus
viribus animae sensitivae ... Huiusmodi autem vires, licet quodammodo immaterialiter formas rerum suscipiant, non tamen eas suscipiunt
absque organo corporali.   Si qua igitur processio in huiusmodi viribus
animae inveniatur, quod procedit, non erit aliquid corporale, vel corporaliter distinctum, vel coniunctum ei a quo procedit, sed incorporali-
ter et immaterialiter quodammodo, licet non omnino absque admi-
niculo organi corporalis.   Sic enim procedunt in animalibus formatio-
nes rerum imaginatarum, quae quidem, sunt in imaginatione non sicut
corpus in corpore, sed quodam spirituali modo ... 3) Si autem secundum operationem imaginationis procedit aliquid non per modum
corporalem, multo fortius hoc accidet per operationem partis intellec-
tivae, quae nec etiam in sui operatione indiget organo corporali, sed omnino eius operatio immaterialis est.   Procedit enim verbum secundum
operationem intellectus, ut in ipso intellectu dicentis existens, non
quasi localiter in eo contentum, nec corporaliter ab eo separatum,
sed in ipso quidem existens secundum ordinem originis : et eadem
ratio est de processione quae attenditur secundum operationem voluntatis, prout res amata existit in amante, ut supra dictum est. " *Comp.*
c. 52, 90.

Word is not distinct from the one producing it in the line of
substantial being, but only in the line of what it is for one
reality to proceed from another. The same must be said of
the Holy Spirit.

Hence, there is nothing to prevent the Word of God,
His Divine Son, from being one with the Father in substance,
and yet distinct from the Father in the relation that follows
upon procession ("secundum relationem processionis"). It is
clear, therefore — St. Thomas returns to his original problematic — that this is not an instance of some one and the
same reality originating or proceeding from itself. For the
Son as proceeding from the Father is distinct from the Father ;
and the Holy Spirit as proceeding from both the Father and
the Son is distinct from both the Father and the Son.[16]

Moreover, these relations whereby the divine Persons are
distinct from one another are real, not merely rational. For
they are consequent upon what obtains in the order of reality,
as opposed to what is apprehended only in the mind.[17] Furthermore, since real relations existing in God cannot possibly
accrue to the divine substance in any accidental manner, it

---

[16] " Est igitur commune in omni intellectu, ut ex dictis patet,
quod oportet id quod in intellectu concipitur, ab intelligente quodammodo procedere, inquantum intelligens est, et sua processione ab ipso
quodammodo dixtinguitur [sic — the point being made, however,
dependence of distinction upon procession, as in the parallel *C. G.*,
IV, c. 11, 13, and the very construction of the sentence, would seem
to require " distingui "]. sicut conceptio intellectus quae est intentio
intellecta, distinguitur ab intellectu intelligente ; et similiter oportet
quod affectio amantis, per quam amatum est in amante, procedat a
voluntate amantis inquantum est amans. Sed hoc proprium habet
intellectus divinus, quod cum intelligere eius sit esse ipsius, oportet quod
conceptio intellectus, quae est intentio intellecta, sit substantia eius,
et similiter est de affectione in ipso Deo amante. Relinquitur ergo
quod intentio intellectus divini, quae est Verbum ipsius, non distinguitur a producente ipsum in hoc quod est esse secundum substantiam,
sed solum in hoc quod est esse secundum rationem procesionis unius
ex alio : et similiter est de affectione amoris in Deo amante, quae
ad Spiritum sanctum pertinet. Sic igitur patet quod nihil proihibet
Verbum Dei, quod est Filius, esse unum cum Patre secundum| substan-
tiam, et tamen distinguitur ab eo secundum relationem processionis,
ut dictum est. Unde et manifestum est quod eadem res non oritur
neque procedit a seipsa : quia Filius, secundum quod a Patre procedit, ab eo distinguitur ; et eadem ratio est de Spiritu sancto per comparationem ad Patrem et Filium. " *Comp.*, c. 52, 91.

[17] *Comp.*, c. 53, 92.

follows also that the same relations are necessarily subsistent.[18] Finally, it is through these same subsistent relations, that the distinction of Persons in God is constituted.[19]

Thus, St. Thomas himself makes it explicit, that his treatment of the Trinity in the *Compendium*, is, notwithstanding the unevenness caused by the anticipation already observed, according to the basic lines and movement of understanding through synthesis. The same point receives additional confirmation as Aquinas goes on, in the chapter immediately following, to resume his exposition, and once again stress the order of internal dependence — Persons upon relations, relations upon procession — in the course of explaining why it is impossible that there should be more than these Three Persons.[20]

Moreover, it is only in the full perspective of the Thomist synthetic design, that one can give a truly satisfactory answer to the question of whether or not the way St. Thomas approached the processions at the beginning of his treatise in the *Compendium* involved some measure of apologetical intention or at least the unsuspected creation of an apologetical argument.

For while it is possible, and to some extent even necessary, to show that the discussion actually began with a simple statement of the mystery as revealed, and was developed within the larger context of what was contained in Sacred Scripture and the apostolic creed, there always remains the possibility of some subordinate idea of apodictic demonstration as being involved, one might say automatically, in St. Thomas' use of what might seem to be purely rational structure. But the only way to show conclusively what the pur-

---

[18] *Comp.*, c. 54, 93.

[19] " Quia ergo in divinis distinctio est per relationes quae non accidunt, sed sunt subsistentes, rerum autem subsistentium in natura quacumque intellectuali est distinctio personalis, necesse est quod per praedictas relationes in Deo personalis distinctio constituatur. Pater igitur et Filius et Spiritus sanctus sunt tres personae, et similiter tres hypostases, quia hypostasis significat aliquid subsistens completum. " *Comp.*, c. 55, 94.

[20] " Plures autem in divinis personas tribus esse impossibile est, cum non sit possibile divinas personas multiplicari per substantiae divisionem, sed solum per alicuius processionis relationem, nec cuiuscumque processionis, sed talis quae non terminetur ad aliquod extrinsecum ... " *Comp.*, c. 56, 95.

pose and nature of Aquinas' theological exposition was not, is simply to show, in a more positive manner, what it was.

As in the *Summa*, therefore, so likewise in the less perfectly drawn, but fundamentally similar, design of the *Compendium*, the ultimate and most telling reason why St. Thomas had no intention to demonstrate the processions, and why, moreover, such a demonstration could not possibly have had any rôle, however implicit and unsuspected, in the eventual theological achievement, is simply because, in light of the synthetic order he himself had chosen to follow, the fact of procession was presupposed, and necessarily presupposed, from the very beginning. For in the order of synthesis, one starts off with the divine procession because the divine procession is first in reality, and already known to be first in reality, inasmuch as it is first in the line of internal cause. But this is the line of understanding, not the line of certitude.

Once the order of synthesis is set down as the plan to be followed, the entire question of certitude as to the fact is laid aside. It no longer has any place within the essential structure. If it is raised at all, as Aquinas does raise it while speaking of the Persons in the *Pars Prima*, the time to do so is when the *ordo doctrinae* has completed its course from the first internal reason down to the last consequence, down to what was first known, therefore, and from knowledge of which knowledge of the successive reasons or 'causes' was previously obtained — or putting it another way, at the time when it might be thought well to remind the student, as Aquinas does, that such a presupposition is essential to the order of understanding through synthesis.

At the same time, the presupposition is not made loosely or arbitrarily. St. Thomas begins with the divine procession because the divine procession is known to be first in the line of internal reason. But this means that the legitimacy of postulating such a priority has been scientifically established.

Or concretely, it means that from the divinely revealed data of Three distinct Persons in one indivisible God, human intelligence — not 'pure reason', but reason enlightened by supernatural faith — has come to understand this mystery, to the limited extent such understanding is possible, in terms of subsistent real relations following upon immanent procession through intellect and will in the divine nature. Once this analytical reduction has been performed, then, and only then, can the same theological reason presuppose as the ultimate and first ' cause ' of the distinction of Persons immanent procession through intellect and will in the divine nature — and go on from this primordial supposition to construct the synthesis of trinitarian understanding.

In the *Summa*, and also in the *Compendium*, this process of analysis is not explicitly recorded. In neither treatise, does St. Thomas begin with an account of the individual Persons as portrayed in character, association, and salvific activity, in the pages of Scripture, then continue by showing how it is necessary to take or understand the personal distinction thus described as based upon subsistent real relations, and finally conclude by showing how it is necessary to understand these subsistent relations, in turn, as following immediately upon immanent processions of origin in intellect and will. Yet clearly, these steps are present, by necessary implication, in the inverse order of synthesis.

As was noted, however, at the end of the preceding chapter, the fact that such a *via analytica* is actually implicit in the text, for all that it is not explicitly presented in either the *Pars Prima* or the *Compendium*, and that St. Thomas himself wished his *ordo doctrinae* to be interpreted precisely in this light, is a point deserving of more direct and detailed attention. An attempt will be made to do so in the chapter immediately following.

THE PRIOR 'VIA ANALYTICA' AND SOLUTION TO THE PROBLEM OF 'PURE PERFECTION' IN THE GENERALIZATION ON PROCESSION OF INNER WORD

When all is said and done, the challenge of apologetical design, of offering, however unintentionally, some manner of purely rational proof for the a priori necessity of the divine procession, which might be brought against the Thomist '*de Trinitate*', becomes the more specific challenge that Aquinas somehow 'concludes' divine procession from the philosophical properties of intellect. In his more mature works, in the *Summa*, in the *Compendium*, and one might add the ninth question of the *De Potentia*, St. Thomas at least approaches the procession of the Divine Word, and subsequently the procession of the Holy Spirit, from what is absolutely essential to intellectual being.

To explain this procedure, and thus to test the legitimacy and strength of the challenge, the study of the text had to move through several successive steps. It was necessary to show, first of all, that in the passages where the difficulty was thought to be found, the root fact or existence of the trinitarian processions was at least not the precise matter Aquinas had set out to prove, or even confirm. For wherever the question of the existence, fact and certitude of the mystery was concerned, St. Thomas always took care to observe that the substance of the mystery was known to man through revelation, and through revelation only.

Secondly, it was necessary to show, again from the text itself, that according to the inherent logic of the very plan or order Aquinas intended to follow in these same expositions — the plan or order, moreover, he explicitly defined in the *prooemium* to the '*de Trinitate*' of the *Pars Prima* — the point from which he began his doctrinal elaboration, the universality of really distinct intellectual or spiritual emanation, was not, and could not possibly be, the principle from which further facts, beginning with the generation of the Son, were to be deduced. For the principle itself was known only through theological analysis of the revealed mystery.

In the *prooemium* just referred to, St. Thomas had been at pains to clarify this point. His proposition was to treat first the divine procession — not, however, because divine procession in its ' metaphysical ' character as the archetype of intellectual emanation was what is the *primum motum*, but rather because the divine procession so described is the ultimate ' cause ' or *ratio* of the trinitarian relations, and hence of the plurality of Persons.

Thirdly, it was necessary to show, still from the text, that adoption of such a plan or order of exposition involved at least two serious consequences. In the first place, it meant that Aquinas had explicitly laid aside as the objective of this particular exposition, and of any others that would be substantially parallel, the ideal of certitude or verification of fact in favor of the quite distinct ideal of theological under-standing. For to proceed from the ultimate explanation or reason of a fact, is to presuppose prior knowledge of the fact, not to undertake its proof or demonstration. But in the second place, it also meant that through some previous process of theological analysis the ultimate explanation or reason of the fact had itself already been determined.

St. Thomas proposed to begin his trinitarian exposition with the treatment of procession as such *because* it is the relations of origin, or procession, that distinguish the Three Divine Persons — " *quia* personae divinae secundum relationes originis distinguuntur." But how was the fact of this depen-dence known ? On precisely what ground was it determined ?

Fourthly, therefore, it was necessary to point out the actual, albeit implicit, theological analysis which underlies the *ordo doctrinae*. In the twenty-eighth question of the *Pars Prima*, when Aquinas introduced the real trinitarian relations, his exposition at this juncture contained the analytical proof that the only possible foundation for real relations within the divinity was immanent procession in intellect and will. In the following questions, when he introduced the Persons, his exposition then contained the further analytical proof that the only possible explanation for personal distinction in God is that of subsistent relations.

The existence of this prior theological analysis, therefore, is not in any sense a gratuitous inference. For it is clea- from the text itself that as St. Thomas advanced from pror cession to relations, from relations to Persons, the *prius notum*, all along so to speak, was simply the Persons and the Persons as known through the revelation of the mystery.

As the order of synthesis moved forward, each of the successive steps in the prior analysis were formally and explicitly indicated. Only the order itself had been reversed, and hence, only in this sense was the *via analytica* not recorded. It is not possible to understand a plurality of Divine Persons, Aquinas argued, except in terms of subsistent real relations. It is not possible to understand subsistent real relations in God except in terms of procession *ad intra*. It is only, then, because, theological analysis had previously arrived at this latter point, that Aquinas was able to commence his strictly synthetic account, not with the Persons, but with procession as such — not, therefore, with what is first in the knowledge of experience, but with what is known to be first, or more accurately *understood* to be first, in the order of things as they are in themselves.

In both the *Summa* and the *Compendium*, then, St. Thomas' presentation is according to the order of understanding through synthesis — not, of course, merely because he keeps to the schematic sequence : procession, relations, Persons, but because he takes care to assign as the reason for this sequence the order of internal dependence : of Persons upon relations, and of relations upon Persons. In the same synthetic presentation, moreover, he continues to underscore the original process of analysis, or *reductio in principia*, whereby the priority of the real as understood was grasped.

It remains, however, that while each of the essential steps in the analysis is clearly marked, with the result that its underlying presence in the *Pars Prima, Compendium, De Potentia*, q. 9, a. 5, is unmistakable, nevertheless the methodological structure of these particular expositions is still synthesis, and hence the process of analysis as such is only implicit. One might ask, then, whether at other times, and in the context of this specifically different theological design, the analysis itself was worked out more explicitly ? One might also ask whether St. Thomas actually extended such a theological analysis, not merely to the divine *processio ad intra*, but to formulation of the universal or transcendental principle that really distinct intellectual and volitional procession is an essential property of intellectual nature?

I. The Fundamentally Analytical Method of the "Sentences"

In point of fact, and despite the methodological clumsiness of the work, the '*de Trinitate*' of the *Sentences* shows Aquinas already engaged with theological analysis in the technical sense of attempting to determine, through rational process illustrated by faith, how what had been revealed must be interpreted or understood. This was shown earlier in the present study, of course, when the text of the *Sentences* was under examination, but now that the further significance of the *via analytica* as the presupposition of synthesis in the *ordo doctrinae* of more mature works has been brought out, the same matter should be viewed once again, though in summary form, from the perspective of this larger context.

It will be recalled, then, that when Aquinas passes from the unity of God and the divine attributes to a consideration of the Trinity, his opening question is simply whether there is in God a plurality of Persons.[1] Next, he poses the further question, whether this plurality is real as opposed to merely rational.[2]

St. Thomas' first concern, therefore, is with the certitude of the mystery, the fact of the real plurality of Divine Persons, as revealed. But immediately after having affirmed that Christian faith attests this plurality, and also, since the opposite insinuates the Sabellian heresy, strictly real plurality, he announces that it is yet to be seen how such a real plurality in God is possible. In explanation, Aquinas appeals to the personal property as a relation, at once only rationally distinct from the divine essence, but really from the *alterum*, to which, in virtue of the proper formality of relation, it is referred.[3]

---

[1] *In I Sent.*, d. 2, q. 1, a. 4.

[2] *In I Sent.*, d. 2, q. 1, a. 5.

[3] " Respondeo dicendum, quod dicere personas distingui tantum ratione, sonat haeresim sabellianam : et ideo simpliciter dicendum est, quod pluralitas personarum est realis. Quomodo autem hoc possit esse videndum est. " *In I Sent.*, d. 2, q. 1, a. 5 sol.

Thus, as was noted at the time, St. Thomas first established the existence of the mystery : the revelation that there is in God a real plurality of Persons, and then proceeded to reduce this datum, through theological analysis, to its principles — to the personal property which, as relation, is to be identified with the divine essence, and yet distinguished from its correspondent, or opposite.

The same basically analytical process was conspicuous again in the discussion of the Son's generation. The fact of this generation is established solely on the authority of faith. But once the fact is thus established, it becomes the function of theological reasoning to see how it must be understood.

When perfections discovered in the created universe, St. Thomas explains, are to be attributed to God properly, and not metaphorically, they must be divested of whatever potentiality and imperfection belongs to the creature. Generation, therefore, in its generic aspect, or as a type of change, cannot be predicated of God. But generation in its specific aspect as communication in the line of act, and hence in the order of pure excellence, can be predicated of God. It is in this way, then, as *actus perfecti* involving no actuation of any potency, that the generation of the Son, once revealed, has to be understood.[4]

A bit later, after having analysed the rôle of the Father, as supposit, or *principium quod*, and that of the divine essence, as *principium quo*, Aquinas was able to transpose the simple revealed datum : God the Father generates the Son, into the more theologically refined doctrine : God the Father (as supposit, *principium quod actuum*), in virtue of the divine essence (as *principium quo actuum*, rationally distinct from supposit), generates (*actus perfecti*, communication of the divine essence in the line of pure act) the Son (as supposit, Divine Person, corresponding to the Father, recipient of the Father's communication, but without any actuation being involved). [5]

It could be said, in fact, since elements of true synthesis, as St. Thomas would later understand it, are almost totally lacking in this early work, that whatever process of theological reasoning is actually present in the *Sentences*, it is strictly and exclusively the process of analytical reduction. This ob-

---

[4] *In I Sent.*, d. 4, q. 1, a. 1, and ad 1m.
[5] *In I Sent.*, d. 5, q. 1, a. 1 sol.

servation, on the other hand, must not be taken to mean that the analysis itself, particularly where the Trinity of Persons is concerned, is at all complete.

Thus, while there is a clear reduction of the Persons to real relations, there is no clear reduction of the relations themselves to the two immanent processions — *per modum intellectus* and *per modum voluntatis* — that are solely possible in spiritual nature. As was noted previously in this study, excessive preoccupation with the formula *per modum naturae vel intellectus* to designate the first procession prevented St. Thomas, in the *Sentences*, from making an intellectually satisfying identification between the generation of the Son and the conception of the Divine Word. Though Aquinas saw clearly at this time that the divine generation as such had to be understood in terms of communication in the order of pure act, his notion of the inner word was still quite obscure, and hence he had no adequate means for understanding this same communication simply as the procession of what is conceived in intellect.

The sprawling ' *de Trinitate* ' of the *Sentences*, therefore, reveals unmistakably the intent and method of theological analysis, but such as remained, at least in contrast with later works, hesitant and unfinished in its achievement. More particularly, inasmuch as the effort here to attain some partial understanding of the revealed mystery touches only superficially on the intellectualist character of the divine procession, this first recorded analysis of St. Thomas does not reach what will eventually become the specific presuppositions of the *ordo doctrinae*.

At the same time, the basic structure of the *via analytica* is already in evidence. The significance of this observation for the subsequent development of Aquinas' thought should not be minimized.

II. The Fulfilment of the Trinitarian Analysis in Contra Gentiles IV

The more mature and more expertly worked treatise of the fourth book *Contra Gentiles* shows the analysis begun in the *Sentences* carried, for all practical purposes, to its conclusion.

As was noted earlier, the processes of theological reasoning in *Contra Gentiles IV* are not exclusively analytical. A
careful study of the two key chapters, the eleventh and the
nineteenth, indicates a certain attraction toward introducing
the more synthetic approach in the course of the analysis.
The same processes, nevertheless, are at least predominantly
analytical, as will be demonstrated with greater precision presently. Hence, the *via analytica* here is not merely implicit,
as subsequently in the *Compendium* and the *Pars Prima*, but
actually recorded step by step in the idiom and structure of
the composition itself, clearly moreover, though perhaps just
a bit unevenly due to the tendency toward an anticipation of
synthesis already mentioned.

As in the *Sentences*, then, but in obvious contrast to the
plan later adopted in the *Compendium* and the *Summa*, St.
Thomas begins, it will be recalled, by considering the documents of Sacred Scripture in which the mystery of the divine
fatherhood and sonship, which is the mystery of the divine
generation, is proclaimed. The approach at this point is strictly exegetical: to examine these biblical testimonies, and to
prove from an ensemble of related texts, that it is God Himself Who is being described as the begotten Son of the Father.

Some confusion might possibly arise from the fact that
the notion of 'generation' was likewise introduced here. One
might be led to surmise, therefore, that St. Thomas was speaking of procession as internal cause of personal distinction, at
least as between the Father and the Son. This is not the
case, however. The notion of generation which Aquinas brought
into his opening chapter was simply the unrefined biblical notion that was no less immediate to the text than fatherhood or
sonship. He did not stop here to discuss anything like an
order of internal dependence.[6]

With the mystery itself thus established on the authority
of Sacred Scripture, St. Thomas turned to a consideration of
the Photinian, Sabellian, and Arian heresies. And here his
basic methodology became that of theological analysis.

In discussing the created sonship of grace and adoption,
which he attributes to the Photinians and others, Aquinas first

---

[6] *C. G., IV*, c. 2. A comparison with c. 15 and the parallel usage
of 'procession' in connection with the Holy Spirit will confirm the
observation made with regard to the notion of generation as introduced here by St. Thomas.

describes the heterodox position itself, then indicates the chief
biblical passages claimed in support, and indicates as well the
fundamental aprioristic assumption which had given rise to
this tendentious exegesis : namely, the impossibility of assigning to one who was God *per naturam* the many contingent
and created properties and events with which Sacred Scripture
speaks of the personality of Christ.

By way of reply, St. Thomas cites several passages of
Scripture, in which, as he sees it, the eternal generation of
the Son, unique and in every sense divine, is amply demonstrated. But before leaving the Photinians, he returns as well
to the rational assumption just mentioned, and refutes this
latter by appealing to the theological principle of the two
distinct natures. Because there are in the Incarnate Christ
these two natures, human and divine, it is possible and necessary to predicate of Christ both what is proper to the
divine nature and what is proper to the human nature.[7]

The principle itself enjoys, of course, the authority of Christian teaching. Aquinas is quite aware of this, as his use of
the expression " confitemur " makes clear.[8] It is, nevertheless, an instance of Church authority having given official
sanction, on the occasion of heretical pressures, to the only
possible way in which the testimonies of Sacred Scripture can
be understood, and its basic character as development through
the process of theological analysis must not be lost sight of.

In succeeding chapters of this fourth book of the *Contra
Gentiles*, St. Thomas will adhere to the same method — not,
to be sure, in the sense that for each and every further point
his analysis will determine, he could, or would, claim a like
degree of authentic sanction. Moreover, as he passes on to
treat of the Sabellian, and especially the Arian, heresies, the
greater complexity of his material will suggest some departure
from the simple plan he was more easily able to follow in
treating of the Photinians. Thus, after having exposed the
main tenets of Sabellianism and Arianism, along with the
biblical exegesis each had appealed to in confirmation of their
position, he will give in answer his own presentation of the
orthodox biblical apologetic, but he will postpone his discus-

---

[7] *C. G., IV*, c. 4.
[8] The passage is quoted above on page 142, note no. 21.

sion of the rational or philosophical assumptions contained
in the two heresies until he has first completed the lengthy
and positive doctrinal account of how the mystery has to be
understood beginning in the eleventh chapter.[9]

This account itself, once Aquinas gets into it, shows many
faces. First, and as previously remarked in this study, it
occupies a central and climactic position in the tract on the
divine generation. It has every sign of being, so to speak,
the moment St. Thomas had been waiting for.

Secondly, as will be explained presently, the passage taken
as a whole — comprising chapters eleven through thirteen
— has much of the quality of synthesis in it as well as of pure
analysis. Thirdly, however, and notwithstanding the observation just made, the account represents, more than anything
else, the final and most significant step in the process of analytical reduction which Aquinas had begun when he discussed
the initial false assumption of the Photinians, and went on
to reject this by appealing to the theological principle of two
distinct natures.

The transition in chapter ten brings out this basically
analytical perspective and intention. In view of what has
been said thus far, St. Thomas summarized, it is the evident
testimony of Sacred Scripture with regard to the divine generation, that the Father and Son, though two distinct Persons, are nevertheless but one God, sharing one essence or nature in common. With this, he introduces a further theological principle, and one more directly concerned with the
Trinity as such than the previous christological principle on
the two natures. Then Aquinas draws his transition. Yet,
since the idea of two distinct supposits sharing the same single
essence is quite foreign to human experience, the human reason naturally encounters many difficulties in its understanding.[10]

In context, this transition introduces what is to follow
as an exposition of theological analysis. For immediately

---

[9] The Sabellian position is outlined in *C. G.*, *IV*, c. 5, and the
rational assumption: God is one; hence Father and Son are united
in supposit, is indicated in par. 12. See above, pp. 143-144. Arianism
is discussed in cc. 6-9, its assumptions, along with other rational objections, recounted in c. 10, solutions being postponed to c. 14. See
above, pp. 144-147.

[10] *C. G.*, *IV*, c. 10, 1.

after detailing these rational difficulties, St. Thomas postpones their specific solution for the moment, and instead, begins right away with his positive doctrinal account, inasmuch as the positive and comprehensive exposition will render specific solution all the more easy when the time comes. Accepting, then, Aquinas continues, everything that the Sacred Scriptures relate of the divine generation and the Son of God, it remains to see how this mystery must be taken or understood.[11]

First, St. Thomas proposes at considerable length the metaphysics of emanation — the merely transient activity of inanimate bodies, the successive stages of vegetative, sensory, and intellectual life, the further levels of human, angelic, and divine intelligence, until in God the height of emanation is attained in the perfect absolute identity between what emanates and its source. Next, he offers a more particular explanation of what precisely it is that emanates in intellectual being : namely, the *intentio intellecta*, and contrasts the specific characteristics of this *intentio*, or *verbum*, as found respectively in human and divine understanding. St. Thomas concludes this preliminary part of his exposition, remarking that, in the light of this theory of emanation, it is now possible to see how generation in God has to be taken.[12]

In point of fact, there is an obvious parallel between the foregoing discussion on emanation in general and the similar account, likewise introductory, in the *Compendium*.[13] This parallel has already been noted.[14] A difficulty, however, arises here. For the *Compendium* passage is clearly synthetic in structure and movement, with the *via analytica* supposed, not explicitly recorded.

In the writer's judgment, that there is a certain synthetic quality to the *Contra Gentiles* passage as well, can readily be allowed. Nevertheless, the difference between the two passages are more significant, at least from the methodological point of view, than the similarities.

In the *Compendium*, the order throughout has been that of synthesis — of the *priora quoad se*, moving progressively from procession, to relations, to Persons. In the fifty-second chapter, moreover, this same basic line of internal dependence

---

[11] *C. G.*, *IV*, c. 10, 14 ; c. 11, rub. See above, p. 147.
[12] *C. G.*, *IV*, c. 11, 1-8. See above, pp. 147-151.
[13] *Comp.*, c. 52, 90.
[14] See above, pp. 270, 273.

is explicitly drawn, and in this context, the doctrine of general emanation has the more or less summational function of restating the first trinitarian procession in the precise terms of intellectual emanation as ultimate ' cause ' or reason. Paraphrased in its simplest form, the argument would read as follows : there is emanation in all things, properly in living things, more properly still in beings endowed with intellect and will, first and foremost, then, in God Himself ; from this divine emanation, or procession, there originates real relations ; and by these relations, are constituted the Three Persons of the Trinity.

In the *Contra Gentiles*, on the other hand, the order has been throughout that of analysis — of the *priora quoad nos*, moving progressively from what is first known, fatherhood, sonship, generation in God, as revealed in the testimonies of Sacred Scripture, to what is known subsequently, when, and inasmuch as, theological reason seeks to reduce the revealed message to its internal principles, according to the way the mystery itself, once revealed, has to be taken or understood. In the early part of the eleventh chapter, the theory of emanation is presented, not so much as the beginning from what is first in the order of reality — though the fact itself is implicit here also — but rather as the background of rational structure, the applicability of which to the mystery of God's generation will then be tested.

For while the *Compendium* continues without interruption from the discussion of divine emanation, as the highest mode of emanation in the universe of being, to introduce the relations as immediate consequence of this divine emanation, the *Contra Gentiles* breaks off at the same point to examine how, in the light of this rational structure, the mystery itself is to be understood.

St. Thomas excludes first inanimate emanation. It is impossible to understand the divine generation in terms of material activity and change. Next he excludes the emanation proper to the vegetative soul, then that proper to the sensory soul. Intellectual emanation alone is left, but even here, it is impossible to understand the conception of the Divine Word as substantially distinct from either the object that is understood, or the act of understanding itself, as is proper to the inner word of the human intellect.[15]

---

[15] *C. G.*, *IV*, c. 11, 8. See above, pp. 150-151.

All of this, however, was dispensed with in the *Compendium*. In the *Compendium* account, there was no longer any need to show how the divine generation had to be understood in rational theology. Here, it was clearly presupposed that it had to be understood according to intellectual emanation or procession. In the *Contra Gentiles*, on the other hand, this necessity was precisely the point Aquinas wished to elucidate, and did so through a detailed analysis.

The analysis, moreover, is not yet completed. For in the *Contra Gentiles*, but again not in the *Compendium*, St. Thomas continues with a step by step reduction of what is held in connection with the mystery of the divine generation to the intellectualist account as conception of the Divine Word. The understood, as such, exists in the one understanding. In knowing Himself, therefore, God exists in Himself as the understood in the one understanding. Further, since the divine intellect does not pass from potency into act, it follows that the Divine Word is eternal. Further still, since the divine intellect is not only in act, but is itself pure act, there is complete identity between the divine intellect and the divine act of understanding, and hence also between the Divine Word and the nature, essence, and existence of God. The Divine Word, therefore, is truly God, sharing the numerically same divine nature.[16]

Next, Aquinas introduces the matter of real distinction. Though the components, so to speak, of the divine being are unequivocally identified in absolute reality, one must still assign to each of these components whatever is essential to this formal perfection. But it is essential to the inner word as such, that it proceed from the one understanding, upon the act of understanding, as the quasi term of intellectual operation. Hence the Divine Word is referred to God understanding, Who utters this Word, as to the one from whom it has its being. At the same time, because of the perfect identity between God understanding, the divine act of understanding, and the Word itself, the distinction involved here can be only that of relation.[17]

Once again, therefore, there is an element of the theological progression characteristic of synthesis. St. Thomas moves

---

[16] *C. G.*, *IV*, c. 11, 9-12. See above, pp. 151-153.
[17] *C. G.*, *IV*, c. 11, 13. See above, pp. 153-154.

for the moment from procession to relations in virtue of the
internal dependence of the latter upon the former. The main
thrust of the argument, however, is still analytical. For Aquinas' central purpose is still that of reducing what is contained
in the mystery of generation to its intellectualist principles.
In the sections immediately following, he describes the Divine
Word as image of the invisible God, as image according to
substance and communication in the same nature with God
Who utters it. Finally, St. Thomas explains how, in God,
the utterance is necessarily natural, and with this, he completes
his analytical reduction. The Divine Word is the Eternal
Son; His generation from the Father is perfectly identified
with the Father's conception and utterance.[18]

What Aquinas has done, therefore, is simply take the
mystery of God's generation, as revealed, to show how rational theology must understand this mystery (*quomodo accipienda*) in terms of the procession of inner word in the divine
understanding. In later chapters, he will perform the same
analysis for the Person and procession of the Holy Spirit.[19]

The analysis, then, which has already been seen to be
necessarily implicit in the *ordo doctrinae* of the *Pars Prima*
and the *Compendium* is actually worked out in the *Contra
Gentiles*. The essential methodology had made its appearance
as far back as the *Sentences*, but in the absence of a clear doctrine on the emanation of inner word, the final achievement
of the analysis had to await the writing *Contra Gentiles IV*.

If, on the other hand, the trinitarian *via analytica* as expressed by St. Thomas is less than perfectly satisfying, or if
there seems to be something missing, and even in the *Contra
Gentiles*, this is due to the fact that, although the precise
analysis implicit in the *Summa* and *Compendium* is explicitly
developed and recorded in the *Contra Gentiles* so far as sub-
stantials are concerned, there are, nevertheless, peripheral differences and one at least that may be more than peripheral.
The analysis implicit in the *ordo doctrinae* of the *Pars Prima*
moves from the revelation of the Three Persons, to the real
relations by which these Persons are constituted and in terms
of which they are to be understood, to the divine immanent

---

[18] *C. G.*, *IV*, c. 11, 14-17. See above, pp. 155-157.
[19] *C. G.*, *IV*, cc. 15-19. See above, pp. 189-198.

processions which ground the relations, and in terms of which the relations themselves are to be understood.

In the present study, it has already been demonstrated, sufficiently it is hoped, that this analysis is an absolutely necessary inference to be drawn from an examination of the *ordo doctrinae* itself. The purpose, therefore, in looking in other works for the same analysis as explicitly recorded was not to establish a point for which there was as yet only partial or inadequate proof, but merely to confirm that point by adducing clear textual evidence. But the question might well be asked : does the account of the analysis contained in the *Contra Gentiles* actually accomplish this ? Or to put it concretely : has St. Thomas, in the *Contra Gentiles*, actually begun with the revealed mystery of the Three Persons, then moved on, through reduction, to, first the real relations, and then the immanent processions ?

That he begins with the revealed mystery of the Three Persons, is quite evident. In light of the apologetical or pastoral rôle assigned to his treatise, in connection with which he planned to treat separately the heretical doctrines pertaining to the divinity and personal altereity of the Son, on the one hand, and those pertaining to the divinity and procession of the Holy Spirit, on the other, St. Thomas divides his subject matter into two neat parts. First, he discusses only the Father and Son and the divine generation. Next, he discusses in parallel fashion the Holy Spirit. This simple division, however, does not substantially alter his treatment. As the approach taken in both sections from the testimonies of Sacred Scripture makes clear, the essential and constant movement throughout the treatise is from the revealed mystery — the mystery of the Three Persons, moreover, though subdivided to meet his particular purpose — to its understanding in rational theology.

But is Aquinas' first step in this theological analysis from the Persons to the real relations ? Is it, in other words, precisely the same first step as that taken in the analysis which is implicitly contained in the *ordo doctrinae* ?

In point of fact, it is not — at least not as explicitly worked out and recorded in the passages which have already been examined above. St. Thomas moves rather from the revealed Persons to the two immanent processions *per modum intellectus* and *per modum amoris*. The treatment of the real relations, on the other hand, is incorporated into the discussion on immanent procession — with the consequence, as remarked earlier, that there is, in the course of the analysis, some anticipation of the more strictly synthetic design. There is thus an ellipsis of sorts in the analysis itself.

The significance of this ellipsis, however, should not be exaggerated. The basic and prevailing structure of the doctrinal exposition presented in *Contra Gentiles IV* is manifestly the analysis whereby what is the ' first known ' in the knowledge of experience — here, the mystery as revealed — is ' reduced ' through understanding to its ultimate causal, or in the case of the divine, quasi causal, principles. The analysis, moreover, is carried by St. Thomas to its term: understanding of the plurality of Persons as internally dependent upon intellectual emanation in the divinity.

III. MORE PRECISE INTEGRATION OF THE RELATIONS INTO THE STRICTLY ANALYTICAL STRUCTURE IN THE BRIEF PRESENTATION OF DE POTENTIA, Q. 8, A. 1

If the slight unevenness in design occasioned by a certain anticipation of synthetic order in *Contra Gentiles IV* with the introduction of the relations should leave any doubt as to whether or not Aquinas had explicitly recorded each and every step of the analysis which is demonstrably implicit in the *ordo doctrinae* of the *Pars Prima*, and in perfect parallel with this latter, this doubt should be removed by a careful reading of the text in the first article of the eighth of the *Quaestiones Disputatae de Potentia*.[20]

In this passage of the *De Potentia*, as one would tend to expect inasmuch as the question itself is directly concerned with the trinitarian relations, the ellipsis of *Contra Gentiles IV* mentioned above does not occur. The passage is, in fact, despite its comparative brevity, an explicit and perfect representation of the identical process of analysis present, albeit implicitly, in the doctrine as synthetically elaborated in the *Summa*.

---

[20] As previously noted, this section of the *Quaestiones Disputatae* would be later (Walz: 1265-1267) than *Contra Gentiles IV*. In Synave's distribution, the eighth question is assigned to 1268, which means it would date from about the same time as the *Pars Prima*.

Aquinas begins with the customary categorical statement whenever the matter to be discussed pertains to authentic Christian teaching. In the light of Christian doctrine, one must recognize in God the existence of real relations. For catholic faith proclaims that there are Three Persons in God sharing the one divine essence.

The mystery, therefore, is affirmed, and St. Thomas embarks upon his theological analysis. Every case of number or enumeration, he observes, follows some sort of distinction. Hence, there must be distinction in God too, not only with respect to creatures, which differ from God essentially, but also with respect to whoever subsists in the divine essence.[21]

Now this distinction cannot be according to anything absolute. For whatever is predicated of God absolutely, signifies the divine essence. To distinguish the Persons according to something absolute, therefore, would be to introduce distinction into the divine essence itself — which is Arianism. Hence, the distinction of the Divine Persons is necessarily and exclusively relative.[22]

The process here is obviously analytical. From the mystery of Three Persons as revealed, rational theology must accept the fact that there is in God personal distinction. But the only way this distinction can be understood (*qualiter accipi*) is according to the distinction which obtains between such things as are only relative.

This relative distinction, moreover, Aquinas continues, must be real, not merely rational. For things which are only rationally distinct from each other can be predicated of each other. Only a nominal distinction, therefore, would separate the Father from the Son. But this is Sabellianism.[23]

---

[21] " Respondeo. Dicendum quod, sententiam fidei catholicae sequentes, oportet dicere in divinis relationes reales esse. Ponit enim fides catholica tres personas in Deo unius essentiae. Numerus autem omnis aliquam distinctionem consequitur : unde oportet quod in Deo sit aliqua distinctio non solum respectu creaturarum, quae a Deo per essentiam differunt, sed etiam respectu alicuius in divina essentia subsistentis. " *De Pot.*, q. 8, a. 1, 1.

[22] " Haec autem distinctio *non potest esse secundum aliquod absolutum* : quia quidquid absolute in divinis praedicatur, Dei essentiam significat, unde sequeretur quod personae divinae per essentiam distinguerentur, quod est haeresis Arii. Relinquitur ergo quod per sola relativa distinctio in divinis personis attenditur. " *De Pot.*, q. 8, a. 1, 2.

At this juncture, St. Thomas takes explicit notice of his analytical procedure. It remains, he says, that the divine relations are certain realities (" res "), and taking the suggestions of the saints, one must examine just how this is (" qualiter sit "), even though reason cannot fulfil this aim perfectly. Thus, since real relation cannot be understood (" intelligi ") except as following upon either quantity, on the one hand, or action or ' passion ', on the other, it is necessary that relation be attributed to God according to one of these modes.[24] Quantity, of course, is easily ruled out.[25]

The divine relation, therefore, must be consequent to some type of action. Aquinas explains, however, that this action cannot be the type which passes into the recipient (*patiens*). For in God, since there is no matter, there can be no recipient. But if the relation were to something outside of God, upon which God had acted, the relation itself would no longer be real.[26]

The only action, then, which can ground the divine relations is such as remains in the agent. But in God, the only possibility of such immanent action is the operation of intellect and will.

With this, St. Thomas has brought his theological analysis from the initial revelation of the Three Persons, through the real relations which alone can explain number and internal diversity in the Divine Persons, to the immanent operations of intellect and will which alone can account for the existence

---

[23] " Haec tamen distinctio *non potest esse rationis tantum* : quia ea quae sunt sola ratione distincta, nihil prohibet de se invicem praedicari ... et ita sequeretur quod Pater est Filius et Filius Pater, quia, cum nomina imponantur ad significandum rationes nominum, sequeretur quod personae in divinis non distinguerentur nisi secundum nomina : quod est haeresis Sabelliana. " *De Pot.*, q. 8, a. 1, 3.

[24] " *Relinquitur ergo* quod oportet dicere, relationes in Deo quasdam res esse : quod qualiter sit, sequendo sanctorum dicta, investigari oportet, licet ad plenum ad hoc ratio pervenire non possit. Sciendum est ergo, quod cum realis relatio intelligi non possit, nisi consequens quantitatem vel actionem seu passionem, oportet quod aliquo istorum modorum ponamus in Deo relationem esse. " *De Pot.*, q. 8, a. 1, 4.

[25] *De Pot.*, q. 8, a. 1, 5.

[26] " Relinquitur ergo quod oportet in eo ponere relationem *actionem* consequentem. Actionem dico non quae in aliquod patiens transeat : quia in Deo nihil potest esse patiens, cum non sit ibi materia ; ad id autem quod est extra Deum, non est in Deo realis relatio, ut ostensum est. " *De Pot.*, q. 8, a. 1, 6.

of such relations. He must yet show, however, that it is
the divine understanding precisely as conception of the Word
that grounds the relation between the Father and the Son.
For, as Aquinas goes on to note, in the act of understanding,
he who understands is ordered to four things : that is, to the
object of his understanding, to the intelligible species actuating intellect, to the very operation of understanding as such,
and to the intellectual conception.[27]

To accomplish this final step, St. Thomas first proposes
to study the distinction of the concept from the three other
elements just mentioned. Since, then, the object understood
can exist outside the mind itself, while the concept cannot,
and since, moreover, the concept is ordered to the object as
to an end, the concept must differ from the object. It must
differ likewise from the intelligible species, whose rôle is rather
that of the form through which intellect is actuated. It differs, finally, from the act of intellect, as term of this act and
its quasi product. For it is in virtue of this act, that intellect forms its definitions and propositions. In this manner,
Aquinas isolates the conception of intellect, which is, as he
notes here, the reality immediately signified by external words,
and hence, in human beings, itself given the proper name of
' word. ' [28]

---

[27] " Relinquitur ergo quod consequatur relatio realis in Deo *ac-*
tionem manentem in agente : cuiusmodi actiones sunt intelligere et
velle in Deo ... Intelligens autem in intelligendo ad quatuor potest
habere ordinem : scilicet ad rem in quae intelligitur, ad speciem intelligibilem, qua fit intellectus in actu, ad suum intelligere, et ad conceptionem intellectus. " *De Pot.*, q. 8, a. 1, 7.

[28] " Quae quidem conceptio a tribus praedictis differt. *A re* quidem intellecta, quia res intellecta est interdum extra intellectum, conceptio autem intellectus non est nisi in intellectu : et iterum conceptio intellectus ordinatur ad rem intellectam sicut ad finem : propter
hoc enim intellectus conceptionem rei in se format ut rem intellectam
cognoscat. Differt autem *a specie* intelligibili : nam species intelligibilis, qua fit intellectus in actu, consideratur ut principium actionis
intellectus, cum omne agens agat secundum quod est in actu ; actu
autem fit per aliquam formam, quam oportet esse actionis principium.
Differt autem *ab actione* intellectus : quia praedicta conceptio consideratur ut terminus actionis, et quasi quoddam per ipsam constitutum.
Intellectus enim sua actione format rei definitionem, vel etiam propo-
sitionem affrmativam seu negativam. Haec autem conceptio intellectus in nobis proprie *verbum* dicitur : hoc enim est quod verbo exteriori significatur : vox enim exterior neque significat ipsum intel-

This inner word, St. Thomas continues, the medium through which the human mind understands something external to itself, at once arises from another, and represents something other. It arises from the intellect through the latter's operation, and it is the similitude or likeness of the object which is being understood. But in the special instance of intellect's self-understanding, the same inner word is both offspring and likeness of the intellect understanding itself. This follows from the general principle, that effects are assimilated to their causes according to their form. But the form of intellect is the thing which is understood, and therefore the inner word originating from intellect is the similitude or likeness of the thing understood, whether this be the intellect itself or something else.[29]

Next, Aquinas draws an essential distinction between the human inner word and the divine. The human inner word is not extrinsic to the operation of intellect, for it is necessary to the completion of this operation. But it is extrinsic to the natural being (*esse*) of the intellect, as a quasi 'passion' or perfection received.[30]

In God, however, the Divine Word is extrinsic neither to the operation of intellect, nor to the natural being of intellect. For in God, understanding and being are identified. God's Word, therefore, does not exist outside the divine essence, but is rather coessential with the divine essence.[31]

---

lectum, neque speciem intelligibilem, neque actum intellectus, sed intellectus conceptionem qua mediante refertur ad rem. " *De Pot.*, q. 8, a. 1, 8.

[29] " Huiusmodi ergo conceptio, sive verbum, qua intellectus noster intelligit rem aliam a se, ab alio exoritur, et aliud repraesentat. Oritur quidem ab intellectu per suum actum ; est vero similitudo rei intellectae. Cum vero intellectus seipsum intelligit, verbum praedictum, sive conceptio, eiusdem est propago et similitudo, scilicet intellectus seipsum intelligentis. Et hoc ideo contingit, quia effectus similatur causae secundum suam formam : forma autem intellectus est res intellecta. Et ideo verbum quod oritur [ab intellectu, est similitudo rei intellectae, sive sit idem quod intellectus, sive aliud. " *De Pot.*, q. 8, a. 1, 9.

[30] " Huiusmodi autem verbum nostri intellectus, est quidem extrinsecum ab esse ipsius intellectus (non enim est de essentia, sed est quasi passio ipsius), non tamen est extrinsecum ab ipso intelligere intellectus, cum ipsum intelligere compleri non possit sine verbo praedicto. " *De Pot.*, q. 8, a. 1, 10.

[31] " Si ergo aliquis intellectus sit cuius intelligere sit suum esse, oportebit quod illud verbum non sit extrinsecum ab esse ipsius intel-

Thus it is, St. Thomas concludes his analysis, that there can be discovered in God the origin or procession of one from another — of the Word from the one uttering this Word — with the unity of the divine essence still perfectly intact.[32] Toward the beginning of his exposition, St. Thomas had spoken of the two immanent operations, that of will as well as that of intellect, which ground the trinitarian relations. In this particular passage of the *De Potentia*, however, the procession of love is not otherwise treated.

There can be no doubt, then, that St. Thomas did in fact presuppose the initial process of theological analysis which can and must be inferred from the strictly synthetic exposition of the *ordo doctrinae* in both the *Summa*, and the *Compendium*. For in the *De Potentia* — more succinctly, but in certain respects more obviously than in the *Contra Gentiles* — he actually worked out and explicitly recorded all the essential steps of the very same analytical reduction that is implicit, though patently demonstrable, in the *ordo doctrinae* itself.

But what precisely is the significance of this fact for the present study ?

When the time had come to examine in detail the ' *de Trinitate*' as presented in the *Summa*, and also in the *Compendium*, it was pointed out, that the problem of an apologetical intention or perspective on the part of Aquinas might seem to be more justly raised here than in the works previously studied, and raised, moreover, right from the very beginning of each treatise. For in both these works, Aquinas began, not with a discussion of the trinitarian mystery as contained in the Sacred Scriptures and the teaching of the Church, but with an apparently rational exposition of the internal procession of inner word and love as a strictly universal characteristic of intellectual nature from which one could deduce the revealed processions in the Trinity.

A closer examination of the text, however, showed that throughout both the *Summa* and the *Compendium*, and even in the initial passages taken up with the divine procession as

---

lectus, sicut nec ab intelligere. Huiusmodi autem est intellectus divinus : in Deo enim idem est esse et intelligere. Oportet ergo quod eius verbum non sit extra essentiam eius, sed ei coessentiale. " *De Pot.*, q. 8, a. 1, 11.

[32] " *Sic ergo* in Deo potest inveniri origo alicuius ex aliquo, scilicet verbi et proferentis verbum, unitate essentiae servata. ..." *De Pot.*, q. 8, a. 1, 12.

such, Aquinas never ceased to affirm the dependence of his doctrinal elaboration upon the revealed word of God. Furthermore, the same examination of the text also showed that at no single moment in his entire treatment, did St. Thomas ever make the fact of procession itself the thing which he was demonstrating, or to which he was in any true sense concluding. The fact of the divine procession was rather that which was being presupposed.

Yet, the presupposition was seen to have been more than merely a fact. It was rather an essential and necessary consequence of the order of treatment Aquinas himself had chosen to follow — the order of internal causality, which he explicitly so designated when, in the *prooemium* to question twenty-seven of the *Pars Prima*, he proposed to treat first of the divine procession because the Persons were dependent upon the relations, and the relations in turn upon the processions.

It was this same order of internal causality, the order of the *priora quoad se*, moreover, that provided the ultimately most meaningful and satisfactory key to the apologetical problem. The reason why there was never the slightest question, however implicit, of demonstrating in any manner at all the fact of the divine procession, was simply that St. Thomas had necessarily to presuppose this fact as already determined. For whatever else might be said on the point, at least Aquinas was not and could not be determining this supposition in the opening passages of the *Summa* and the *Compendium*.

It remained, then, to show on just what grounds or from just what source St. Thomas had been able to make this supposition in the first place — if not here at the beginning of the *Summa* and *Compendium*, then where?

This latter question was answered in two ways. First, the supposition was shown to derive immediately and necessarily from the theological analysis implicit in the *ordo doctrinae* itself. By assigning the relations as internal 'reason' of the Three Persons, and the two immanent processions as internal 'reason' of the relations, St. Thomas made it clear, that he had previously arrived at relations as the only way in which the distinction of Persons, that is, the revealed mystery as such, could be understood, and had then arrived at immanent procession of inner word and love as the only way in which the relations themselves could be understood.

But the supposition was also shown to rest on the more obvious and positive evidence of the Thomist text. If not in the *Summa* and *Compendium*, where his purpose was exclusively that of synthesis, at least in the fourth book of the *Contra Gentiles* and in the eighth of the *Quaestiones Disputatae de Potentia*, St. Thomas had left a written record of the fact that he had actually performed the theological analysis which gave him the right to presuppose as the starting point of the *ordo doctrinae* in his synthetic treatises the *processio ad intra* of intellect and will as the only way in which the plurality of Divine Persons could be taken or understood.

A final question yet remains. Is not the real starting point in the '*de Trinitate*' of the *Summa* and the *Compendium* and the summary account in *De Potentia*, q. 9, a. 5, not precisely the *divine* procession, but rather, at least in the *Summa* and *De Potentia*, the universal or transcendental principle that there must be procession of inner word wherever there is intellect, for this is of the essence of intellectual being? And is it not possible to transpose the equivalent first step in Aquinas' argument into the simple syllogistic form : in every instance of intellect, there must be procession of inner word ; but God is instance of intellect ; therefore in God there must be procession of inner word?

The same question could be expressed a bit differently. If the actual point of departure in St. Thomas' synthetic exposition were the divine procession as ultimate ' cause ' or reason of the Three Distinct Persons, it could be conceded that this particular truth had previously been determined through analysis of the revealed mystery. By the same token, it could also be conceded that beginning with such a truth in synthetic exposition did not in any way involve the apologetical design of a priori demonstration.

But if, on the other hand, the actual point of departure is rather the affirmation of what is absolutely and universally essential to intellect as such, where in the analysis has this generalization been accounted for? And if Aquinas himself has not accounted for it, is not the problem of apologetical design still unsolved?

It seems, therefore, that the present study should not be concluded until the difficulty that might arise here has been adequately explained.

IV. THE PROBLEM OF 'PURE PERFECTION' IN THE GENER-
     ALIZATION ON PROCESSION OF INNER WORD. SOLU-
     TION IN THE 'VIA ANALYTICA'

First, it is necessary to recall the extent to which this problem had already been taken care of in earlier sections of the
present study.

In the first chapter of part three, immediately following
the detailed examination of the key passages *S. T.*, *I*, q. 27,
a. 1 and *De Pot.*, q. 9, a. 5, it was shown that certain provisional conclusions with regard to the Thomist generalization
on procession of inner word could be made right away. Aquinas does affirm in these passages, not only that inner word
is *de facto* found in every intelligence, but also that procession of such an inner word is an essential property of intellectual nature — " de ratione eius quod est intelligere " (*De
Pot.*, q. 9, a. 5). On the other hand, however, both in the
very same passage of *De Potentia* and in the twelfth article,
twelfth question, of *Pars Prima*, he makes it equally clear that
he does not understand this generalization as a purely rational
principle, or purely philosophical law. For, by showing that
it is impossible for human reason, even enlightened human
reason, to know in this life *quid est Deus* ; and hence the *quid
est* or *quomodo est* of the divine intelligence, St. Thomas removes from the competence of reason that alone in virtue of which
his generalization could rest on purely rational or philosophical insight : reason's grasp, that is to say, of the causal nexus
between the divine intellect and its Divine Word.

For Aquinas, then, it was concluded that the generalization itself is a strictly theological principle, dependent at
once on the revelation of the first trinitarian procession and
the exercise of illustrated reason seeing that the trinitarian
procession thus revealed has to be understood in intellectualist terms, on analogy with the procession of inner word in
the human spirit. Natural reason grasps the emanation of
the intelligible in its own understanding. Natural reason also
grasps that God is intellect, and even, since this is a philosophical property of intellect, that there must be in God therefore " intellectum in intelligente " — all as succinctly expressed in the thirty-seventh chapter of the *Compendium*.

But where God Himself is concerned, natural reason cannot more than assert the unequivocal absolute identity in God between the *intellectum* and the *intelligens*. That notwithstanding this absolute identity, there is nevertheless in God the real, but relative, distinction between the same *intellectum* and *intelligens*, and hence that real procession is a universal or transcendental property of intellectual nature, is something natural reason cannot possibly grasp, and consequently is known to man only through revelation.

At this point, therefore, the question of the logical genesis of the universal or transcendental principle in St. Thomas' thought was already answered. But the further question of its 'historical' genesis had not yet been solved, at least not directly. For it could still be asked whether the argument showing that, for Aquinas, the ultimate formulation of this principle depended on the revelation of the first trinitarian procession could be supported by further evidence from the text itself showing Aquinas actually arriving at the formulation of his principle in the course of theological analysis?

In point of fact, in the two places already seen — *C. G.*, *IV*, c. 11 and *De Pot.*, q. 8, a. 1 — where the intellectualist analysis is worked out, St. Thomas does not explicitly add as the very last moment in his analytical process something to the effect : ' Et ita ergo est de ratione eius quod est intelligere, quod procedat in eo intra ipsum interius verbum '. In the writer's judgment, however, two observations might be made with regard to such an 'omission'. First, the generalization itself is really not called for in the formally analytical exposition. Its proper place is only at the beginning of the strictly synthetic *ordo doctrinae*. Secondly, on the other hand, and more positively, at least all of the essential elements warranting the generalization are already obtained, and precisely as the conclusion of the analytical process.

In both passages, the essential necessity for inner word proceeding in human understanding is presumed as known to reason. In both passages, the essential necessity for a Divine Word proceeding in the divine understanding has just been arrived at as the conclusion of rational theology attempting to grasp, to whatever extent possible in this life, how the revealed mystery must be taken or understood. Except, then, for the problem that might be raised with regard to the angels, the final results of the theological analysis have given St.

Thomas all the justification he will need for setting down as the point of departure in his trinitarian synthesis the universal or transcendental principle that procession of inner word is essential to intellectual being.

Before leaving this question, however, a look should be taken at the first chapter of Aquinas' commentary on St. John's Gospel. In this particular text, belonging, moreover, to the final period of St. Thomas' career, the generalization on procession of inner word is explicitly added, and even the angelic instance is specifically introduced.[33]

In this well-known passage, Aquinas proposes to determine how *Verbum* as used by the Evangelist in the opening words of the Gospel must be understood: " Ad intellectum autem huius nominis *Verbum* ..."

To explain St. John's meaning, St. Thomas first studies the inner word of the human spirit, beginning with the relation of this latter to the external word of oral discourse. Next, he points out that this human *verbum* is distinct from the faculty, species, and operation of intellect. For the word of specch, which signifies the word of intellect, does not signify any of these three. What is properly called inner word, on the other hand, is what is formed in or through understanding by the one who understands — the definition, therefore, or the enunciation. Such, then, is the meaning, Aquinas concludes, of this name *Verbum*.

From what has thus far been said, he continues immediately, it is possible to conceive that the inner word is always something proceeding from intellect in act, and likewise that it is the *ratio* and similitude of the thing understood. Hence, if the one understanding and the understood are the same, it follows that the inner word is *ratio* and similitude of the intellect itself from which it proceeds.

Up to the moment, St. Thomas has been preoccupied exclusively with the correct understanding of the *Verbum* in St. John's prologue. But in the very next paragraph, he pushes his analysis to the transcendental generalization. It is clear, therefore, that in any intellectual nature it is necessary to posit an inner word. For it is essential to understanding that something be formed by intellect in its act of understanding,

---

[33] The date 1269-1272 (the second Paris period) is generally accepted. See CHENU, *Introduction*, p. 211.

and this formation is called inner word. And hence, in every instance of understanding, it is necessary to posit an inner word. Finally, since intellectual nature is itself threefold, human, angelic and divine, inner word is also threefold, the human word, the angelic word, and the Word of God.

St. Thomas completes his account by observing that the word to which the Evangelist is referring is not the human, nor the angelic, but clearly the Divine Word. For St. John says : " In principio erat Verbum, " and he goes on to describe this *Verbum* as the " verbum non factum. " [34]

Since the composition of this passage in its larger context adheres to the exegetical design of textual commentary, and is therefore less than rigidly systematic, it would be perhaps a bit gratuitous to assign it in strict terms either the analytical or synthetic structure of exposition. From at least the literary standpoint, there would be difficulties with either approach.

The reader will have observed, for example, that the Word is the Word of St. John's prologue right from the start, and obviously St. Thomas considers this Word to be the Word of God. But he does not say so immediately. There is, in fact, a sort of didactic suspension. The Word is introduced

---

[34] " Circa primum autem videndum est quod sit hoc quod dicitur *In principio erat Verbum.* ... Ad intellectum autem huius nominis *Verbum,* sciendum est quod, secundum Philosophum (I Perih. lect. ii) ea quae sunt in voce, sunt signa earum, quae sunt in anima, passionum. ... Si ergo volumus scire quid est interius verbum mentis, videamus quid significat quod exteriori voce profertur. In intellectu autem nostro sunt tria : scilicet ipsa potentia intellectus ; species rei intellectae ... et, tertio, ipsa operatio intellectus quae est intelligere. Nullum autem istorum significatur verbo exteriori voce prolato. ... Illud ergo proprie dicitur verbum interius, quod intelligens intelligendo format. Intellectus autem duo format ... definitionem ... enunciationem. ... Sic ergo habemus significationem huius nominis *Verbum.* Secundo, ex his quae dicta sunt, concipere possumus, quod verbum semper est aliquid procedens ab intellectu in actu existente Iterum quod verbum semper est ratio et similitudo rei intellectae. Et si quidem eadem res sit intelligens et intellecta, tunc verbum est ratio et similitudo intellectus, a quo procedit ... Patet ergo quod in qualibet natura intellectuali necesse est ponere verbum : quia de ratione intelligendi est quod intellectus intelligendo aliquid formet ; huius autem formatio dicitur verbum ; et ideo in omni intelligente oportet ponere verbum. Natura autem intellectualis est triplex, scilicet humana, angelica et divina : et ideo triplex est verbum ... " *In Ioan.,* c. 1, lect. 1, 24-25.

from the first line of the Gospel text. The objective of the ensuing account, as indicated explicitly by Aquinas, will be to determine how this Word must be understood. To accomplish this task, he explains the notion of inner word as such, beginning with the conception of human understanding and ending with the generalization that procession of inner word is essential to intellect, and hence found in men, in angels, and in God Himself. But since the Word here spoken of by St. John is the Eternal and Uncreated Word, the Word of the Gospel text must necessarily be understood as the Word of God.

Such a mode of exposition, insofar as it seems to move from what is universally true in the ultimate line of cause, is to this extent synthetic. On the other hand, since the very pericope St. Thomas is studying does not consist of the single word " Verbum ", but rather of the complete expression " In principio erat Verbum, " it is not very likely that the force of " in principio " — Aquinas' simple proof at the end that it is the Word of God which is being spoken of — is meant to be suspended in any realistic fashion. In the writer's judgment, therefore, the exposition is rather more analytic in structure, with St. Thomas reaching, at the end of his analysis, the explicit formulation of the general law that procession of inner word is essential to intellect, and making this generalization precisely inasmuch as and insofar as analysis of the revealed mystery, whose existence is implicit throughout the account, has just arrived, so to speak, at the divine instance.

* * *

As mentioned more than once during the course of this study, the intention has been throughout, not to engage in controversy, but rather to accept the challenge put forth by Dom Vagaggini that the problem of some species of demonstrative proof in the trinitarian theology of St. Thomas was a matter which stood in need of a fresh examination from start to finish. Now that the investigation of the text has been completed, however, at least to the writer's own best ability to do so, it seems that a modest suggestion with regard to the very statement of the question in Dom Vagaggini's criticism would not be out of place. The writer has in mind

Vagaggini's introduction into this problem of the concept of 'pure perfections'.

In Vagaggini's reading of the text, as seen in the introductory chapter of this study, Aquinas seems to conclude to the first trinitarian procession from the universal principle that procession of a really distinct inner word pertains to the *ratio formalis* of intellect itself. But such an approach, Vagaggini feels, is simply to reproduce in trinitarian theology theodicy's argumentation based on the notion of pure perfection. Thus, everything in the created universe which can be divested through rational or philosophical analysis of all potency and imperfection must be attributed to God according to its *ratio formalis*. But for St. Thomas, in Vagaggini's view, the really distinct *verbum cordis* is precisely an instance of this rationally or philosophically isolated pure perfection. Moreover, it was conceded above that if certain texts, particularly *De Potentia*, q. 9, a. 5, are read, so to speak, too close to the canvas, it might well appear that Aquinas himself had explicitly adopted just this procedure.

Nevertheless, a more painstaking examination of the Thomist '*de Trinitate*', including most emphatically the passage *De Potentia*, q. 9, a. 5, proves conclusively, in the writer's mind, that the principle some might consider the 'major' of the argument — the generalization, that is to say, on procession of inner word as essential to intellectual being — was not understood by St. Thomas to be a rational or philosophical principle at all. For in St. Thomas' thought, its ultimate formulation depended quite clearly on the divine revelation of the first trinitarian procession. Without this revelation, theodicy would know that God is intellect, and that therefore there must be in God the understood in the one understanding — " intellectum in intelligente. " But theodicy would also be forced to assert that these were utterly identified in the absolute order — the only order theodicy would have cause, apart from revelation, to consider pertinent. For inasmuch as human reason, not only when left to its natural resources, but even, as Aquinas insists time and again, when enlightened by supernatural faith, cannot know *quid est Deus*, nor, consequently, the *quid* or *quomodo* of the divine intellect, the causal nexus between the divine understanding and the really, but only relatively, distinct Divine Word cannot possibly be grasped by the human intelligence.

Moreover, analysis of the text went further still. As was pointed out at the time, it would be one thing to give a satisfactory explanation of a difficulty actually inherent in a given passage, and yet quite another to be able to show that had the passage in question been correctly interpreted in the didactic and literary context of the author's intention, the difficulty itself need never have arisen.

It is not a case, therefore, of merely proving that the problem actually occasioned by St. Thomas' strange procedure of introducing the *verbum* principle at the beginning of his systematic exposition is neatly solved by the fact that the principle was not meant to be purely rational or philosophical, but theological in the strictest sense of the word. The fact is true, but it does not go far enough. For once St. Thomas' synthetic exposition, especially as presented in the *ordo doctrinae* of the *Pars Prima*, has been correctly understood, it becomes immediately clear that the procedure itself is not strange in the least. Rather, it is of the very nature of the synthetic design to begin from what is first, not in the knowledge of experience, but in reality as understood.

Finally, now that the *via analytica* which stands as the necessary and implicit presupposition throughout the synthetic exposition has been brought into clearer focus, it is possible to add still further confirmation to what has already been seen with regard to the origin and rôle of the *verbum* principle in St. Thomas' thought. From the implications surrounding its introduction and use in synthetic passages, it is evident that the principle is not merely rational, not a purely philosophical generalization, but a statement of universal truth having meaning and validity only in rational theology. But from the study of the analytical process whereby Aquinas, beginning with the revealed mystery, advanced in strictly theological *reductio ad principia* to the conclusion that the revealed plurality of Persons has to be understood as dependent in the line of first ' cause ' or *ratio* upon the divine *processio ad intra*, it is further evident that it was precisely the theological analysis, as opposed to a purely rational or philosophical process, that had originally given St. Thomas the same universal or transcendental principle.

In *Contra Gentiles IV*, and in the particular passage *De Potentia*, q. 8, a. 1, St. Thomas had perfected the intellectualist account of the divine generation on analogy from the procession of inner word in human understanding, and in so doing, had gathered, as it were, all of the essential elements necessary to make the generalization that such procession is a transcendental property of spiritual being. But since he was not going to use this generalization in the basically analytical expositions — for its proper place is really in synthesis — there was no special need to state the fact in so many words. In the quite late and exegetical passage *In Ioannem*, c. 1, lect. 1, however, it is not improbable that to note the ' historical ' origin of the *verbum* generalization as precisely the final moment in the trinitarian *via analytica*, was actually a part of Aquinas' specific intention.

When all is said and done, therefore, it is frankly impossible to consider St. Thomas' formulation and employment of the *verbum* principle as a case of ' pure perfection ', certainly not as the term would be introduced in philosophy or theodicy. But neither is it sufficient to say that granting its strictly theological origin and character, Aquinas at least used the principle in a process of exposition which sought to imitate the purely rational process as closely as possible.

The recognition of pure perfections in the created universe gives the philosopher a means of ascertaining the existence — *an sit* — of certain perfections, such as wisdom and goodness, in God. The pure perfection in theodicy, therefore, exercises a rôle, not only in the line of understanding, but also and antecedently in the line of certitude. But the exercise of such a function in the line of certitude is precisely what St. Thomas' generalization on procession of the word does not and cannot achieve. Its place, therefore, is exclusively in the order of understanding.

Putting it another way, the pure perfection of philosophy or theodicy stands as the *prius notum* through means of which the existence of certain divine properties can be determined. The principle of the universal *verbum*, on the other hand, stands rather as the *posterius notum*, itself determined only insofar as theological analysis of the revealed mystery has arrived at its consequence at the conclusion of a process, not of certitude, but of understanding. Again, when the same principle is introduced as the point of departure in the exposition of theological synthesis, it stands, not as the first known, through whose knowledge further truths will be determined, but rather as the first in reality, already understood to be the first in reality, upon which, therefore, the *prius notum* and the *primum notum* are known to depend ontologically.

In the writer's judgment, then, to seek the explanation for St. Thomas' theological procedures along the lines of an attempt to reproduce the rational or philosophical processes centering on the concept of 'pure perfections', is simply to seek the explanation where it can never be found. For it is hard to call the imitation of a thing that which actually took, on each and every substantial point, a quite opposite turn.

CONCLUSION

In view of the comparative length to which it was felt necessary to go in the preceding analysis of the Thomist '*de Trinitate*', it might be well to observe here in the conclusion that the theme discussed was nevertheless quite simple and compact. On the one hand, there was the particular *status quaestionis* which in this case imposed upon the writer the critical obligation of inspecting, not selected texts and sections from the works of Aquinas, but large blocks of consecutive passages comprising organic units, and even entire treatises. For what was at issue was not some single point of doctrine, but rather the more comprehensive point of scientific ideal and basic methodology. Yet on the other hand, the same *status quaestionis* also imposed upon the writer strict adherence to the methodological theme itself. Thus, there was never any intention in this analysis to give an account of the Thomist '*de Trinitate*' in the full complexity and richness of its theological detail.

The immediate occasion for the present study was the recently published contribution of Dom Cyprian Vagaggini in the commemorative volume *Spicilegium Beccense*.[1] It was this contribution, moreover, taken together with certain *obiter dicta* directed to the same point by other modern theologians, that was allowed to establish both the breadth and restriction of the precise question to be investigated.

Concretely, it was Vagaggini's challenge that historical and theological interpretation of St. Thomas' trinitarian doctrine had not yet come to grips with the problem of some species of aprioristic rational or philosophical demonstration latent in the idiom and structure of the Thomist theological exposition. For Aquinas, as Vagaggini reads the text, at least appears to conclude in some fashion to the very existence of the revealed mystery — the trinitarian processions

---

[1] See above, pp. 1-20.

— from what pure reason or human philosophy ascertains as the essential properties of intellectual being.

By way of a suggested explanation — and in the writer's judgment, Vagaggini's intention was rather to stimulate a critical reexamination of the problem, than to propose a personal solution — Vagaggini points to the " rationes necessariae " and the ideal of apodictic proof which had been the theological objective of St. Anselm. Like so many others of his day, he asks, did not St. Thomas himself eventually come to make his own the Anselmian objective ? For does not an objective reappraisal of the Thomist ' de Trinitate ' show that its author sought, if not perfectly to reproduce, then at least to imitate as closely as possible, the apodictic demonstrations of Anselm ?

The problem therefore, is not so much that of a point of doctrine, as of basic methodology. Moreover, as Vagaggini is careful to insist, there is no serious question with regard to St. Thomas' position on the level of theory. The emphatic statement first made in the *Sentences* that unaided human reason simply cannot demonstrate the Trinity of Persons, Aquinas would continue to repeat time and again to the end of his life. But on the level, so to speak, of practice, Vagaggini finds it much more difficult to see how this negative protest can be reconciled with the appearances of *de facto* demonstration in St. Thomas' most mature works.

The same basically methodological nature of the problem was likewise seen to have been brought out by other modern theologians commenting, though less purposefully than Vagaggini, on the question whether or not the use of rational principles, particularly the *verbum* analogy, involved proof or demonstration touching on the roots of the mystery. Writing in 1951, eight years therefore before Dom Vagaggini's challenging article, Père H. Paissac had called attention to the Thomist distinction between rational process as employed in proof of a basic fact and rational process employed in explanation.[2] As far back as 1931, the Abbé M. T.-L. Penido had made the same observation, in the writer's opinion with rather more clarity and precision.[3] In 1949, in the final article of his series on the concept of *verbum* in the thought of St. Thomas,

---

[2] pp. 24-28, 30-32.
[3] pp. 45-48, 48-49.

Father B. Lonergan had stressed the necessity of recognizing the full and decisive implications of the Thomist scientific ideal as ' understanding ' precisely as opposed to ' certitude ', and at the same time went considerably further than Dom H. Diepen in insisting that Aquinas' principle of universal procession in intellectual being had to be taken in the strict context of one — Aquinas, that is — who was writing, not as a philosopher, but exclusively as a theologian.[4]

Consequently, before turning directly to the texts of the Thomist ' de Trinitate ', it was possible, and in light of the academic dialogue to this extent necessary, to frame the status quaestionis quite clearly and quite succinctly in terms of the strictly methodological problem.

Dom Vagaggini points an accusing finger at the trinitarian expositions contained in St. Thomas' mature works, and believes that he has discovered here, if not apodictic proof in a more serious sense of the notion, at least its very close imitation, its " illusion esthétique. " [5] Whoever understands, by this alone that he does understand, there must proceed within him a distinct inner word. But God understands. Therefore there must proceed within Him the distinct Divine Word. What is one to make of this line of reasoning, Vagaggini asks, if not at least the semblance or illusion of rational demonstration according to the manner in which the ' pure perfections ' of philosophy or theodicy — in this case, the ' pure perfection ' of really distinct inner word as an essential property of intellect as such — are to be assigned to God Himself in the ratio formalis ?

The status quaestionis of the present study, then, was readily formulated.[6] Thus, whatever the basic intention and perspective of St. Thomas had actually been — demonstration's " illusion esthétique ?", explanation ?, understanding ? — is it possible to give an account from the text itself, from its inherent design and methodology, for the peculiar and, judged by contemporary standards, perhaps unusual procedure whereby Aquinas introduces at the very beginning of his more mature trinitarian expositions, in the idiom and structure of

---

[4] For Lonergan's position, see above, pp. 50-53, 54-55 ; for Diepen's, pp. 36-39, 40-41.

[5] Cited above, p. 18.

[6] pp. 56-60 ; especially 60.

the syllogistic ' major ', the universal or transcendental principle that procession of inner word pertains to the *ratio formalis* 'of intellect as such ? Is this, or is this not, argument from ' pure perfection ' ? If not, then why not ? Is the problem some might discover here a problem that truly belongs to the text, in the sense that a strange procedure on St. Thomas' part is ultimately responsible, even though a careful examination of his works can give a satisfactory explanation ? Or is it rather that, had Aquinas' own theological ideal and method been interpreted more correctly from the start, the problem would never have arisen ?

In any case, it should at least be clear that the only satisfactory way such a problem could have been investigated was through a fairly lengthy and sufficiently detailed study of the Thomist ' *de Trinitate* ' as a whole. For it was precisely the scientific structure and methodology of the treatises as St. Thomas himself composed them that was really in question.

It was quite necessary, moreover, that the expositions belonging to the early and middle periods of Aquinas' career not be omitted. If it could be assumed that only texts from the later period presented the exact difficulty pinpointed by Vagaggini, and indirectly by others as well, someone might justly doubt why the earlier works had to be included. But the reason for examining these earlier works was not at all to test the reasonableness of such an assumption. It was rather because the ultimate question was methodological.

In the writer's judgment, if a personal evolution in St. Thomas' thought can be demonstrated on any given point, it can certainly be demonstrated on the very basic point of his concept of rational theology as science of the divine. Moreover, as became clear during the course of the lengthy textual analysis, the best, if not only satisfying, way to prove what Aquinas' theological ideal and methodology was not, is simply to prove what it was. But this ideal was a long time in forming, and it is most uncertain that what it became in the maturity and precision of later works could be accurately assessed if the process of development itself were not first exposed to a rather painstaking scrutiny.

In the *Sentences*, then, there is no immediate problem with regard to a trinitarian demonstration, intentional or even unintentional. At each point in the text where the *quaestio-*

nes inserted by St. Thomas into the loose structure of his commentary take up the matter of the Three Persons, the generation of the Son, the procession of the Spirit, Aquinas begins with the flat and sufficiently emphatic statement that these truths are known to man only through revelation.[7]

Moreover, at least in the *Sentences*, even the possibility of an unsuspected demonstration is effectively ruled out. On the one hand, St. Thomas was so preoccupied at this time with the double formula " per modum naturae et intellectus " to characterize the first trinitarian procession, that his analysis of the divine generation was primarily as *operatio naturalis*, and his attempt to reconcile with this account the secondary account which would be more strictly intellectualist was only indifferently successful.[8] On the other hand, not having as yet worked out a theory of intellectual emanation in the human spirit, Aquinas lacked what would someday afford him a satisfactory *media* for penetrating in some limited way to the inner ' cause ' or *ratio* of trinitarian procession in the divine essence.[9]

The significance of the *Sentences*, however, is not restricted to this exclusively negative evidence. For at least two essential points in the emergent theological ideal and methodology of St. Thomas are already coming into relief.

First, when treating of reason's fundamental incompetence to attain knowledge of the distinct Persons, and doing so precisely in the context of divine cognoscibility, Aquinas does not let the matter rest with a simple denial of fact. Rather, he gives his explanation for this incompetence. While the divine being is eminently intelligible and understood in itself, and hence *per se notum quoad se*, the same divine being is not *per se notum quoad nos*. What man knows of God in this life, therefore, he knows only through knowledge of creatures. But this knowledge from creatures leads reason no further than God as ultimate cause and exemplar of all created perfection. Consequently, reason can attain the oneness of the divine being and essence, and knowledge of the rationally distinct attributes, but reason cannot attain the Trinity of really distinct Persons.[10] At the moment, at least in the writ-

---

[7] pp. 69-71, 76-78, 85, 96.
[8] pp. 85-88, 92.
[9] pp. 94-97, 98-110.

er's judgment, this distinction — *per se notum, per se notum quoad nos* — lacks the precision St. Thomas is about to accord it in the *In Boethii de Trinitate*. For it is the immediacy of divine knowledge that is being excluded, with its essentially vicarious or substitutional quality left rather to be inferred. Nevertheless, the point actually scored is of primary importance as showing that even now Aquinas' rejection of the possibility of trinitarian demonstration is not lightly or incidentally asserted as a ' pious ' observation or as a theological commonplace, but is radicated in what is in process of becoming the basic structure of his own theological ideal.

Secondly, it is further to be noted that, again even at this very early stage, the rôle assigned to reason in the exploration of revealed mysteries is exclusively that of theological analysis, and in no sense that of proof or demonstration touching upon the fact or existence of the mystery itself. Thus, there is a highly significant contrast between the approach St. Thomas makes in the *Sentences* to truths which he recognizes to be within the *per se* compass of rational or philosophical inquiry, and the approach he makes to those truths that are known only from divine revelation.

After explaining, at least briefly, how reason can attain the unity and simplicity of the divine essence, he goes on to show how reason can also penetrate into the divine essence to the extent of affirming in God the existence of the rationally distinct attributes, whose distinction nevertheless is rooted objectively in the divine being. Even if one prescinds from the more highly polished third article most likely interpolated from a much later *quaestio disputata*, it is still abundantly clear in the two articles remaining that Aquinas considers the rôle of reason in this first area to extend all the way to the determination, and hence demonstration, of what might be called specifically new elements or specifically new ' data '.[11]

In the same passage, however, when he passes from the essence and attributes to the plurality and real plurality of Persons, the fact itself, the existence of the mystery, is based exclusively on revelation. Yet even in this second area, reason is not summarily excluded. For immediately after asserting on the authority of christian faith that the plurality of

---

[10] pp. 74-77.
[11] pp. 64-69, 71-72.

Persons is unequivocally real, St. Thomas proceeds to see
'how this can be'.   And to do so, he makes application from
the philosophy of relations : the Three Persons, as constituted by subsistent relations, can be at once both identified absolutely with the divine essence, and still distinct from one
another in terms of the formality of relation which is to be
ad alterum.[12]

Later in the treatise, he will apply a similar analysis to
the divine generation, distinguishing the generic notion ("mutatio ") from the specific difference, which is communication
in the line of act ("operatio," "actus perfecti "), free from
all potency and actuation and hence from the imperfection
which cannot be attributed to God.[13]

The method, then, for all that its achievement (in the
first instance) may be found wanting, is the method of theological analysis.   What has been revealed is now utterly presupposed, nor is there the slightest evidence in the text that apologetical corroboration or confirmation is envisioned as the
objective, or even part of the objective, in subsequent inquiry.
In this second area, the rôle assigned to reason is exclusively
that of explanation, interpretation, understanding.   There is
no discovery of new elements, no determination of specifically
new 'data', but simply the transposition of what is already
known, through revelation, to a new level of understanding,
as reason, not pure reason but reason enlightened by faith,
attempts to probe into the revealed mystery in search, to
whatever extent possible, of its ultimate 'cause' or *ratio*.

Though the methodological treatise *In Boethii de Trinitate*, composed during the roughly ten years separating the
'*de Trinitate*' of the *Sentences* from that of the *Contra Gentiles*, does not itself contain still another trinitarian exposition,
its importance for showing the growth of St. Thomas' theological ideal would be hard to exaggerate.   For in this explicit
and well-articulated account of the nature, scope, limitations
and positive objectives of theology as science of the divine,
there is a distinct advance by way of clarification and finer
precision in the same two lines of thought just observed in the
Sentences.

---

[12] pp. 69-71, 72-73, 283-285.
[13] pp. 85-92, 283-285.

Once again, then, Aquinas addresses himself to the question whether human intelligence can achieve knowledge of the Trinity of Persons, and situates his question within the larger context of the divine cognoscibility. In the *Sentences*, he had already explained how the divine being is not *per se notum quoad nos*, and how God therefore could be known only in, and to the extent of, what is implied for the divine being in knowledge from His created effects. Here in the *In Boethii de Trinitate*, however, this theme is considerably developed and sharpened.

The human mind, not only when left to its own natural resources but even when illuminated by supernatural faith, cannot know God in this life " per formam Dei, " but exclusively " per formam effectus. " Immediate quidditive knowledge of God is thus excluded. But the limitation goes much further than this. Since even in the knowledge through created effects, no such effect is proportionate to the power and reality of the divine cause and no finite similitude or analogy capable of perfectly representing the divine essence, quidditive knowledge of God that would be only mediate is also excluded. It follows, therefore, that in this life man can know of God, not 'what' God is (" quid est Deus "), but only 'that' God is (" an est Deus "), along with what St. Thomas describes as 'certain conditions' of the divine existence, such as immateriality.[14]

The restrictive point made by Aquinas in this treatise, then, is more precise and more far-reaching than that which he had previously scored in the *Sentences*. The full implications of the fact that God cannot be known in this life " per formam Dei " are now brought out. What is excluded is not merely immediate knowledge of the divine being, but any knowledge whatsoever that would be strictly essential or quidditive. What St. Thomas now emphasizes is that knowledge of God achieved through science of the divine is consequently vicarious or substitutional, contoured at every step to the form of the created effect inasmuch as the form of the object itself is in this instance inaccessible. And it is precisely in this context of a fully expressed doctrine of epistemological limitation that he repeats once again his earlier and constant assertion that human reason cannot attain to the Trinity of

---

[14] pp. 115-121.

Persons. For the Trinity of Persons pertains to the internal ' what ' (" quid est ") of the divine existence.[15]

The observation made above, therefore, with regard to reason's basic incompetence in this area as affirmed in the *Sentences* is all the more applicable to the repetition of this denial in *In Boethii de Trinitate*. The denial is not made lightly, or in the manner of asserting a theological commonplace, but derives from the deepest foundations of St. Thomas' personal synthesis.

But the methodological treatise also shows a distinct advance over the *Sentences* in the more positive point of how exactly Aquinas was coming to understand the nature and scope of theological science. In the *Sentences* the rôle of illuminated reason in exploring the revealed mysteries was restricted in practice to explanation, interpretation and limited understanding. Here in the *In Boethii de Trinitate*, the epistemological theory on which such a restriction was based is clarified and further developed.

Even in this still early period of his career, St. Thomas gives his own reply to those who conceive the function of rational theology, and perhaps of Thomist rational theology in particular, as application of principles and processes of reason to the given ' data ' of divine revelation. For the place Aquinas here assigns to the articles of faith and internal belief is not that of data, or object, or ' *materia circa quam* ', so to speak, but rather the place of being the " quasi principia " in the basic movement and elaboration of theological science.[16]

It is the strictly genetic quality of these principles, moreover, which he wishes to emphasize. Because of the radical dependence of human understanding on abstraction from the sense phantasm, man cannot know God in this life " per formam Dei, " and hence cannot know God here and now as He is known to Himself and the saints. Nevertheless, even in the restrictions of his present existence, man can participate, however remotely, in precisely this knowledge of the divine as divine, through faith.

Through faith, through adherence and conformity to the divine truth " propter seipsam, " man is able to share, by way of reliance upon the authority of a ' superior knower ',

---

[15] pp. 121-123, 130-133.
[16] pp. 123-129.

in the knowledge of the superior knower which is here and now not directly accessible to him, and through this very same faith to form certain conclusions of theological science. And by so acting, St. Thomas explains, man gives scope and forward motion to internal faith in the proper prosecution of its connatural *finis*, which is understanding of the divine.[17]

Finally, it is also important to note in this treatise that not only does Aquinas leave no room here alongside the ideal of understanding for a simultaneous or subordinate ideal of certitude and demonstration, but even excludes this latter explicitly. While the articles of faith already known and pre-supposed as known can be defended against the attack of unbelievers, the same articles of faith in rational theology are not themselves the conclusions of demonstrative process, but rather its principles. For scientific reason engenders assent, not to principles, but to subsequent conclusions. In rational theology, therefore, the " principia fidei " being the source of demonstrative process leading to conclusions in the order of understanding cannot themselves be the object of the same demonstrative process. For the process has no existence or meaning except inasmuch as and insofar as certitude of the principles is simply presupposed.

It was not until some few years later, with the composition of the fourth book *Contra Gentiles*, however, that St. Thomas would implement the methodological ideal of the *In Boethii de Trinitate* in his second systematic presentation of trinitarian doctrine. But now the theological analysis first in evidence, for all its imperfections, in the *Sentences* is brought, so to speak, to its natural term. And the means through which this is seen to have been accomplished, moreover, is quite clearly the rational structure provided by a now fully developed theory of intellectual emanation. Nevertheless, despite this growth in Aquinas' thought, and despite the introduction and decisive use of this rational structure, the particular difficulty recognized by Vagaggini has no real basis in the text of *Contra Gentiles IV*. For whatever else St. Thomas may be doing here, at least he does not approach the revealed mystery from the philosophical properties of intellectual nature.

In a sense of the term quite different from the usage in the present study, the *Contra Gentiles* is apologetical, and so

---

[17] pp. 124-128, 133-136.

also is the treatise ' *de Trinitate* ' in book four. For the entire work quite clearly envisions the defense of authentic christian belief against infidel and heretical errors. But at least in the treatises concerned directly with the orthodox interpretation of revealed mysteries, including therefore this ' *de Trinitate*", St. Thomas introduces his exposition with the explicit statement that his purpose is to take up the revealed mysteries as contained in the testimonies of Sacred Scripture, which are proved (" probantur "), he remarks, not by natural reason but exclusively on the authority of the word of God, and to defend these mysteries by showing how the biblical doctrine must be taken (" qualiter accipi ") or understood (" qualiter intelligi ").[18]

The apologetic Aquinas presents here, therefore, is the apologetic which formally and explicitly presupposes the certain knowledge of what has actually been revealed. The further purpose, so to speak, of submitting to some sort of aprioristic demonstration, regardless of how qualified, the basic fact or existence of these same mysteries is deliberately excluded. In perfect accord with the distinction drawn in *In Boethii de Trinitate* between rational process as demonstration (" demonstratio ") and rational process as elucidation or manifestation (" manifestatio "), St. Thomas proposes here in the fourth book *Contra Gentiles* to accept the proof and certitude of the mysteries exclusively from revelation. So far as certitude is concerned, this is simply the end of the matter.

When, then, he passes on to a strictly positive account of the trinitarian mystery in theological exposition, and does so with the observation that only in this way can a satisfactory answer be given to heretical interpretations, he characterizes his use of rational process repeatedly and without the slightest deviation in the obviously technical idiom of understanding. As in the theoretical explanation of the *In Boethii de Trinitate*, so again here in the ' *de Trinitate* ' of the *Contra Gentiles*, it is the " principia fidei " which are assigned the rôle of ultimate source and basic intellectual energy in the attempt of rational theology to achieve some measure of understanding: " qualiter accipi, " " qualiter intelligi. "[19]

---

[18] p. 139.
[19] pp. 146-154, 191-203, 285-289.

21

At the same time, the particular and essential *media* through which, in the eleventh chapter of *Contra Gentiles IV* St. Thomas achieves this understanding concretely is his psychological and metaphysical concept of intellectual emanation as derived from the procession of inner word in human understanding.[20] The problem was raised, therefore, inasmuch as it had been suggested in Vagaggini's criticism, whether use of this rational principle and structure on Aquinas' part did not, in effect, compromise his purpose by introducing into his explanatory account an element of *de facto* demonstration. It was noted, however, that there are three distinct questions here, not one.[21]

First, it is certainly evident from the text that a decisive evolution had taken place in St. Thomas' psychological and metaphysical understanding of the *verbum cordis*. In the *Sentences*, he was not at all clear on the point of whether the intellectual conception was to be distinguished from the operation of intellect. But here in the *Contra Gentiles*, book four, and for the greater part even in the earlier fourth question *De Veritate*, Aquinas accepts the reality of this distinction.[22]

Secondly, now that his understanding of the inner word had been perfected, it is likewise clear from the text of *Contra Gentiles IV* that St. Thomas made use of this doctrine to give a vastly more mature and different account of the trinitarian processions from that which he had offered in the *Sentences*. In the *Sentences*, he did not see the cogency of the argument that proper predication of the Divine Word had to be personal as opposed to essential. It was rather christian tradition that settled the matter. But here in *Contra Gentiles IV*, and earlier in the fourth question *De Veritate*, he maintains that the proper usage is necessarily and exclusively personal. For he is now aware of the essentially relative quality of the inner word. Consequently, in this second exposition of his ' *de Trinitate* ' Aquinas is no longer embarrassed, as he was in the *Sentences*, by having no adequate means for reducing the divine generation to a purely intellectualist account. As God understands Himself, there proceeds within

---

[20] pp. 150-154.
[21] p. 162.
[22] pp. 162-170.

Him upon the divine act of understanding the really distinct
Divine Word.   For such procession is essential to inner word.[23]

Thirdly, on the other hand, there is not the slightest textual evidence that this development in the psychology and
metaphysics of the *verbum cordis*, entailing, as it did, a parallel development in the theology of the processions, involved as
a still further parallel consequence a change of position on the
question of a priori demonstration.   Nor can the contrary be
shown by contrasting the negative reply to an objection in
the *In Boethii de Trinitate* with the present positive account
in *Contra Gentiles IV*.

In the passage of the *In Boethii de Trinitate* which might
be alleged the state of the question is frankly apologetical.
Aquinas does not deny in this earlier passage that procession
of inner word is essential to intellect.   In fact, since the opposite is his teaching in the fourth question *De Veritate*, and
since the two works most likely issue from the same period
of time, it is highly probable that the opposite teaching is also
his mind on the matter when composing the *In Boethii de Trinitate*.   What Aquinas denies rather is the ability of natural
reason, as claimed by the challenger in the objection, to affirm
in God the existence of this procession on the mere ground
that God understands.   The reply, that is to say, is addressed
to the precisely apologetical context of the objection —
all as one should normally expect.[24]

But here in *Contra Gentiles IV*, the context itself is the
quite different context of explanatory theology.   It is not
the fact or existence of the Divine Word, or the first trinitarian procession, that St. Thomas is attempting to establish.
The existence of the procession and of the Divine Word has
been presupposed throughout the exposition, as also that the
word, when used of God, is used in a strictly proper sense. [25]

Moreover, it is important to note that the precise point
made by Aquinas in this passage of the *Contra Gentiles* is not
that procession of inner word is essential to intellectual being,
and hence must be found in God as well, but rather that to
proceed with real distinction from its principle is essential to
inner word.   The absolute universality of procession as essential

---

[23] pp. 170-172.
[24] pp. 173-178.
[25] pp. 178-181.

to intellect is the virtual, though unstated, conclusion which
St. Thomas reaches at the end of his theological exposition.
For his theological analysis has arrived at such strictly intellectual procession in God. But in no sense is the universality
of procession a premise in his argument.

The basic structure of the argument is simply as follows.
Christian faith attests to the existence in God of the Divine
Word, and the predication is proper. But it is of the *ratio
formalis*, not of *intellect*, but of *inner word*, that this word
proceed in intellect upon the act of understanding with real
distinction from its principle. Therefore, such is the procession of the Word of God in the divine understanding. [26]
Having reached this conclusion of strictly theological analysis,
St. Thomas may then generalize and assert the universality
of procession in intellectual nature, though he does not do
so explicitly.

Moreover, it is clear now why the particular difficulty
discovered by Vagaggini has no real place in the text of
Contra Gentiles IV. There could be some ground for this
difficulty, one might say, in those later works of Aquinas
where the process of exposition actually moves out from the
essential properties of intellectual being. But this is not the
process here in the *Contra Gentiles*. As an examination of
the text makes quite evident, St. Thomas approaches his
understanding of the first trinitarian procession from what
is essential to inner word once the existence of the Divine
Word is presupposed, but not from what is essential to intellect.

In the two major presentations of the Thomist ' *de Trinitate* ' still remaining, however, the masterful treatise of the
Pars Prima together with the abbreviated and most likely
earlier exposition of the *Compendium*, St. Thomas does, in fact,
introduce the trinitarian processions in the precise context
of what is essential to intellect. In *Contra Gentiles IV*, his
argument had been : given inner word, such and such is its
necessary consequence ; or more concretely : given from revelation the existence in God of the Divine Word to be interpreted in the strictly proper sense, it follows, in theological
analysis, that this Word must proceed upon the divine understanding as term of the divine understanding really distinct

---

[26] pp. 183-189.

from its corresponding principle. The procession of the Divine Word was not deduced, therefore, but rather presupposed as already known and then reduced, through theological analysis, to its intellectualist principles. At the very beginning of the trinitarian expositions in the *Pars Prima* and *Compendium*, on the other hand, the procession of the Divine Word itself is made to follow, at least in some fashion, upon the universal or transcendental principle that procession of inner word is necessary to intellect as such.

In the *Compendium*, more clearly in the *Pars Prima* and in a parallel though summary account in the ninth question *De Potentia*, Aquinas does not conclude with what is therefore universally true of intellectual being, as he did, at least virtually, in *Contra Gentiles IV*, but actually begins with what is universally true of intellectual being. Whoever understands, he writes in the *Pars Prima*, by this alone that he does understand, there proceeds within him an inner word. Moreover, if someone should doubt the strictly essential force of such a general statement, the more technical expression " quae est absolute de ratione eius quod est intelligere, " used to qualify procession of the concept in the ninth question *De Potentia*, settles the matter.[27]

Hence, the question has been asked : is this not equivalently a purely rational or philosophical demonstration for the first trinitarian procession ? Or if to say this would do too much violence to the text, insofar as St. Thomas continues to repeat, even in these later works, that demonstration in this area is quite impossible, is this not at least demonstration's " illusion esthétique ? " For is not St. Thomas arguing : where there is intellect, there must be procession of inner word ; but in God there is certainly intellect ; therefore in God there must be procession of a *Verbum Divinum* ?

To close with this difficulty, it was necessary to approach the problem in two distinct steps. First, it was necessary to accept, provisionally at any rate, the *status quaestionis* of one who would presume that the difficulty itself was inherent in the text. From the very same passages, then, it was shown that St. Thomas is clearly presupposing throughout his exposition the fact or existence of trinitarian procession as known to man only through revelation. For in each of the accounts,

---

[27] pp. 208-213, 219-223, 273-277.

he affirms this dependence upon revelation explicitly. It was also shown that just as earlier in *Contra Gentiles IV*, so again in these later works, the rôle explicitly assigned to theological reasoning is exclusively that of attempting to see how what had been revealed must be taken or understood. Finally, it was pointed out how in a preceding section of the same *Pars Prima*, and in the very same passage of the *De Potentia*, Aquinas reaffirms as his basic argument against the possibility of trinitarian demonstration his constant principle that human intelligence cannot know in this life " quid est Deus, " nor therefore the " quid " and " quomodo " of the divine understanding. But only through the quidditive knowledge thus denied it, could human intelligence ever grasp the causal nexus between the divine understanding and procession of the Divine Word.[28]

Secondly, however, it was necessary to ask if the difficulty one might feel he has discovered here is, when all is said and done, actually inherent in the text itself ? For among other things, it is clear that the problem as posed is expressed according to a particular mentality — the mentality, that is to say, which considers the certitudinal and the demonstrative as the proper, if not exclusively possible, ideal of scientific process, and hence of theological process as well. But it cannot be presumed that such was the ideal of St. Thomas. The further question remains, therefore, whether the problem would ever have arisen if Aquinas' personal intention and methodology had been correctly assessed from the start.

In this second perspective, then, detailed attention was given to the highly significant *prooemium* to the ' *de Trinitate* ' of the *Pars Prima*. In this *prooemium*, Aquinas proposes to treat first the divine procession, then the relations, and lastly the Three Persons. Moreover, he explicitly sets down his reason for following such a plan or order of exposition. He will treat first origin or procession, then relations, and finally the Three Persons, precisely because the Persons depend upon the relations, and the relations in turn depend upon procession or origin. The " ordo doctrinae " he intends to follow, therefore, is the order of internal ' cause '.

It was necessary to show, then, what this " ordo doctrinae " involves. To begin with what is first in the line of

---

[28] pp. 212-214, 217-219, 220, 222-224, 269-270.

cause, is to begin, not with what is first or *primum notum* in the knowledge of human experience, on analysis from which further truths could be determined in understanding, but with what is first in reality, and is itself understood to be first in reality only in virtue of a previous analysis from what is first in the knowledge of human experience.

In the interiority of the divine being, there is, of course, no strict "priority" or 'cause'. But according to the only possible and perfectly valid way in which the human mind, and hence rational theology, can achieve some limited and vicarious understanding of the divine being, there is an order of internal dependence. What is first known in the knowledge of human experience is the Three Persons, as revealed by God, and as portrayed concretely in their salvific activity, personal interrelationships and character in the testimonials of christian faith. Analyzing this revelation, the illuminated reason of rational theology comes to see that the only way this distinction and plurality of Persons can be taken or understood is according to the subsistent relations through which the Persons are constituted. Prolonging its analysis, the same illuminated reason further comes to see that the only way the subsistent trinitarian relations can be taken or understood is as grounded upon the two "processiones ad intra" — the one through intellect, and the other through will — which alone are possible in a purely spiritual being.[29]

Not only in the *prooemium*, but also and in more detail when he passes on to treat of the processions, then the relations, and finally the Persons in the three major divisions of his treatise, St. Thomas makes it abundantly clear that he is following this order of internal dependence throughout the entire exposition. At this point, therefore, there is at least no problem over the fact that in the twenty-seventh question of the *Pars Prima* and in the parallel passages of the *Compendium* and *De Potentia* Aquinas begins with the divine procession, and precisely in its intellectualist understanding. For it is divine procession so understood that is ultimate 'cause' or *ratio* of the Three Persons in the order of things as they are in themselves, and is known to be such through a previous analysis, each of whose essential steps is clearly indicated as

[29] pp. 205-208.

the processions, relations and Persons are systematically introduced.[30]

But what of the fact, someone might object, that St. Thomas begins his exposition in all three of these mature works, not with the *divine* processions in particular, nor even with *divine* procession in general or, so to speak, in the abstract, but with *procession as such* — with procession as a universal or transcendental property of intellectual nature? While it may be true that he assigns revelation as the source of man's knowledge of the divine procession, does he not at the same time conclude to the divine procession in an apologetical process which seeks at least to imitate apodictic demonstration, inasmuch as he concludes to the divine procession from the philosophical nature of intellect?

That St. Thomas is not doing this, however, is clear from the exigencies of the " ordo doctrinae " to which he adheres. For the very same theological analysis which necessarily preceded this order of synthesis, which is implicit in this order of synthesis, and whose basic steps are actually recorded in this order of synthesis, had arrived in its quest for understanding, not only at the divine " processio ad intra " as first in the line of internal cause, but also, at least virtually, at the universal or transcendental principle that procession is therefore an essential and absolute property of intellectual being.

At the conclusion of his theological analysis in *Contra Gentiles IV*, and also in the neatly summarized analysis in the eighth question *De Potentia*, Aquinas was able to affirm procession of a distinct inner word following upon the operation of understanding as the ultimate ' cause ' or *ratio* of the plurality of Persons. But the precise *media* which he employed in his theological analysis to achieve this measure of understanding was procession of the *verbum cordis* and *amor* in the human mind. If one prescinds, then, from the angelic instance which was not explicitly introduced in either of these accounts, it is clear that the analysis has arrived at the point where the generalization wants only formal statement. Moreover, in the first chapter of his commentary *In Ioannem*, where the angelic *verbum* is explicitly introduced, and the generalization formally expressed, there is supporting textual evidence to confirm the point that St. Thomas himself undoubt-

---

[30] pp. 239-241, 245-250, 264-265.

edly considered the generalization as at least virtually attained in the theological analyses of the *Contra Gentiles* and the *De Potentia*.[31]

When, therefore, St. Thomas commences his strictly synthetic exposition in the *Pars Prima*, *Compendium*, and ninth question *De Potentia*, with the universal or transcendental principle that procession of inner word is an essential property of intellectual being, his intention is simply to begin at the most utterly first moment, so to speak, in the order of things as they are in themselves — and precisely inasmuch as they are thus understood to be at the most utterly final moment in the preceding theological analysis. Nor is he in any sense whatsoever concluding to the existence of the divine procession from the same principle. For understanding of the divine procession in its precisely intellectualist description has first to be achieved before the principle itself could possibly be formulated.[32]

As a last consequence, then, the Thomist generalization on procession of inner word is not a purely rational principle, or a purely philosophical law. Nor is Aquinas making use of this principle to construct an argument, however qualified, from 'pure perfections' to demonstrate what must exist in God on the basis of what is known in creatures and has been divested from all vestiges of potentiality and imperfection. Human reason and human philosophy cannot pass beyond the absolute identity in God of the 'understood' and the 'understanding' to affirm as well the relative but real distinction that exists between the two. For human reason does not, and in this life cannot, know " quid est Deus, " and hence the " quid est " and " quomodo est " of the divine understanding. Philosophy knows, therefore, that intellect is a perfection from whose *ratio formalis* all potentiality and imperfection can be excluded, but philosophy does not know that procession of the really distinct *verbum cordis* is an essential property of the *ratio formalis* of intellect. Theodicy can affirm in God the existence of intellect, therefore, analogously but formally. On the other hand, theodicy cannot affirm in God the existence also of a distinct word. For apart from the revelation of the Trinity of Persons, human under-

---

[31] pp. 303-306.
[32] pp. 306-310, 224-231.

standing cannot see how the potentiality and imperfection attendant upon the real distinction of the *verbum humanum* might be totally excluded so that through theodicy's *via remotionis* a similarly distinct *Verbum Divinum* might be predicated of the divine understanding as well.

The Thomist generalization, then, is rather a theological principle in the strictest sense. For its formulation is and can be made only at the term of a theological analysis whereby illuminated reason, beginning with the procession of the Divine Word as revealed, has first come to understand in some measure the divine instance.

Moreover, when St. Thomas introduces this generalization at the very beginning of his trinitarian synthesis, there is not even a remote imitation of the argument from " rationes necessariae " or ' pure perfectionis '. As was remarked earlier in this study, it is difficult to conceive as the imitation of something that which takes, on every last significant turn, a precisely opposite direction. The argument from pure perfections, certainly such as Vagaggini attributes to St. Anselm, envisions certitude and demonstration of fact, itself serves as the *prius notum* in virtue of which knowledge and certitude of the *posterius notum* will be obtained. But the Thomist principle of the universal *verbum*, on the other hand, stands, not as the *prius notum* in the knowledge of human experience, but as the *posterius notum* at the end of a process of theological understanding, in which knowledge of something already known, whose certitude was no longer in question — in this case, the procession of the Divine Word — was actually and necessarily presupposed.

In conclusion, therefore, the difficulty some might be inclined to discover in St. Thomas' procedure of beginning his trinitarian synthesis with the universal or transcendental principle that procession of inner word is essential to intellect can be explained, in the writer's judgment quite satisfactorily, by showing from the text itself that it was ever his explicit intention to presuppose on the exclusive authority of divine revelation the fact and existence of the mystery. Nevertheless, it also seems to be quite clear that had St. Thomas' own ideal of theological science been accurately grasped from the onset, the difficulty itself would never have arisen. For the Thomist ideal is not that of certitude or demonstration of fact, but simply, in a word, understanding.

BIBLIOGRAPHY

I. Books

AQUINAS, SAINT THOMAS, O. P., *Scriptum super Libros Sententiarum Magistri Petri Lombardi*. P. Mandonnet, O. P., editor, Tom. I et II. Paris : Lethielleux, 1929.

——, *Expositio super Librum Boethii de Trinitate*. Bruno Decker, editor, 2§ editio. Leiden : E. J. Brill, 1959.

——, *Quaestiones Disputatae*. Vol. I : *De Veritate*. P. Raymundus Spiazzi, O. P., editor, 9§ editio revisa. Turin : Marietti, 1953.

——, *Quaestiones Disputatae*. Vol. II : *De Potentia, De Anima, et al*. P. Bazzi *et al*, editors, 9§ editio revisa. Turin : Marietti, 1953.

——, *Opera Omnia*. Vol. XV : *Summa Contra Gentiles, Liber Quartus*. Rome : Commissio Leonina, 1930.

——, *Summa Theologiae*. Institutum Studiorum Medievalium Ottaviensis, editor, 2§ editio emendata. Ottawa : Commissio Piana, 1953.

——, *Quaestiones de Trinitate divina Summae de theologia*, l. I, q. XXVII-XXXII. Bernhardus Geyer, editor. Bonn : Petrus Hanstein, 1934.

——, *Opuscula Theologica*. Vol. I : *De Re Dogmatica et Morali*. P. Raymundus A. Verardo, O. P., editor. Turin : Marietti, 1954.

——, *Super Evangelium S. Ioannis Lectura*. P. Raphaelis Cai, O. P., editor, 4§ editio. Turin : Marietti, 1952.

CHENU, M.-D., O. P., *Introduction à l'étude de saint Thomas d'Aquin*. 2§ éd. Montreal : Institut d'Etudes Médiévales. Paris : Librairie J. Vrin, 1954.

LONERGAN, BERNARD J. F., S. J., *De Deo Trino. Pars Analytica*. Rome : Apud Aedes Universitatis Gregorianae, 1961.

——, *Divinarum Personarum Conceptio Analogica*. Rome : Apud Aedes Universitatis Gregorianae, 1957.

——, *Insight. A Study of Human Understanding*. New York : Philosophical Library, 1957.

PAISSAC H., O .P., *Théologie du Verbe. Saint Augustin et saint Thomas*. Paris : Les Editions du Cerf, 1951.

PENIDO, M.T.-L., *Le rôle de l'analogie en théologie dogmatique*, Vol. XV of *Bibliothèque Thomiste*. Paris : Librairie Philosophique J. Vrin, 1931.

II. Articles

BAYART, J., S. J., "The Concept of Mystery According to St. Anselm of Canterbury," *Recherches de théologie ancienne et médiévale*, IX. (1927), pp. 125-166.

BOUILLARD, H., "La preuve de Dieu dans le *Proslogion* et son interprétation par Karl Barth," *Spicilegium Beccense. Congrès International du IXe centenaire de l'arrivée d'Anselme au Bec.* Paris: Librairie Philosophique J. Vrin, 1959. Pp. 191-207.

CHENU, M.-D., O. P., "La date du commentaire de saint Thomas sur le *De Trinitate* de Boèce," *Les Sciences Philosophiques et Théologiques*, II (1941-1942), pp. 432-434.

DIEPEN, H., O. S. B., "De Analogica Nostra Sanctissimae Trinitatis Conceptione," *Angelicum*, XXIII (1946), pp. 89-125; XXVI (1947), pp. 33-46.

DONDAINE, ANTOINE, O. P., "Saint Thomas a-t-il disputé à Rome la question des ' Attributs Divins ' ? " *Bulletin Thomiste*, X (1933), pp. 171*-182*.

————, "Saint Thomas et la dispute des attributs divins (I Sent., d. 2, a. 3), authenticité et origine," *Archivum Fratrum Praedicatorum*, VIII (1938), pp. 253-262.

DONDAINE, H., "Le *Contra Errores Graecorum* de s. Thomas et le IVe livre du *Contra Gentiles*," *Les Sciences Philosophique et Théologiques*, XXX (1941), pp. 156-162.

DUMONT, C., S. J., "La réflexion sur la méthode théologique. II : Le dilemme théologique," *Nouvelle Revue Théologique*, LXXXIV (1962), pp. 17-35.

GLORIEUX, P., "Pour la chronologie de la Somme," *Mélanges de Science Religieuse*, II (1945), pp. 59-98.

LONERGAN, BERNARD J. F., S. J., "The Concept of *Verbum* in the Writings of St. Thomas Aquinas," *Theological Studies*, VII (1946), pp. 349-392; VIII (1947), pp. 35-79, 404-444; X (1949), pp. 3-40, 359-393.

PENIDO, M.T.-L., "La valeur de la théorie 'psychologique' de la Trinité," *Ephemerides Theologicae Lovanienses*, VIII (1931), pp. 5-16.

SYNAVE, P., "Le problème chronologique des Questions Disputées de S. Thomas d'Aquin," *Revue Thomiste*, XXXI (1926), pp. 154-159.

VAGAGGINI, CYPRIAN, "La hantise des *rationes necessariae* de saint Anselme dans la théologie des processions trinitaires de saint Thomas," J. Evrard, trans., *Spicilegium Beccense. Congrès International du IXe centenaire de l'arrivée d'Anselme au Bec.* Paris: Librairie Philosophique J. Vrin, 1959. Pp. 103-139.

WALZ, P. A., "Thomas d'Aquin. Ecrits," *Dictionnaire de théologie catholique*, XV-1. Paris: Librairie Letouzey et Ané, 1946. Col. 635-641.

INDEX TO CITATIONS FROM ST. THOMAS

(In the Textual Analysis of Part Two and Part Three)